History of Scandinavia

A Captivating Guide to the History of Sweden, Norway, Denmark, Iceland, and Finland

Free Bonus from Captivating History (Available for a Limited time)

Hi History Lovers!

Now you have a chance to join our exclusive history list so you can get your first history ebook for free as well as discounts and a potential to get more history books for free! Simply visit the link below to join.

Captivatinghistory.com/ebook

Also, make sure to follow us on Facebook, Twitter and Youtube by searching for Captivating History.

Youtube: Captivating History

Table of Contents

Part 1: History of Sweden

A Captivating Guide to Swedish History, Starting from Ancient Times through the Viking Age and Swedish Empire to the Present

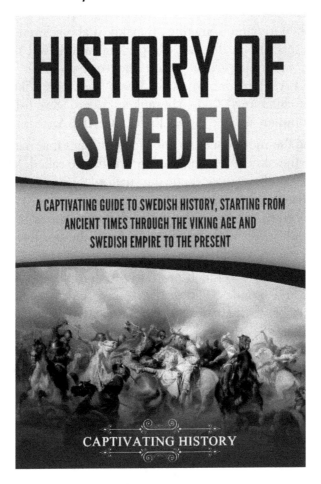

Introduction

When asked to name something they know about Sweden, many people (especially in the English-speaking world) will name the following, in no particular order: the ready-to-make furniture brand IKEA, the famously safe Volvo cars, the Vikings, the somewhat infamous Old Milwaukee Beer "Swedish Bikini Team" commercials, the Nobel Prize, and ABBA.

Among the more concrete and serious things that many know (or think they know) about Sweden are the so-called "cradle to the grave" welfare state and the nation's famous neutrality. Sweden has not been involved in a war in some two hundred years. Recently, many might know that Sweden is starting to struggle with issues over immigration from the war-torn Middle East, especially since 2015.

Obviously, there is much more to Sweden than Vikings, cars, furniture, and blondes. (Though a recent study concluded that somewhere between 50 and 80 percent of Swedes have light hair, not all are blonde, although they are some of the tallest people in the world.) In Captivating History's *History of Sweden*, you'll find out all you want to know about this famous Nordic country.

Chapter 1 – Just the Facts

Let's begin with a few facts about the country before we delve into its history. If you think about it, Sweden has been mentioned numerous times in the news recently, whether on an international issue like climate change (the issue in which Swedish teenager Greta Thunberg made a name for herself in the last few years) or its place in between Russia and Europe/NATO. There is the Nobel Prize and Sweden's stellar performance at the 2022 Winter Olympics. However, Sweden is home to just over ten million people. That is only about a million more than the number of people living in New York City. Yet Sweden has been playing an important role in world events for hundreds of years, and at one time, it was a considerable world power.

In a list of the population of European countries, Sweden ranks about midway between Russia, with 146 million, and the small independent principality of San Marino, with 34,000 (we're not counting Vatican City, home of the pope). But even the geographically smaller nations of Holland and Greece have more people than Sweden.

However, in terms of geographic size, Sweden ranks fifth (and it would be third if Russia and Ukraine were left out, which is sometimes done). Sweden comprises 173,860 square miles (450,295 square kilometers), which pulls it just ahead of its other large Scandinavian neighbors, Norway and Finland. However, these countries are not always included as part of "Scandinavia," which is traditionally seen by many as the triad of Sweden, Denmark, and Norway, although some include Iceland.

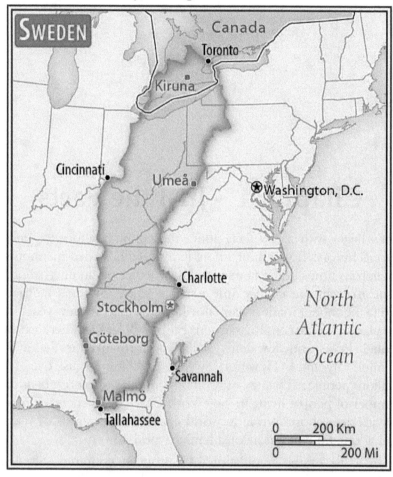

Sweden in comparison to the United States of America.

Sweden's widest part, the south of the country, is 310 miles (500 kilometers) wide. North to south, however, Sweden is 1,000 miles (1,600 kilometers). Think of it this way: from the southern part of Sweden to Italy is about 1,000 miles, which means the north of Sweden is quite far from the capital of Stockholm in the south. Thus, there are some significant differences in the country, primarily the weather but culturally as well. Another way of picturing the size of the country is this way: Sweden is about the size of the US state of California. And California and Japan are roughly the same size area-wise.

Another important comparison is that, unlike California, Sweden does not have much arable land. What it did grow was rather limited (at least until relatively recent times, before the advent of many advances in agriculture). In this way, Sweden is very similar to Japan, and both nations have depended on the sea in various ways, such as for trade, food, and defense.

Many people believe Sweden to be cold year-round, and while about 15 percent of its area lies north of the Arctic Circle, much of the country is warmer than similarly situated nations. Though Sweden is at about the same latitude as Greenland, northern Siberia, and Alaska, it is kept relatively warmer by the Gulf Stream, which swirls around the coasts of the nation from west to east. Still, the nation is not exactly Jamaica either. In the winter, the people living in that 15 percent of the northern part of the country sometimes experience sub-zero temperatures (up, or rather down, to -40°F/-40°C).

As you can likely imagine, the population of the country is mostly Swedish, comprising about 81 percent. The massive influx of refugees from the war-torn Middle East has had a huge impact on the country, which we will discuss toward the end of the book, but the numbers are quite small, at least comparatively. Together, Syrians and Iraqis make up about 3.2 percent of the population, and most live in the major cities in the south, particularly Stockholm. Finns comprise about 1.4 percent, and others, mostly Poles, Ukrainians, Turks, and people whose origin is in the Baltic countries of Lithuania, Latvia, and Estonia, make up about 15 percent altogether. Many of the Eastern Europeans arrived in the 1990s after the fall of the Soviet Union, but guest workers from Poland and Ukraine still come to Sweden, sometimes on a temporary work visa.

In Sweden's prehistory and into the Middle Ages, the country was dominated by two tribes: the Goths and the Svears, from which Sweden takes its Swedish language name of Sverige. Also making up part of the population in both ancient and modern times is the Sámi, who for many years were called "Lapps" (a name that they regard as derogatory since it was given to them by foreigners). Today, the Sámi people are found in Sweden,

Norway, and Finland, as well as on the Russo-Finnish border area.

Within Scandinavia, the Sámi have struggled and won the right for their own parliaments, but these are limited in power when it comes to questions of the Sámi culture. Each Scandinavian nation has a Sámi Parliament, but Russia does not (we are going to include Finland in Scandinavia for our purposes here, though some writers, historians, and politicians do not). All of the Sámi of Scandinavia have the right to cross the borders of other Scandinavian countries. For centuries, the Sámis' primary source of income and food was the large reindeer herds they managed. Today, there are only about twenty-five thousand people who identify as solely Sámi in Sweden, but they have ties with Sámi in Norway and Finland. Like many minorities around the world, the Sámi were long persecuted by the majority population, particularly as Sweden became Christian and as the nation became industrialized in the 18th and 19th centuries.

"Sápmi," the Sámi homeland today.

Relative to the size of its population, Sweden is an economic powerhouse. Among the nations in Europe that have about the same number of people (the Czech Republic, Greece, Portugal, Hungary, Belarus, and Austria), Sweden's gross domestic product (GDP) is the highest. Of Europe in total, it ranks tenth with a GDP of $540 billion (Germany is first at $3 trillion).

Sweden's main economic goods, for both domestic consumption and export, are engines and engine parts (both airplane and automotive), motor vehicles, and telecommunications equipment. Timber has been an important product of the country since the early Middle Ages, and the region also has iron, coal, and copper.

As you will read later, Sweden has a high standard of living. This is based both on its relative wealth and the existence of its world-famous welfare system. Today, Sweden ranks tenth in per capita income among European nations at just over $50,000 a year.

Along with its much talked about and much debated social welfare system, Sweden is likely best known to non-Swedes as being one of two European countries (the other being Switzerland) that has declared itself "neutral." Aside from United Nations Peacekeeping Missions (some of which have included combat, as in Afghanistan), Sweden has managed to avoid the catastrophe of war since the early 19th century. This does not mean Sweden has no self-defense forces. The Swedish military has some of the most technologically advanced weaponry in the world and maintains about 50,000 soldiers with a reserve of over 2.5 million men *and* women. Between 2010 and 2017, Sweden did away with the military draft, but it was reinstated in 2018 since volunteer numbers dwindled. A sizable minority of the Swedish population has had some military training.

Though Sweden is officially neutral, it is an open secret that the country is more aligned with the nations of Western Europe and the United States than Russia, with whom it has had a long and violent history. In recent times, Russian submarines have been identified in Swedish waters near important installations and Stockholm. Sweden takes this very seriously, and its navy has repeatedly chased out these intruders.

But to fully understand how modern Sweden came to be, we have to take a look at its past. We shall start at the very beginning, with Sweden's prehistory.

Chapter 2 – Ice to Iron

Swedish history, or rather prehistory, happened about ten thousand years ago in 8000 BCE when the Great Ice Age began to wane. Around that time, glaciers and snow covering the ground in Scandinavia began to recede in the southern and central parts of the region. In the very far north of Sweden, the ice from the Great Ice Age only began to recede around the time that Sweden was beginning its conversion to Christianity, which was only a millennium ago.

The earliest human settlement in Sweden found to date is located near the town of Segebro near the capital of the province of Scania, Malmö. The culture here (called the "Brummekultur" in Danish/Swedish for the village where artifacts were first found in 1944/45) was a hunter-gatherer society that moved into northern Germany and Denmark as the ice receded. Malmö and Segebro are just across the Øresund Strait from Denmark. Another settlement was found even farther north in what was then Finland (1944) but is now Russia, which dates to about 700 to 1,400 years later. Later settlements developed near Gothenburg and the town of Ageröd in the south.

(An important note—as you read, remember that at various times, much of Scandinavia was under either Swedish or Danish control. In 1809, when Finland was ceded to Russia, it had belonged to Sweden for centuries. Finland won its independence from Russia in 1917.)

As more ice melted from the northern climes, other peoples and tribes moved into the area. As the Paleolithic ("Old Stone Age") moved into the Neolithic ("New Stone Age") about 10,000 BCE, other people groups from both the south and the east moved into Scandinavia. As time went by, the cultures became less and less nomadic and more settled, though they depended on hunting and fishing for their survival. They were settled enough to build massive stone tombs for their elite around 2000 BCE, which were found near Luttra in the Västra Götaland County.

Like many of the people groups and cultures in difficult or hard-to-reach places at the time, the people in Sweden lived relatively isolated lives with little contact with the outside world. However, there was some trade flowing between the far south of Sweden and what is now Denmark. This all changed with the development and arrival of bronze.

The Bronze Age began about 3200 BCE in the Aegean Sea region near Greece. Over time, the knowledge to make bronze moved northward. In about 1500 BCE, the Bronze Age began in Scandinavia. Prior to this, people had used copper for a variety of things, but they discovered that the combination of copper, tin, and other metals made a stronger and more useful new metal: bronze.

Within a very short time, bronze dominated the trade between what would become Swedish territory and future Denmark, as well as people around the Baltic Sea. With the advent of bronze, trade around Europe increased greatly. Bronze was used not only for weapons and armor but for a variety of tools, including those for agriculture. (By this time, most of the people had settled into a life of farming rather than hunting and gathering; the Sámi people are one of the major exceptions to this). They also used bronze to create household tools, jewelry, and other decorative arts, such as the fasteners for the wool clothes they began to wear instead of animal skins.

Throughout southern Sweden and Norway, the people began to record their lives in the granite rocks that covered the land. These petroglyphs depicted wars, raids, farming, animals (both wild and domestic), and supernatural beings. (See the bibliography for a really interesting modern take on petroglyphs by the band Heilung.)

The exchange of goods and ideas at trading posts throughout Europe and the world led to more rapid developments, the most important of which was the use of iron. The Iron Age began somewhere between 800 BCE and 600 BCE, depending on where you look on the map. In the area of Sweden, it appears that the use of iron began around 500 BCE. Iron was introduced to Sweden by Celtic people moving in or trading from the south. (Remember, though, there was no "Sweden" at this time—it was just a territory filled with smaller and larger kingdoms of similar cultures.) So, you see, rather than what many historical dramas would like you to believe, the people of Scandinavia knew about the peoples and cultures to the south and east, and they would eventually trade with people in Britain before the Viking age.

Obviously, iron is much stronger than bronze, and its first serious application during the Iron Age was likely weaponry. However, iron or iron-edged implements were much more efficient and longer-lasting too.

At about the same time that the Iron Age was arriving in what is now Sweden, so did terrible weather. This halted some but not all of the trade going in and out of Scandinavia. One of the societies that remained in contact with the people in Sweden was the Romans. Roman goods were considered to be some of the best at the time, and finely made glassware, decorated pots, and other goods from Rome have been uncovered in Sweden over the years.

Another development taking place around this time was writing. The original runes, the "alphabet" of the Scandinavian area, looks as if it used many Latin characters. These scripts, which did not accurately reflect all of the sounds of the language, are called Futhark for the first seven runes. The original script had twenty-four "letters," but over time, this was whittled down to sixteen. Futhark continued to be used in Sweden well into the first decades of the establishment of Christianity.

A benefit of Sweden's location on the Baltic Sea and near the North Sea was the ease of trade. Being just about two and a half miles across, the Øresund Strait provided easy access to the

European continent for the tribes of southern Sweden. In current literature, shows, and movies, there is the idea that the Vikings did not know of the Roman world or believed it existed. Seemingly every month in the last few years, new and amazing archaeological discoveries have been made in Sweden, Norway, or Denmark, changing the way many people perceive the Viking world (see bibliography for articles).

While the Baltic and North Seas were not the busy commercial and military routes they would become, it is certain that Scandinavia was connected to Eastern Europe via trade with the coast of Poland and the present-day Baltic states. They were also connected to what is now France, Holland, Denmark, and Germany. How far Scandinavian traders penetrated into Europe is unclear, but we do know that the range of goods found from the time period indicates an impressive array from many different and far-flung lands.

The Scandinavians hadn't yet developed the shallow-draft oar- and sail-powered "dragon ships" that were to be their hallmark in the coming centuries. However, both remnants of vessels (most often preserved in the icy bogs in northern Europe and Scandinavia) and petroglyphs from the time show fairly large rowing vessels similar in shape to those famous ships.

The Roman historian Tacitus, who wrote in the early 2nd century CE, mentions the people living in what would later become Sweden. This means the Roman world knew of the people in the north. Tacitus mentions that the people of future Sweden were called Svears, and they were united and governed by one king. This likely is the product of hearsay and guesswork, as just a few centuries later (6th century CE), the Eastern Roman historian Procopius (whose work is generally much more reliable) described *thirteen* different tribes in Sweden, all having a king of their own.

Today, we're still not exactly sure of the make-up of the land, but historians after Procopius tend to describe Sweden as being populated by two tribes: the Svears (from which modern Sweden gets its name) and the Goths (which quite a few cities and other geographical areas, especially in the south, are named after). Ancient sources have the Svears (sometimes spelled as "Svea") and Goths controlling vast areas of land, almost dividing the country between them. Today, it is believed that the Goths predominated in southwestern Sweden and the island of Gotland ("Land of the Goths"). The Svears mostly occupied the area near the present-day city of Uppsala, which even then might have held an important religious and spiritual place in the lives of the Swedes.

Another famous feature of the Viking age was the *thing*. A *thing* was a regular meeting of the free people of an area, tribe, or kingdom to help decide the matters of the day. They were set up at various intervals throughout history. As many nations do today with their local, state, and federal systems, there were *things* on smaller and larger levels. In Norse, these are sometimes referred to as the Althing, which was actually just the kingdom-wide meeting in Iceland. In Sweden, it is called Disartinget, with "ting" being the operative part of the word. We know the Svears met together in this manner, and religious, economic, and legal matters were discussed. Another useful aspect of the *thing* was to bring unity to the different branches of the Svears in the areas around Uppsala, which would serve them well in the future.

By the beginning of the Viking age (c. 780), the Svears were by far the most dominant tribe in Sweden by all accounts, as the power of the Goths had already begun to fade, at least in Sweden. By this time, Gothic tribes of various parts of northwestern Europe had descended on the Western Roman Empire and helped to bring about its fall.

In 865, at the height of the Viking age, a Scandinavian wanderer named Wulfstan visited the court of Alfred the Great in England. Wulfstan reported that most of Sweden was dominated by the Svears. A century and a half later, King Olof Eriksson Skötkonung united both the Svears and Goths in most of the country under his banner. This is generally looked upon as the beginning of centralized Sweden.

Of course, there was one other people group living in Sweden at the time: the Sámi. Remains of settlements have been found on the western Swedish coast of the Gulf of Bothnia and inland in the north of the country. Trade between the Sámi and the Svears and Goths consisted mostly of timber, reindeer skins, and meat, likely in return for more finely made goods and weapons.

Chapter 3 – The Swedish Vikings

Today, interest in the Vikings is at a new high. There are thousands of Viking fictional titles (I recommend James Nelson's ten-book *The Norsemen Saga* series), TV shows and streaming series, and movies. This latest wave of interest in the Vikings was started by the History Channel's series *Vikings*. There was a huge Viking fad in the late 19th century, which unfortunately gave birth to many erroneous and sometimes harmful notions about Viking history and culture.

However, a high percentage of these books and series focus on the Vikings of Norway (and possibly Denmark) rather than those of Sweden. There are many reasons for this. First and foremost is the fascination people have had with the Vikings' "voyages of discovery" to Iceland, Greenland, and North America. Then there are the many chronicles still extant in England and France (two highly literate societies at the time), which describe the Norse Vikings who raided throughout Britain, Ireland, and France. The accounts left by the victims of the Viking raids were hardly flattering, but they are gripping, horrific stories and were widely read by the elites of the time.

As you might imagine, after looking at a map of Scandinavia, the Vikings of Norway and Denmark raided to the west. The Swedes, given their location and the probable interference of

Danish and Norwegian Viking fleets if they attempted to move into the North Sea and beyond, raided east into Poland, Ukraine, and, most of all, Russia.

In the late 1800s, the Romantic movement in Europe, particularly operas by Richard Wagner, spawned new interest in the Viking age. However, to fit in with Romantic ideas, Vikings were seen as "noble savages," heroes, and horn-helmeted raiders. In an ever-more industrial society, Vikings were held up as "natural," "free" spirits living in opposition to Christianity, which was incredibly prevalent in Europe at the time. Many Romantic writers and others were beginning to chafe against the "oppressiveness" of Christianity. Unfortunately, around the same time, new ideas about health, race, evolution, and economic and cultural developments spawned the theory of white supremacy. The image of the Vikings, especially the rare one with blond hair and blue eyes, came to symbolize this new idea. Much harm was done to the truth in the process.

While today's TV shows *Vikings* and *The Last Kingdom* take liberties with the truth and the timeline, they seem to have gotten a few things correct. First is the idea of women warriors. This is not a book on the Viking age, but suffice it to say that current discoveries and new technologies have shown us that it is likely that female Viking warriors existed, but their number was likely far less than that depicted on TV. In the later seasons of *Vikings*, a number of people from other cultures are shown, not only in their own homelands (as in the desert of North Africa and Spain) but also in Kattegat, the fictional capital of the main characters.

Even the word "Viking" is under new scrutiny. Various schools of historical thought assign different meanings to the word. Some believe it refers to the Norse word *vik*, meaning "bay." Others believe that the word means something akin to "rower." Still, others posit that a "Viking" was originally a person from the area of "Vik" in Norway. Some believe it was a word from Old English that meant something like "pirate." In the 19th century, most people saw Vikings as "pirates" and "raiders," and this is the meaning that has stuck.

However, there are some people who call anyone from Scandinavia a Viking; this usually pertains to men but sometimes women as well. From both foreign sources of the Viking age and later accounts (specifically the sagas of Icelander Snorri Sturluson in the 12th and 13th centuries), "Vikings" were the people that went out on raids or to war. They were not the average citizens of Scandinavia, though it is highly likely that a large percentage of the Norse male population went on raids overseas.

As mentioned previously in the text, the Vikings who went west were mostly Danes and Norwegians (all of whom were usually called "Northmen" rather than "Vikings"). However, there were likely some Swedes with them. (During this time, as now, the Scandinavians spoke mutually intelligible dialects or languages—in this case, "Old Norse.") In Ireland and Scotland, the Vikings were more successful when it came to interacting and intermarrying with the native population. New cultures, a hybrid of both, developed as a result. In many cases, many Irish and some Scots "turned" Viking, as did Frisians from the coast of present-day Holland and Germany.

We have less information about the Swedish Vikings. We know for certain that they raided to the east, specifically down the large rivers of Russia and Ukraine to the Black Sea and beyond. Were there Norwegians and Danes on these voyages? It is likely, as many Swedes, especially in the upper classes, had important economic, political, and family ties to Norway and Denmark. Their numbers were likely very small and their presence irregular.

Swedish Vikings began to move into the hinterland of Poland, Ukraine, and western Russia in the early 800s. The city of Novgorod (known to the Swedes as Holmgard) in western Russia, just south of where St. Petersburg stands today, was built by Swedish Vikings, local Russian elites, and, of course, slaves. In 840, Kyiv (sometimes seen as "Kiev," especially in older historical manuscripts) in today's Ukraine was founded by Kievan Rus—the Swedish Vikings.

The Swedes, like all Vikings, did not simply raid and take what they wanted, especially when they were far from home and away from reinforcements. They traded as well. The Swedes bartered all sorts of goods with the many tribes of western Russia and Ukraine. They traded fine goods from Western Europe, ivory (which they had traded with the Sámi for), and much else. They also sold slaves, which were taken on their raids. The Swedish Vikings mainly took slaves from Poland, the Baltic states, and the far west of Ukraine. Slavery was likely the most lucrative "product" the Swedes sold to the various kingdoms they met on their way downriver.

The areas along the major rivers of Russia and Ukraine were naturally occupied by other people. In the north, many of these people were Slavic, but they would soon become known as Russians of one variety or another. As the Vikings ventured south toward the coast of the Black Sea and the Caucasus borderlands, they encountered various other people groups. Particularly in the plains of the south, some Slavic and/or Turkic tribes had carved out large and powerful kingdoms.

However, in the north and western parts of Russia and Ukraine, the Vikings carved out the foundations of what would become the first recognizable Russian state. At first, the Swedes traveled to trade with the towns and settlements along the great river systems of the Volga, Don, and Dnieper Rivers. Through trade, threats, and the occasional battle with local tribes, the Swedish Vikings carved out a large territory.

Varangian/Rus trade routes in the east. The Rus states are marked clearly in the northern part of the country. As you can see, Swedish trade routes reached the Persian Empire and the Holy Land.

As you can see, the territory controlled to one degree or another by the Swedes was vast. In actuality, though they came to quickly dominate the economy and trade, the number of Vikings in Russia was too small for them to control the country completely. Before we discuss how the Swedes came to give birth to the first ruling dynasty of Russia, let's discuss what they were called. This is likely the most well-known bit of information about the Swedes in Russia.

Though there is still some debate over the origin of the name, most people accept that the Swedes moving into the borderlands of Russia from their homeland in Sweden were called Ruotsi by their wild Finnish neighbors. "Ruotsi" means "ones who row," which obviously refers to the longboats with which the Swedes (and their Norse and Danish cousins) used to establish a far-flung trading and raiding empire. The Estonians, who are related to the Finns, called the Swedes Rootsi, which has the same definition. This is the likely meaning, though there is another theory that says the Swedes were called Rus for their red hair, red beards, and ruddy red faces. Thus, though what is now Russia was filled with many different tribes of many different ethnic groups, the first people called "Rus-sians" were likely the Swedish Vikings.

Along the Black Sea coast and in the Byzantine Empire, some Swedes were known as Varangians, which is a word derived from Old Norse, along with medieval Greek and Old Slavic languages. Beginning in the late 800s and early 900s, many Swedes were tempted by the unbelievable wealth of the Byzantine Empire and Constantinople (today's Istanbul). They hired themselves out to not only the emperor but also the upper classes in the city. Varangian means something akin to "pledged companion" or a "foreigner who has pledged to a new lord."

As they became a dominant force in the region, especially along the vital rivers, the Swedes, to a degree, actually became a uniting force. For centuries, the various tribes along the important rivers fought against each other for control of trade routes or at least part of them. If they had control over them, they could impose taxes on those wishing to pass through. This was a seemingly never-ending cycle. One tribe would establish dominance for a time, then another would take over until they were kicked out, ad infinitum.

In the late 850s, a semi-legendary Swedish prince named Rurik seized the area around the town of Novgorod, south of present-day St. Petersburg. (Today, Novgorod is also known as Veliky Novgorod, meaning "Great Novgorod," as opposed to the more easterly "Nizhny Novgorod," meaning "lower new town.") There is no direct evidence for the existence of Rurik other than what was written about him four centuries afterward, which was based on hearsay and legend. Most historians believe there *was* a Rurik, but the details remain elusive.

As the story goes, the Varangians and Rurik were approached by a number of native "Russian" tribes and asked to act as peacekeepers between them. According to the story, these Russian tribes believed that war would never stop between them until someone made them stop. And that someone was Rurik and the Swedish Vikings.

Portrayal of native tribesmen trading with the Swedes and asking for their help in ending the endless warfare in Russia at the time.

It is said that Rurik and his men, with the aid of slaves and local people, built Novgorod into a powerful fortress and trading hub. It then became the center of Swedish/Varangian/Rus/Viking life in Russia until one of Rurik's family members, Oleg, established his fortress city of Kyiv in today's Ukraine. Prince Igor, believed to be the son of Rurik, is considered to be the founder of the first Russian dynasty, the Rurikids, which lasted from around 862 to 1598. The famed Ivan the Terrible or Ivan IV (r. 1547–1584) was possibly the most famous of the Rurikid dynasty.

In Constantinople, the Varangian Guard became the Eastern Roman emperor's version of the Praetorian Guard of ancient Rome. Members of the Varangian Guard were mostly Swedes, but both Danes and Norsemen made their way to the Byzantine Empire to seek their fortune in the court of one of the richest kings in the world. The Varangian Guard was virtually all-Scandinavian until the later 1000s when both Anglo-Saxons from England and Normans made their way to the area.

The Varangian Guard not only protected the emperor but also took part in his campaigns in the Middle East and southern Europe. At times, support of the Varangian Guard was needed when the old emperor died and a new claimant sought the throne. As you may know, the word "Byzantine" has come to signify something that is secretive, intricate, and hard to deduce; this comes from the incredibly intricate plotting and counter-plotting that took place after the death of a Byzantine emperor or in plots against him. Eventually, claimants to the throne paid massive bribes to the Varangians for their support. At times, the Varangians took what they wanted in true Viking style. In 860, a massive Viking raid believed to have been organized in Kyiv swooped down on Constantinople. A great deal of wealth was taken, and a great deal of destruction was left in their wake.

The chance to make a fortune in the Varangians Guard lured so many Swedes and other Scandinavians that, for a time, there was a real dearth of military-aged men in their homelands. Many different areas within both Sweden and Norway passed laws that made it impossible for anyone "in Greece" (as they called the Byzantine Empire) to inherit wealth or property as a means of forcing men to stay or return home.

As you can see, the Swedes were at the root of the first ruling dynasty of Russia, but within a century or two, intermarriage and the intermingling of customs brought forth a new culture that was in many ways similar to that of pre-Christian Sweden. For example, the people adopted Russian gods that were similar in aspect to the Norse gods. Still, the culture was unique in many other ways, including the evolution and adoption of Russian as its language.

(In the last season of the popular History Channel show Vikings, *a "Rus" invasion of Scandinavia is portrayed, led in part by Ivar the Boneless, who likely never set foot anywhere near Russia, and Russian/Swedish Princes Oleg and Igor. While it makes for an interesting couple of episodes, it should be remembered that there was never a Rus invasion of Scandinavia.)*

While much of the later wealth generated in Russia stayed in Russia, for most of the Viking age, many of the raw goods seized, traded for, or bought in Russia went back to Scandinavia. This wealth may have been gathered together by princes or their families at home to secure positions of power, or it was traded for higher prices in silver and, more rarely, gold.

For the Swedes and much of the Scandinavian world, trade was conducted in many places, but the two most famous trading stations were the island of Gotland in the Baltic Sea on the east coast of Sweden and the island of Birka in Lake Mälaren, west of Stockholm. There, goods from Russia, Europe, and even Arabia were bought and sold, such as furs, walrus ivory, and amber. Slaves were the other major "commodity," and they were taken or bought from almost every area the Vikings raided and traded.

Birka thrived from between circa 800 to 975. Eventually, its distance to major trade routes began to be prohibitive; it is likely that the rivers that led to the lake and island silted up and were no longer navigable by ships big enough to make trade worthwhile. It was supplanted by the large island of Gotland, which is just off the coast of Sweden in the Baltic. Though many coins were likely used as "hack-silver" (pieces of silver used as currency), much of the trade done in both Gotland and Birka was through Arab dirhams (coins), which were made with purer silver than the Vikings knew how to refine. This is just one piece of evidence that shows the Vikings were linked with the rest of the world, not only in violence but in peaceable trade.

Birka has been much in the archaeological news for the past few years, as large numbers of Viking age relics have been found on the island with new technology, such as ground-penetrating radar (LIDAR). The most famous of these is the "warrior woman of Birka," a skeleton that was originally found in 1899 and believed to be male. The skeleton was found with typical male grave goods. According to a paper published in the *American Journal of Physical Anthropology* in 2017, "a sword, an axe, a spear, armour-piercing arrows, a battle knife, two shields, and two horses, one mare and one stallion" were found there. An in-depth study of the bones determined it was female without a doubt; it is likely the 1899 discovery had assumed it was male. However, questions remain. Was this woman a warrior or a queen of such high rank and/or popularity that she was given warrior status? If she was a warrior, how common were female warriors? The Scandinavian sagas and other accounts report women fighters, but other than that, hard evidence for a large number of Viking warrior women or "shield-maidens" is lacking.

The Viking age ended in the mid-11th century. Decisive defeats, unified and centralized kingships, strong defenses, and the wish for more peaceful trade helped to bring about the end of the Vikings. However, the greatest impact on the end of the Viking age was the advent of Christianity. In Sweden, Christianity spread more quickly and more peacefully than it did in Denmark and especially Norway.

In 829, the first recorded Christian missionary, Ansgar, a monk from France, was allowed to teach in Sweden, at least for a time. Over the next 160 years or so, various other monks visited Sweden to spread the Gospel. Some were met with acceptance, while others were thrown out. A number were killed, though. The first regional Swedish king to become Christian did so sometime during the mid-900s to 980 after returning from war in Denmark, where he had been exposed to the new religion. However, sometime after returning to Sweden, he reverted to the worship of the Norse gods Odin, Thor, and Frey, just to name a few. The first king of all Sweden, Olof Eriksson Skötkonung, converted to the new faith sometime between 980 and 990. Many Swedes converted shortly thereafter.

Chapter 4 – Christianity, Killing, and Kronor

Despite the efforts of Ansgar and other monks, as well as the conversion of King Olof Skötkonung and his promotion of the new religion, it took some time for Christianity to take root among the Swedes. Olof invited numerous Catholic priests into the country, and these men brought not only knowledge of the faith but also other skills, most notably building, with them. During the reign of Olof and his three sons, churches were built in many places in southern and central Sweden, most notably near Uppsala, the "Mecca" of the old Norse belief system.

The missionaries found a way to appeal to the Scandinavians by incorporating elements of their old religion into their teachings. They would allude to the idea that Jesus Christ might have been the reappearance of the Norse god Baldur. According to Norse myth, Baldur, the handsome, generous, and kind son of Odin, was said to be destined to come back to Earth after his death at the hands of the trickster god Loki and the end of the world, which is known as Ragnarök. Monks and priests allowed the Swedes to believe that Christ was Baldur by another name and that a new "golden age" would ensue if they worshiped him.

From 1015 to 1070, church building and missionary work slowed to a crawl due to the lack of funds and the Swedes' attention to wars, which were constantly occurring with their neighbors in Norway. This would be a recurring theme in Scandinavian history.

In 1070, one of the great missionaries of the Middle Ages, the monk Adam of Bremen, arrived in Sweden. Under his guidance, the powerful noble families of Sweden all converted, as well as much of the population except for the Sámi in the north. They would hold onto their old ways until the 1500s, and to a degree, they still do.

Those Swedes who would not convert of their own volition were pushed toward it by laws, which made the worship of idols, sacred trees, and stones illegal. Additionally, more and more churches were built throughout the country, allowing the message of Christ to reach more people. Local lords "urged" the population to go. In Scandinavia, maybe more so than in any other European land, some harmless old pagan traditions were incorporated into the Christianity taught there. The Christmas tree and the old practice of the Yule log are two of them. Helping matters was the notion that Christ had been born in December, which was around the time of the winter solstice, the period of longest darkness. However, this is also when the days begin to become longer. The winter solstice was an important pagan holiday, and placing Christmas on this date greatly appealed to the Scandinavians. This aided in the idea that Christ might be a resurrected Baldur. (Historians, astronomers, and biblical scholars believe that Jesus was actually born in the spring, likely April.)

Another bonus for the Swedes in becoming Catholic was the opening of much greater trade with Europe. In the eyes of Catholics, other Catholics were much more trustworthy than pagans.

By the early 1100s, most of Sweden was Catholic. It must be remembered that this was the only Christian sect at that time in the country, as the Protestant Reformation wouldn't begin until the 1500s.

Throughout the 12th and 13th centuries, Christianity spread throughout Sweden, save the most remote hinterlands of the north. Many of the famous Scandinavian wooden stave churches were built in the major cities (barely more than large towns in most cases), and the educated clergymen coming to Sweden from other parts of Europe spread new architectural ideas. Thus, the building of a number of stone churches and a small number of cathedrals began. Oddly enough, the models on which these stone structures were built were Gothic. The various Gothic tribes of Europe, having converted to Christianity in the 5th, 6th, and 7th centuries, had developed a new style. It reflected their desire to both emulate and stand out from the Roman Empire. Perhaps the most important of these structures in Sweden was at Uppsala, where the pagan religion had been centered and where an archbishopric was set up to guide the church in Sweden.

Another result of the Christianization of Sweden was its unifying force. The worship and practice of one deity and a written doctrine (both the Bible and the writings of great early Christian thinkers) could not help but unify the country to a degree. Additionally, the Catholic Church was linked with the ruling houses of Europe in terms of the economy and its blessing of certain leaders. Having the support of the church and the pope was a powerful tool for anyone seeking power.

During this time in Europe, a handful of universities were started and run by the church. In 1309, it was recorded that at least thirty Swedish students attended university in Paris. Other universities in Italy and Germany opened their doors to Swedish students, some of whom were destined to become part of the clergy. Members of the nobility also attended.

By the mid-1500s, Christianity had spread to all corners of Sweden, and in the latter half of the century, attempts were made to convert the Sámi. Though many of them retained elements of their pre-Christian religion (just as others did in Sweden and Europe), the majority converted. However, it is difficult to say how enthusiastic they were about this change.

Dynasties Come, Dynasties Go

The history of the early Christian rulers of Sweden is a bit confusing. Actually, the politics of power remained rather complex in Sweden for quite some time. After the death of the first Christian king, Olof Skötkonung (d. 1022), the rule passed from his eldest son Anund (d. 1050) to his youngest son, who became known as Emund the Old, as he was quite old when he took the throne. This was the Munsö dynasty, named for the place where the family originated.

The next dynasty, named after its first ruler, was the Stenkil dynasty, which lasted from about 1060 to 1126. Four of the ten men of this dynasty were killed in successful attempts to take the throne. Two of them were killed in battle, one was assassinated by supporters of the founding king of the next dynasty, and another was believed to have been poisoned by his wife.

The violent overthrows of Swedish kings did not end with the next dynasties, the Houses of Estridsen, Sverker, Erik, and Bjelbo. These mostly interrelated and sometimes partly foreign (meaning Danish) dynasties ruled Sweden from 1126 to the late 1300s. Other than King Olof Skötkonung, the most well-known Swedish king was King Erik IX (ignore the numerals—Erik was not the ninth of his name to rule all of Sweden. The IX likely refers to him being the ninth prince named Erik in his family line or from his native region). Erik IX is better known as Erik "the Saint" ("Erik den helige" in Swedish). Erik reigned from 1156 to 1160.

Erik is known to history as one of the few European kings who were later sainted by the Catholic Church that really deserved the title. He was a keen supporter of the church, giving it lands and helping with the building of new stone churches in the central and northern parts of the country. The former pagan "Mecca" of Uppsala was named the seat of the first Swedish archbishop under Erik, and the king ordered monks and missionaries to Finland to begin the conversion of that area. At the time, it was under Swedish control, and it would be for some time.

On May 18th, 1160, Erik was killed by a rival while in the midst of Mass. This rival, who took the throne and set off a short civil war, was known as Magnus II. Magnus was killed in battle by the next king, Charles (Karl) VII, who was the son of a previous king. He only ruled for one year before being killed by St. Erik's son Canute (who became King Canute I Erikson and ruled from 1167 to 1196). The ascension of Canute I brought thirty or so years of stability to the country.

That stability ended when Canute's successor, Sverker the Younger, was forced from power in 1208. Although Sverker took the throne with Canute's blessing, he was from another dynasty, as Canute's sons were too young for the throne at his death. Canute's now-grown son, Erik Knutsson, was the one behind the throne change. He became Erik X. Sverker returned in 1210 from exile in Denmark, and a short civil war began. At the Battle of Gestilren in July, Sverker was killed, and the rule of Erik X was secure.

Erik X's wife gave birth to a son after Erik's sudden death by an unknown illness in 1216. The son of Sverker the Younger took the throne. He is known to history as John the Child, for he died in 1222 at the age of twenty-one. As you may have already deduced, the line of Erik X came back to power at that point, with his son, Erik the Lisp and Lame (Erik XI), ruling from 1222 to 1229. He was then overthrown by a cousin, who ruled as Canute II the Tall from late 1229 to 1234. After Erik deposed Canute II, he began his second reign, which lasted from 1234 to 1250.

Erik XI died childless. Valdemar, the son of the powerful Birger Jarl, an influential noble of the House of Bjelbo, was the next to come to power. His house would rule Sweden until 1364. In reality, Birger Jarl was the power behind the throne until he died in 1266.

In some ways, Birger Jarl can be said to be a distant forefather of the progressively-minded Sweden that came to be in the 19th and 20th centuries. During his time in power, Birger Jarl began many economic and social reforms, two of which were remarkably forward-thinking for the time. One of these was the abolition of trial by fire, which, as amazing as it sounds, is the notion that a person was innocent of a crime if they could walk across burning coals (no, not the kind that is popular at some self-help retreats) or walk through flames and survive. You would be right in guessing that most people subjected to a trial by fire were found guilty, which often had dire consequences for their families. In addition to abolishing trial by fire, Birger Jarl also introduced reforms that began to limit the abuses of serfdom (a state of virtual slavery in which one was indebted to a local lord with few, if any, rights).

Kronor

Today's Swedish currency is known as the kronor ("crown" in English), and it has been known as such since the Early Middle Ages. In the time of the Vikings, currency from other kingdoms (such as Arabia) was used for trade, as were precious metals that were weighed. This is the reason so many of the Viking hoards found in England and elsewhere have numerous chunks of silver of various sizes included in them. Amazingly, though it was different in many lands, most traders along the more common trade routes knew how much something was worth in the metal, goods, or foreign coinage used in the north and elsewhere.

With the establishment of a country-wide currency, trade values and exchange rates developed, along with advances in banking, which were brought to the country by both clergy and traders from Europe. ("Modern" banking was founded in Italy in the Early Middle Ages with the development of two-columned accounting, which took into account both credits and debts and expenditures.) With the establishment of a national currency and modern accounting, the European economy began to separate itself from the rest of the world.

Along the coast of northern Europe, from today's Belgium through Holland, northern Germany, Poland, parts of Denmark, and the Baltic states, a primitive economic league began. It is "primitive" by today's standards, but for the time, it was quite advanced. This was the Hanseatic League, which began in the German city of Lübeck in 1159 when that city was being rebuilt after a costly war among regional nobles.

The word *Hanse* in German refers to a guild, a precursor of the modern union. However, while there were guilds throughout Europe, most of these consisted of the collective ownership of small urban businesses and their workers, such as leather-workers, carpenters, wool-makers, candle-makers, etc.

The merchants and producers on the northern coast of Germany had united, to a degree, to regulate prices and for self-protection. Each guild was required to send men for the army when asked. In the independent cities of northern Germany, the guilds and their leaders were the government, so aside from economic control, these guilds, or "Hansa," came to control the politics of the region.

United together to a large degree and each with various and sometimes unique ties to foreign lands, the guilds of northern Europe expanded their trade into the North Sea, the Baltic, Russia, and down the river systems of central Europe. Before long, the major northern European coastal cities of the time had banded together. Each city was a state in and of itself (at least most were at the beginning), but they agreed to work with each other for the economic common good. This included the formation of merchant and naval fleets that soon gave the Hanseatic League a foothold in Scandinavia.

Hamburg was another important city, as was the port city of Bremen, which is just south of both Hamburg and Lübeck. There were other cities in the league, which reached all the way to Bergen, Norway, and into Russia. The town of Visby is located on the age-old Viking trading station, the island of Gotland.

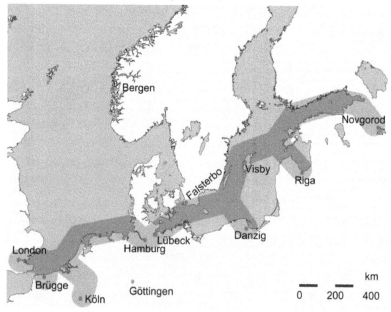

The main trade routes and system of the Hanseatic League.
https://commons.wikimedia.org/wiki/File:Haupthandelsroute_Hanse.png

At times, regional nobles would attempt to gain control of Hansa cities in his area of influence, but the Hansa cities were powerful, both economically and militarily. When threatened, they often banded together and/or hired mercenaries to defend themselves (this sometimes included naval ships as well). At the same time, the cities would often begin to wage economic warfare against their foes. Most of the time, at least until the early 1600s, this worked, though, at times, there were reverses.

If one city went "rogue" and attempted to undercut prices or edge into markets traditionally dominated by other cities, wars might erupt. It should be noted that the regulations were often verbal agreements or rather "loose" in their wording. War also occurred with foreign powers, such as England in the 1460s and Russia in the 1490s.

The Hanseatic League was dominated by German cities. German traders and Hansa officials (often one and the same) settled throughout their trading areas around the North and Baltic Seas. From the mid-1200s, one of these areas was Sweden, though, for much of the time, Denmark controlled the southwestern portion of the country. In Stockholm, Uppsala, and Visby (as well as other minor ports and towns), German Hanseatic merchants carved out enclaves where they enjoyed protection from the local laws due to their influence. They slowly became enmeshed in both the Swedish economy and politics.

Sweden was rich in raw materials, and the island of Gotland and its port of Visby was perhaps the most important trading hub in the Baltic. Over time, Sweden became more and more intertwined with the Hanseatic League. With Hansa control over the richest trade routes in northern Europe, Sweden became increasingly dependent on the Hansa for trade. Sweden grew rich at this time, but the Hansa merchants grew richer. Due to their riches and control of the trade routes, the Hansa and its German representatives, workers, and naval and merchant vessels began to have more and more influence on Sweden's economic and political life.

Throughout their areas of control, especially in Norway, Sweden, and Novgorod in Russia, Germans settled and formed cultural and economic enclaves. In Sweden, the economic control of the Hansa and their special treatment, both economic and legal, would cause resentment. This grew over the years, especially when Hansa cities allied with those who would do Sweden harm, such as King Christian II of Denmark when he attempted to place himself on the throne of Sweden in the early 1500s.

By the 1300s, the Hanseatic League had firm control of most of the important trade hubs and routes in the north of Europe, spanning an area from Norway down the Rhine River into Germany and east into Sweden and Russia. In a very real sense, the Hanseatic trade routes, as well as those dominated by the Italian city-states in southern Europe and in the Middle East and beyond, were the first globally integrated trade systems. This allowed for a wide variety of goods and riches that could have only been dreamed of a hundred years before.

However, these trade routes also increased the spread of disease. In the late 1340s, the most infamous disease of all time, the bubonic plague (better known as the Black Death), spread throughout Europe, North Africa, and western Asia.

Sweden lost about one-third of its population to the plague, which was roughly the same as other parts of Europe. We know that trade routes played a huge role in the spread of the disease. For instance, even though Finland was part of Sweden at this time, it was barely affected by the plague due to its remoteness. The plague was devastating in the short term, both socially and economically. For the wealthiest, the death of so many agricultural workers and the taxes collected from them and on their crops meant a reduction in income and influence. Conversely, after the plague had passed in the early 1350s, the reduced number of workers meant that laborers were in a better position economically. The lack of labor meant higher wages for those who remained, as well as greater choice and increasing economic and political power.

Chapter 5 – Empire and Intrigue

Ask many Chinese students what the worst part of history class is, and you'll likely get this reply: "Memorizing the dynasties and emperors." There were twelve major dynasties, a few minor ones, and an untold number of emperors. Ask many Swedish students what the worst part of history class is, and you'll likely get a similar reply, although it's kings and queens in Sweden, not emperors. There were eleven Swedish dynasties, which includes that of today's royal family, and a number of Danish rulers as well.

Suffice it to say that for the purposes of this book, we will not be listing all of the kings and (three) queens of Sweden who ruled the country from the 900s onward. Rather, we shall say that those who ruled Sweden came to do so through a combination of economic and political intrigue and military force.

Another characteristic of Swedish politics from the 1200s onward is the upward mobility of the lower classes, at least as rights and security were concerned. Though this did not happen quickly and was fraught with problems, Swedish history mirrored English history to a degree. Over the centuries, power devolved from an absolute monarchy to a constitutional monarchy in which various checks on the monarch's power were put in place.

As in England, the history of Sweden can also be said to be a gradual but continuous evolution of the rights of the majority. Though in both countries, violent outbursts and even civil conflicts broke out, the rights for the average person increased over time, usually in a peaceful manner. This was unlike what happened in other parts of Europe, where extreme and sometimes world-shaking violence was usually the precursor to change.

The Kalmar Union and Baltic Expansion

In the 13th century, the Swedes fought against both the Danes and the Norwegians in a variety of wars and battles. These were mostly fought over Norwegian territories, as Norway was the weaker of the three Scandinavian countries at that time. It was also geographically divided and isolated. Thus, many local nobles claimed kingship, oftentimes with the support of one of the other two Scandinavian kingdoms.

The Kalmar Union

Primarily because of the economic and political challenges coming from the Hanseatic League, the three Scandinavian countries united under the guidance and leadership of a remarkable woman, Queen Margaret. She became the ruler of all three countries in 1387 through a tangled web of inheritance. However, because she was a woman, it was agreed that she should provide the three northern kingdoms (remember, Finland was Swedish at this time) with a king as soon as possible. Her only son died before she came to the throne, and he had no heir. After some debate, Margaret adopted her sister's grandson and chose him to be king, which was approved by the noble councils of the three kingdoms in 1397. However, Margaret retained the title of regent and ruled behind the throne until she died in 1412.

Erik (r. 1397–1439) eventually lost all three crowns due to his harsh rule and relatively unsuccessful wars. Just less than one hundred years later, the Kalmar Union was essentially over in all but name, though it officially continued until 1570. The union never really got off the ground. An official agreement spelling out the laws and rights within the union was never produced, and in each of the three kingdoms, nobles and rivals for the thrones did not want to see an all-powerful lord of all three countries. On top

---

of this, there were the countries' possessions, which included Finland, Iceland, Greenland, and some of the islands off the north coast of Scotland that had been conquered in the Viking era.

The ascension of Gustav Vasa as the undisputed king of a united Sweden in 1523 effectively ended the Kalmar Union, which went on in name for a few more decades. However, the Kalmar Union was one of the first voluntary steps in European history in which countries attempted to unite for mutual benefit.

Baltic Expansion

For Sweden, the only real place for economic expansion without serious competition (at least for a time) was Russia. Sweden was located on the Baltic Sea along with Russia, and the Swedish territory of Finland bordered the huge but sparsely populated and economically primitive nation. In the early 1300s, there was a conflict with Russia over the eastern border of Sweden/Finland. This led to the first territorial settlement between the two kingdoms, the Peace of Nöteborg (1323).

Russian trade with the city of Novgorod was productive, but by the early 1400s, competition with the Hanseatic League led the rulers of Sweden to look for expansion, both economically and territorially, across the Baltic Sea. Sweden wanted the territories that are now the countries of Lithuania, Latvia, and Estonia.

On July 15th, 1410, the famed Teutonic Knights were defeated at the Battle of Grunwald by an alliance of the Kingdom of Poland and the Grand Duchy of Lithuania. This created a power vacuum in the area of today's Baltic states, one which Swedish King Erik XIII (also known as Erik of Pomerania), the adopted son and nephew of Margaret I (ruler of the Kalmar Union), was eager to fill.

Erik built the fortress of Elsinore on the (currently) Danish side of the straits leading into the Baltic Sea and strengthened the fortress of Kärnan on the opposite side of the narrow waterway in an attempt to tax and control traffic going in and out of the Baltic. (You may recognize the name Elsinore; it was made famous in William Shakespeare's play *Hamlet.*)

This effort was a bit self-defeating since it was aimed at the Hanseatic members, which were forced to pay tolls going through the straits. As you can imagine, this led to conflict with a variety of those cities, especially Lübeck, which was the most powerful.

The imposed tolls and the closeness of Erik's kingdom to Lübeck posed a threat to the Hansa. Though battles were not continuous, the Hansa generally got the upper hand, which was aided by some of the earliest examples of economic warfare. Certain goods, including food, were withheld to weaken Erik. At the same time, his gifting of castles and lands in his extensive kingdom to Hanseatic merchants, leaders, and diplomats was both counterproductive and unpopular. Erik, as you read above, was deposed in 1439 after a series of internal rebellions, though he remained the powerful duke of Pomerania until his death twenty years later. (At the time, Pomerania consisted of lands on both sides of the modern borders of northern Germany and Poland.)

Chapter 6 – Plots, Counter-plots, and Civil War

During the latter part of Erik of Pomerania's reign, rebellions both small and large erupted within Sweden. These mainly had to do with the currency manipulation Erik attempted, which disrupted the Swedish economy. There were also conflicts surrounding the appointment of Erik's choice for the archbishop of Sweden. This was opposed by a large number of Swedish nobles on the high council and in the countryside, who had their own man in mind, partially to act as a balance against Erik's power.

Attempts to settle this problem by submitting the two candidates for the election made things worse, as bribery and vote-rigging were rife. This, in turn, led to an open revolt against Erik in 1434. This was led by a rich noble named Engelbrekt Engelbrektsson (he controlled a large iron mine in the area once known as Dalecarlia in the central part of the country). Questions involving an unpopular sheriff in the town of Västerås also played a part in the rebellion. (Yes, it's pronounced almost exactly like the region of Westeros in George R. R Martin's *A Song of Ice and Fire*, the inspiration for the TV series *Game of Thrones*, though his inspiration for Westeros actually came from a Scottish town named Wester Ross.)

Engelbrekt had much support in the center of the country and gathered an army. Important nobles in the area threw their lot in with Engelbrekt and moved south to take Stockholm, which fell to the rebels with little opposition. The rebellion spread throughout southern Sweden, and violence occurred when the rebels attempted to expel Erik's appointed sheriffs, most of whom weren't even Swedish.

King Erik formed a fleet and asked for military help from the unlikeliest source: the Hanseatic League. It was reluctant to support him, but it did so out of fear of economic uncertainty and the anti-foreign tone of the Swedish uprising. Erik took Stockholm, but the uprising was now supported by much of the country. Still, Erik was the rightful king, and talks with the rebels in May 1435 established a truce. Erik agreed to respect the laws of Sweden and not give his castles and lands to non-Swedes.

Unfortunately, three of the most important castles and fortresses were to remain exempt from the agreement. Erik also still had the power to tax, which increased to the point where the rebellion began again in earnest later that year. Engelbrekt was named commander of the rebel armies, but since he was a minor noble from an outlying region, he did not have the support of the more powerful nobles in the army. These men supported another popular noble, Karl Knutsson Bonde, for the position. Engelbrekt was later murdered by a man with whom he had a legal dispute. That man was later given protection by Bonde, leading to the belief that Engelbrekt was assassinated. If this is true, Karl Knutsson Bonde "thanked" the assassin by seizing his lands later on.

In 1439, violence broke out once more, with arson and anti-foreign riots taking place not only in the countryside but also in the major city of Uppsala. In Denmark itself, where Erik had his throne and (theoretically) the most control, the Danish Council, which was supposed to guide and advise the monarch, turned against him. By this time, Erik knew his time was up. He relinquished the throne to his nephew Christopher of Bavaria and wisely removed himself to Pomerania.

The removal of Erik took the steam out of the Swedish rebels, and the Swedish Council agreed to the accession of Christopher because they believed him weak and pliable. To a large extent, this was true. Many substantial changes in the way Sweden had been governed and organized began, including a prohibition on the king moving Swedish wealth out of the country. In addition, the money deposited in the new state treasury was to be used only within the borders of Sweden. At the time, this was an almost revolutionary step in Europe, although some Italian city-states had similar laws. The rebel commander, Karl Knutsson Bonde, who aspired to sit on the throne of all Scandinavia, was essentially exiled to his fortress in Finland. A couple of islands were granted to him by the council.

The reign of Christopher (king of Sweden 1441–1448) was relatively short and marked by economic hardships, which began with crop failures. This was made worse by the fact that Christopher was involved in plundering royal estates for his own gain outside of the country.

In 1442, Christopher agreed to a new legal code that, among other things, granted the nation's castles and their extensive lands to the nobles of the council, not his German favorites. This did "buy" him some support, but his defeat at the hands of the former king, Erik, for the control of the rich island of Gotland, combined with economic hardships and his financial schemes, caused rebellion to break out in 1448. Another long civil war seemed to be averted when Christopher suddenly died, likely of natural causes, in that same year. The council agreed on Christian of Oldenburg (today, as then, a German city just south of the Danish border) as the new king of Denmark, Norway, and, theoretically, Sweden.

We say "theoretically" because Karl Knutsson Bonde heard the news of Christopher's death and moved to a base near Uppsala. There, he began his attempt to become not only the king of Sweden but also of the entire Kalmar Union. He began this attempt at Uppsala since, by tradition, the kings of Sweden were traditionally made king at the Stones of Mora, which is near the important central-eastern city. The Swedish Council was literally made to proclaim him king at spear-point, as Karl had summoned his army and supporters to the Stones of Mora for the surprise coronation.

For the next nine years, Karl Knutsson Bonde (now known to history as Karl or Karl VIII of Sweden) and Christian I of Denmark would fight a bloody war for not only control of Sweden but also a weak and divided Norway. In 1449, Norwegian supporters of Karl named him king of the country at the cathedral in Trondheim. However, his kingship over the Norwegians ended when Christian, who was the stronger military power, enforced his claim on Norway. The Swedish Council then withheld its support of Karl, not wanting to fight Denmark over Norway.

However, this did not mean that the war between Norway and Sweden continued. From 1451 to 1457, Karl VIII was politically outmaneuvered by Christian, who was supported by some very powerful Swedish nobles. Karl VIII was exiled once again, but he did not give up on his dream of being king of both Sweden and Norway.

Christian had secured the support of not only some powerful noble families but also the Swedish archbishop in Uppsala, who represented some powerful families, not all of whom liked Christian. Christian was the king of Sweden from 1457 to 1464. During this time, plots, counter-plots, and uprisings occurred throughout the country.

Behind the scenes, powerful families plotted against Christian, among them the Stures, the Oxenstiernas, the Totts, and, most importantly, the Vasa family. In 1464, a realigned council recalled Karl VIII back to the throne, and he ruled until his death in 1470. The next year, Christian I attempted a return to the Swedish throne. He summoned an army and built a new fleet, but he and his Swedish supporters were defeated by his opponents, most notably the Sture family. Sten Sture, the leader of the house, had seized control of the council and ruled as regent from 1471 to 1503, although he was removed for a few years beginning in 1497. He took this role until a king suitable to the entire council could be found.

During the reign of Sten Sture, Sweden made arrangements with the powers in charge of present-day Latvia and established a Swedish economic and military presence there. This set Sweden on a course of conflict with not just one but two of the major powers of the time: Denmark and Russia. By establishing Swedish outposts in Latvia, Sture hoped to check both Russian expansion westward and Danish expansion eastward. Sweden would engage in conflicts with both powers for the next three and a half centuries.

In 1495, the Russians attacked two Swedish outposts in Finland. Over the course of two years, Sweden and Russia fought a number of small battles in the area before making a tenuous peace.

The Danes did not stop in their attempts to regain rebellious Sweden and spent much of the last five or six years of Sture's regency maneuvering behind the scenes to regain control of the country. Many of these maneuvers involved the archbishop of Sweden, who was a Danish supporter. For a time, conflict broke out between the archbishop and Sture, who assaulted the clergyman's properties with armies of his supporters. It was a war that Sture could not win, for he was both excommunicated by the archbishop and had Danish armies moving into his territory. Therefore, he negotiated a Danish withdrawal, which, strangely enough, ended with Sture receiving personal control of two important castles, one in Finland and one on the coast of Sweden. In late 1503, Sten Sture died. His place was taken by Svante Nilsson.

Under Nilsson, who died around eight years later in 1512, Sweden and Denmark continued their conflict. The Danes still controlled two important Swedish fortresses and castles at Kalmar and Borgholm. The former allowed the Danes to control much of southwestern Sweden, and the latter was an important island on the east coast of Sweden, which threatened trade in the area. The new regent was no friend of the Danes, and he attempted to take the two fortress castles mentioned above in 1510.

When Nilsson died two years later, his political opponent Erik Trolle was elected leader of the council. As you may have anticipated, this was not the beginning of a new era of peace and stability in Sweden, as Sten Sture the Younger (the son of Svante Nilsson) was playing a game of his own. He wanted to be regent instead. Sture was fortunate that his father had received the fortress of Borgholm on the island of Öland in addition to the one in Finland, as well as his family lands throughout the country.

In 1514, Erik Trolle managed, through political maneuvering and bribery, to have his son appointed archbishop of the country. The two worked together to prevent Sture the Younger from attaining his goal. This conflict included an ever-increasing number of battles in Sweden itself. The conflict between the two Swedish nobles and their supporters remained a largely Swedish affair until 1517 when the king of Denmark, now Christian II (r. 1513–1523), decided the time was right to get involved and return Sweden to Danish control.

Using the danger to the archbishop as an excuse (and also to strengthen ties with the pope in Rome), Christian II sent a fleet to the Swedish coast near Stockholm. To the surprise of many, Christian's force was defeated, and what remained retreated back to Denmark.

Rather than strengthen the position of the archbishop and his family, Christian's actions stoked the anti-foreign fire that had always been burning in the background of Swedish politics. The archbishop was forcibly removed from office in 1517, despite the protests of Rome.

In response to the removal of the archbishop, Christian II gathered a new fleet and an army of mercenaries and landed once again near Stockholm. Though the Danes sustained losses there, they were successful in driving into central Sweden and taking the strategic and economically important island of Öland with Sture's fortress at Borgholm.

Danish support increased when the Catholic Church in Denmark decreed excommunication against the rebelling Swedes. Excommunication was more than just a spiritual decree; it also forbade any Catholic from associating with the excommunicated in any manner (in this case, economically being the most important). Excommunication was also threatened to anyone supporting them.

In 1520, the Danes invaded near Uppsala, and Sten Sture the Younger was mortally wounded in a battle fought on a frozen lake. When he died shortly thereafter, resistance against the Danes fell apart. The newly restored Archbishop Trolle negotiated between Christian II and the leading Swedish rebels. In the fall of 1520, Christian II became the king of Sweden, as well as Norway and Denmark.

After the defeat of Sten Sture the Younger, Christian spread the word that he would forgive his enemies and move on. In the first week of November 1520, Christian was crowned king of Sweden, and a week or more of festivities was planned.

If Christian II had lived up to his word to truly forgive his enemies, Scandinavian history might have been much different. On the night of November 8th, 1520, many of the king's "former" enemies were invited to a dinner to celebrate a new era and reconciliation. Instead, one of the most, if not *the* most infamous, event in Swedish history took place: the "Bloodbath of Stockholm." Over one hundred of Christian's enemies were slaughtered, including bishops and a powerful noble of the Vasa clan, Erik Johansson Vasa, who had a son named Gustav. Gustav had been doing business among the Hanseatic cities of northern Germany when Christian had come to power in Sweden. Before his father's death, he was arrested while traveling through Denmark to go home. He was held as a hostage to ensure the good behavior of his father back home. He managed to escape and return to his family home at Räfsnäs in central Sweden, west of Uppsala.

Chapter 7 – Father of Sweden

The Bloodbath of Stockholm had a number of important consequences. One of them was the negative impact it had on support for the Roman Catholic Church, as the archbishop was believed to have played a central role in the massacre. The victims had been given a mock trial based on trumped-up charges of heresy before their execution that night.

Another important consequence was that Christian II's betrayal and Erik Johansson Vasa's death gave rise to the man who is still called the "Father of Sweden" by many Swedes and historians today: Gustav Vasa.

When Gustav heard the news of the bloodbath and the death of his father (along with a nephew), he was determined to not only fight and remove the Danish king from the throne but also take it for himself and end two centuries of instability. Before arriving in Sweden, he had been held hostage in Denmark but escaped before his father's murder. Gustav fled his family estate and headed into Dalecarlia in the interior of the country (known in Swedish as Dalarna; it borders Norway in the west). He went there to gather support from the region, which had been the birthplace of many of the rebellions over the years.

Gustav Vasa, dressed in local costume, rallying the men of Dalecarlia in this 19ᵗʰ-century painting by Johan Gustaf Sandberg.

Gustav Vasa was related to the widow of Sten Sture the Younger, whose base of power was in Dalecarlia. Many of the families that had supported Sture the Younger now rallied to Gustav Vasa.

Vasa and his supporters defeated a force gathered by the local pro-Danish governor at the village of Brunnbäck in Dalecarlia, just east of Uppsala, and then moved to Uppsala itself. There, he defeated the forces that had gathered around the infamous archbishop of Uppsala, Gustav Trolle. Uppsala was a much more important city back then. It was where Swedish kings were crowned and where the Swedish Council met.

When Uppsala fell to Vasa and his army, much of the country supported him. In August 1521, Vasa was elected head of the council. Over the next year, the armies under his command took control of much of Sweden, except for fortresses on the Finnish coast and the important cities of Stockholm and Kalmar.

Vasa was a very shrewd man, and he approached the leaders of the Hanseatic League for their support against what was a common enemy (or at least, in the case of the Hansa, a rival)—Denmark. Vasa and nearly everyone else believed that Christian II would attempt to secure control of Sweden once again. Surprisingly, both economic and political pressure, which was applied by the Hanseatic League and Christian's rivals within

Denmark, forced him to flee the country. He lived in exile in the Netherlands until further political machinations and the effects of the Protestant Reformation caused his arrest. He died in prison in Denmark in 1559.

Vasa became the elected king of Sweden in 1523. In 1528, he had himself crowned as king at Uppsala, having spent the last five years maneuvering to become the last elected king of the 16th century of Sweden and its first truly autocratic monarch. In 1531, Vasa, working with the Hanseatic League, seized the southernmost region of Sweden, Scania, from the Danes, a land that had been Danish for centuries.

Gustav Vasa by German artist Jacob Binck, 1542.

Vasa ruled Sweden until his death in 1560. He stayed in power by being perhaps just as ruthless as his former enemy, Christian II of Denmark, and establishing a nation-wide bureaucracy that was ultimately responsible to only him. He also secured the support of a powerful Swedish family with his second marriage in 1536. He married for the third time in 1552. Nine of his children survived into adulthood. This is amazing, as healthcare was relatively primitive, the infant mortality rate and disease rate were high, and the life expectancy rate was low. Three of his sons would sit on the throne after his death.

In 1536, Vasa rejected his alliance with the Hanseatic City of Lübeck and formed a working relationship with Lübeck's main rival, the eastern German port city of Danzig (now Gdańsk in Poland). Vasa was rightfully skeptical of keeping too close of ties with Lübeck, as they had influenced Sweden greatly for more than a century.

At the same time Vasa was marginalizing Lübeck (at least in regards to Sweden), he imported experts in administration from Germany, using their knowledge to form the previously mentioned bureaucracy. Vasa was extremely skilled at placing rivals against themselves in the fight for influence in Sweden, all the while keeping both from gaining too much influence.

In 1527, Vasa felt strong enough in his position to call together the Swedish Council at Västerås. This was made up not only of nobles but also clergy, merchants, and influential members of the free peasant class, who actually had more political rights than one would imagine. The council did two extremely important things: they established a Swedish parliament (known as the Riksdag) and, more importantly at the time, separated the church in Sweden from that of Rome.

Many historians have compared Gustav Vasa with his contemporary in England, Henry VIII of England. Both were intensely ambitious and temperamental. Both were faced with rebellions that they put down ruthlessly. Both Vasa and Henry VIII eventually turned on their allies. (In the case of Henry VIII, they were Cardinal Thomas Wolsey and the devoutly Catholic philosopher and chancellor Thomas More. Vasa similarly turned on men who helped him achieve and consolidate his power.)

They were both quick to joke and loved music. (The Swedish Royal Court Orchestra, which is still in existence, was established on Vasa's orders in 1526, and Henry VIII wrote music.) Recurring infections of the leg (and, in the case of Vasa, the jaw) contributed to the death of both monarchs.

Henry separated England from the Catholic Church over his desire to have his first marriage to Catherine of Aragon annulled in favor of wife number two, Anne Boleyn. The church's refusal to bend to Henry's will led the English king to adopt many of the tenets of the new Christian sect spreading throughout northern Europe. This was Protestantism or "Lutheranism," which was named after its founder, Martin Luther of Germany.

In Sweden, though the purpose and the means of the break from Catholicism and Rome were different, the result was the same. In England, Henry founded the Church of England, also known as the Anglican Church. In Sweden, Vasa established the Church of Sweden.

When Henry broke with the Catholic Church, he also came to realize that he could more easily confiscate church lands and wealth in the country. In Sweden, Gustav knew that the removal of the Catholic Church from Swedish political life would give him additional power, especially when the new religious sect was beholden to him for land and influence. Gustav, like Henry, also knew that the Catholic Church in Sweden had been rich, although it was not as wealthy as its English counterpart. He could use these riches not only for his own political gain and personal wealth but also to bolster the Swedish economy. He began to build a national military (especially Sweden's navy) rather than depend on volunteers or mercenaries.

Both countries benefited from their isolation; England is surrounded by water, and Sweden is so far in the north and across the Baltic Sea that people tended not to bother them as much. Thus, neither of them suffered nearly as much as France and especially the many states of Germany in the religiously motivated conflicts that would embroil Europe for the next hundred years.

In England, there was much resistance to Henry's rebellion against the Catholic Church, especially compared to Sweden.

There were a number of reasons for this, one of them being the age of the Catholic Church in England. By the time of the Protestant Reformation, the Catholic Church in England was nearly one thousand years old. The Catholic Church had only been established in Sweden in the 12th and 13th centuries.

Another factor contributing to the rise of Protestantism in Sweden was its proximity to Germany, the birthplace of the Reformation. The invention of the printing press in Germany some ninety years prior allowed for the quick dissemination of information, and many of Luther's works (and those of other leading Protestant reformers) were quickly translated from German into Swedish.

Though the literacy rate in Sweden and Europe as a whole was generally low, much of the nobility were able to read, along with many of the merchants in urban areas. Even for those who could not read, word spread quickly, and Swedes read the rebellious tracts voraciously.

As you may know, Luther and other Protestant leaders believed that the Catholic Church's insistence on using Latin in all of its texts, including the Bible, meant that the vast majority of the people in Europe had to rely on priests to read them the Bible and tell them what it meant. The Protestant Reformation changed this. Luther was the first to translate the Bible into German, which made it accessible to millions of people and allowed them to challenge many of the Catholic Church's beliefs and interpretations. For the Swedes, it was easier to translate Luther's German-language Bible into Swedish than from Latin.

Henry VIII's rebellion against the pope was based on his desire to leave his first wife. In Sweden, Vasa used the popularity of Protestant ideas for his own ends, and there was little resistance against it. Two of Vasa's allies, the Petri brothers, became high officials within Gustav's government and in the Church of Sweden. But, like Henry, Gustav eventually turned on them and placed them in prison for a time. (Similar to Henry, Gustav had many of his enemies beheaded.)

By the time of his death in 1560, Gustav had put down a number of rebellions, some of which ended in the torture and quartering of his enemies and the display of their head on pikes as a warning. He also secured the Swedish Council's agreement that he had ruled by divine right (the belief that his position as king had been ordained and blessed by God) and that his sons and grandsons should be the future kings of Sweden. He also had, for the most part, united the country behind his rule and that of his family. Though the Vasa dynasty would end with the abdication of the extraordinary Queen Kristina in 1654, Gustav laid the groundwork for an efficient national government, national unity, and Swedish national identity.

Chapter 8 – A Real Game of Thrones

The next chapter of this short introductory book on the history of Sweden will discuss the reigns of some of Gustav Vasa's descendants and the rise and fall of Sweden as a European power. However, history is not just kings and wars; it is about the lives and cultures of the people, health and medicine, science, inventions, law and justice, fashion, and so much more.

This includes the arts. Unfortunately, we do not have the space to go into a detailed history of the development and evolution of Swedish art, architecture, and culture, so a brief introductory chapter will have to suffice.

At the start of the book, you read and saw some of the earliest examples of artistic expression in Sweden, the petroglyphs of the pre-Viking "Vendel Period" (c. 500-750 CE) and the Viking age runestones that dot the Swedish countryside.

Most of the runestones in Sweden are actually not about the Viking raids or their spiritual beliefs, though some are. Most of those come from the late Viking age and early Christian era (c. 1000-1150). As you read earlier, a great many runestones include Christian references.

With the establishment of Christianity in Sweden and the appointment of an archbishop (the direct representative of the pope), both art and architecture in Sweden developed along religious lines, as they did throughout Europe. The only true exception to this in the Middle Ages were the portraits of monarchs, nobles, and high clergy, as well as paintings and tapestries depicting important events in their lives. At this time, art was meant to promote religion and elevate the ruling class.

With the ascension of the Hanseatic League and the development of the Kalmar Union, more and more foreigners (most notably Danes and Germans) came to Sweden for trade and politics. As you saw, the rise of the Hanseatic League in both Europe and Sweden allowed for much economic development and the establishment of valuable trade routes. By the 1300s, the Hanseatic League dominated the economic life of Sweden, and large enclaves of foreigners (mostly Germans and Danes) rose up in Swedish cities and ports throughout the country.

The Danes and Germans, who were located "on" the European continent itself as opposed to Sweden and Norway, meant that people in both countries had established ties with the other states of Europe. While it is true that increasing numbers of Swedes traveled into Europe after their conversion to Christianity, more foreigners came to Sweden than the other way around. That meant that Danish and German cultural influences did as well.

The most obvious example of this can be seen in the architectural skills, styles, and expertise that German architects had that most Swedes did not. This meant that growing Swedish cities, especially Stockholm and Uppsala, began to display a distinctively German style.

The first Christian churches in Sweden were constructed of wood. With the arrival of increasing numbers of Danes and Germans, most of the large churches were rebuilt, becoming cathedrals in both Stockholm and Uppsala. These were built in the German Gothic style, which was all the rage in northern Europe at the time.

Likewise, many of the artworks within the churches and palaces of the time were done by foreign artists. Artworks in churches obviously had a religious theme, and the paintings, woodwork, and sculptures within the church or its grounds looked much like what could be found in other northern

European nations.

With the coming of the Protestant Reformation came the removal or destruction of much religious art, not only in Sweden but also throughout northern and central Europe, where Protestantism took root. The reason for this was the Protestant belief that the Catholic Church had strayed too far from the edicts against idolatry, which is the worship of idols and images rather than of God.

In the early days of the Reformation and before Vasa's establishment of the Church of Sweden, iconoclasts (people who saw the display of religious images as blasphemous) sporadically rose up throughout the country. As you might imagine, these riots and the hostility toward religious images in general at a time when religion was almost as important as food caused a decline in the arts.

However, as time went by, people throughout Protestant Europe, including Scandinavia, began to portray non-religious scenes and images. These were not only paintings of monarchs, nobility, and rich merchants but also "everyday" people, such as farmers and builders.

Chapter 9 – The Swedish Empire

When Gustav Vasa died in September 1560, his deathbed wish was that his family remain united. He knew from both experience and history that many times after the death of a strong and long-reigning king, disunity and a struggle for power would begin.

Gustav's eldest son Eric became king after his father's death. Eric became Eric XIV when he took the crown, though his claim to be the fourteenth was based on the reigns of local tribal leaders of the past and Swedish cultural mythology that included many kings, most of them nonexistent. Adding "XIV" to his name added a touch of historical continuity to his reign, which was needed after the death of a great king who was the first in his line.

Everything about Eric seemed to point to a long and stable reign. His father had insisted on the finest education available, and Eric, along with his half-brother John, seemed to like learning. He mastered several foreign languages, had a decent knowledge of the latest scientific theories and breakthroughs, and loved math. He was also quite versed in history, which would provide him with much of the knowledge he would need as the king.

By the time he became king, Eric had already been in charge of a number of fiefdoms, so he was familiar with ruling. One of his territories was the city of Kalmar on the southern coast, an exceedingly important trading station and fortress.

Like other European royals of the time, Eric searched the royal houses of Protestant northern Europe for a wife. In the 2007 movie *Elizabeth: The Golden Age*, Eric is seen at the court of Elizabeth I of England, seeking her hand in marriage. This is Hollywood at work again. Eric never voyaged to England, but he did exchange letters with the queen and sent her a portrait. In the film, Elizabeth was portrayed as being in her prime, but in actuality, she only had a few more years left to reign. She put Eric off like she did all others.

Gustav I had instructed his son not to pursue Elizabeth, likely because of her age and inability to have children, but Eric persisted to the point of almost creating a rift between father and son. Eric also lobbied many other royal and noble houses for a wife. Eventually, he married his mistress, a Swedish noblewoman, who became queen of Sweden for a short time.

Eric XIV suffered from increasing mental instability as he grew older. His reign was also fraught with difficulties. There was an on-again, off-again war with Denmark over Norway, and the Danish kings continued their claims on Sweden, which depleted the state treasury. This forced Eric to raise taxes and to further deplete the decreasing yields of Sweden's main silver mine. Another difficulty was the nobility of Sweden, who likely saw the chance to weaken a new king in the first years of his reign and regain some of the power they had lost under Gustav I.

However, what gave Eric the most trouble and what led to his truly bizarre and tragic downfall was the conflict he had with his half-brother, John. John had married into the Polish royal family, the Jagiellonian dynasty, which gave him influence in that powerful kingdom. And he did this in spite of Eric's explicit demands to not do so. John was also the ruler of Finland as its grand duke. Finland was an autonomous part of Sweden, meaning it was ruled directly by John, not Eric. Making things worse, John had both negotiated for and invaded the Baltic states of Estonia and Latvia. (The third, Lithuania, was a ruling partner with Poland in their informal union. Their lands extended quite far into Russia and Ukraine and had great influence in central Europe at this time.) By gaining these territories, John was seemingly setting himself up as a rival to Sweden and surrounding it with hostile states.

Making things worse, Eric picked an unpopular adviser, at least among the nobility. Göran Persson, who had been an enemy of Gustav I, was a political survivor and had befriended Eric in his rebellious youth. Persson would bring Eric into conflict with many nobles and the king's half-brother John.

Despite all of these issues, which were issues that virtually every king faced at the time, Eric's biggest problem was, well, Eric. For reasons that may remain forever unknown, Eric began showing signs of serious mental illness and instability early in his reign. Like many other unstable rulers throughout history, part of Eric's madness was increasingly intense paranoia, which was fed by his adviser Göran Persson.

In 1566, the king began to suspect the powerful and influential noble Sture family. (You may remember that members of the Sture family had played an important role in Sweden before the reign of Gustav Vasa.) In a truly bizarre series of events, Eric had five Stures arrested and jailed. At first, the king seemed to be wracked with guilt. He went to one of the cells holding the leader of the noble family, Svante Sture, and asked for forgiveness while on his knees, assuring Svante that everything would be all right and that he would soon be released. Sometime later, the king returned and stabbed Svante's son Nils in the chest or arm. It is believed one of the king's cousins, who was a bodyguard, finished Nils Sture off.

The king then went back to Svante Sture's cell. He dropped to his knees once again and sadly pronounced that while he had promised to release the elder Sture, he now could not, as he could not expect Sture to forgive him for his son's murder. In the end, three Stures were killed, along with two of their supporters.

After the murders, Eric apparently descended further into insanity. His personal tutor, whom the king had known for years, followed the king outside, where he was found in a state of great agitation. The tutor, Dionysius Beurraeus, attempted to calm the king but apparently said something wrong. The king ordered his personal guards to kill the tutor and then took off into a nearby forest.

Things were made worse by the fact that the king remained in the forest for three days and nights. During this time, Göran Persson had a decree passed in the king's name that endorsed all past and future sentences against those arrested. Many of the votes were likely secured from noble supporters of the prisoners, for Persson ordered the news of their deaths to be kept secret.

After the king was found, dressed in peasant clothes in a nearby village, he was brought back to the castle. The first person who saw him was the widow and mother of the Sture victims, who was met by a (once again) kneeling king, asking for forgiveness. In return, the widow was promised not to be arrested herself. A statement was issued saying that the victims were innocent, and Göran Persson was arrested and sentenced to death by the Privy Council of Nobles. However, he was only imprisoned, not killed. Persson, though he did play a significant role in the murders, was being set up as a scapegoat for the king's actions. Part of the promise Eric made to the widow was to "arrest all those responsible for the actions and behavior of the king." It was a convenient out for Eric and a way to avert a possible civil war.

Later that year, the king seemed to regain his senses. He continued his campaign against Denmark and restored Persson's power. This and the king's murder of his own personal secretary with a fire iron caused an uprising against Eric, which was waged by his two half-brothers (John and Karl). In January 1569, Eric was deposed by order of the Privy Council and the Riksdag (the Swedish parliament).

Eric was kept in a variety of prisons, sometimes with the company of his family but mostly alone. He lapsed back into insanity, and when it looked as if the nobles supporting his cause might rebel and free him, his brother John, following a decree of the Privy Council, had his brother killed. Everything, including a recent investigation of Eric's remains, points to arsenic poisoning in the pea soup given to Eric for dinner that fateful night in January 1569. Persson was arrested and executed upon news of Eric XIV's death.

Eric's half-brother John became king of Sweden, and he had the support of the Privy Council and most of the nation. He ruled the country until his death in 1592. John III is primarily known for his attempts to reconcile the Lutherans of Sweden (which were the majority by that point) with the Catholic Church. He allowed the nobility to regain many of the rights taken from them by his father and brother, and he exempted them from forced military service.

During John's reign, Sweden forged strong alliances with two other Protestant powers—England and Holland—thereby increasing trade, especially of iron and copper. (Sweden was Europe's largest supplier of these two metals at the time.) This trade, however, was not enough to keep Sweden afloat financially, and the unpopular move to tax nobles' estates did raise money but made enemies, as they had previously been exempted from taxes.

John III's son, Sigismund, became both king of Sweden and Poland upon John III's death in November 1592. He became the king of Sweden after his father's death, but he had been on the throne of Poland since August 1587. His mother's father was King Sigismund I of Poland, who ruled from 1506 to 1548.

Many of the people in Sweden, while comfortable with the idea of being part of a much larger empire, realized that the Polish-Lithuanian Commonwealth (which was established in 1569) had problems that had nothing or very little to do with Sweden. Some of those problems would lead Sweden into conflict with Russia and involve it in European power politics in a way the country had not been before.

Among the issues brought to Sweden by the ascension of Sigismund III was the fact that he had been raised Catholic. As you might remember, Sigismund's Swedish grandfather, Gustav Vasa, had separated Sweden from the Vatican, seized most of its assets in the country, and ordered the independent and Protestant Church of Sweden into existence. These actions had caused much bloodshed and strife within Sweden, and many Swedes were afraid that Sigismund would attempt to bring them back into the Catholic fold. By this time, the vast majority of Swedes were Lutheran, and in the forty-plus years since the Reformation, they had raised their children and possibly grandchildren as Protestants who believed Catholics were idolatrous.

Sigismund did not allay the Swedes' fears when he arrived from Poland in September 1593. Sigismund almost immediately began an effort to "re-convert" Protestant Sweden. Shortly after his arrival, he ordered Catholic Masses to be held in Stockholm and began a political process by which he intended to bring back Catholicism.

One must wonder if Sigismund was so convinced of the rightness of his cause that he never believed he could be stopped. Perhaps he was naive or just stupid, for almost as soon as he began his attempts to bring back the Catholic faith, the Swedes (led by his own powerful uncle Karl, Gustav I's last remaining son) began to push back—hard.

The support for Duke Karl and the opposition to Catholicism was so great that Sigismund was forced to accede to the Uppsala Resolution of 1594, which stated that Lutheranism would be supported and defended by the government. It forbade Catholics from teaching or holding appointed offices and severely limited Sigismund's ability to raise taxes without his council's consent. This last term was not religious in scope, but it should be mentioned that Sigismund's council was made up of Lutheran nobles.

Sigismund could have relented. He had spent most of his life in Poland anyway. It would have been easy to leave his uncle in charge of Sweden as the grand duke. However, that was not the way Sigismund thought. He wished to be an absolute monarch before the true Age of Absolutism began. He expected obedience from everyone. Unfortunately for Sigismund, he inherited the throne of two of the most independent-minded nations in Europe: Sweden and Poland. (In Poland, the nobility frequently and often challenged the monarchy's power.)

Throughout his reign in Sweden, Sigismund attempted to subvert the rules imposed on the monarchy in any way he could. Swedish governors were told to stop persecuting Catholics, which they did, as they owed their power and prestige to the king. One of Sigismund's appointees, the governor of Stockholm, was Catholic; riots and unrest ensued in the city.

Sigismund also decreed that the Riksdag could not meet without the monarch's consent. The parliament met the next year anyway. Sigismund's uncle and his many supporters in the Riksdag announced that Karl would henceforth become regent and rule the country, along with the Privy Council, while the king was out of the country, which was almost always.

Most Swedes agreed with this, but the nobles of Finland objected, as they knew Karl was their ruler as duke of Finland. Their leader, a regional governor named Klas Fleming, was an ally of Sigismund's and declared Karl a rebel. This led to open bloodshed in Finland. Karl organized a local rebellion against Fleming, which lasted from 1596 to 1597. This was essentially a civil war between Sigismund and Karl, along with their respective noble supporters.

For the next two years, civil war raged in Sweden. It ended when Sigismund, who had organized a powerful fleet of warships carrying Polish soldiers, German mercenaries, and Sigismund's Swedish supporters, was defeated by a fleet of Swedish warships (among the most modern in Europe at the time). At a meeting at Linköping Castle in southeastern Sweden, Karl and Sigismund reached an agreement. Karl would become regent of Sweden and rule the country until Sigismund's son, Prince Władysław Vasa, came of age to take the throne. The only hitch for Sigismund was that his son had to move to Sweden immediately and be raised as a Lutheran. Not having any choice due to his fleet and army being defeated, Sigismund agreed and vacated the throne in favor of his son with the understanding that Karl would rule until Władysław was of age.

Sigismund left immediately for Poland, never to return. He also did not send his son to Sweden. After not hearing from Sigismund for some time, Karl convinced the Riksdag to declare himself king, which happened in 1600 (though by an old Swedish custom, he was not coronated for another three years until it was confirmed by the Council of the Estates). He then officially became Karl IX (also known as Charles IX), and his descendants were confirmed as being the future rulers of the country.

Contemporary portrait of Karl IX.

Karl IX ruled Sweden from 1600 to 1611, though some histories list him as king only from his coronation in 1604. However, he was the undoubted ruler and king of Sweden after he was confirmed by the Riksdag in 1600. During his reign, Sweden was embroiled in a series of wars against Poland, Denmark, and Norway, the latter of which was still in a union with Denmark under a Danish monarch. Karl also meddled in Russian politics, attempting to sway one faction or another into opposing Poland, which would potentially limit the growing Polish power in the Baltic and create a new chapter in the history of Swedish trade in Russia.

The war with Poland ended with the death of Karl in 1611, but it had, on the whole, been a disaster for Sweden. Though it did not have to give up much land in the treaty that ended the war, Sweden's economy and prestige were diminished by its defeat.

In their war with Denmark and Norway, the Swedes, though victorious at times, were forced to sign a peace treaty that cost the country important coastal Swedish cities like Kalmar, as well as a huge reparations bill that the country could not easily pay. The Kalmar War with Denmark lasted from 1611 to 1613. The war ended with the Treaty of Knäred, which cost Sweden two important southern cities. The Danish also temporarily controlled the Swedish province of Västergötland until Sweden could pay Denmark the million kronor agreed to in the treaty.

Sweden paid off this debt in six years, partially by raising taxes and partially by securing loans from Holland. Holland was the up-and-coming northern European trading power, and it was eager to see Sweden back on its feet as a counter-weight to the Danes, whom the Dutch wished to weaken.

Holland's loans, its similarity in religious outlook, and a shared enemy in Denmark drew Sweden and Holland closer together. Aside from the financial support, the Dutch also provided military aid of all kinds to the Swedes, whose military might was inferior to Denmark's. Perhaps most importantly, Dutch traders and technicians were brought to Sweden to teach the Swedes about the latest industrial developments and economic theories.

Sweden provided Holland and other friendly nations, like England, with iron ore, which was plentiful in Sweden. Dutch technicians showed the Swedes how to improve their mining techniques, which resulted in iron production increasing by nearly 100 percent from 1550 to 1600. Copper mining, which began losing its influence to iron, was still a major export, and it, too, was improved by Sweden's adaptation of new Dutch and other European ideas.

During the latter part of the 1500s and into the 1600s, Sweden's population grew, and the old cities of Stockholm and Uppsala expanded both in size and modernity. This held true for other Swedish cities and towns, especially in the south of the country.

It would be up to the only Swedish monarch dubbed "the Great" to avenge these losses.

Chapter 10 – Gustavus Adolphus and Kristina

Historically speaking, it seems to be an axiom that one war simply leads to another. This was especially true for Sweden in the 16th and 17th centuries. In actuality, this was true for most of Europe and had been for some time. One kingdom would win some territory or treasure from another, then tempers and egos in the defeated kingdom would simmer for a while. Eventually, a new war would break out, which did not solve much.

Of course, there were exceptions. For instance, the Hundred Years' War (1337-1453) between France and England ended in France driving the English from its soil and ending England's claims to any French territory. Of course, there were exceptions, and quite a few times, two nations that had previously been at war would become allies in the next. This is all to say that Europe had been a battlefield for a long time, and it would remain so for a long time to come (something to remember when you read about Sweden's decision to be a neutral nation after the downfall of Napoleon).

However, in the second decade of the 1600s, a war in Europe broke out over religious freedom and, of course, power that would consume much of central Europe and cost the lives of an estimated four to eight million people. This was the Thirty Years' War. Sweden would play a major role in the latter part of that war, and its king would play a major role in bringing the conflict to an end.

The only king ever to be called "the Great" in Swedish history was Gustav II Adolf. He is most often called by the Latin version of his name, although it is sometimes spelled as Gustav II Adolph. His nickname was the "Lion of the North," for he became one of the greatest military commanders of all time and expanded Sweden's territory, power, and influence. Gustavus Adolphus was also one of Napoleon Bonaparte's heroes, and many military experts recognize the influence of Gustavus Adolf in the way the Frenchman structured his military and carried out some of his battles.

Gustavus Adolphus was the son of Karl IX and took the throne upon his father's death in 1611 at the age of sixteen. When the young man became king, Sweden was facing war on its doorstep in the Kalmar War against Denmark and Norway.

The king, who had just been crowned and was only sixteen, relied on the very able advice of nobleman Axel Oxenstierna to navigate the waters of war and government administration when he assumed power in 1611. Still, the new king led troops in battle in Norway and southern Sweden.

In addition to the Kalmar War, Gustav II inherited wars with Russia (the Ingrian War, 1610–1617) and Poland, which ebbed and flowed in four phases from 1600 to 1629. In both cases, Gustav's military leadership and the diplomatic skill of his advisers led to positive results for Sweden in the form of territory. The territories gained from Poland (namely Latvia and Estonia) gave Sweden a continental base of operations in the greater war that was to come.

Gustavus Adolphus as a young man. Many portraits of the king showed him on horseback as an energetic military commander.

https://commons.wikimedia.org/wiki/File:Gustav_II_Adolf_of_Sweden.jpg

In 1618, the Thirty Years' War began, though, at its start, no one could have predicted the conflict would spread over a large segment of Europe. The war began when a new king, Ferdinand II of Bohemia, was crowned in the important central province of the Holy Roman Empire. Not helping matters was the fact that Ferdinand was devoutly Catholic. He aggressively promoted Catholicism throughout his life. In addition, Ferdinand was from the House of Habsburg, which was again growing in power. The Habsburgs were Catholic like the ruling house of France, the Bourbons. However, though they ruthlessly persecuted Protestants in their own country, the French were arrayed against the Habsburgs in the Thirty Years' War. France was concerned that the Habsburgs would grow even more powerful and influential than they already were. Not only did the Habsburgs sit on the throne of Bohemia, but they also ruled Austria, and a branch of the family ruled Spain. France felt hemmed in by the Habsburg family and worked with anyone to weaken it.

The war began with the famous Defenestrations of Prague (*fenestra* meaning "window" in Latin). In 1618, Calvinist rebels who were against Ferdinand and Catholic domination literally tossed two Catholic members of the Bohemian royal council out of a castle window. It was a seventy-foot drop! Amazing, the council members survived but only because they landed in an immense heap of manure being stored for fertilizing. This act of rebellion and its disgraceful but somewhat laughable beginning began a chain reaction that resulted in the deaths of millions of people.

Calvinism was a new and more radical sect of Protestantism that began with the French theologian John Calvin in Switzerland. While some Protestants were willing to at least try to "live and let live" with the Catholic Church, the vast majority of Calvinists were not. They believed Catholicism was heresy and were determined to either lead Europe's Catholics "into the light" or kill them in the process. Shortly after the war broke out, Catholics in Europe reciprocated the feeling. In many ways, the Thirty Years' War (much of which took place within the borders of the German states or near them) was a genocidal conflict as well as a religious one. Both sides committed massacres, and horrific atrocities took place throughout the war.

The war rapidly spread. The Catholic powers of Bavaria and the Holy Roman Empire restored Ferdinand II to the throne after the Calvinist rebels had driven him from the country and placed the Calvinist Frederick V on the throne. The king of Bavaria, Maximilian I, gained territory in western Germany, and many Protestants fled.

Between 1620 and 1625, events in Germany led Lutheran Denmark to feel threatened by the growing Catholic influence near its borders. Four years and a number of defeats later, Denmark signed a treaty in which it vowed not to meddle in the German states' affairs again.

By 1630, it looked as if Catholicism was, at the very least, solidifying its hold on many of the German states. This alarmed Gustavus Adolphus and many other Swedes, as much Swedish trade was done in the German states. On top of this, Poland was already Catholic. If Sweden did not act, the Catholic powers might end up controlling much of central Europe. They would then be in the position to both militarily and economically isolate the Swedes.

Over the course of the next two years, Gustavus Adolphus became a hero to not only Swedes but also many Protestants in

Germany and elsewhere. Even today, quite a few schools, public buildings, and roads are named after the Swedish king in the northern part of modern Germany, which is predominantly Protestant.

Gustav had built a professional army in Sweden in the time between the wars, and he had equipped it with the finest foreign and homemade weapons, especially artillery. Many innovations were introduced, such as the use of small, mobile artillery as a sort of primitive tank. An emphasis was placed on movement, maneuvering, and securing good positions before a battle. This helped Gustavus Adolphus and his relatively small army defeat one enemy after another from 1630 to 1632, all the while looting and pillaging along the way. Much of the riches left to Gustavus Adolphus's daughter Kristina was pillaged in the German states and sent home to Sweden.

Unfortunately for Sweden, Gustavus Adolphus was killed while leading his men at the victorious Battle of Lützen in southeastern central Germany on November 16th, 1632. Both sides were wounded and exhausted by this time and negotiated the Treaty of Prague in 1635, which led to a brief respite in the fighting before the French decided to become involved that same year.

The war would continue until 1648. The Swedes were commanded by able generals and the future king, Karl Gustav, but Sweden was under the rule of Gustavus's daughter, Queen Kristina (r. 1632-1654). The Treaty of Westphalia, which Kristina pushed for after Swedish troops defeated Catholic forces and looted the incredibly rich Prague Castle, bringing home many priceless classics in books and artwork, ended the Thirty Years' War. Generally speaking, this benefited both Sweden, which gained riches and territory, and France, which became the predominant power in Europe.

Queen Kristina

Kristina has been the focus of many studies since her death in 1689 at the age of sixty-two. In many ways, Sweden had missed much of the Renaissance, and the strict Protestantism in the country limited intellectual curiosity.

Kristina, who was born in December of 1626, became queen at the age of six, though Sweden was ruled by her regent, Axel Oxenstierna, and the Privy Council. She was crowned queen of Sweden in 1650, although she had essentially ruled the country (with the aid of Oxenstierna) since she came of age in 1644.

She became queen in more than just name at the age of eighteen (1644). To say that she was as ready to rule as could be is perhaps an understatement. Many scholarly articles, contemporary accounts, books, movies, and documentaries point to her intelligence and learning. She was multi-lingual, speaking German (her mother's family was German), French, Italian, Dutch, and Danish, which would prove quite useful during her reign and beyond. She was also able to speak Hebrew and Arabic.

Kristina was an "enlightened monarch" before the Enlightenment truly began. She famously corresponded with famed French philosopher and academic René Descartes and even had him visit her court. (Though, when they were together, it seemed they could not tolerate each other, despite cinematic accounts showing a close friendship. Descartes would die of pneumonia in Sweden after only a short time in the country.) Kristina was interested in an amazing variety of topics, including history, many of the sciences (especially biology), math, philosophy, religion, and much more. Many books and websites describe her as "one of the most educated women of the time." In actuality, she was one of the most educated *people* of the time.

Before the queen came of age, the powerful noble Axel Oxenstierna essentially ran the country and government. He had been a trusted adviser of Kristina's father, and when she took the throne to rule herself, Oxenstierna remained at her side as a trusted counselor. He was much more versed in the politics of the country and also had a greater understanding of the people of Sweden.

Kristina gave Oxenstierna wide leeway, especially in regard to foreign affairs. As a diplomat, Oxenstierna made peace with Denmark (war had begun again in 1643) and gained a significant number of important territories for the Swedes, including the island of Gotland.

In 1648, the Thirty Years' War ended with the Peace of Westphalia. In the agreements that ended that exceedingly bloody war, Kristina and the Swedes gained quite a bit of territory across the Baltic Sea along the coast of present-day Germany and Poland, as well as control of a number of important coastal German cities. This not only increased Sweden's area and prestige, but it also gave it a vote in the Diet (parliament) of the Holy Roman Empire. As mentioned previously in this chapter, before the Peace of Westphalia, Kristina's army assaulted and looted Prague, where Holy Roman Emperor Rudolf II kept many of his treasures, including ancient manuscripts, books, and priceless artworks. The looting of Prague was a spur to peace, but it also satisfied Kristina's desire to possess some of the most important pieces of classical art and literature in the world. She also gained an immense treasure, which helped to finance some of her other endeavors at home.

Kristina in 1661 as portrayed by Dutch artist Abraham Wuchters.
https://commons.wikimedia.org/wiki/File:Portr%C3%A4tt._Drottning_Kristina._Wuchters_-_Skoklosters_slott_-_47811_(cropped).tif

By the time Kristina came to power at the age of eighteen, Protestantism and especially its offshoot, the more fundamentalist Calvinism, had taken firm root in Sweden. The country had just taken part in the Thirty Years' War, a conflict largely fought along religious lines. Catholicism was not banned in Sweden, but it was heavily persecuted, and those Swedes who remained Catholic either kept it to themselves or were very circumspect about displaying any sort of religious identity.

However, from a young age, Kristina was fascinated by Catholicism. Its pageantry and history impressed her, and by the time she became queen, many scientific and artistic freedoms existed in the Catholic world that simply did not exist in Sweden and many other Protestant areas. This greatly impressed the queen, who often spent hours or days removed from anyone, studying and reading.

Kristina was also controversial, at least within the inner circle of the government and nobility, for her sexual preference. Though it has not been proven conclusively, it is believed that the queen was in love with the noblewoman Ebba Sparre, who was also one of the queen's ladies in waiting (whether there was a physical dimension to this relationship is not known with any certainty). There has been much speculation in recent times about Kristina's sexuality and even her gender; an evaluation of her skeleton revealed her to be anatomically female.

Kristina likely did have some type of intimate relationship with women, and she did not exactly dispel rumors by her dress and mannerisms. As a child, her father, Gustavus Adolphus, treated her much like the son he never had. He taught her to ride in the male style, hunt, and study war just as he would have with a boy. She also adopted a masculine way of dressing when she was not at court or in official meetings.

Kristina befriended not only Descartes but also another Frenchman: the ambassador Pierre Chanut. He is believed to have taught her about Catholicism and perhaps contributed to her later conversion. At the time, the Catholic Church was conducting what is now called the Counter-Reformation in an attempt to both control the spread of Protestantism in Catholic-dominated countries and perhaps roll back Protestant gains in others. One byproduct of the Counter-Reformation is that while many of the strictures against other Christian sects remained, an artistic and limited philosophical explosion occurred in many Catholic areas, most notably in Rome and the Italian city-states.

Despite increasing the size of the Swedish nobility (at the expense of the common people), Kristina was the target of many plots to remove her from the throne or at least sideline her. This would have likely happened even if she had been a man (as you have read, Sweden was a land of plot and counter-plots for hundreds of years). However, rumors of her interest in Catholicism and women, as well as her reckless spending, meant that plots were almost always afoot.

In 1649, after being under much pressure to marry and have an heir and not wishing to do so, Kristina named her cousin Karl (Charles) as her heir. This was done with one condition—her inner circle and the nobles could not pressure her to marry and have an heir. For the next nearly four years, Kristina ruled in an increasingly erratic manner and became less and less popular, both with her nobles and her people. During this time, it seems as if she was carefully planning to abdicate the throne, for she arranged for a permanent annuity to be paid to her and seemingly gathered much state wealth.

The main reason for her decision to abdicate in June 1654 was her decision to convert to Catholicism, which would likely have caused a civil war in the country had she attempted to stay on the throne. By the time she left Sweden in disguise, she had moved considerable wealth from her castle in Stockholm to places overseas. Despite this, she was soon almost broke due to her lavish lifestyle while traveling through Europe. This caused her to sell off many of her treasures and also secure a large loan to maintain her lifestyle. She also hid her conversion until she arrived in Rome in December, where she was met by Pope Alexander VII and given a new name, Christina Augusta, though she adopted the name Christina Alexandra.

In Rome, she took up residence in the palace of the duke of Parma and began a life that included creating an intellectual salon for the discussion of current events, the sciences, philosophy, and the arts. The highest nobility in the land and visiting dignitaries attended these meetings. Kristina's conversion made her popular with the Catholic hierarchy; perhaps they saw a way to spread

Catholicism to Protestant areas through her.

It is also important to note that despite its religious nature, Rome, the Vatican, and the Italian/Catholic nobility enjoyed a very liberal atmosphere as long as it was not too openly displayed. It is believed that Kristina indulged her sexual desire for women and likely some men as well, although we do not know this for certain. Although Pope Alexander liked her personally and supported her intellectually and, to a great degree, financially, he left a quote about the former queen. Though tainted by time and culture, it gives us a picture of Kristina's life in Rome: "A queen without a realm, a Christian without faith, and a woman without shame."

In 1660, Kristina returned to Sweden to attend the funeral of her heir, Karl Gustav X. The king's son, who would become Karl XI, was only five years old. Kristina attempted to regain power by becoming regent until the boy was eighteen, but she was denied due to her conversion. She left Sweden for Germany and then Rome for another five years, but scandal and an increasingly strained relationship with Alexander VII caused her to return to Sweden in 1667. She was limited to living in a Swedish-controlled province in Germany.

Her remaining years included a very close (platonic) relationship with Alexander's successor, Clement IX, and she traveled to and from Rome a number of times. She also went to Poland, where she put her name forward as a candidate for queen, but she was rejected.

Kristina died in 1689. She had fostered the arts in Rome and patronized both theater and music for decades by that point.

Chapter 11 – Poltava and Bernadotte

After Kristina, Sweden, which had set itself on a course of conquest, colonization, and influence in Europe, was ruled by a series of kings, virtually all of whom can be said to have been gifted with military genius to one degree or other.

Kristina's abdication in 1654 not only marked the end of her tumultuous and controversial reign but also brought an end to the House of Vasa, which had ruled Sweden since Gustav I Vasa had come to power in 1523. As you read in the prior chapter, Kristina officially "adopted" her cousin Karl Gustav, whose mother was the daughter of Karl IX and whose father was John Casimir, a nobleman from the Wittelsbach family in Germany. Karl Gustav was the first of the Wittelsbach kings of Sweden, which ruled the country until 1720.

Karl X Gustav (Karl is the equivalent of Charles" in English), his son Karl XI, and his grandson Karl XII all saw the value in expanding Sweden's domains, both for prestige and power. In the case of Karl X Gustav, he wanted to expand to loot or win reparations from his foes, as Kristina's reign had left Sweden's economy on the verge of collapse.

Over the course of the next sixty-four years, Karl X Gustav, his son, and his grandson increased the size of Sweden's empire and solidified the rule of the king over the nobles. Finally, after decades of power struggles of one kind or another, the Swedish Council of Nobles voted to give Karl XI absolute power in 1693. This was both a blessing and a curse, for while the increase in royal power did add stability, it also placed the country at the whim of the monarch.

Karl XI (r. 1660–1697) was thought to be "slow" as a child. He was likely dyslexic but proved to be an able ruler and military commander.
https://commons.wikimedia.org/wiki/File:Kung_Karl_XI_till_h%C3%A4st_(1670-1697).jpg

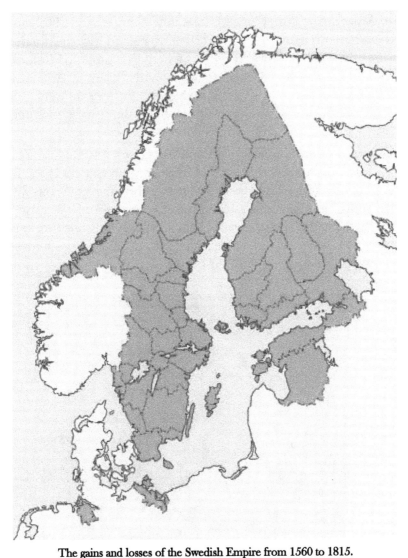

The gains and losses of the Swedish Empire from 1560 to 1815.

The course of Sweden's wars and international affairs during the time of the Wittelsbach dynasty can be confusing to even the most experienced historian. Suffice it to say that between 1654 and 1718 (not counting the short reign of the last Wittelsbach monarch, Queen Ulrika Eleanora, who ruled from 1718 to 1720), the Swedes and their neighbors continued the wars and intrigues that had been going on for centuries. Alliances shifted, and kingdoms farther afield, notably France and Holland, involved themselves in Scandinavian wars and power politics. Essentially, though, the rivals remained the same (Denmark, Norway, Russia, the German states, and Poland). At times, Sweden found itself at war with a majority of these powers, and though there were setbacks, on the whole, the Swedish Empire grew.

The most formidable of Sweden's enemies was Russia. This was especially so after Peter the Great became tsar in 1682; he ruled Russia until 1725. Peter is famous for many reasons but none more than his efforts to modernize Russia and put it on a European path. Peter journeyed throughout northwestern Europe as a young man, learning about Western cultures, economics, science, and especially military tactics and technology.

Peter the Great, Sweden's nemesis.
https://commons.wikimedia.org/wiki/File:Inconnu_d%27apr%C3%A8s_J.-M._Nattier,_Portrait_de_Pierre_Ier_(mus%C3%A9e_de_l%E2%80%99Ermitage).jpg

One of Peter's main goals, at least internationally, was to give Russia a port that would be open most of the year and allow the new powerful Russian Navy access to the Baltic and North Seas. (Peter is considered the "Father of the Russian Navy.") But to do this, he would first have to defeat the great power that sat on his border—Sweden. Sweden controlled today's Finland. At the time, that included forts and fortified towns in what is now Russia, near what would be the future St. Petersburg, which was named after Peter.

In 1697, Karl XII came to power in Sweden at the age of fifteen. Unlike many of his predecessors, he took power almost immediately. Three years later, the Russians, Danes/Norwegians, and the combined kingdom of Poland, Saxony, and Lithuania had built up their strength and were prepared to launch an attack on Sweden and her interests on the Baltic coasts. This was the Great Northern War, which lasted, with temporary peace agreements halting action for varying amounts of time, from 1700 to 1721.

Britain and Holland were allied with Sweden and helped it both at sea and economically. On land, the Swedes were joined by rebel Polish nobles, a number of smaller German states with ties to the Swedish royal family or nobility, and a sizable number of Ukrainian Cossacks who sought greater autonomy or independence from Russia.

Sweden's land army was almost always outnumbered, but inspired leadership from the king and a number of Swedish and German generals, as well as a military made up of highly trained mercenaries and a Swedish army that had begun to modernize in many ways, made up for that. One of these ways was in the training they received. At this time, most European armies were made up of a small core of experienced troops and large numbers of relatively untrained peasants and townspeople.

At the start of the war, Karl XII and the Swedes surprised everyone. The king learned quickly, and he was not afraid to delegate responsibilities to his older and more experienced officers. In August 1700, the Swedes defeated the Danes at Travendal in today's northern Germany, as well as the Russians in the Battle of Narva in today's Estonia in November of the same year. Narva was an utter disaster for the Russians, who outnumbered the Swedes by three to one.

The Battle of Narva was a Pyrrhic victory for the Swedes. While they did gain a temporary advantage over the Russians, it also caused Peter to accelerate the pace of reforms in the Russian army and gave him more than ample reason for revenge. Believing the Russians to be finished, at least for the time being, Karl turned his attention westward and engaged in a number of victorious battles against the Poles and Saxons from 1701 to 1706, which resulted in Swedish gains in both territories.

While the Swedes were fighting in the west, Peter retook Narva and the Swedish fortress of Nyenschantz, which sat at the mouth of the Neva River and was located in present-day St. Petersburg, which Peter began to build almost at once.

By 1707, Karl XII had defeated and deposed the Polish king and imposed a costly peace on his enemies in central Europe. He was then determined to turn east and defeat Russia, if not for good, then at least for the long term. For his part, Tsar Peter wished to buy time to continue his building of St. Petersburg and to rebuild and reform the Russian army. In 1707, Peter offered to return the border province of Ingria to the Swedes but not the area around St. Petersburg. Karl refused this offer. Rather than offer his own peace terms, he invaded Russia in 1708.

Though Napoleon Bonaparte's and Adolf Hitler's invasions of Russia (in 1812 and 1941, respectively) are better known due to their sheer size and effect, Karl's invasion was similar in a number of ways. He was outnumbered, the Russians gave ground but burned what they couldn't use or move, and, as you might guess, the Russian winter of 1708/9 was one of the worst winters of the century. Disease, hunger, and desertion reduced Karl's army. In the spring, when Karl moved south to Ukraine to recover and possibly join forces with his ally Ivan Mazepa (the leader of a sizable number of Cossacks), he was defeated by Peter's generals at the Battle of Poltava.

The Battle of Poltava (July 8th, 1709) was a defeat from which Sweden never recovered, and from the Swedish point of view, it should never have been fought. The Swedes had defeated the Russians many times before with a much smaller force, so they believed they could do it again and launched an ill-fated attack on a fortified Russian position. Confusion in communications and the absence of the king, who had been severely wounded in the foot in June, all contributed to the Swedish defeat, as did superior Russian tactics.

After Poltava, Karl began a strange and roundabout journey back to Sweden, which took almost five years and included him being the honored guest of Russia's traditional enemy, the Ottoman Empire. When the king finally returned to Sweden, he was forced to relinquish much of his power back to the nobility. During the rest of his reign (he died in 1718), the Swedes invaded Norway twice, both times to disastrous effect, and continued the wars against their other enemies.

However, the Battle of Poltava marked the beginning of the end of the Swedish Empire. Sweden continued to hold a number of small enclaves on the north German coast but lost the Baltic states in 1721 and Finland in 1805. Sweden would never again be a world power, and to the surprise of virtually the entire world, it would fight its last major battle in 1814. It defeated Norway, and the two nations were united until 1905.

The author of Sweden's victory over Norway was not a Swede but a Frenchman who had been one of Napoleon Bonaparte's most gifted field marshals: Jean-Baptiste Bernadotte. He became known as Karl XIV Johan ("Charles XIV John," r. 1818-1844), King of Sweden and the founder of the nation's current dynasty.

Bernadotte is known to many as the "Father of Swedish neutrality," and he did, in fact, begin a foreign policy in which Sweden kept itself out of the wars of the later 19th century and the disasters of WWI and WWII. However, while this seems a wise, peaceful policy on the surface, it was grounded in practicality and did not truly begin until Sweden had gained Norway for itself and Bernadotte had lost all chances to become the leader of France after Napoleon.

In 1809, after a war with Russia that cost Sweden the possession of its territory of Finland, Swedish nobles overthrew King Gustav IV Adolf (r. 1792-1809) and replaced him with an aged, childless prince, who became Karl (Charles) XIII (r. 1809-1818). These nobles also pushed through what is known as the

Instrument of Government on June 6th, 1809, which marks the date of Sweden's National Day. The Instrument of Government limited the monarchy's power after nearly two centuries of absolutism that tended to involve Sweden in constant wars and economic crises.

The monarch was still left with considerable power, but at his relatively advanced age and with the nobility watching him carefully, most people knew he was a caretaker king. His adopted Danish son and heir died of a stroke in 1810, and the powerful men in the royal court and the nobility began to cast a net for the next king. They found their next monarch in France.

As you have might have noticed, it was not unusual for someone with foreign roots to become a monarch in Sweden, but the idea that a revolutionary Frenchman, who had risen to command by fighting the French monarchy and the idea of the monarchy itself, seems a rather odd choice for a Scandinavian king.

The Frenchman in question, Jean-Baptiste Bernadotte, had been born to a lawyer. He wasn't poor, but he was far from rich and definitely not of the aristocracy. Jean-Baptiste joined the army in 1780, nine years before the French Revolution began. Like French society, the French Army was split between those who supported the monarchy and those who did not. When the French Revolution broke out in France, Jean-Baptiste supported the revolutionaries and their cause, which eventually evolved into the belief that the kingship should be abolished and replaced by a republic.

The French Revolution was felt keenly in the army, and one positive coming from the great changes taking place was that soldiers from non-noble backgrounds could rise to become officers. In 1792, Bernadotte was promoted to lieutenant. A mere two years later, he was made brigadier general. Bernadotte led his brigade to battles in Germany and is now Belgium, Holland, and Italy, where he met Napoleon Bonaparte in 1797.

Bernadotte as a Marshal of the Empire.

Bernadotte's relationship with Napoleon was initially friendly, and in 1798, he even married Napoleon's former fiancée, who was also the sister-in-law of Napoleon's brother Joseph. Bernadotte was an immensely talented commander, and he rose rapidly through the ranks. This was helped by his relationship with the Bonaparte family. In 1799, he was appointed minister of war by the government of the time, the Directory, which lasted until Bonaparte's coup d'état in November 1799, which Bernadotte did not support or oppose.

Bernadotte was appointed councilor of state in 1800, and he held that office, as well as commander of the Army of the West (essentially the French home army, which helped keep order and Napoleon in power) until 1802. Whether it was Bernadotte's republican tendencies, their personalities, or the paranoia that sometimes comes with power, Bernadotte and Bonaparte had a very contentious relationship. Sometimes Bernadotte was "in," and sometimes, he was "out." In 1802, he was "out" after having been rumored to have been part of a republican plot to overthrow Napoleon, a rumor that was never proven. In 1804, Bonaparte made Bernadotte a marshal of the French Empire, which was one of the highest positions in France. In 1805, he commanded a corps at Napoleon's stunning victory at Austerlitz.

In 1810, the Swedes began looking for a new "son" and heir apparent to the elderly Karl XIII, who was easily influenced and more interested in women and the occult than matters of state. Any crown prince would be in a position to have considerable power almost immediately.

The only place the Swedes truly considered looking for a new king was France. Having gone from an absolute monarchy to a republican revolution, in which the king was beheaded, France might seem a strange place to have looked for a new king. However, in 1804, Napoleon had declared himself emperor of the French, instantly turning his family and trusted associates into a new aristocracy.

Seeking to "get in" with the powerful French emperor, the Swedes asked him for a recommendation as to who in France he would choose to put forward as a candidate as the new king of Sweden. Napoleon's choices, which were his four brothers, worried the Swedes and were politely rejected. While deciding on a new candidate, a minor Swedish noble, Baron Karl Otto Mörner, who was in France, approached Bernadotte and offered him the throne, which he had no authority to do.

Bernadotte told Napoleon of this plan, and despite initially believing it to be a joke of some kind, he believed it was a good idea. When the Swedish noble returned to Sweden, he was arrested, but within a short time, the idea gained followers. Baron Mörner was released, and Bernadotte accepted the offer.

The choice worked for both sides. Bernadotte was an ambitious man, and his ambition had led him to great heights in France, but he had gone as far as he could go there. Although he had held anti-monarchist feelings as a young man, Bernadotte saw the possibility of being king of what could be an important nation in European affairs. One requirement of the Swedish king was that he become Lutheran, something that did not trouble

Bernadotte (it had been a sticking point among the Bonapartes).

For the most part, the Swedes were happy with the choice. Bernadotte was a "man of the people," which would appeal to the middle and lower classes in Sweden. He had also been a soldier in one of the most successful armies in world history, which satisfied the officers and men in the Swedish military, which were not quite done with matters in Scandinavia. Most nobles believed that the "outsourcing" of the crown to a man everyone could agree on would help avoid the strife between royal families when a dynasty was in trouble.

It did not hurt that during Bernadotte's time as general in Germany, the Swedish soldiers fighting there were treated well as prisoners under his orders. He was seen as a respectable man, which might cause potential enemies (meaning Denmark and Russia) to hesitate before attacking too ruthlessly. He was also reported to be a very competent administrator, as he had governed northern German cities and coastal towns where many Swedes did business. On top of this, he was a confidante of the French emperor. The Swedes officially offered Bernadotte the title of crown prince and heir to the Swedish throne. They also gave him command of all of Sweden's armies. During the years he waited to become king (1810–1818), Bernadotte *was* the king in all but name.

When Napoleon agreed to allow Bernadotte to go to Sweden, he asked that Bernadotte swear to never take up arms against France, something which Bernadotte could not commit to. Obviously, this was not an answer that pleased Napoleon, who reportedly replied to the future Swedish king, "Go, and let our destinies be accomplished!" Both men would be a thorn in one another's side for the rest of Napoleon's rule, although they did ask one another for military aid (in Napoleon's fight against Great Britain and Bernadotte's fight against Norway). Napoleon refused Bernadotte's request for help, though. Although the Swedes essentially had to comply with Bonaparte's request, they went to war with Britain in name only and continued trading with the British. This would bring Sweden and France to blows and Bernadotte into an alliance against his former ruler and commander.

In 1813, Bernadotte attacked Napoleon's ally, Denmark, as Russian, Prussian, and Austrian forces surged westward against Bonaparte. The defeat of Denmark resulted in its loss of Norway, which became a semi-autonomous province of Sweden until 1905, when it gained independence.

Toward the end of the Napoleonic Wars (1803–1814), Bernadotte entered into agreements with both Russia and Britain. Norway, which under an outdated and meaningless agreement decades before was British (in name only), was now officially Sweden's. Despite the hopes of some Swedes, Finland was given to Russia, although some border adjustments were made.

Along with the rest of the European nations involved in the Congress of Vienna, which attempted to find a conservative path to peace after Napoleon, Bernadotte instituted his own policy for Sweden, which he had written in 1812. The was the Policy of 1812, and it was the foundation stone of Sweden's policy of neutrality, which lasted until the early 2000s.

Sweden would be defended, but its army was never to be used to aid one side or another in a foreign war. Business was to be done with both sides equally, and the government would be utterly neutral in the press and its own statements from that point forward. After the end of the Napoleonic Wars, Swedish troops were used as peacekeepers, even before the establishment of the United Nations, but the number of Swedish troops involved in combat (at least under the Swedish flag) has been minimal. Sweden has not experienced war on its own soil in centuries.

In 1818, Bernadotte officially became King Karl XIV Johan of Sweden. Despite never learning Swedish, the king was relatively popular in Sweden and Norway until near the end of his reign. The king became ultra-conservative as he grew older and placed increasing restrictions on freedom of the press and speech. While this affected his popularity at the time, he was never under threat of being deposed. The Bernadotte dynasty is still the ruling monarchy in Sweden today, although it is more of a national symbol than a political power.

Chapter 12 – The World Wars

In the years between the death of King Karl XIV Johan (Bernadotte) and World War I, Sweden underwent many changes—too many to include in this introductory history. In the last years of Bernadotte's reign, Sweden became much more conservative in regards to many of the freedoms espoused by the French Revolution, which had spread throughout Europe between 1789 and 1815 with the fall of the French Empire. Freedom of the press, religion, and speech were all curtailed. While this did cause anger and resentment among many Swedes, peace and economic developments were more important to many in the country.

Like many other Western European nations in 1848, Sweden experienced a wave of liberal reactions to the conservative laws and attitudes in the country. While the changes in Sweden were gradual and not violent as they were, for example, in Germany, most of the ideas from the revolutions in the middle of the 19th century were eventually adopted. Most importantly, Sweden gradually began the process of creating a constitution, which was put into writing in the 20th century with the Constitution Act of 1974. It stated, among other things, that the monarch would "no longer rule the Kingdom alone" and that "all public power in Sweden derives from the people."

Sweden had begun to change from an agricultural economy to a mainly industrial one in the late 1700s with aid and knowledge from Britain and the Netherlands. Throughout the 1800s, the pace of economic and industrial changes quickened. By the early 1900s, Sweden was still a primarily agricultural nation, but the factories in its cities produced many of the nation's own industrial goods and exported many as well, primarily to Russia. Sweden remained one of the leading metal exporters, and it was a major source of iron, copper, lead, and tungsten for the nations of Europe, particularly Germany.

In the late 19th century, as you may know, Germany, under its young Kaiser Wilhelm II, was becoming a problem for many of its neighbors, particularly Britain and France. Germany had defeated France in the Franco-Prussian War of 1870–71, which had resulted in the final union of the German states and the loss of significant French territories on the borders of these two nations.

In the late 1800s, another round of European colonization took place, this time mainly in Africa and Asia. Since Germany was a "new" country, it was already behind in the race for new territories, but the kaiser was determined to gain "a place in the sun." He began to claim territories that were unclaimed by the other powers of Europe. These territories were economically backward, desolate, and more of a liability to Germany than an asset, but it did allow Wilhelm and the Germans to proudly announce the German Empire to the world. This and a number of ill-timed statements and actions, combined with the awesome size and ability of the German Army and a rapidly growing navy, put the world on alert.

As you have read, Germany (or rather the various German states until Germany was united in 1871) and Sweden had a long relationship. Wars had taken place between them, but they had also been allies. Sweden had controlled parts of Germany, and between 1654 and 1720, a German family, the Wittelsbachs, had sat on the Swedish throne. Trade was one of the more important elements of each nation's economy, and strategically, both were worried about the power of Russia, which bordered both.

However, in the late 19th and early 20th centuries, Sweden's culture had changed. Neutrality was becoming a part of the Swedish psyche, and its government resembled that of Britain and France more than belligerent and boastful Germany. While Germany was attempting to gain an empire, in 1905, the Swedes and Norwegians peacefully agreed that Norway should be a self-governing country. Swedish colonies in the Americas had been sold in the 1800s, and the nation had only one African colony on the northwestern coast of the continent, which was given up in 1663.

Germany's growing navy was also right across the Baltic from Sweden—not shelling distance but close. Sweden also did much business with France and Britain, and the Swedes knew that even if Germany's navy controlled the Baltic, Britain controlled access to the North Sea and the Atlantic. Its official policy of neutrality aside, Sweden was walking an economic tight-rope. One wrong move toward either side could be catastrophic.

Neutrality was truly the only way for Sweden when WWI began in 1914. Its army was small, and its navy was no match for Germany, Britain, or France. It also had to take into consideration the position of Russia. Allying with Germany put Sweden at risk of Russian attacks via Finland, and it would cause Britain to blockade Swedish trade. Joining the Allies meant losing its number one trade partner (Germany) and possibly subjecting itself to German naval bombardment or even invasion. Above all else, however, was its policy of neutrality and peace.

Still, despite officially declaring itself neutral, Sweden did suffer (to a relatively small degree) during WWI. Much of this was due to the near-famine conditions that occurred in the country in 1916 as a result of the British blockade of the North Sea. Since Swedish goods purchased overseas might eventually go to help Germany, and since Germany was buying all the minerals it could from Sweden for its war effort, the British began to stop a great deal of Swedish trade. The unrestricted submarine warfare declared by Germany in 1917 meant that any merchant vessel suspected of trading with Germany's enemies was a target. This policy, as well as the United States' entry into the war, tipping the scales in the Allies' favor in 1917, caused the Swedes to establish better relations with the Allies. Toward the end of the war, an agreement allowed Sweden to import goods (mostly food) from the West in return for limiting its exports to Germany. Sweden's large merchant fleet would also be at the Allies' disposal if needed. By this point in the war, it was becoming increasingly clear that Germany was on its way to defeat; Sweden knew dealing with the Allies was the better choice.

World War II proved a challenge to Sweden's neutrality as well, and throughout the war, the Swedes had to walk another fine line. Even after the rise of Hitler, Germany was the biggest importer of Swedish resources and goods. However, Joseph Stalin's Russia, despite facing famine in many parts of the country, sent food products to Sweden in exchange for hard currency. Making the Swedes' situation even more tenuous was the fact that much of its trade still went out into the North Sea to the Atlantic and beyond, and Britain still ruled the waves. Once again, neutrality seemed the only way.

During the late 1930s, as Hitler began becoming more of a threat to all of Europe, Sweden increased its military budget and called up more men to arms. When war came, however, Sweden had to make a choice: allow German troops through its country to attack Norway or face German occupation as well. A small number of German troops entered Swedish territory on the way to Norway.

Sweden's unaligned status and location meant that Hitler knew he would benefit more from leaving Sweden alone than occupying it. He also had hopes that Sweden, a nation that he saw as a Germanic cousin, would gradually evolve one way into a fascist or Nazi state as well. In 1941, Sweden was forced to allow German troops to cross its borders to attack the Soviet Union. It should be remembered that a small number of right-wing Swedes did join Hitler's Waffen-SS, though this ugly truth is somewhat unfortunately downplayed in Sweden today. More Swedes did join the fight for the Allies, fighting in Norway. A significant number of US men who were born or raised in Sweden joined and served in the US Armed Forces.

Though Sweden remained neutral and at times attempted to broker peace between the Western Allies and Hitler, it, unfortunately, did more trade with Hitler than many are comfortable with. The Swedes also knew more about the Holocaust than much of the rest of the world. Sweden garnered criticism after the war for its seeming indifference to the situation since it had benefited from trade with Germany.

On the other hand, the Swedes did allow nearly five thousand German Jews to emigrate to the country before the war, and it famously admitted about eight thousand Danish Jews (almost the entire Jewish population of that country), who escaped their occupied nation with the help of their countrymen in the autumn of 1940. A number of individual Swedes also put their lives at risk to rescue the Jews in Hitler's Europe, most notably Raoul Wallenberg.

Wallenberg

Raoul Wallenberg was the second foreigner to be given honorary American citizenship. The first was Winston Churchill. The reason for this honor? Wallenberg helped to rescue many Jews from the horrors of concentration camps. The exact number of Hungarian Jews rescued directly by Wallenberg or as a result of his efforts is unknown. Low estimates are in the few thousands, but they go as high as 100,000. Either way, Wallenberg was responsible for the rescue of thousands of people when the Holocaust began in full in Hungary in 1944.

Wallenberg was born into a life of privilege. His family had been at or near the center of Swedish politics and business since the mid-1800s. Today, the Wallenberg family owns significant parts of or controls many famous Swedish companies, including telecommunications giant Ericsson, appliance maker Electrolux, Scandinavian airline SAS, and others. They are one of the wealthiest families on the planet and were when Raoul was born in 1912.

Raoul's twenty-four-year-old father died three months before his son was born, and Raoul was raised by his grandfather, a diplomat. Raoul traveled to many countries and was fluent or passable in a number of languages, including German. In 1935, he got his master's degree in architecture from the University of Michigan, and the next year, he was a bank officer for a Dutch firm in Haifa, then British-controlled Palestine through a League of Nations mandate (today, it is Israel).

There, he met many European Jews who had the good fortune to have fled Hitler's Germany. They spoke to him of the worsening persecution of the Jews in Germany. In the early

1940s, after the war had been raging for two years, Wallenberg took a job with a food-exporting business whose owner was Jewish. This meant that Raoul traveled to Hitler's Europe on frequent trips since his boss could not risk his life doing so.

One of the countries Wallenberg visited often and which had (until the spring of 1944) maintained its autonomy by refusing Hitler's demands for its Jewish population was Hungary. However, Hungary, which was allied with the Nazis and had sent troops to fight on the Eastern Front, was beginning to waver in its loyalty to Germany, something that even its right-wing generalissimo, Miklós Horthy, could see. Horthy was also under increasing pressure from a virulent and growing anti-Semitic fascist party in Hungary, the Arrow Cross movement.

Hitler was worried that Hungary might flip sides, and he knew he could use the nation as a buffer between the Red Army of the Soviet Union and Germany in the south. In March, Hitler invaded. As soon as German troops arrived, they began to round up Hungary's Jews: an estimated 500,000 to 600,000 people. Most people don't know this, but by the spring of 1944, most of the six million-plus Jewish victims in areas under Hitler's control had already been killed. The Hungarian Jews were deported into a system of industrial murder that had already been "perfected." By the mid-summer, most of the Jews of Hungary outside Budapest (Hungary's capital) had been deported to Auschwitz-Birkenau and killed. In July, when Wallenberg arrived in Budapest, there were only around 200,000 Jews left.

Wallenberg was sent to Hungary by the Swedish government after a request by the US-based War Refugee Board to see if Sweden could use its good offices to obtain the release of whatever Jews were left in Hungary. ("Good offices" refer to international negotiations, in this case between the Nazis and the War Refugee Board.) Wallenberg, having traveled throughout Hitler's empire and especially in Hungary (he spoke Hungarian, as well as German and English), was an ideal and well-known candidate. He was also known to be appalled at the treatment of the Jews or at least what he knew of it, and he was trusted by many.

Wallenberg's first actions did not make him any friends, at least not among the SS leadership responsible for carrying out the genocide of the Jews in Hungary, chief among them being the now-infamous Adolf Eichmann. Wallenberg situated his offices, which were declared part of the Swedish Embassy, near the largest Jewish ghetto in Budapest and immediately granted diplomatic immunity to four hundred Jewish workers to assist him in his "diplomatic work." He gave them Swedish diplomatic credentials, which gave them immunity from Nazi persecution. He immediately began to cultivate friendships among the Jews in Budapest and with German officials who were either anti-Hitler or in need or want of money or other treasure, especially since many could see the writing on the wall in the shape of the ever-approaching Soviet Red Army. Wallenberg also established safe houses that became hideouts for Jews smuggled out of the ghetto, and what's more, he had the Swedish flag flown over these houses, declaring them officially part of the Swedish Embassy. Within the buildings, the Jews were safe, at least for the time being.

By the fall of 1944, Wallenberg had survived an assassin sent by Eichmann and had personally handed out Swedish diplomatic immunity papers to Jews on a death train to Auschwitz. The dumbfounded Hungarian fascist guards and German soldiers were stupefied by this move, and hundreds of Jews were brought into Wallenberg's safe houses and other places. (It should be known that a number of other diplomats in Hungary joined Wallenberg's efforts, and they also provided shelter of one sort or another.)

By the end of October, Wallenberg had managed to negotiate the safety of the Jews remaining in Budapest. He also paid significant bribes to a number of German and Hungarian officers to forestall their plans until the Soviets entered Budapest, which they did on October 29th, 1944. Wallenberg had saved many thousands.

In January 1945, Wallenberg was summoned to the headquarters of Soviet Marshal Rodion Malinovsky to "answer some questions." By this time in the war, the paranoia of Stalin and the Soviet regime had kicked into full gear once again. The Soviet Union had already begun to anticipate a conflict of one kind or another with the West, particularly the United States. No one knows exactly what happened next. Raoul Wallenberg simply disappeared.

In 1947, the Soviet foreign ministry announced that Wallenberg was not in the country and that he had likely died in the siege of Budapest in 1944. Ten years later, confronted with contradicting accounts, the Soviets admitted that Wallenberg had been imprisoned by them but that he had died of heart trouble in 1947. No one uttered a word about why he would have been in a Soviet prison in Moscow, and the mystery continued.

By the 1970s, Wallenberg had become an international figure. His role in WWII became known in its entirety, except for his death. Much pressure was put on the Soviet Union, but it was not until the fall of the USSR in 1991 that the Russians admitted that he had been "wrongfully" held in a Soviet prison. They said nothing about his death, which by that time had begun to be reported as a likely execution, with accounts coming from ex-guards and ex-prisoners who had known him. Today, Russia admits nothing regarding his death, but most people believe he was killed, along with thousands of others of Stalin's so-called "enemies of the state," in 1947.

In addition to being named an honorary US citizen in 1981, Wallenberg was named "Righteous Among the Nations" by Israel, an honor reserved for those who saved Jews in WWII.

One of the many statues worldwide honoring Wallenberg. This one is in England.
Statue of Raoul Wallenberg. Gt. Cumberland Place by Derek Voller, CC BY-SA 2.0
<https://creativecommons.org/licenses/by-sa/2.0>, via Wikimedia Commons
https://commons.wikimedia.org/wiki/File:Statue_of_Raoul_Wallenberg._Gt._Cumberland_Place_-_geograph.org.uk_-_1997555.jpg

Chapter 13 – Sweden and Famous Swedes since WWII

Today, Sweden is still an officially neutral country, but in 2009, it joined a number of defense treaties with its neighbors to the west and with Denmark and Norway. While it is not a member of NATO (North Atlantic Treaty Organization), it is clear that in any major war that involved NATO or a Russian movement to the west, Sweden would side with the Western powers (the US, UK, Germany, France, etc.). Sweden also has an effective air force with its own highly regarded Swedish fighters and a highly competent navy. The military draft was eliminated in the early 2000s, but not enough volunteers entered the military, so a form of the draft was implemented once again in 2019.

One of the main factors pushing the Swedes into a more Western-oriented orbit is the increasing number of aggressive moves, both in Europe and throughout the world, by Russia. Most significantly for Sweden, this involves more and more incursions into Swedish territorial waters by Russian submarines. At each suspected violation, the Swedish Navy makes it clear that intruders are not welcome.

How do women's rights fare in Sweden? It's often cited that women in the Viking age were able to divorce their husbands. In many places, they were able to inherit land if their husband died without heirs. But with the introduction of Christianity in

Scandinavia in the 1000s and 1100s, the restrictions on women increased over time. Despite the glorification of Scandinavian women in modern TV shows and movies, women of all ages were subject to all kinds of abuse for which they did not have recourse. If they came from a powerful family, there might be some pushback if her husband was abusive, but most women did not. Those on the lower part of the social ladder were subject to domestic abuse on a likely frightening scale, as well as sexual abuse and exploitation.

The situation for women worsened with the arrival of Lutheranism and its offshoot Calvinism in the 1500s and 1600s. It was not until the later years of the Industrial Revolution that things began to change, mostly because many men were out of the house working in factories. Women slowly began to take on a greater role in the economy as well.

In the mid-1800s, a number of middle- and upper-class women, most notably Fredrika Bremer (1801–1865), began to push for the legalization of women's rights, such as the abolition of corporal punishment for domestic servants (this did include male servants as well, but as you can likely imagine, it was more of a concern for women than men) and property rights for women over twenty-five.

In the later 1800s, the Fredrika Bremer Society was founded in order to push for increased women's rights, most notably the vote. They also pushed for the inclusion of a passage in an 1884 law that granted women over twenty-one the same legal rights as men. Suffrage was not a part of this; it was made law, as in many other nations, including the US, in the early 1920s.

Since that time, women in Sweden have made great strides, and they enjoy legal, financial, and societal equality with men, including legalized abortion. Though both Denmark and Norway have had women prime ministers since the end of WWII, it was only in 2021 that Sweden elected its first female prime minister, Magdalena Andersson.

Of course, one of the most famous elements of Swedish society is its social security system. Sweden has had some form of social welfare since the late 1700s. This, of course, was rudimentary and generally involved the very poor. It was often administered by the clergy. With the advent of the Industrial Revolution, the pace of social change grew, along with the need for a "safety net" (a 20th-century term) for those in need. Sweden was one of the first nations to grant medical leave and insurance, and though it was very basic, it was light-years ahead of almost all other Western countries at the time, with the possible exception of Germany after 1871.

In the 1960s and 1970s, Scandinavian social welfare programs and the involvement of the government in their administration gave rise to a new phrase: the "Third Way," a middle way between what was seen in Scandinavia as the unrestrained capitalism of the United States and the communism of the Soviet Union.

The "Third Way" was a trade-off to a great extent. In return for seemingly ever-increasing taxes, the Swedish, Norwegian, and Danish governments provided a level of medical care and employment insurance not seen anywhere else in the world. In most cases, education (including most colleges and universities) was free and of a very high standard.

However, heading toward the end of the 20th century and into the 21st, the Swedish welfare state model came under increasing criticism both overseas (where much of it was misdirected hysteria on the part of right-wing politicians and pundits in the United States) but also at home. While the Swedish "Third Way" gave the government a huge role in the individual lives of Swedes, it did not in any way restrict their political freedoms. However, as the rest of the world shifted into a new and dynamic economy, with the advent of computerization and the demise of the Soviet Union in Eastern Europe, Sweden's tax burden impeded its economic growth and innovation. A number of wealthy and influential Swedes began to speak out against many of the elements of the welfare system, especially taxation.

By the mid-2000s, the people began to shift away from the high taxes and government involvement. Despite this shift away from the "heyday" of the Swedish "Third Way," Sweden still enjoys a much more advanced and effective social welfare system than much of the rest of the world.

However, the ability and willingness of many Swedes to pay into that system have been challenged in recent years, most notably since 2015, the year that Europe faced the Middle East refugee crisis. That year, literally millions of people attempting to escape war, terrorism, economic hardship, disease, and much else began to stream into Europe. A small but significant minority of people of Middle Eastern descent (mostly from more modern and secular Turkey) had lived in Sweden for some time by that point and had, in many cases, become Swedish citizens. But now Sweden was faced with a huge influx of refugees, who mostly settled in the south of the country and in the capital of Stockholm. Like many other nations at the time (and at the time of this writing), many Swedes have questioned why they are paying for these refugees' care.

Of course, there is an element of exaggeration on both sides. Many Swedes, especially those in the lower-income bracket, see the refugees (mostly those from Syria and Iraq) as competition for jobs and education. Many of the refugees believe that the Swedish government is not doing enough to help them in their new country.

The truth lies somewhere in between, but the huge and sudden influx of foreigners has led to the rise of more conservative and even extreme right-wing parties in Sweden, as well as elsewhere in Europe. Their rise is also due to the formation of gangs within the refugee community, which rose both for protection and criminal activity. In 2021 and 2022, Sweden has seen a marked increase in gun violence in some of its major cities, especially Stockholm and the southern port city of Malmö. The immigrant situation is the most important issue facing Sweden as we enter the third decade of the 21st century.

Conclusion

You've reached the end of your introductory journey into Swedish history. As we noted above, the immigration question is likely *the* problem of Sweden today, and the country is tentatively attempting to find a workable solution to the many problems the largest wave of immigration to the country has brought to its shores.

In this book, you have read about the Swedish Vikings, the foundation of early Russia, the expansion of the Swedish Empire, its conversion to Protestantism, its many wars, and the plots and counter-plots facing a number of Swedish monarchs. Lastly, you read about the development of the famous Swedish policy of neutrality that kept it out of the two most costly wars in human history.

Unfortunately, we haven't mentioned the many Swedes of the 20th century and today who have had a major impact (considering the size of the country and its relatively small population) throughout the world.

Perhaps the most famous Swede of the last two hundred years was Alfred Nobel, the industrialist, philanthropist, and scientist who is responsible for the invention of dynamite, which led to other developments in the area of weapons and explosives. As a result of the guilt he felt for having introduced a tool with such destructive potential, the Swedish inventor established a philanthropic society, whose prizes for work in the fields of international peace, science, and literature are known as the Nobel Prize. It is perhaps the most prestigious award in those fields.

You read about the heroic and unfortunate hero of WWII, Raoul Wallenberg, but other Swedes have been involved to a great degree in the field of international relations for some time, especially after WWII. The most famous of these was Dag Hammarskjöld, the second secretary-general of the United Nations. He led the organization from 1953 to 1961 and was respected throughout the world for his efforts in building world peace and understanding. The plaza outside the UN building in New York City is named after him.

Two Swedes in particular (who shared the same last name but were not related) rose to fame in the field of entertainment: Ingmar Bergman, the highly regarded and somewhat controversial film director, and Ingrid Bergman, who won three Academy Awards and is famous worldwide for her role as Elsa in the classic WWII-era film *Casablanca*.

Most recently, another Swede has captured the attention of the world: teenager and environmental activist Greta Thunberg, who has drawn the world's attention (in sometimes admiringly blunt ways) to the problems of climate change and the environment. She has sparked a movement throughout much of the world, particularly among young people.

We hope you have enjoyed this book. Please see the bibliography for further reading!

Part 2: History of Norway

A Captivating Guide to Norwegian History

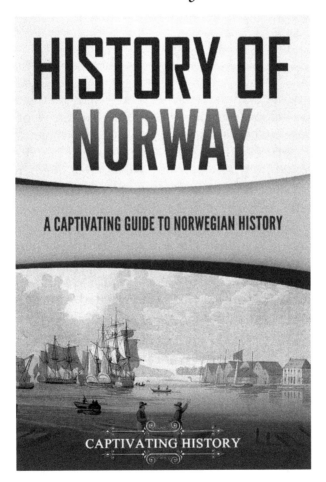

HISTORY OF NORWAY

A CAPTIVATING GUIDE TO NORWEGIAN HISTORY

CAPTIVATING HISTORY

Introduction

The history of Norway is deeply connected to its geographic location. Scandinavia lies far on the northern fringes of Europe, with Norway being just a small part of it. This whole region was covered in glaciers during the last glacial period that ended around 12,000 BCE. No humans inhabited this area of the world at the time due to the harsh environment. However, with the retreat of the ice, life started sprouting, and tundra vegetation consumed the peninsula. The southern regions soon started growing thick and wild forests that attracted many animals, such as elk, deer, and aurochs (now extinct wild cattle). The first humans followed. They were hunter-gatherers, and they came to inhabit the Norwegian coast because it offered perfect conditions for catching fish and seals.

With the people came the first settlements and the development of the first Scandinavian cultures. The migratory people of central Europe followed the northern paths and brought the Proto-Germanic language, which would later take the shape of Old Norse and finally Norwegian. These people also brought cultures that were developed in central Europe, but in Scandinavia, they took some unique aspects, mainly due to the lack of raw materials and the need for imports. This would also be the reason why different periods came late in Scandinavia.

Other things were imported from parts of Europe. During the Bronze Age, the ideas of agriculture, permanent settlements, and the design of tools and houses penetrated Scandinavia. In Norway, some areas proved to be very fertile, and this was where the first farms were established. But the Scandinavian farmers couldn't rely only on agriculture, mainly due to the harsh winters and cold climate. They also engaged in the fur and skin trade, which they exchanged for luxury items from Jutland (continental Denmark and northern Germany).

The Iron Age saw a sudden increase in the population of Scandinavia, and more forests needed to be cleared for the establishment of new farms. Local chieftains rose to power and created a new society based on clans. Conflict often rose between different clans and villages, which led to the development of a warrior society. During the Iron Age, the Norsemen traded with the Romans, though it is unknown if the Norwegians did so directly or through their neighbors, the Danes and Swedes. But it is evident that some Scandinavians even served in the Roman army.

The Viking Age is the period separating the Iron Age from medieval times, though some historians consider it to be the culmination of the Iron Age. The Vikings were Norsemen who expanded their Scandinavian territory and trade. For a long time, it was thought that Vikings were raiders who would attack foreign settlements across the sea and quickly escape with the plunder. But the Vikings were more complex than that. They were also farmers, traders, explorers, and settlers. They developed longships and navigation techniques so they could travel far into the unknown. They were pagans and fearsome warriors. They were often considered to have supernatural powers by the God-fearing Christians.

But the Norwegian Vikings were mainly explorers. The lack of arable land in western Norway forced people to search for their fortune somewhere else. The Norwegians first inhabited Iceland and the Faroe Islands, and they formed colonies on Shetland, Orkney, and even as far as Greenland.

Norway was Christianized during the Middle Ages, and many kings chose to do it through violence. In Norway, the Middle Ages were a period of frequent succession struggles and conflicts but also church development. The population of Norway continued to rise, which led to the reshaping of the farming system. The land was mostly owned by the king, church, and the elite levels of society, and the farmers had to rent it. Nevertheless, the tenants remained free men and had more freedom than the medieval serfs of other European kingdoms.

During the 14th century, Norway entered its golden age. The country was in continuous peace, and trade was booming. But this is also the period when the plague took many lives, causing famine and the severe reduction of the Norwegian population. Germany started playing a significant role in the political and economic life of Norway with the establishment of the Hanseatic League in Bergen. Eventually, the league took complete control over Norwegian trade. Although some scholars see this as oppression since the domestic society was not allowed to develop itself, many more scholars believe that the league propelled Norway into its future. The end of the league came when Olaf Haakonsson succeeded both the Norwegian and Danish thrones.

When the union fell apart, Norway was politically weak, and it couldn't escape Danish dominance. Norwegian history was once again profoundly bound to the history of its neighbors. However, the union with economically powerful Denmark brought the first industrialization to Norway. Norway started benefiting from many European wars that increased the demand for raw goods. Being on the fringe of the continent, war never came to Norway, so it was always a safe place.

After the Napoleonic Wars, Norway was invaded by Sweden. Denmark and Sweden were on opposing sides in the wars, and this conflict continued into the fight over Norway. In 1814, Norway finally broke from its union with Denmark, but it could do so only by entering another union, this time with Sweden. Sweden was a highly constitutional kingdom, and it promised Norway that it would be an equal partner in the union. Thus, Norway gained its independence, though it was still bound to another neighboring country. The Norway-Sweden union lasted only for ninety-one years, and it ended due to disagreements over foreign policy.

Norway finally gained complete independence, and when World War I broke out, it chose to remain neutral so it could build up the young state. Realizing how well the policy of neutrality had worked, Norway attempted to stay out of the conflict during the Second World War too. However, having an established border with Russia, the country became of immense strategic importance for both Germany and the Allies. Unfortunately, the Nazi Germans were quicker, and they occupied Norway in April of 1940.

After the end of the war, Norway started recovering from the immense destruction it went through. Norway established a welfare system, which is still considered to be one of the best in the world. Through rationing and hard work, the Norwegians managed to build up their country and have one of the highest-rising post-war economies. But the real development of Norway started during the 1960s with the discovery of oil.

Nevertheless, Norway remains known for its stunning natural beauty. Many fjords cut through the country, and where the fjords end, the mountains start. It is no wonder it was so difficult to connect the country in the past, as sailing was the only way its population could easily get around. The geographic position and shape of Norway determined its history. It is because of it that the Vikings invented navigational systems and longboats that were capable of long-distance sailing. Even in modern times, Norway's geographic position allows it access to oil, the black blood of the earth. Due to the discovery of oil and the establishment of a prosperous oil industry, Norway became the influential country that it is today.

Chapter 1 – Scandinavia in Prehistory

Satellite image of Scandinavia from March 2002.
https://commons.wikimedia.org/wiki/File:Scandinavia_M2002074_lrg.jpg

To understand the history of Norway, you must understand its geographical position and the history of the whole of Scandinavia. Scandinavia is not strictly a geographical term. It is used to designate culturally, linguistically, and historically similar countries: Denmark, Sweden, and Norway. In a geographical sense, Scandinavia is a peninsula, and as such, it includes mainland Norway, Sweden, and parts of Finland and Russia. But in a cultural sense, Scandinavia is often expanded to include the Faroe Islands, Iceland, the Åland Islands, Svalbard, and Greenland. Norway is part of this cultural and geographical region, and its early history is very connected to its neighboring countries. This is why when researching the earliest history of Norway, the best thing to do is look at the history of the whole of Scandinavia, both in the geographical and cultural sense.

The prehistory of Scandinavia started more than thirteen thousand years ago at the very end of the last glacial period. Global warming started, the ice melted, and new lands for flora and fauna to thrive opened up. The first humans then came to live in the Scandinavian region and started their Stone Age culture. In Scandinavia, the Stone Age is divided into three phases: Old or Hunter Stone Age (Paleolithic period), Middle Stone Age (Mesolithic), and New or Farmer Stone Age (Neolithic period). The Stone Age in Scandinavia lasted from 13,000 to 1700 BCE. The Bronze Age lasted between 1700 and 500 BCE. The next was the Iron Age, which lasted from 500 BCE until the start of the Viking Age, approximately 750 CE. However, although this periodization is largely accepted for the whole of Scandinavia, it cannot be applied to the northern regions. There, the climate was such that development was often halted, and some changes didn't appear at all. For example, the true Neolithic period never really arrived in the north since agriculture was impossible due to permafrost.

The first societies of Scandinavia, those belonging to the early Paleolithic, are almost invisible to archaeologists and history in general. They were hunters, and they inhabited mainly the western shores of the peninsula, where they had easy access to reindeer and seals. Their tools were made of stone, animal bones, and antlers, and they were scattered across the landscape. It is hard for scholars to determine what kind of social structure these early societies had, if they even had any. But with the Neolithic period came the first permanent settlements on the western shores, although they were very small. Several huts and burial places belonging to this period were discovered, as well as flint items, seashells, and fish bones, which points to a culture capable of utilizing resources from the sea. The first pottery appeared in the late Mesolithic period, but it became much more common in the Neolithic.

In the Neolithic period, the societies of Scandinavia turned to farming. The first farms were established in inland Scandinavia, where the land was more fertile. Pastures for cattle were also more available there. This is also the period where the people started burying their dead in monumental tombs, which held tens, sometimes even hundreds of bodies. During the early Neolithic period, copper items appeared, and they became common later in this period. Although some houses and many tombs from the Neolithic period were preserved, especially in southern Scandinavia, not much is known about the society. However, with the start of the Bronze Age, this changed.

The Bronze Age is best known for the usage of this metal, but it was also the first appearance of social structures. The tribes were led by chiefs, who resided in large timber halls, and were buried with their riches and weapons, many of which had their origins in other parts of Europe. The rest of the people were simple farmers living on scattered small farmsteads. The commoners were still buried together, but some prominent individuals and even whole families had special, designated burial spaces within the common burial complex. This whole period was dominated by rich individuals, and most of the archaeological and historical evidence belongs to the chieftains. The rest of Scandinavian society remains almost invisible to history.

During the Iron Age, true villages emerged. Many large and small farms have been excavated, and flint and stone completely perished as a material used for tools and weapons. With the villages came more powerful leaders who were capable of directing the economic and social developments of their people. Military and religious activities became apparent, and the chieftains often assumed the roles of military and religious leaders. Society was divided into distinct classes, such as warriors, shamans (or priests), artists, and craftsmen. The people of the Iron Age started changing the landscape of Scandinavia as they built roads and bridges, erected walls around their settlements, and built fortresses. The burial mounds became larger so they could accommodate more people, more treasures of the chieftains, and sometimes even whole ships.

The Founders of Scandinavia

Human ancestors first arrived in Europe more than a million years ago. But they were mostly concentrated in the south and southwestern regions of the continent, as the climate there allowed them to thrive. They were hunter-gatherers, and they led a nomadic way of life. They were constantly on the move and in search of food sources. When the ice melted in the north of Europe, it left behind a wide territory covered in tall grass and thick wild birch forests. These were the perfect conditions for the migration of animals. While the birch forests became home to large elk, the grasslands and plains of the northern tundra attracted reindeer. For a very long time, it was believed that the first Scandinavians came from southwestern Europe as they followed the migration of large elk, and although this is true, they were not the only ones. At approximately the same time, another group of people migrated to the western shores of Scandinavia, and they came from the east. They were the nomadic people of northern Russia, and they came to the far west of Norway by traversing the arctic routes of Russia, Finland, and Sweden, all while following the migration of reindeer.

The earliest known Scandinavian body ever discovered is Koelbjerg Man, and it was discovered in Denmark. His remains were carbon-dated to around 8000 BCE. Later, the remains of a settlement were found approximately two kilometers south from the site where Koelbjerg Man was found. This settlement was also dated to the year 8000 BCE, and it is quite possible the man lived there. However, these discoveries are not the oldest ones in Scandinavia. In the north of Norway, the first archaeological findings were dated to 9000 BCE, and they were tools and items belonging to the people who came from the east and settled on the western shores of Scandinavia. It is believed that these people then constructed crude vessels made of animal skins and sailed to the south, where they eventually met the migrating southwestern Europeans.

It is from the mingling of the southwestern and northeastern migratory nomadic tribes that the first cultures developed in Scandinavia. The two most prominent ones in Norway were the Hensbacka and Fosna cultures. A third one was discovered in the Alta region in northern Norway and was named the Komsa culture after Mount Komsa. However, most recent discoveries proved that the Komsa culture was, in fact, the same as Fosna, but due to the lack of flint and some other materials in the northernmost reaches of Norway, the Komsa culture lacked diversity in their tools. The Hensbacka culture was mainly concentrated on the shores of western Sweden and the Oslofjord in Norway, while Fosna/Komsa spread from the central (Trøndelag county) to northern Norway (Finnmark). Even though archaeologically these two cultures were different, they are generally called the Fosna-Hensbacka culture due to their undeniable similarities.

The Fosna-Hensbacka culture is typically dated between 9000 and 8000 BCE, and the tools belonging to it are usually large flake axes and artifacts with distinctive tanged points. The design of the flake axes suggests they were used as an adze instead of an ax, as the blade was perpendicular to the shaft. They were also very similar to the *ulu* of the Inuits, a long crescent-shaped blade used for butchering seals and food preparation. Flint was the main material from which the tools of the Fosna-Hensbacka culture were made, but Scandinavia had very few sources of flint. The earliest source came from Denmark and southwestern Sweden. It is believed that flint was taken from these parts and traded elsewhere either as already prepared tools or as a raw material. Later, flint sources were found along the southwestern beaches of Norway, and it is believed that the early people used icebergs to transport flint to the northern areas. In other areas of Scandinavia where flint was sparse or didn't exist, the people used other materials to construct their tools, such as chert, rhyolite, tuff, jasper, rock crystal, and fine-grained quartzite.

For a long time, it was believed that the north of Norway and Scandinavia in general were populated much later than the south. For this reason, the history of northern Scandinavia was often neglected, and no archaeological excavations were performed. However, once archaeological findings were discovered, scholars were shocked to learn that the northernmost reaches of the peninsula were inhabited at the same time as the south. All the items found in the early northern settlements were as old as those found in the southern settlements. But their similarity with the southern inhabitants came as the result of the mixing between the early migratory peoples.

Just as in the south, the northern society was sea-oriented. The eastern parts of the Scandinavian Peninsula were still covered in ice, and glaciers dominated the area. But the shore was habitable, and the sea was filled with life. Most of the settlements above the Arctic Circle were concentrated on the western shores of Norway and the coast of the Russian Kola Peninsula. The materials most often used here were various quartzites, cherts, and flint of very poor quality. But it is there, in the far north, that the earliest rock art was discovered. In the Nordland region, at the end of the Komsa period, the people started carving shapes of animals into the surrounding rocks. These animals were usually whales, reindeer, elk, and bears, and they were dated to 8000 BCE.

The Hunters

Scandinavia is a vast territory, and as such, it has different conditions for life in the southern and northern areas. The Old Stone Age, also known as the Hunter Stone Age because this was the period when hunter-gatherer societies thrived, lasted approximately from 9700 BCE until 4000 BCE. However, in the far north, where the land couldn't be cultivated due to climate and permafrost, the hunter-gatherer societies existed much longer than in the south; some even exist today. But these societies left very little behind, and we know almost nothing about how they lived and what their social structure was like.

Their main tools were adapted to hunting, and various arrowheads and spearheads have been found that tell the story of their development. At the beginning of the Stone Age, arrowheads were narrow and long. While they would easily reach their target, they would slice through animal tissue, causing little damage. As time passed, the northerners adapted their weapons and started producing wider arrowheads that would smash bone tissue and cause much more damage to the animal, which made hunting more efficient.

At the end of the Stone Age, pottery was introduced to Scandinavia. More and more jars and different varieties of pottery containers can be found in the Mesolithic archaeological sites that were dated after 4800 BCE. It was believed that pottery was introduced to Scandinavia from southern Europe. However, recent discoveries proved that Scandinavian pottery came from the east, following the northern routes from China through Russia and Finland. There might have been more than one source from which Scandinavian pottery originated, but the prevailing opinion is that it was introduced from the east. In southern Scandinavia, where the climate was milder, other materials were used for producing tools and ornamental objects, such as bones, antlers, amber, wood, tree bark, and fungus threads.

The climate during the Scandinavian Stone Age was warming up, and thick forests of birch, pine, and hazel developed in places that previously belonged to the tundra. Over time, as the warming up continued, elm, oak, and lime trees started appearing. The different types of trees and forests attracted different types of animals, which people could hunt. Red deer, wild pig, and roe deer became the most valued prey, and they drove the economy of the hunter-gatherer societies of the north. Marten, otter, wildcat, and squirrel were other animals hunted for their fur and meat. The Hunter Stone Age is also the period in which the first dogs started appearing in the tombs of humans, a clear sign of domestication. Thus, dogs were the first animals to be domesticated, even before the development of agriculture. Although it is unknown where and when the first dogs joined humans, one theory suggests it happened in northern Siberia.

After the last glacial period, most of the Scandinavians lived by the sea, and the warming climate made the waters abundant with life. The main diet of the Scandinavian hunter-gatherers came from the sea in the form of fish, crustaceans, mollusks, seals, and even whales. Freshwater fish was also popular among the early Scandinavian societies, as the melting glaciers formed a great number of lakes and rivers. The equipment they used to extract fish and sea mammals was very elaborate. They used rods, hooks, spears, and even nets made out of bark and fungus threads. Because most archaeological sites contained a very large number of animal bones and antlers, it was believed that land mammals were the main diet of the Stone Age hunter-gatherers. However, the carbon isotope ratios in human bones from the Mesolithic period correspond to those of the Greenlandic Inuit, whose diet primarily consisted of marine sources. The human remains of the Neolithic period when farming was introduced have a carbon isotope ratio appropriate for a diet based on plants and domestic land animals. Today, it is believed that the Scandinavian hunter-gatherers had 75 percent of their diet coming from the sea. The shift in diet was very sharp once farming was introduced to southern Scandinavia.

What little is known about these early Scandinavian societies seems to be much different than what is generally believed about the European hunter-gatherers. While in central Europe, these societies were very small and constantly on the move in search of prey, in Scandinavia, they were much larger, and they preferred to stay in one region. This might be because the density of people in central Europe was very small during the Stone Age, and in the north, people concentrated around the seashores where the climate was warmer and food resources abundant. But that doesn't mean that all societies in the Scandinavian Stone Age were sedentary. Some people followed large land animals, mainly reindeer, as they migrated to the colder north, although their numbers were very small since the majority preferred to stay near the sea.

The First Farmers

The most important event in human prehistory is the transition from hunting and gathering to farming. This shift from foraging for food to producing it changed the way of living for humans across the globe, and it was no different in Scandinavia. This is why scholars are very interested in finding out and explaining what pushed the people to make such a change and how this transition influenced all aspects of life. Scientists started researching this topic in the early 19th century, and even Charles Darwin engaged in the research of the domestication of plants and animals. In Scandinavia, agriculture began with the appearance of the Funnelbeaker culture (named so because of the shape of the ceramics found in the archaeological sites).

The Funnelbeaker culture appeared first around 5000 BCE in what is today northern Germany, but it reached Scandinavia only one thousand years later. Once it arrived, the life of the people abruptly changed. Scholars are still researching what exactly caused this sudden change. Domesticated animals and plants appeared as if out of nowhere, and it took only a few hundreds of years for the whole Scandinavian society to change its way of life. But this wasn't the case only in northern Europe. Wherever agriculture appeared, change came surprisingly fast. The first items signaling the arrival of agriculture were the T-shaped axes made out of copper and jadeite, as well as some copper ornamental items, such as rings and bracelets. These were imported into Scandinavia directly from Germany and Poland, but the domestication of animals and plants had yet to come.

There is not a lot of evidence for farming during the first part of the Neolithic period. Several settlements were discovered, and there are only a few signs of purposeful deforestation, which would have opened the fields for agriculture. But around 3500 BCE, the development of agriculture exploded. But it is yet to be discovered how farming first arrived in Scandinavia. Three main theories could explain the appearance of farming in northern Europe: 1) the colonization of the Scandinavian Peninsula by the southern Europeans, 2) the adoption of agriculture by the indigenous people, 3) or the combination of the two elements, with small groups of new settlers bringing the idea of agriculture, which was then quickly adopted by the indigenous people.

The contact between the Danubian farming societies and the southern Scandinavians existed even in the late Mesolithic and early Neolithic periods, which can be seen from the import of tools and jewelry. But it is suspected that the idea of agriculture didn't get adopted early simply because the sea-oriented Scandinavians didn't have much use for it. The waters were abundant with food, and coastal life was thriving. So, the reason they suddenly changed from hunting and fishing to agriculture remains a mystery. Perhaps it was the increase in population or the decline of available resources that made the people turn to growing their own food. Some scholars even propose that it wasn't any natural cause that caused the transition to farming but a socio-economic change. The hunter-gatherer societies started forming classes, and the elites needed to create a surplus in food to keep their social position. This could only be achieved through farming.

The first plants that were grown in Neolithic Scandinavia were emmer, einkorn, naked barley, wheat, and probably spelt. Oil-rich plants were also domesticated early, as well as some berries, apples, and nuts. Aside from plants, the Neolithic Scandinavians domesticated animals, such as pigs, cattle, sheep, goats, and dogs. As discussed earlier, dogs were the first animals to appear alongside humans. The other animals didn't appear in Scandinavia until approximately 3800 BCE. During the Funnelbeaker culture in Scandinavia, around 90 percent of animal bones found in archaeological sites belonged to domesticated animals.

It seems that cattle were the most prominent animal. They were highly regarded for their meat and milk, which could be consumed, and also because of their skin, horns, and bones, which were used for tool production. Cattle were so widespread that they came to represent 80 percent of domestic animals in later Neolithic sites. Pigs were also popular, but they were mostly kept in the settlements away from the sea where they could roam the forests. Sheep and goats were also present but not as widespread as cattle and pigs. It is therefore unlikely that wool was used for textile production at this period and that the main material for garments was probably leather and fur.

With agriculture came a wide change in the society of Scandinavia, and different cultures started developing. Some focused on their warrior lifestyle, while others started practicing nomadic cattle herding. Some were completely sedentary societies that developed early forms of village life, while others chose to move around, following animal migrations or simply conquering their weaker neighbors. But the prevailing culture of the late Neolithic period was the Bell Beaker culture (named after the pottery shape they used the most). It seems they were mostly traders in northern and central Europe. They produced and exchanged flint daggers, spears, and tools, and they introduced the first metals to Scandinavia. The southern people had already discovered metals, especially copper, gold, and later bronze, and they used them in trading. Following the economic network of late Neolithic Scandinavia and Europe in general, these metals found their way to the north.

The introduction of metals, just like agriculture, started a new series of changes within Scandinavian society. Mainly, the society started dividing itself by class, and powerful warrior chieftains became the leaders of small or large groups of people. Due to this power, they were able to conquer their neighbors and establish long-distance trade routes that would bring them even more riches. But all these changes mainly occurred in the southern regions of Scandinavia, where agriculture bloomed. Northern Norway and Sweden felt the influences from the south, and they started using newly developed and imported tools and materials, but agriculture was still impossible there. This is why the social changes were almost nonexistent in northern Scandinavia. Nevertheless, the Bronze Age arrived in Scandinavia, and it would become one of the most remarkable periods of Scandinavian prehistory.

Chapter 2 – Bronze and Iron Age Warriors

Reconstructed longhouse at the archaeological site at Borg, modern Viking Museum.

The Bronze Age (1700-500 BCE)

The European Bronze Age originated in the Aegean area, where it started around 3000 BCE. But it came late to Scandinavia, just as agriculture did. The Scandinavian Bronze Age started in 1700 BCE and lasted until 500 BCE, and it was followed by the Iron

Age. However, bronze items were already in use in Scandinavia before the proper Bronze Age came. This is because of the extensive trade network the Scandinavians developed with the rest of Europe, especially with areas that are today central Germany and Poland. From there, copper and bronze items, such as tools and jewelry, entered the north, although Scandinavians didn't start producing their own metal items yet. The Bronze Age is not only about the use of metal; it also brought social and economic changes. Although the metal was in use in Scandinavia as early as 2800 BCE, the social changes didn't occur until 1600 BCE.

Although the Bronze Age started late in Scandinavia, it was a very productive period, as there are more bronze artifacts found in this peninsula than anywhere else in Europe. However, flint continued to be used for the production of daggers and scraping tools. Metal items used in Scandinavia were mostly imported. It was only during the Late Bronze Age that production started. However, once it was set in motion, metal production became the basis of the Scandinavian economy. Almost all of the production sites were concentrated in the southern parts of the peninsula, but ingots were imported. Middle Sweden and southern Norway have rich copper veins, but these were not excavated during the Bronze Age. Nevertheless, the items produced from imported ore and ingots were usually for local use and often found in the burial mounds. The most common bronze items produced in Scandinavia were richly decorated shields and lures (also spelled as lurs; they are very long horns used to make music).

Most of the raw ores for the production of bronze items were imported from the western Mediterranean world, and it is believed that the Scandinavians sailed the Atlantic routes for trade. But the style of the items produced in Scandinavia wasn't Mediterranean-styled. Instead, they preferred central European aesthetics and were influenced by the items they saw in central Germany, Poland, and even Latvia. With the new metals and stylistic designs came new ideas, and these were also borrowed mostly from central Europe. By the second millennium BCE, northern Europe started producing a great number of innovative items, such as chariots and new weapons. But the most intriguing change came within the society, as the first social institutions were created. Agriculture was no longer the only viable foundation for the economy. Now trade, crafts, and production entered the scene and started competing with farming.

The new economic foundations brought an even greater accumulation of wealth and power, and competition became fierce. This led to an increased number of conflicts and open wars between different groups of people. The result was a constant change in trade alliances, the creation of new ones, and old trade ties being cut off. The differences in the social status of individuals became very prominent, and the idea of land ownership was introduced into Scandinavian society. Wealthy individuals were able to afford extra workers in their chosen industries, and captured enemies became slaves. The differences in social status are observable today, as the burial mounds from the Bronze Age were well preserved. These mounds often contain enormous riches, such as weapons, clothes, household items, chariots, and animals. The chieftains and high-status individuals were buried in stone and wood coffins, while the commoners were buried without any protective layer around them. The Late Bronze Age saw the widespread use of cremation, and although it often signaled the equal treatment of the dead in the afterlife, in Scandinavia, the ashes of prominent individuals were buried with their riches to put an accent on their high status during life.

The Warrior Society of the Bronze Age

The Bronze Age excavations led to extraordinary discoveries in Scandinavia. One was the existence of a new social class: the warriors. Separate graves were found in which warriors were buried with special honors. They were different from the graves of the chieftains and commoners, as the items they contained pointed to a lifestyle of continuous warfare. These individuals were always buried with their armor and weapons. The main items found in these tombs were swords, shields, and items for personal hygiene, such as combs, trimmers, and mirrors. The Early Bronze Age saw the redesign of arrows and spears, as these were weapons adapted from hunting. However, when swords and battle-axes came into use, their number significantly decreased.

The sword was the first weapon specifically designed for battle, and they were meant for close hand-to-hand combat. Bronze weapons were also used as a symbol of high social status, as they must have been expensive to produce. Copies of these bronze swords were also produced out of flint so they could be used by less fortunate individuals. All bronze and flint swords excavated in Scandinavia that date to the Bronze Age display signs of frequent usage. They were often sharpened and contained many nicks, though these were often removed before burial. Swords that were placed as offerings were never repaired and sharpened. In Scandinavia, two types of swords were in use: ones with a solid metal hilt riveted to the blade and those that had the blade and the hilt cast together.

Although warriors represented a new social class that rose in response to the increased need for the defense of communities, their bodies rarely displayed signs of violent death. But this could be due to the poor skeletal preservation of the Early Bronze Age. During the Late Bronze Age, the bodies were cremated, and there is no way of concluding how they died. Nevertheless, scholars estimate that the life expectancy in Scandinavia during the Bronze Age was around forty years.

One archaeological site in Norway, near the city of Trondheim, serves as evidence that violent deaths did occur. This place named Sund is actually a part of a wider excavation area that extends to another dig site named Tunds. It seems that the people of these two sites were two parts of the same society. Sund proved to be a mass grave, where the bones of humans were mixed with those of animals. The human bones belonged to men, women, and children. Around 50 percent of the discovered remains belonged to children. They were dated to approximately the same period as the remains found two kilometers to the west in Tunds.

But there was a massive difference between these two sites. The burials in Tunds were done appropriately for the period, and many personal items, weapons, and armor were found together with human remains, which were buried separate from each other. In Sund, all remains were found together in one massive grave, and they had no personal items with them. Further exploration of the remains proved that the ones found in

Tunds belonged to healthy individuals, all aged above forty. Those found in Sund displayed various signs of malnutrition and bone defects that are common for hard-working people (spondylosis and osteoarthritis). Bone cuts could often be seen on the remains of the adult individuals from Sund but not on the children. Some of these cuts healed, but some were made immediately before death and had no time to heal. The bone cuts are a perfect sign of the violence these people must have experienced.

Scholars believed that the inhabitants of Sund were warriors due to the signs of violence their remains showed and the lack of these signs on the remains of the children. However, the deformities of the bones caused by malnutrition and hard work are not found among any other remains of warrior societies around the world. Therefore, it must have been that the Sund people were oppressed, probably by their very close neighbors of Tunds. In fact, there is a high possibility that Sund and Tunds were the same community, with the first one being the slums in which the slaves lived and the latter being home to a warrior society. This would explain the malnutrition and bone deformities and wounds, as well as the fact that they were all buried in a single grave. The Sund inhabitants possibly died all at approximately the same time, either due to violence or disease.

Bronze Age Settlements

The typical form of settlements in the Scandinavian Bronze Age were farmsteads. They were rarely fenced, and they were close to each other. A group of such farmsteads formed a community, and the chieftain had the largest land allotment and the largest house, which was typically in the middle of the settlement. Farmhouses were more simple and smaller than the houses of the Late Neolithic period, probably because of the lack of wood for construction. The forests were cut down long before to make room for farms n. Typically, the longhouse belonged to the chieftain, and it served as a hall. However, it also housed the extended family of the Bronze Age leaders. Some houses in southern Sweden had a separate room with a hearth that housed a family and another one for the animals. However, sheltering the animals wasn't practiced anywhere else in Scandinavia until the Iron Age.

Some of the houses had cellars in which food was stored, but these were rare. The houses were built on or near the site of an old house that was deteriorated. Repairing houses wasn't profitable, and the Bronze Age people preferred to build a new one once the old house was no longer usable. Nevertheless, the settlements were very stable, and they remained inhabited for long periods. Families often buried their dead on their farmsteads, which took up several square kilometers. The distance between farmsteads indicates that the settlements weren't yet proper villages. The typical layout of the settlement was one large farmstead, which belonged to a chieftain, that was surrounded by many smaller farms.

The Bronze Age settlement development in the north of Scandinavia was very much different than in the south. There, farming finally arrived, but due to the climate, it could only be practiced in the coastal regions. The tools used by these northern farmers remained largely made out of stone, as metal hadn't yet entered this region. Nevertheless, farming spread north of Trondheim to the Altafjord in Norway, and the people learned how to grow their food. Hunter-gatherers still thrived, though. The seas were still rich in fish, and although plant-based food could be cultivated, the Bronze Age north Scandinavians continued to hunt and fish. Hunter-gatherer societies continued to exist in inland areas and the far north, but they formed new alliances and trade connections with the southerners. In exchange for new tools and weapons, they traded meat and fur.

The Bronze Age might have been the period when the Sámi people first appeared in Scandinavia. However, it is impossible to conclude how long they roamed the peninsula due to their constant nomadic way of life, which they have managed to preserve even today. Nevertheless, the connection of the Scandinavians with the Russians, Finnish, and Eastern Baltics increased during the Bronze Age, especially in the north. The eastern ideas continued to flow into Scandinavia, and they can be easily seen in clothing decorations, asbestos-tempered ceramics, and elongated stone projectiles. In the north of Norway and Sweden, distinctive rock carvings with elaborate drawings of animals, people, boats, and abstract objects and shapes have been discovered that can be connected to the shamanistic religion of the period. These carvings and drawings can be found in northern Norway, Sweden, Finland, and the Russian Kola Peninsula. The wide area in which they are found might be explained by the nomadic way of life of the northernmost societies.

The Iron Age (500 BCE–750 CE)

The Scandinavian Iron Age came later than in the rest of Europe, and it is divided into three periods: pre-Roman, Roman, and Germanic. The names of this division can be confusing since the Romans never conquered Scandinavia, and they barely even knew about these northern regions. Nevertheless, the Roman influence on the whole of Europe was so great that it was felt even in the far north. The Iron Age was followed by the Viking period, which some scholars see as the peak of the Scandinavian Iron Age, as it happened just before the beginning of the medieval period and the spread of Christianity in the north. But even though the Viking period can be considered part of the Iron Age, more about it will be said in the next chapter.

The Romans never sent their legions to Scandinavia, and they never spread their military influence to the peninsula. In fact, they never went east of the Rhine River, and their politics never concerned the northern people. So, how did they manage to spread their influence without stepping on Scandinavian soil? The Roman Empire was one of the largest empires in the world, and it was the most significant empire in the history of Europe. As such, it had an extremely vast economic network that spread as far as China in the east and to the westernmost coast of Europe. This economic network also included Scandinavia. Roman goods and commodities moved across Asia and Europe, and some of them would reach Scandinavia. The northerners traded raw materials and slaves to acquire Roman glass, pottery, weapons, and various exotic metal objects that came from all corners of Europe and even Asia.

Although the Scandinavians never extracted metal during the Bronze Age, after 500 BCE, they started excavating iron from local deposits. They sold it as a raw material, but the Scandinavians also developed iron products. The newly discovered material was stronger than bronze; therefore, it was more suitable for the production of weapons and farming tools. The excavation of iron in northern Europe was much different than in the rest of the continent. Iron was typically mined from the mountains, such as the Carpathians, the Alps, or the Holy Cross Mountains in modern-day Poland. But in the lowlands of southern Scandinavia, iron could be found by forming a thin layer in the boggy ground.

Because of this, the Scandinavians couldn't simply adopt the excavation methods from other Europeans. Instead, they had to look to western Asia and adapt their own method of iron extraction. They had to collect the bog iron sand and use sophisticated furnaces and technology to melt and separate iron. The production of iron was very expensive because it demanded time, plenty of raw materials, and a labor force that would mind the furnaces for hours. To make just one kilogram (2.2 pounds) of iron, a furnace needed to work continuously for 25 hours and consume 10 kilograms (22 pounds) of charcoal. Only wealthy individuals were able to start iron production in Scandinavia.

The settlements of the pre-Roman Iron Age remained the same as during the Bronze Age, but the size of the farmhouses started varying more. This is a good indicator of the divisions of society, which became much wider with the introduction of the new metal and new economy. Certain individuals were rich and able to build larger farms and houses, while the rest had to be satisfied with smaller ones. During the Roman Iron Age, the farms gained true fences. Suddenly, people started reinforcing their position against their neighbors. This meant that the relationships within a community changed. Although the main unit of a settlement remained a farm, the communities slowly started taking the shape of true villages.

The settlements in eastern and central Scandinavia were suddenly abandoned during the 6th century CE, even those that were permanently inhabited for over a thousand years. Between 536 and 545, a climatic catastrophe occurred in Eurasia, but modern scholars are unsure what exactly happened. The mainstream opinion is that it was a combination of several volcanic eruptions and a meteorite crash. The written accounts from Europe of the period talk about the sun barely showing, as if a veil of dust had enveloped the earth. The summer temperatures dropped by 4°C (7°F), and the sky was always darkened. Thus, the plants couldn't grow.

This natural catastrophe was so great that even Mesopotamia recorded frost and snow during the summer of 536. In Scandinavia, this period saw an increase of sacrificial items, which suggests that people tried to fend off the natural catastrophe with religious rituals. Some scholars even believe that this period was a source of inspiration for the myth of *Fimbulwinter* ("Great Winter," which lasted for three years without a summer), a prelude to Ragnarök, the end of the known world and the birth of a new one.

But the abandonment of the settlements wasn't uncommon in the Iron Age. As farmers exhausted the land that they grew food on, whole communities would move to a new area with more fertile land. This movement caused the development of different types of settlements during the Late Iron Age. Some remained small, but there is no doubt the size of settlements continuously grew and that communities often merged to form larger villages. The community leaders also grew more powerful, and their titles became hereditary. Local chieftains turned into true rulers, resembling medieval kingship. These powerful rulers had the means to extend their trade network beyond the Rhine and Germany into the Roman Empire. They even started several important economic centers in Scandinavia, such as Uppåkra, Gudme, Sorte Muld, and Gamla Uppsala.

Iron Age Warfare

The culture of Iron Age Scandinavia was even more warrior-oriented than the one of the Bronze Age. The first iron items produced were weapons, and they were used to defend and conquer new lands or people. Warfare was the norm throughout Europe during the Iron Age, and it was no different in Scandinavia. The territories were divided, militarized, and fortified. The excavated bodies that belong to the Iron Age display clear signs of violent deaths, and more male bodies were buried with weapons and armor. This pattern of warfare, which started in the Late Bronze Age and culminated during the Iron Age, would remain a constant in European history.

The Roman Iron Age period was when the conflict in Scandinavia reached its peak. Chiefs and rulers constantly competed for fertile land and followers, who would become their military force. Those who were in power remained so because they had the means to defend themselves and conquer others. During the Iron Age, the Scandinavians started building their first defensive constructions, such as walls, ramparts, bridges, and roads. Although it is difficult to determine their age, some ring fortifications in Sweden are believed to have originated from the Late Iron Age, although they were similar to the ring forts of the later Viking Age. Nevertheless, during the Iron Age, the Scandinavians started constructing hill forts, which were fortified large settlements that rested on the top of a hill. Even some smaller villages were fortified or at least raised in an easily defensible position.

The practice of sacrificing weapons to the gods was still prevalent during the Iron Age, and many of them were placed in sacred bogs, which proved to be excellent for the preservation of items. This is why we now have exemplary evidence and fairly accurate knowledge of the military equipment of Iron Age Scandinavia. The weapons and armor were intentionally broken or burned before they were placed into the sacred bogs with the remains of sacrificial animals (cattle and horses). Human remains were rarely placed in bogs as a sacrifice. It is unclear whether this was done on purpose or if the individuals simply happened to die there.

The practice of sacrificing items to the sacred bogs was distinct to the Germanic people, who rose in Scandinavia during the Bronze Age and spoke the Proto-Germanic language. During the Iron Age, they developed the Proto-Norse language, which would become Old Norse in the Viking Age and eventually divide into the many Scandinavian languages that exist today. Also, during the Iron Age, the first Germanic tribes that would later inhabit continental Europe started migrating southward and occupying the territories between the Elbe and Danube Rivers. By the 4th century, they would establish their kingdoms in the territory of the Roman Empire.

All the weapons sacrificed in the sacred bogs belonged to the destroyed enemies. The lack of human bodies that would typically accompany weapon sacrifices means that the enemy warriors were killed elsewhere or taken as prisoners. Among the sacrifices were boats that were either completely sunk into nearby lakes and rivers or hauled to the bogs in pieces. The weapons came in all possible forms and included battle-axes, single and double blade swords, spears, shields, arrows, and sometimes even armor. They were all bent, broken, or burned so that they could no longer be used against those who captured them in the first place. The most interesting find among the sacred bog hoards was a completely preserved piece of mail armor that consisted of twenty-three thousand metal rings and several scabbards that were lined with fur on the inside. It is believed that this fur was oiled and served as a means of weapon preservation.

The Iron Age in the North and the Sámi People

In Norway, the Iron Age societies were mainly farmers, and they occupied the territories from the south up to Trondheim. They were well connected to southern Sweden and Denmark. Although there were smaller farms on the western shores of northern Norway up to the Tromsø area, these never had the same connection to the developing southern societies as central Norway. Nevertheless, iron deposits existed in the north, and the people extracted them, though in much smaller quantities. They even produced items made of iron, as suggested by the existence of furnaces, and several prominent centers were developed, such as Borg in northern Norway. These farming/iron production societies traded with southern Scandinavia, but it is unclear if they ever traded directly with the rest of Europe.

The farming societies of northern Norway continued to develop more or less the same as during the Bronze Age. The settlements concentrated around the biggest farm, which belonged to the chieftain. However, there is one innovation in the Iron Age settlements of northern Norway that is hard to explain. The large central farm consisted of several buildings for human and animal housing, a longboat, and a central courtyard made out of side-by-side foundations that formed the shape of a horseshoe. No evidence explains what the purpose of these courtyards was. Perhaps barracks were built there, or maybe they were maintenance buildings for the chieftain's farms. But the lack of building material in these courtyards suggests that they were left as open spaces. Some scholars believe these were the spots in which a *thing* would occur. The Scandinavian *thing* was a gathering of people who held legislative and judicial authority. The courtyard might have been assembly places, but more research is needed to fully understand them.

Just like in southern Scandinavia, the northern regions also had local rulers. On the west coast of Norway, inside the Arctic Circle, there is an archipelago with spectacular natural beauty named Lofoten. The evidence of humans inhabiting the Lofoten Islands spans to at least eleven thousand years ago. In the Iron Age, the archipelago was home to a society that didn't mind the complete darkness from December to January, as the sun never rises on Lofoten during this period. Despite the lack of sun, the archipelago has very mild winters. The Atlantic Ocean currents keep the climate temperate, and the sea rarely freezes there. This made the Lofoten Islands the perfect spot for the development of fishing societies, as access to the water was always open. Lofoten was one of the biggest stockfish producers and exporters until very recently.

The waters around the Borg regions were especially filled with fish, mainly cod. This was due to the winter migratory routes. In this region, archaeologists made a stunning discovery concerning the Iron Age settlement of the northern region of Norway. At Borg, the longest Viking longhouse was discovered. In total, it was 83 meters (272 feet), but further excavations proved that this longhouse was much older and that the Viking rulers only expanded it. Originally, the longhouse was 67 meters (220 feet) long, and it was built during the 5th century CE. It had four rooms and two entrances, one on each side of the longhouse. Later rulers added one more room and created five separate entrances. The longhouse was built completely out of wood, and although it was destroyed in the 9th century, archaeologists managed to reconstruct it and build a replica in the vicinity. This site is now the Lofotr Viking Museum; it's open to visitors and hosts an annual Viking-themed festival.

Aside from the longhouse, the Borg excavation site was rich in various items dating from the Iron Age. Among these items were sickles, scythes, various hooks, racks for drying fish, many tools made of iron, arrowheads, and four swords. There were also many items made of gold and glass, which testifies that Lofoten had a good connection with the rest of Scandinavia and was open for trade, maybe even warfare. The discovery of high-status gold-foil figures indicates that the Borg rulers were rich, respected, and of importance to the region and period.

The inland areas of northern Scandinavia remained populated by hunter-gatherer societies, which were believed to be the ancestors of the Sámi people. The Sámi people are indigenous to northern Norway, Sweden, Finland, and the Russian Kola Peninsula. They are known for preserving the semi-nomadic lifestyle of reindeer herders, though, in modern times, most of them are well integrated into the rest of the Scandinavian societies. Only around 10 percent of the Sámi are devoted to reindeer herding. Although reindeer herding is a traditional way of life for the Sámi people, it appeared relatively late, in around 1500 CE.

In the 19th century, Scandinavian historians believed the Sámi people occupied only the northernmost territories. However, new evidence disproved this theory, and it is now a consensus that the Sámi used to live anywhere between central Norway, Sweden, Finland, the Kola Peninsula, and the far north. It is also believed that the Sámi had been present in Scandinavia since the Stone Age, but they only began developing their social and ethnic identity during the first part of the 1st millennium CE. In prehistory, the societies of Scandinavia were pretty homogenous, but in time and due to contact with the societies of southern Scandinavia and continental Europe, some groups of the population started developing unique cultures and identities.

Although it is not known when the Sámi people formed their separate identities, it is obvious that they were a distinctive group during the Scandinavian Iron Age. They lived parallel to the farming societies of the western coast of northern Norway and occupied the inland regions, where they were free to hunt and lead nomadic and egalitarian lives. (Unlike the farming societies, the Sámi never had class divisions.) The Sámi and the Scandinavians had a symbiotic relationship that was based on marriages, gifts, and trade. It is believed that the Sámi of the interior first introduced falcons, walrus ivory, and fine fur to the south. The farmers of northern Scandinavia may have acted as the middlemen between the southerners and the Sámi, and they collected taxes on the Sámi trade. The Sámi also became very dependent on the products from the southern Scandinavians, especially iron tools.

The archaeological and historical evidence suggests that the relationship between the Sámi and other Nordic groups of people was based on respect and cooperation rather than on violence and oppression. However, in more recent years, the Sámi people were oppressed and discriminated against. These major problems came about when the governments of Scandinavian countries wanted to assert sovereignty over the northern lands. They forced Scandinavization and Christian baptisms on the Sámi. They wanted to forcefully integrate the indigenous people, and they banned the Sámi languages and culture.

Chapter 3 – The Viking Age in Norway

Norwegian petty kingdoms, circa 872.
https://commons.wikimedia.org/wiki/File:Norwegian_petty_kingdoms_ca._872.png

The Vikings were Scandinavian raiders, farmers, poets, and singers who dominated the seas approximately between 750 and 1066. However, the modern meaning of the word "Viking" is very different from what it used to be throughout history. The exact origin of the word is still unknown, although many theories have been put forward. But the meaning of the term is known. When it first appeared in the Old English language, it was never used to designate a nation or belonging to a Scandinavian ethnicity. It was simply used to describe the foreign raiders as pirates. In the Latin translation, the Old English word "wicing" was translated to "pirata." The first appearance of the word "Viking" was in written evidence in Old English, but that doesn't mean that was its origin. The word may have a Proto-Germanic or Old Norse origin and a meaning somehow related to sailing and nautical activities. In any case, the term Viking today has a different meaning, as it designates the Scandinavians who lived in a certain historical period that we often refer to as the Viking Age. This modern meaning was invented (and romanticized) during 19th-century nationalism.

The Vikings never called themselves by that name. They lived in communities occupying certain geographical regions. They referred to each other by the names of these regions; for example, they would call each other men of Jutland, Hordaland, Vestfold, and many others. They didn't have a national identity, and they expressed loyalty only to their local leaders. In this regard, they named each other followers of Thorkell, Olaf, Cnut, or Svein. But they did form alliances and fought together against common enemies. They spoke the same language—Old Norse—and enjoyed the same culture and religion. They also shared the runic writing system, fashion, art, and way of life. Only later did a sense of national identity develop. They started calling themselves by their national names, such as Danes or Norse. In the medieval period, the Danes were all Scandinavians of the southern regions, while the Norse were those who inhabited the northern regions.

Not all Scandinavians were Vikings—only those who indulged in raiding and pirating. The majority of Scandinavians remained farmers and craftsmen; only the minority were practicing "Vikings" Modern scholars prefer to use the term Vikings just for the raiders and Scandinavians for the rest of the people who inhabited the peninsula. Sometimes they even like to separate the northerners and call them Norse simply to make the differences between them and the inhabitants of the southern regions of Scandinavia.

The term "Viking Age" refers to the end of the Iron Age and the beginning of the medieval period, but the term itself was coined in the 19th century to make the periodization of excavated items in the Copenhagen Museum easier. Since then, the term's meaning was expanded, and the public started using it to designate a period of very much romanticized barbarians of the past. With this new meaning, the "Viking Age" entered popular culture and expanded outside the borders of Scandinavia.

During the Viking Age, Norway was defined as a geographic entity for the first time. It became obvious that the people who inhabited the Norwegian territories saw themselves as a separate community from the rest of Scandinavia, and they started developing an independent identity. They had separate rulers, kings, and chieftains who would ally themselves with the Danes and Swedes in their efforts to colonize the new lands. But conflicts between different Scandinavian groups weren't uncommon either. At this point, Norway begins to differentiate itself as one nation. However, through alliances and constant contact with other Scandinavians, Norway remained bound to the history of the whole peninsula. Norway's connection to neighboring states would remain visible until the 20th century.

The Viking Age in Norway

Until recently, it was thought that the Viking Age started with the first recorded raid on the abbey of Lindisfarne, England, in 793. However, later excavations proved the presence of early English and Irish items in the graves of Norwegian chieftains of the early 8th century. This means that the first contact was established much earlier than originally thought. There were many significant social and cultural changes in Scandinavia that occurred during the late 7th and early 8th centuries that led to the first overseas voyages and early contact between the Vikings and the Brits and Celts. The most important was the development of much larger ships capable of sailing in the open waters of the vast seas and oceans. Previously, the Scandinavians sailed in much smaller canoes that were able to safely navigate the shallow coastal waters.

The modern countries of Scandinavia didn't exist during the Viking Age, but the clear separation between the communities existed. Most of Europe and the British Isles had already accepted Christianity and formed kingdoms that more or less resembled the modern states. But this wasn't the case in Scandinavia. During the early Viking Age, the Scandinavians remained pagans and maintained their tribal divisions, with many chieftains forming the aristocracy of the Scandinavian society in general. But this changed by the 10th century. Many Viking leaders sailed to Europe, where they adopted not only the new faith (Christianity) but also new ideas of governance. When they returned to their homeland, they tried to implement these new ideas. By the 12th century, Christianity had been largely adopted, and the royal authority and kingship were set in place. The Viking leaders were no longer simply chieftains but kings that ruled by laws, edicts, and various privileges. By the 13th century, each Scandinavian country became a nation-state in its own right.

During the early Viking Age, Norway was composed of several petty kingdoms and earldoms. They were of different sizes, with the smallest ones comprising only several villages and the biggest one occupying the territory of several modern counties. Little is known about this period since written sources didn't exist. Almost everything we know comes from archaeological discoveries, and the many kings and earls of Norway are mythological and legendary figures, which means their actual existence is questionable. Nevertheless, the territory occupied by all these small kingdoms and earldoms was already referred to as a single geographical entity.

One of the Norwegian chieftains of the 9th century, Ottar fra Hålogaland (English: Ohthere of Hålogaland), visited the king of Britain, Alfred the Great (r. 871–899), and told him stories of his travels. His account was documented in *Seven Books of History Against the Pagans* by a Roman priest named Paulus Orosius. Ottar talked about his homeland, which was, according to him, situated in the northernmost of all Norse lands. It is believed that his kingdom, which he called Hålogaland, occupied the territories of the southern Troms og Finnmark district between Namdalen Valley and Lyngen Fjord. But Ottar talked about his kingdom as part of the land of Norsemen, which he called *Norðweg*, or "Northern Way" (Norway). The chieftain also spoke of *Dena Mearc* (Denmark) and *Sweoland* (Sweden), clearly making a difference between the three Scandinavian nations. He even mentions the Sámi people naming them the *Finnas*, but he also gave an account of *Cwenas* and *Beormas*, who also spoke the Sámi language and are considered different tribes of the Sámi people.

Ottar continued his traveling stories and described Norway as a long and narrow country. He also claimed that north of Hålogaland, there were no permanent settlements until one sailed to the southern shores of the White Sea in what is today Russia. It is through Ottar's account that the Norwegians and Norway entered history as a separate, individual country with very distinct people. Ottar considered himself a leader of his people and equal to the Anglo-Saxon king. But his farmstead had no more than ten cows, twenty pigs, and some arable land. Nevertheless, he was considered a wealthy man in Norway, and most of his wealth came from hunting, trading, and taxing the Sámi people.

At this point in history, the Norwegians shared the same language, culture, and religion with the rest of the Scandinavians. But they considered themselves a separate people, and it is possible that they were seen as such by their neighbors. They were separated by natural boundaries. Thick forests and mountains in the east divided Norway from Sweden. In the south, the Danes had their domain, which was separated from Norway by the lay of the land. It is possible that due to this obvious separation, the Norwegians started developing their own cultural and ethnic identity.

The farm continued to be the main unit of land and source of livelihood. However, Norway's geography is such that, even today, with all the modern technology available, only 3 percent of the land is arable. Mountains rise from the western shores of Norway and expand across the country to enter Sweden. The population was confined in the small ledges and plains in the fjords, where they didn't have much land that would produce food. It is believed that the lack of land that could be turned into farms was one of the reasons for the Viking expansion, especially when the population started rising. It was also the reason the Norwegians turned to the sea and started sailing farther away.

The difficult terrain of Norway also made the land routes impossible to traverse. This is yet another reason why the Norwegians turned to sailing. One of their goals was to establish sea communication routes, and naturally, they turned to the west. The first Vikings who approached the British Isles were probably the traders from Hålogaland, but it didn't take long for these traders to turn to raiding. They were also the first settlers in the western and northern islands, such as Greenland, Iceland, and the Faroe Islands. From these islands, in the year 1000, the Norsemen sailed farther west to the coast of North America. They landed in the area of Newfoundland (*Vinland*). However, they never managed to establish permanent settlements there.

The Vikings' expansion wasn't limited only to the west. They entered continental Europe and reached the shores of the Mediterranean. The Vikings even served in the armies of the Byzantine Empire and were influenced by Christianity. They also crossed the Baltics and traversed Russian territory, sailing the rivers to the Black and Caspian Seas. But these were mostly the works of the Danish and Swedish Vikings, as the Norwegians concentrated their efforts to the west and sometimes to the east, where they would sail to the White Sea. No matter where they settled, the Scandinavians had a lasting impact on the area, and they even organized little kingdoms within these new territories. In Ireland, they founded Dublin, and in England, the Norse kings ruled in York. They quickly adopted the more sophisticated forms of rulership that were already in place in medieval Europe, and they realized the significance of the urban centers. The Scandinavians brought the idea of these cities back to their home country.

The Unification of Norway

While Ottar fra Hålogaland was giving his account to the Anglo-Saxon king, Alfred the Great, Norway was going through political changes. The last three decades of the 9th century saw the settlement of Iceland, and during this time, the famous Battle of

---

Hafrsfjord took place. The battle was well documented by the Norse skaldic poets and chroniclers, but its exact date is lost. It is believed it took place anywhere between 872 and 900. The Viking chieftain Harald Halvdansson (later known as Harald Fairhair) won the battle and started the process of unifying Norway. In reality, this battle brought Rogaland and Agder under Harald's control and nothing else. But in the popular imagination of Norwegians, this battle was the key moment of the unification of the whole country.

Modern scholars believe that the unification of Norway came as a result of a century of internal political changes. Nevertheless, the result was the same as the popular belief about the Battle of Hafrsfjord. Harald Fairhair emerged as the sole ruler of the vast territories of Norway, and he started ruling as Harald I. The *Heimskringla* (sagas about the Norse kings) of 13th-century Icelandic chronicler Snorri Sturluson describes how Harald conquered all the Norwegian petty kingdoms one after the other and how the Battle of Hafrsfjord was just the conclusion of this unification.

The geographical nature of Norway made it very difficult for the early kings to assert power over their neighbors. The most powerful ones who managed to conquer more territories had to sail their ships up and down the rugged coast of Norway to collect products from the farmstead that owed them their allegiance. This was the only way the Norwegian leaders could assert their power, and it was very unlikely they were able to control vast areas at once. But there is no reason for scholars to doubt the story of Harald Halvdansson and his unification of Norway. However, it's very unlikely he ruled Norway alone. With the level of political organization and the instruments of power exercised in Scandinavia during the Viking Age, it is more likely that Harald ruled through alliances with other petty chieftains.

Even though Harald didn't unite Norway under his direct rule, he started the process of unification, which his successors would follow. But Norway's unification wasn't a unique case in Scandinavia. At approximately the same time, Denmark and Sweden underwent the same process. These developments in Scandinavia had a strong influence on the rest of Europe. The expansions and raids made the European rulers consolidate their power and borders. But by doing so, they provided the Scandinavians with lessons of political organization, and the Scandinavian countries started imitating the European kingdoms.

The three Scandinavian kingdoms, now fully organized, started asserting their dominance on each other, and the wars between neighbors started. Alliances were forged and broken, depending on the political trends, which changed often. Norway would help Denmark against Sweden just to suffer Danish and Swedish attacks a year later. The Scandinavian kings also competed for the control of the same territory since they all had territorial ambitions in what is today Norway and Sweden. The Danish kings were the strongest during the Viking Age, and through their wars and their control over southern parts of Sweden and Norway, they asserted their dominance on the whole peninsula and had a deep political influence on it.

The Territorial Consolidation of Norway and the Viking Kings

The unification of Norway fell apart after the death of Harald Fairhair in 930. The sagas mention that Harald allowed his eldest and favorite son Eric (later known as Eric Bloodaxe) to rule alongside him. Eric inherited the throne of Norway after his father's death and defeated the armies of his brothers who wanted to partition the kingdom. However, Eric proved to be a despotic ruler, and he lost the support of the Norwegian nobility. At this time, his younger brother, Haakon, who was fostered at the court of the Anglo-Saxon King Æthelstan (r. 924–939), returned to Norway. The nobility was more than eager to replace Eric and raise his younger brother to the throne. With the help of Sigurd, Jarl of Lade, young Haakon took over Norway. Eric Bloodaxe was forced to flee to Orkney, but his sons remained and fought for their right to rule. The country was yet again partitioned, and a conflict for dominance started, which would last until the 11th century.

This conflict between the Norwegian throne pretenders was just the first phase of the territorial consolidation of Norway. Some jarls were more successful than others, but the permanent success of uniting the country once again eluded them all. It was hard for Eric Bloodaxe to assert his dominance over the land, as he was known to travel, which means he was away from his kingdom for extended periods. According to the sagas, Eric started raiding when he was twelve years old, and he sailed to Denmark, the Baltic, Germany, France, Ireland, Wales, Scotland, and later to Lappland and Bjarmaland. Some Norwegian sources even claim he entered what is today Perm Krai (Principality of Great Perm) in Russia. He is thought to be the same person as Eric, King of Northumbria, but this is often disputed by modern historians since there are no reliable contemporary sources that confirm this claim.

Eric's youngest brother Haakon was nicknamed "the Good" and "Adelsteinfostre" (foster son of Æthelstan). He spent most of his life outside of Norway since he was sent to the Anglo-Saxons at a young age; his father wanted to protect him from his dangerous, power-hungry brothers. This might have been the reason he had trouble keeping Norway unified. Although he had the support of the nobles, as he promised them the abolition of the inheritance tax imposed by his father, not all wanted to follow a foreigner. He had to defend his right to rule against Eric's sons on different occasions. In 953, he fought a battle at Avaldsnes in today's Rogaland county. He proved he was superior to Eric's sons by winning the battle and killing Guttorm Ericson (one of Eric's sons). The next battle against his enemies was in 955, and Haakon again emerged victorious. This time, he killed another son of Eric, Gamle. In 957, the sons of Eric attacked again; this time, they had the support of the Danish king. Haakon once again defeated them.

But he had to pay a high price for the final victory over Eric's sons. In 961, at the Battle of Fitjar, Haakon was mortally wounded. After his death, he was succeeded by Eric's eldest surviving son, who ruled as Harald II and was nicknamed "Greycloak." However, Harald II couldn't persuade all the Norwegians jarls to follow him, and he exercised his power only over western Norway. He was killed in 970 by a fellow Norwegian jarl named Haakon Sigurdsson, who at the time was allied with the famous Danish king Harald Bluetooth.

Haakon became the *de facto* ruler of Norway, and he ruled as a vassal of Denmark, though he managed to preserve Norway's independence. He was firmly against Christianity, which was slowly penetrating the country, as Haakon the Good had tried to convert Norway. Haakon Sigurdsson ruled approximately between 975 to 995. He was a popular ruler at first, as the people liked that he was against Christianity. However, he was a notorious rapist, and he would persuade many noblemen to send him their daughters under the pretense of marriage. He would rape them and send them back to their fathers. These actions made him very unpopular with other jarls and petty kings across Scandinavia. He lost their support just as his enemy and throne pretender Olaf Tryggvason rose to power.

According to the sagas, Haakon was killed by his slave, who hoped to get a reward for his deed from Olaf. Once he became king, Olaf punished the slave for betraying his master and had his head put on a spike next to Haakon. Olaf I was the great-grandson of Harald Fairhair, and he is one of the most important individuals in the history of Christianity in Norway. Legend has it that Olaf I built the first church in Norway, but he used violence to persuade the people to convert. He was the founder of the Norwegian city of Trondheim, which was his seat of power.

The story of Olaf's downfall is a very interesting one, though its historical accuracy cannot be confirmed. The sagas tell a tale of Sigrid, a Swedish widow queen who was proposed to by Olaf of Norway. However, Olaf demanded she convert to Christianity, which she refused. In a rage, Olaf hit Sigrid with his armed glove in front of all of her followers. The Swedish queen was so infuriated that she started gathering all of Olaf's enemies to bring about his downfall. She united the armies of Sweden, Denmark, and Wendland (Pomerania in today's Germany), and the united army fought Olaf at the Battle of Svolder in the Baltic Sea. This is considered the largest naval Viking battle, and it took place in the year 1000. Olaf had only eleven ships, and he faced down seventy enemy ships; he had no chance of winning this battle. Instead, he decided to throw himself in the sea. What happened to him is unknown, but he was presumed dead. Norway was ruled by the jarls who were loyal vassals to the kings of Denmark and Sweden.

The last Viking king of Norway was Harald Hardrada (r. 1046–1066), also known as Harald III. His predecessor, Magnus I, became the king of Norway after the death of Danish King

Cnut the Great. Several years later, he also claimed the crown of Denmark and ruled it until his death in 1047. As his successor, Harald Hardrada claimed the crowns of Denmark and England but was unsuccessful in keeping them. He was the half-brother of Olaf II (later canonized and known as St. Olaf), father of Magnus I. The Danish King Cnut exiled Harald to Kievan Rus, where he served as the military captain of Grand Prince Yaroslav the Wise. This allowed him to gain military experience and later serve as the commander of the Varangian Guard of the Byzantine Empire. When he finally came back to Norway in 1046, his nephew, Magnus I, accepted him as a co-ruler. They ruled together for one year before Magnus died.

Harald's reign was famous for its peace and prosperity, as he established his coin, the first one in the history of Norway, and a foreign trade network that would serve Norway during the Middle Ages. But to achieve sole rule after the death of Magnus, Harald had to fight off jarls who tried to claim the throne. He was successful, and he outlined the Norwegian territorial unification under a single government. He founded the city of Oslo and made it his capital. Harald died in England, where he had gone to claim the throne, in the famous Battle of Stamford Bridge, which ended the Viking Age. The second stage of Norwegian territorial consolidation would occur during the Scandinavian medieval period.

Old Religion and the Spread of Christianity

Like other Scandinavians, Norwegians followed the Old Norse religion. Unlike Christianity, this Old Norse religion was a system of beliefs and rituals, and it had many variations depending on the region in which it was practiced. The Norse gods were not as divine as the Christian God, and they lived and behaved as humans do. They lived on farms, married, and had children. They warred against each other or other supernatural beings, and they acted out in rage and fell in love with each other. Norse gods were even mortal, and one of them, Baldur, died. Norse mythology has very developed myths and stories about the ancient gods, and most modern people have heard at least some of them, as they have been popularized in pop culture (for example, Thor, Odin, and Loki). These gods accepted sacrifices from humans, and the gods would help them in return.

Interestingly, the practitioners of the Old Norse religion didn't have a concept of religion. To them, the gods, rituals, and magic were integral parts of life, just as their farms, wars, and families were. The concept of religion was introduced only with Christianity. This is what allowed the Old Norse religion to accumulate different variations, as it was never canonized, and the people who practiced it were free to do it in their own ways. Different communities had different rituals that had the same goal. Marriage rituals might have been different in Sweden than in Norway, and different gods could be invoked during the ceremony, but the result would still be a marriage between two people.

Aside from the gods, the Norse revered many different supernatural beings. The most widespread ones were the Norns, the female figures who shaped the individual and collective faith of humans. Scandinavians also recognized the powerful beings named *jötnar*, who were the ancestors of the gods but also their main enemies. There were different types of *jötnar*, but many academic texts simplify the variety of supernatural beings and simply designate them all as giants (though they were not necessarily that large). The giants were not evil by nature, as some of them, such as Skadi, belonged to the pantheon of gods. The Norse also believed in the existence of elves, dwarfs, guardian spirits, Valkyries, ghosts, and much more.

The Old Norse religion was one of animism and magic. The solutions for everyday problems were found in magic talismans, charms, and magical rituals. Runes were a script, but they were also magical. Each had a different meaning and purpose. Some protected against diseases, while others protected against natural disasters. Odin was connected to magic the most. He sacrificed himself by hanging to achieve wisdom and learn the magic of the runes. Another deity connected to magic was Freya. Her power was feminine magic called *seiðr*, and only several male supernatural beings were able to wield this power. The only male god able to cast *seiðr* was Odin.

The Sámi people had different beliefs than the Norwegians. Their religion was one of shamanism. Because the Sámi people lived in vast areas in the northernmost territories of Europe, their religion and rituals also had variations, depending on their geographical origin. The Sámi religion is closely related to nature, and an emphasis is always put on one's personal spirituality. Each tribe had a shaman who would perform religious ceremonies and rituals, unlike the Scandinavians, who had no concept of priests or religious leaders. The connection between the Sámi and Norse religions cannot be denied, though, and the Sámi are the last people in the world to revere Thor as a god. Most Sámi practiced their old religion until the 18th century when Christian missionaries were sent to convert them.

Christianity first appeared in Norway in the 8th century, but it didn't take hold. The raiding Norsemen would bring home Christian stories, ideas, and relics, but they were seen only as curiosities. The first king who tried to introduce the new religion to the country was Haakon the Good. He was brought up as a Christian in the court of Anglo-Saxon King Æthelstan. He even brought monks from England to spread Christianity in Norway, but the pagan jarls rebelled against the new religion and killed the missionaries. Some stories claim that these pagan jarls even forced Haakon to apostatize.

Other Viking chieftains and rulers also accepted baptism, but their main motivation was to strengthen their ties to foreign rulers. The attempts at conversion were also used as a political play, as the newly Christian kings could now replace their political enemies and elevate Christian followers in their place. Harald Greycloak was one of the rulers who were baptized during their visits to foreign countries. He accepted Christianity in Northumbria and tried to introduce it to Norway. However, he was quickly forced into exile and didn't have much time to work on mass conversion. After his reign, Norway came under the control of Danish Christian King Harald Bluetooth. He tried to forcefully convert the region of Oslo but not with much success.

It was believed that King Olaf Haraldsson (St. Olaf; r. 1015–1028) completed the Christianization of Norway. But today, modern scholars understand that Christianization was a process and that the significance of Saint Olaf is more symbolic than real. He was a Viking king, and he fully acted as one. Although he was Christian, his worldview continued to be pagan, especially regarding such themes as war and love. Nevertheless, he did impose Christianity on his subjects and used cruelty to do so.

The miracles prescribed to him were later invented so that Norway could have a domestic saint to whom to pray. He even received some attributes of old pagan deities so that the transition to Christianity would be easier for the Scandinavian "heathens." The cult of Saint Olaf served to consolidate Christianity as the national religion, and it gave the Norwegians a foundation for their national identity and unity.

Chapter 4 – Norway in the Middle Ages

Infant king Haakon Haakonsson being taken to safety by the Birkebeinars (19th-century painting by Knud Bergslien).
https://commons.wikimedia.org/wiki/File:Birkebeinerne_ski01.jpg

The last phase of Norway's unification and territorial consolidation was a period of civil wars. Norway lacked political unity, and it was ruled by many kings who once again divided the country. After the death of Sigurd the Crusader, who ruled Norway from 1103 until 1130, his son, Magnus, wished to unify Norway once again. But he was forced to share with Harald Gille, who claimed to be Sigurd's half-brother who was born and grew up in Ireland. They ruled together for four years before Magnus started preparing for war against his co-ruler. Although he initially defeated Harald and forced him into exile in Denmark, he was later captured and blinded, and Harald ruled the whole of Norway alone.

The dispute for the Norwegian throne lasted for the next hundred years, with the Swedish royal family Sverre finally winning exclusive control over the whole country. Their kingdom was known as Birchlegs (Old Norse *Birkibeinar*), named after the political party that opposed the previous Norwegian king, Magnus V. The Birchlegs were so named because it is said they were so poor they couldn't afford pants (or shoes in some sources), and they wore birch tree bark instead. After the death of King Sverre, the Birchlegs fought the Bagler faction, which consisted of the Norwegian aristocracy. The Birchlegs were victorious, and they used it to install Sverre's grandson, Haakon Haakonsson, on the throne of Norway. Haakon's reign marked the end of the civil war and the unification of Norway under a single ruler.

During the rest of the Middle Ages, the Norwegians concentrated their efforts on expanding to the north and east along the coast of Finnmark. Jemtland (Jämtland), which is now part of Sweden, belonged to Norway at this time, although the population was mostly Swedish and belonged to the Swedish church, not Norway's. This resulted in the incomplete integration of Jemtland, which would later bring the loss of this province. To the south, Norway stretched to the mouth of the Göta River, which is also in Sweden today. This was also the point where the three medieval Scandinavian kingdoms met: Norway, Sweden, and Denmark.

The Medieval Church, Aristocracy, and Wide Society

The territorial unification of Norway lasted for so long because it was a process in which it was necessary not only to conquer the land but also to create a national identity that would bind all its people into a unique and singular society. This society had to be independent of the ruler, at least to some extent, so that it could continue being united even after the death of the kings who held it together. All of this was achieved during the 13th century, though significant steps were made much earlier with the first kings of Norway.

The Norwegian aristocracy was a significant factor in uniting the country, mainly the relationship between the jarls and local chieftains with the king. The kings had to bind the aristocracy to themselves to exercise their power in areas that were far away from their capitals. But the chieftains had immediate benefits from being bound to the ruler. In return for their loyalty, they received a portion of the royal income, patronage, and prestige. The kings and chieftains cooperated, but this administration wasn't easy to maintain. The chieftains tended to be loyal only as long as it was beneficial to them. They never felt the need to serve the country as a whole, and there was little to no patriotic drive behind their actions.

Because of this, the monarchy always strived to strengthen its relationship with the aristocracy. To achieve this, the kings would transform the local chieftains into *lendmann* (men of land). This meant that in return for their loyalty and service, the chieftains would receive a portion of royal lands that would be added to the land that was already theirs. The chieftains who refused to become *lendmann* were driven out of Norway or killed. Thus, the early kings secured the territorial unification of the kingdom.

During the Early Middle Ages, the relationship between the Crown and the church was more positive than the one between kings and aristocracy. The kings remained the leaders of the Christianization of the population. But the kings were also the church builders, and they donated the land that would later become ecclesiastical estates. This land was usually confiscated from the peasants who persisted in their pagan faith. The bishops were appointed by the kings, and they often had a place in the king's retinue. Only from the reign of King Olaf Haraldsson (1015-1028 onward did the bishops start to take up a permanent residence. First, they settled in Trondheim and Bergen and later in Oslo.

The Norwegian kings were mostly baptized abroad, and they learned the relationship between the church and the monarchy from other European countries. They wished to bring this relationship to Norway, mostly because they saw how it could be beneficial to the establishment of kingship. Christianity and the church served to break the old pagan society that refused loyalty to a single ruler by constructing a new one under the leadership of the king and the church. In time, the whole country was dotted with local churches. The ecclesiastical network they created across Norway served to bind society into a single countrywide social system.

The kings were the head of the church and its main protector. As such, their power was immense and undeniable. Through the church, the kings were the protectors of society, and their status among the people of Norway was the most exalted and holy. The clergy served the king as counselors and helpers because they were educated. They could also read and write, which was something not all members of the aristocracy were able to do during the Early Middle Ages. The clergy also had connections with the rest of Europe and informed the king of the more advanced social organizations that existed abroad. Through their religious work, they shaped society according to the king's wishes.

The main bulk of the Norwegian medieval society was the peasants. As they represented the majority of the population, it was the peasants' opinion that shaped the political scene of the monarchy. To please them, the kings needed to provide the peasants with a feeling of security and well-being, and they did so through military protection and their ability to uphold the law. Legal and political stability was achieved by pleasing the majority of the population, and in turn, they gave their support to the monarchy.

Some kings were lawmakers, but all of them upheld the laws because it would bring income to the Crown through fines and confiscations. The legal and administrative apparatus had to be built to maintain the law, and a judiciary system was created, which served the kings as yet another power base.

The military protection that the king offered the peasants was based on the mutual help of all involved parties. The king was the military leader, and he guaranteed the safety of the peasants. But it was the peasants who provided the king with ships, weapons, manpower, and food. This led to the creation of a conscripted army, which would become a great naval force. Such a naval force was first organized in Vestlandet during the reign of King Haakon Haraldsson (Haakon the Good), and it later spread to the rest of the country.

The relationship between the peasants and the king had one important feature: the popular assembly known as the *ting*. This assembly has its origins in prehistoric times, where general meetings of the people were organized throughout the country (Alting). The judicial matters and those of common political interests were dealt with during the *tings*. In the Middle Ages, these assemblies were transformed into local bodies, and they operated in both towns and the countryside. Some assemblies were given a special role, for example, the acclamation of the kings, and they had a series of legal ceremonies during which the kings and the peasants exchanged pledges. Because the peasants represented not only the majority of the population but also a very powerful political force, these acclamations were necessary, and all throne claimants sought them.

The Lagting was another form of assembly that formed during the Middle Ages. Unlike the Alting, the Lagting gathered the representatives of various communities that occupied a certain territory. The representatives met to discuss and deal with the things that concerned multiple peasant communities in the area. The Lagting was also the highest judicial assemblies in the kingdom, and they served to ratify the laws. But it was the monarchy that organized the Lagting, and the king's involvement can easily be understood. Through these assemblies, the monarch could legally associate important government initiatives with the people that inhabited large areas of the country. For example, through the Lagting, the monarchs introduced Christianity to the rural areas of the kingdom.

The first towns and cities were formed by the kings in a time when the need for secure administrative and military bases rose. The old estates along the coastal shipping routes were not enough during medieval times because the population grew, and the monarchs also needed to strengthen the kingdom's centralization. But the Crown also wanted to promote and exploit the economic activities that are often associated with the urbanized areas than with the hinterlands. In the Middle Ages, these activities meant trade and crafts. The first established towns were Trondheim, Borg in the Lofoten archipelago, Oslo, and later Bergen. These towns soon became the bastions of royal and ecclesiastical centralization. Soon, the cities became frequently visited by foreign merchants, mainly the Hanseatic League, whose members even started settling in Bergen in the late 13th century.

The Black Death and the Hanseatic League

One of the most disastrous events of the Middle Ages in Europe was the Black Death, an epidemic of the bubonic plague that took anywhere between 30 and 60 percent of Europe's population. The outbreak of the plague lasted from 1347 until 1351, and Norway wasn't spared. In the summer of 1349, the plague reached Bergen. It was introduced by the English seafarers and merchants, and it quickly spread throughout the country. Sweden and Denmark were affected too, but Iceland and Finland managed to avoid the initial pandemic. The Black Death reoccurred in Europe on several occasions until the end of the 14th century.

The population of Norway decreased dramatically during the years of the Black Death, but we do not know the exact numbers. The population decline can only be measured indirectly by observing the societal and economic developments at the time. The farms were abandoned, which was only the first sign of the massive demographic crisis. These farms were a part of the medieval Norwegian economic system, as they produced food and other commodities. Their disappearance meant a steep economic decline.

An economic crisis followed the decrease in the population, and the abandoned farms contributed to the sudden fall in rent prices. But the urban population suffered the fall in rent prices too, as the majority of landowners had a residence in the towns. The rent prices weren't the only ones to drop; taxes and other royal and ecclesiastical revenues were at a loss too. Even the highest layer of society felt the economic crisis. It didn't help that the abandoned farms meant a reduced food supply for the towns, and the urban centers experienced a population decline not only due to the Black Plague but also famine.

The vacuum left by the population crisis, plus the abundance of fish in the Norwegian Sea and timber in the Norwegian lands, attracted investors from abroad, mainly Scotland, the Netherlands, and Germany. They were especially attracted to the towns on the eastern coast of Norway, such as Oslo and Tønsberg. The foreign settlers increased the population of the Oslofjord, where timber activities were very high. The Germans and English were concentrated in Bergen, where the fish industry boomed. The constantly rising prices for dried fish in the world proved motivation enough for many merchants to settle in Norway.

Around 1360, the first Hanseatic trading station (*kontor*) was established in Bergen. The Hanseatic League was a confederation of trading guilds that operated mostly in central and northern Europe, and it was founded in the 12th century. During the second half of the 14th century, the league bought warehouses on the docs (Bryggen) so that their traders could take up residence there. Bryggen is today the main attraction of the city of Bergen, with its many colorful wooden houses dotting the city docks. However, the old medieval houses were destroyed in a fire in 1702; the new ones that were built during the 18th century are still standing. These houses became a UNESCO World Heritage Site in 1979. Most of the medieval settlers in Bergen were German, and they became some of the city's most prominent crafters.

During the Late Middle Ages, the Hanseatic League spread from Bergen and founded offices in Oslo and Tønsberg. While Bergen's *kontor* was controlled by the city of Lübeck, the other Norwegian branches of the league were controlled by Rostock. Both of these cities are today in northern Germany.

The Hanseatic League created a special credit system in Bergen by which they bought the exclusive supply of fish from the northern peasant fishermen. The independent traders that resided in Bergen could not compete with the Hanseatic League, and they came to play a less important role in the city's history.

However, the monarchy issued decrees that were intended to protect the Norwegian merchants. These decrees made the natives sole executors of the retail trade.

The Hanseatic Germans tended to keep to themselves and form closed societies within the Norwegian towns in which they settled. However, they only had a completely separated part of the city in Bergen. They strived to isolate themselves, and they even brought about the law in which marriage with Norwegian women was forbidden. They regularly avoided using Norwegian courts when solving the disputes they had with Norwegian citizens. Their presence in Bergen was so strong that they felt courageous enough to defy the Norwegian authorities. They even imposed serious economic sanctions against their Norwegian competitors. The violence between the native and the German merchants and crafters was a common sight.

Norwegian historians regard the Hanseatic League as a negative influence on Norway's economy, as it prevented the development of the native middle class, and its members constantly exploited the northern fishermen. But they often disregard the fact that the Hanseatic League opened a larger European market to Norwegian products, such as timber and fish, which only served to expand the economy of medieval Norway. The coastal towns bloomed because of this new market that the league had opened. There is no denying that a large part of the trade surplus was drained out of the country, but the Norwegian urban centers developed because of the Hanseatic influence.

Toward the Scandinavian Union

During the Late Middle Ages, the history of Norway once again became a part of the wider history of Scandinavia. Through marriage alliances, the royal families of the three kingdoms— Norway, Sweden, and Denmark—became so intertwined that the succession rights led to the unification of the kingdoms under one crown. It all started with the death of Danish King Valdemar IV in 1375. This was the first time in the medieval history of the kingdom that the male royal line was completely extinguished. The Danish throne was inherited by the Norwegian prince, Olaf II. He was the son of King Haakon VI of Norway, who was married to the daughter of Valdemar, Margaret (later known as Margaret I, Queen of Denmark, Norway, and Sweden).

Olaf was only five years old when his grandfather died, and he became the king of Denmark. Because the law considered a ruler underaged until he turned fifteen, Olaf's mother acted as his regent. But even when the king reached the appropriate age to rule by himself, Margaret continued to rule through him. When King Haakon of Norway died in 1380, Olaf became the king of both Denmark and Norway, and he brought the two crowns together. These countries would remain united for the next four hundred years. Olaf died when he was only seventeen, and Margaret became regent of the united countries. While in Oslo, she was crowned regent for life; the Danish kingdom proclaimed she would be a regent until she chose a new king. In 1388, she concluded an alliance with the Swedish aristocracy who had risen against their king, Albrecht Mecklenburg (Albert; r. 1364-1389). The Danish queen regent sent troops to Sweden and defeated Albrecht in the Battle of Åsle Albrecht. But the war continued after Albrecht's death, and Margaret failed to gain control of Stockholm. Finally, in 1395, she managed to take the Swedish capital and prohibit Albrecht from claiming the Swedish throne. In 1397, the Kalmar Union was formed through which the three Scandinavian kingdoms became one.

The Kalmar Union was a completely Danish project, and even today, it is seen in a negative light in Sweden and Norway. Denmark was militarily and economically the strongest Scandinavian kingdom, and it always strove to conquer its neighbors. But Margaret didn't keep the throne for herself. Instead, she chose the son of her sister's daughter, Eric of Pomerania, as the ruler of the Kalmar Union, though Margaret remained the *de facto* ruler of the union until she died in 1412.

In 1434, a rebellion broke out in Sweden after the king refused to acknowledge the complaints of the Swedish of the Dalarna region against their Danish bailiff. The rest of Sweden quickly offered their support to their compatriots, even the aristocracy. In 1439, they deposed King Eric. Denmark also deposed Eric in 1439 but for different reasons. The Danish aristocracy was against Bogislav IX of Pomerania, who Eric chose as the successor of the Kalmar Union. Norway continued to be loyal to Eric until 1442 when the aristocracy decided to follow the example of Sweden and Denmark. Christopher of Bavaria was chosen as the next ruler of the union, though he met a sudden death in 1448.

It is important to understand that the Kalmar Union was never a complete unification. Each country was legally a sovereign state with its own government. This is why the rulers were crowned separately in each country at different points in time. The Kalmar Union also wasn't continuous. There were several short breaks between 1397 and 1523, but in general, the domestic and foreign politics of all three Scandinavian kingdoms were controlled by the same crown. After the death of Christopher of Bavaria in 1448, Sweden tried to remain independent and break out of the union. It was ruled by a series of "protectors of the realm," but the Danish kings continuously tried to assert their dominance on Sweden. Finally, in 1520, the Swedes started a liberation war and proclaimed the dissolution of the Kalmar Union in 1523. They even crowned their own king, Gustav Vasa. However, the union was officially dissolved only in 1570 when Frederick II of Denmark and Norway renounced his claim on the Swedish throne. Denmark and Norway remained united after the end of the Kalmar Union.

Chapter 5 – Denmark-Norway, 1536–1814

Coat of Arms of Denmark-Norway.

To prevent the further dissolution of the union, the Danish king and nobility decided to transform Norway into a Danish province. To do this, they had to get rid of the Norwegian national council, the only instrument of national sovereignty the country still had. The integration of Norway into Denmark wasn't only political but also cultural, and the Protestant Reformation gave the monarch new ideological tools to achieve this. The Norwegian council was finally dissolved in 1536, and although King Ferdinand I promised he would not impose Protestantism in Norway, he quickly changed his mind, as he considered religion the one thing that could unite the people of Norway and Denmark, securing the union in the process.

The consequences of the Demark-Norway union can still be seen in language. To this day, Norwegian is heavily influenced by Danish, and the Danish writing system was completely adopted in Norway. But the Norwegians managed to preserve their national identity and finally broke out of the union in 1814. It is amazing how the Norwegians preserved their distinctiveness through the next three hundred years and got rid of the Danish absolutism through a union with Sweden. It is even more astonishing that this sudden transition occurred without any social frictions and institutional disturbances.

Some historians believe that Norway was never completely integrated into Denmark. Instead, Danish absolutism allowed Norway to grow economically, ideologically, and socially. They also believe that the Danish rule made Norway strong enough to finally stand on its own feet after 1814. However, the other side of history must be acknowledged too. The 16th century was one filled with political, social, and cultural developments in Europe, so it is possible that Norway would follow these trends, even without the Danish guiding them. Some even think that the Danish rule was holding Norway back and didn't allow this country to reach its full potential.

The Early Modern Period

While the rest of Europe regards the period between 1500 and 1800 as the early modern period, the Norwegians simply remember it as the Danish times or the "time of the union." However, just like in the rest of Europe, this was the period in which Norway grew both in population and economically, which prepared the ground for the later industrial revolution. The economic growth was directly caused by the labor divisions, better communication and road system, and the growth of trade. But this development wasn't directly caused by the union with Denmark; rather, it was a continuation of the developments from the medieval period.

The growth of trade was due to the new land discoveries of the 16th century. Norway wasn't directly involved in the explorations at this time, even though its people were known for their daring voyages during the Viking era. This time, other European countries, such as Portugal, Spain, France, the Netherlands, and England, took the initiative. They founded their overseas colonies and started trade. But trade in Norway flourished, as the demand for fish, timber, and iron increased, all of which the country had in abundance. In exchange for these, Norway started importing corn and various finished products.

Although trade and the economy flourished, Norway remained on the periphery of Europe and not just geographically. As a supplier of raw materials, the country didn't experience the same development of various industries as central Europe. Norway's development evolved at a much slower pace than in other parts of the continent. This certainly resulted in a form of stagnation. Norway was in no position to start its own production of finished products; therefore, the need for innovation was very low.

The years between 1500 and 1800 were also a period of conflict in Europe. The new land discoveries and economic demands led to rivalry and open wars. Norway, whose government was outside of the country, wasn't able to decide its fate. Denmark now had the perfect opportunity to exploit the Norwegians and use them as workers and soldiers to strengthen its position in Europe. However, being on the periphery of Europe, Norway was never in imminent danger of having a war on its territory. This allowed the population to continue developing at a steady pace. However, that doesn't mean that Scandinavia was spared from conflict. Territorial wars lasted until the 17th century between Norway and Sweden. Norway was only spared a larger European conflict, which was often even fought overseas in the various colonies.

From 1643 until 1645, Denmark-Norway was in the Torstenson War, also known as the Hannibal controversy (after Norwegian Governor-general Hannibal Sehested). This war was very unpopular with the Norwegian public, as the people didn't want to fight Sweden. But Denmark didn't care about Norwegian public sentiment, and it ordered the attack on Sweden from Norwegian Jemtland. The result of the war was the loss of Norwegian territory, as the Swedish Army not only occupied Jemtland but also continued toward Østerdalen. When the peace was finally reached, Denmark-Norway had to cede large parts of the territory to Sweden. Jemtland was completely lost, as well as the parishes of Idre, Särna, and Herjedalen (Härjedalen).

The next war that involved Norway was the Charles Gustav War (or the Second Northern War; 1655–1660), which Denmark-Norway joined in 1657. During this conflict, Norway was split into two parts when the Swedish Army conquered Trøndelag, Nordmøre, and Romsdal. But these territories were returned to Denmark-Norway during the final peace settlement, and this is when Norway got its modern land borders. A special treaty was made in 1751 by which the Sámi people were given the right to cross the border between Norway and Sweden undisturbed, but this treaty completely disregarded the fact that the Sámi had to be considered the subjects of either the Danish or Swedish Crown.

Previous Norwegian territories—Iceland, the Faroes, and Greenland—continued to enjoy trade with their motherland. However, when the final dissolution of the Denmark-Norway union occurred in 1814, these island territories remained under Danish control. Norway exited the union much smaller than it was when it entered it in 1536.

Society and the Crofter System

The main source for the early 16th-period demographics is the preserved tax records that survived the time in most areas of Norway. The taxpayers were listed by their names, and it seems that there were around twenty-four thousand taxpayers in the countryside, all of them peasants and farmers, while the towns had registered twelve thousand taxpayers. For each registered taxpayer, approximately six people should be added to count children, wives, and those who were relieved of tax obligations. This would give us a number close to 150,000 people that lived within the modern borders of Norway. Although there are no official records for the medieval period, it is estimated that there were anywhere between 300,000 and 500,000 Norwegians. This meant that since the Middle Ages, the Norwegian population had suffered a steep decline. However, the census performed in 1801 revealed that 880,000 people were living in the country, which is six times more than during the 16th century.

The growth of the urban population was very fast, even faster than in the countryside. At the beginning of the 16th century, 6 to 8 percent of the population lived in urban centers. By the 19th century, this percentage rose to 10. The towns had clear social divisions, with burgesses (town businessmen) and workers. The burgesses always had their businesses in the town, and they mainly focused on trade, shipping, or crafts. They would often join together in guilds so they could regulate recruitment and trade. They also participated in the internal self-government of the towns. Each urban center was allowed a certain amount of autonomy. There was a clear division, even among the burgesses. The merchants represented the elite, while the crafters lived more modestly. The crafters were regarded as having a better standing in society than other workers.

Many of the burgesses were foreign merchants, especially in Bergen, where the Hanseatic League remained in control of foreign trade until the 1750s when it finally passed into Norwegian hands. Most of the citizens of Bergen were Germans, but it is impossible to determine their exact numbers. It is believed that the burgesses represented less than half the population of the towns, but their number certainly varied from one place to another. During the 17th and 18th centuries, most of the foreigners were Danish. They were considered legal citizens, and they were able to take part in local government. Throughout the Denmark-Norway union period, the foreigners were always the elite of the society, while the Norwegians were often part of the lower classes.

Even during the early modern age, the majority of Norway's population were peasants, up to 90 percent. Within the society of peasants, the crofters were the individuals who rented portions of land (crofts) from landowners and farmers. Although the system was in place in Norway since the Late Middle Ages, the population growth during the early modern period changed the system. It seems that during the 16th and 17th centuries, the crofters made up only a small portion of the population. They were usually older people, which meant they came from the ranks of retired farmers. At the beginning of the 18th century, the number of crofters started rising rapidly. New crofters were young people, and there were approximately fifty-five thousand of them against seventy-seven thousand farmers. This means that around 30 percent of the agricultural community of Norway belonged to the crofters. It is presumed that the population growth and the shortage of food supplies of the later years of the Denmark union forced young people into poverty.

There were different types of crofters: those who rented agricultural land and could work it (crofter's holding) and those who rented enough land for a house and a small private garden (crofters without land). Some crofters rented the land by the sea, and they were called "shore sitters." Crofters didn't pay land taxes because they only rented it. The farmers who owned the land paid the taxes. However, they paid rent and had to contribute to the farm as a whole through other means (either production or as a labor force). From the contracts between the crofters and landowners, we can see that the rent was paid either in cash, in a set number of workdays, or even a combination of these two. These contracts lasted for life, or they were signed for a specific number of years. Some could be broken at any time the landowner demanded.

Crofters never had enough land or animals to support their families. They needed alternative ways to earn income, and they did so by working directly for the farmers. They also sought employment in the timber industry, cutting woods and transporting them down the rivers. Similarly, they found work in fisheries, mines, and the transport of goods. Some crofters had their own businesses, such as petty trading and crafting. If they owned vessels, they usually partnered with other fishermen and earned their living on the seas.

The Economy

In the period between the 16th and 18th centuries, agriculture remained the main source of income, as 75 percent of the Norwegian population drew their income from it. Farms were the main economic units, and all the land between the fjord and the fjell (mountain) was considered a farm. The infields were made out of arable land and meadows on which the animals grazed. The arable land was constantly cultivated, and the Norwegians learned to combat soil exhaustion with heavy manuring. In some areas, the farmers preferred to rotate their land and plant crops in the grazing fields while the arable land rested for a year. The farms also included forests, and these were used for timber and firewood. In areas with rich forests, the farmers would cut the wood to sell. The mountainsides were used as pastures, and the people would build little mountain houses, where they would spend the season with their sheep and cattle.

Farms were divided into holdings, and they were occupied by different families. One of the purposes of this farmland division was to give each occupant equal amounts of different land. Even the woods were divided and fenced off. Because of this, the holdings had their land mixed up with the lands of other holdings. The pastures, meadows, and haymaking areas were held in common by all the holdings of one farm, and these were sometimes even shared with other farms. However, the population growth during the union period ended this practice, and the pastures and meadows were divided and bordered.

The Norwegian climate limited cultivation, which is why animal husbandry was of equal value as agriculture. There were almost no areas solely dedicated to the production of grain like in other European countries at the time. Arable land was so sparse that the Norwegians persistently grew grain as far north as Troms, even though the crops usually failed there. But the importance of livestock and their numbers meant that the fields were always well manured and fertile, and they were able to produce year-round. Although arable land was sparse, it was able to produce much more food than the European standard at the time.

The first register of what farms produced and how many animals they housed was created in the 17th century for tax purposes. Due to this register, we can now see what the Norwegians used to produce during the union period and how they divided the land. The usual grains produced were barley and oats or a mixture of two known as *blandkorn*. Potatoes were introduced in the 18th century, but their widespread use culminated only during the 19th century. There were many animal species on the farms, but they were all local varieties. This means they were much smaller than the animals today, which allowed them to survive harsh winters on much less food. However, during the abundant summers, the smaller animals reproduced faster.

Fish was always abundant in the Norwegian Sea, especially cod and herring. However, these fish are not easy to extract, especially with the technology of the early modern period. The fish could only be extracted during the spawning season, which lasts for three months. This is when cod and herring come close to the Norwegian shore. However, their spawn is unstable, and people had no means to predict where exactly the fish would go. The fishing business was very difficult, though lucrative. The fishing population couldn't survive only on fish, as their caloric needs wouldn't be met. Therefore, they had to exchange fish for other food supplies. To do this, they had to preserve the fish. Otherwise, it would spoil in a matter of days. Luckily, with the coming of the Hanseatic League, the Norwegian fishermen gained access to the whole European continent.

Land Ownership

Norwegian historian Halvard Bjørkvik estimated the land ownership at the end of the Middle Ages. He claimed that the Crown owned 7.5 percent of the land, the aristocracy 13 percent, the various private hands had 32 percent in their hands, and the largest part, 47.5 percent, belonged to the church. During the period of the Denmark-Norway union, only one land ownership survey was conducted in 1661 by the office of the Land Commission. The significant change in the amount of land owned by different parties is evident. The Crown now owned 31 percent, the church 21 percent, the aristocracy 8 percent, and the private hands had most of the land, owning 40 percent.

The increase of Crown lands is easily explainable. After the Reformation, the king confiscated the church lands, mainly from bishoprics and monasteries. Only the land owned by parishes remained the property of the church. The king claimed these too, though ineffectively. The decline of the amount of land owned by the aristocracy is explained by the decline of the aristocracy itself and the rise of the commoners. Elite families either died out or simply went bankrupt and were demoted to the ranks of the peasantry.

In both the late medieval period and the period of the union, it remains unknown what percentage of the land belonged to the farmers, peasants, and crofters. Today, scholars estimate that around 19 percent of the land belonged to them for the early modern period. But its distribution varied depending on the region of Norway. In the far north, there were few farms, constituting only a few percent of the arable land. In the southwest, this percentage was much larger since the climate there was more appropriate for farming.

In Norway, the free peasantry was on the rise during the period of the union, but this class of citizens didn't exist in Denmark at all. There was a continuous shortage of cash in Norway, and the king was forced to sell some of his possessions, mostly his public estates. The Crown auctioned off the land in two waves. The first one was in 1660, when most of the confiscated monastic land was sold, and the second was in 1720 (after the Great Northern War), when the private estates were sold. During this period, the Crown also sold off the land belonging to the parishes, and the Norwegian churches became private properties.

Interestingly enough, it wasn't the aristocracy that bought the land from the Crown but burgesses and civil servants (embedsmann), as they regarded this land as a good investment. Only a small part of the land from the 1660 sale was bought by peasants. But the first generation of the buyers soon started, and they divided the land they purchased into small lots and sold them directly to the peasants. Perhaps the Crown was inspired by this development and started selling the land again in 1720, only this time the sale was made in small pieces of land so that peasants could afford it. That is how the Norwegian peasantry was transformed into the freeholders. However, it remains unknown why the king didn't allow the aristocracy to buy the land, although some scholars believe this was done so that Norwegian agriculture remained protected from exploitation.

Constitutional Politics

The Denmark-Norway union falls into two parts when it comes to constitutional politics. Up until the middle of the 17th century, the union was an elective monarchy. Once a king died, he would be succeeded by a person specifically elected by the council of nobles. This council would subject the new kings to the conditions laid down in a formal agreement. This agreement gave the council the real power in the monarchy, even if the elected successor was the previous king's eldest son. Only the Danish nobility had the right to sit on the council, and they chose the members. The king had no right to appoint new council members. This type of monarchy would be described as the "monarchy of the nobles."

Though the nobles elected the king, other social groups had the right to take part in the governance of the monarchy. In Denmark, the peasants didn't have this right, but in Norway, they did. After all, they represented the majority of Norway's population. Different social orders, such as the nobles, clergy, citizens, and peasants, were all summoned to pay homage and swear allegiance to the king and his elected successor. The different orders would also meet to discuss political issues, such as the sanctioning of specific taxes. However, only the king had the right to summon such meetings, and once they gathered, they rarely took the initiative. One such meeting of the Danish order set the stage for the coup d'état, in which the monarch finally seized full power.

In 1660, the council of nobles lost their power, and the new constitutional politics changed the union into an absolutist hereditary monarchy. This all happened because the council refused to pay additional taxes when the state entered an economic crisis following the wars of 1657 to 1660 (the Dano-Swedish War). The king used the military to press the nobles into agreeing to make the monarchy hereditary. This made all the agreements the kings ever made with the council disappear.

The Law of the Realm wrote a constitution in 1665 by which the king was declared the absolute monarch. However, the constitution limited the king's powers in the sphere of religion. Evangelical Lutheranism was acknowledged as the main religion of the state, and the king had no power to change that.

During the union period, the largest administrative unit in Norway was the county (*len*), and it was under the control of the lord lieutenants, who were all drawn from the ranks of the aristocracy. Nine out of ten lord lieutenants of Norway were Danes. Their primary task was to collect the taxes and customs dues for the monarchy. They also had military duties, such as recruitment, and they supervised the legal system and the church. The lord lieutenants worked for a salary and rewards from the king, all of which were drawn from the Norwegian taxpayers.

Although the lord lieutenants had the counties under their control, all administrative work was performed by their servants or bailiffs (*fogder*), who were all picked from non-aristocratic families. The bailiffs were the ones who went out and collected the taxes and dues, attended prosecutions, and carried out the sentences. The king had direct control over the bailiffs because many governmental issues the public had with the monarchy were dealt with during the meetings of bailiffs and the general public. Over time and due to their relationship with the Crown, the bailiffs were transformed from mere servants of the lord lieutenants to the "His Royal Majesty's Bailiffs." They had to swear an oath directly to the king, and it was the king who could appoint and dismiss them.

After the transformation of the bailiffs, more reforms followed. Each of the reforms was designed to weaken the position and influence of the lord lieutenants. During the first decades of the 17th century, a centralized administrative system was set up in Norway. In the rural areas, there were community assemblies. The peasants acted as jurors, but they needed the help of literate and legally competent magistrates (*sorenskriver*). Soon, these rural magistrates came to dominate the community assemblies. The assemblies in towns were made up of a mayor and the town council. These assemblies served the community, and through them, one could contact the court of appeal and high courts if they needed higher legal institutions. In 1604, King

Christian IV published the Norwegian Code, but it was only an extension to the 13th-century Magnus Lagabøte's State Law, also known as *Magnus Lagabøtes landslov*, which was written by King Magnus VI of Norway.

In 1630, the monarchy sharply increased the custom dues, but they also introduced some administrative changes to follow this increase. No longer were the bailiffs responsible for the collection of the dues. Instead, the office of the customs service was founded, and it was under the direct control of the king. Another change in the administration affected the army. Previously, the lord lieutenants were responsible for the recruitment, but the government decided to organize a professional army of Norway. This reform was implemented during the 1640s, and the professional officers, who were mainly from Germany, were hired to train the peasant conscripts.

All of these administrative changes in Norway didn't only limit the influence of the lord lieutenants, but they also firmly linked Norway with the government in Copenhagen. With the introduction of absolutism in 1660, Norway became a kingdom in its own right once again. However, this was only in name. In reality, the country was only a collection of administrative areas that were run by a Danish king from the Danish capital of Copenhagen. However, some of the government departments were now allowed to be exclusively Norwegian: the army, the postal service, and the mining ministry. But even in these areas of government, the Danish Crown preferred to organize them into smaller subdivisions and prevent joint Norwegian administration.

The Norwegian Outlook on the Union

In 1720, the interests in the economic development of Norway were rekindled, and many academically educated Norwegians started considering the natural resources their country had to offer. They created topographical maps of various Norwegian localities, and they described the natural environment and economic conditions of the targeted areas. This work sparked self-awareness in the Norwegian academic circles. The authors of such maps and literary descriptions all agreed that Norway was a rich country with a very energetic and independent race as its inhabitants. The Norwegians started perceiving themselves as different from the Danes. In the 1750s, the Copenhagen government opened a debate about the economic question of the monarchy, and it immediately split into two groups: the Norwegian one and the Danish one. The two countries had different resources, industries, and societies. The Norwegians started recognizing that their country was subjected to Denmark and that the relationship between the two countries was based on the oppression of Norway.

During the 1770s, the first history of Norway was published, and it was written by Gerhard Schøning. His work further inspired the already growing sense of Norwegian pride. He traveled across the country to collect material for his history volumes, which dealt with the Norwegian past, from the early migrations until the year 995. However, this sense of belonging to one distinctive ethnic group never reached the majority of the population, the peasantry. It was a movement strictly reserved for the growing bourgeoisie since they were able to afford academic education. Because the peasantry was unaware of the movement, there can be no talk of nationalization in its true sense. Nationalization typically includes all levels of society, and it also includes culture and language.

But a national movement existed, though maybe a more appropriate term would be Norwegian patriotism, a sense of belonging to a specific geographic and cultural place. But such patriotism presented the union with some controversial political issues. In the second half of the 18th century, the Norwegians started demanding a separate university in their home country. The loudest advocates for this change in education were the *embedsmann*, the Norwegian civil servants educated in Denmark. Their main argument was the cost of education. They had to travel far from their homes since the only close university was in Copenhagen. The second political issue regarded the Norwegian national bank, as the bourgeoisie wanted to conduct their business completely locally.

Censorship in the union was very strict, and the wishes of the Norwegians were seldom heard. Norwegians had to wait a long time for their wishes to be fulfilled. Johann Friedrich Struensee, the minister of the Danish government under King Christian VII of Denmark, lifted the censorship of the press in 1770, and the

Norwegian grievances were finally acknowledged by the wider Danish population. The first university in Norway was opened in 1813 in Christiania (now Oslo). At the beginning of 1814, the Bank of Norway came into existence.

Although it is easy to conclude that Norway and Denmark started drifting apart during the last years of the union, the truth is that they had close administrative contact. Even the economic contact between the two increased in scale in the years before the Napoleonic Wars, which reached Denmark in 1807. The beginning of the 19th century was also a period of increased cultural contact. The Danish government actively worked on equalizing the position of the Danish and Norwegian peasantry through a gigantic agricultural reform, but it never came to be.

Chapter 6 – The Union with Sweden

Map of Norway-Sweden from 1847 by Norwegian historian Peter Andreas Munch.
https://commons.wikimedia.org/wiki/File:Norge_og_Sverige_1847_copy.jpg

The dissolution of the Denmark-Norway union came in 1814, but the path to it was much longer. When tracing the events that led to the break-up between the two countries, it becomes evident that it was the international relations and the whole European stage at the time that brought about the dramatic upheaval. The union had a history of foreign affairs being about rivalry and wars, especially with neighboring Sweden. Denmark always strived to dominate Scandinavia, but it could only do so at the expense of its neighbors. Norway had already suffered from being dominated by Denmark, but Sweden wouldn't give up its imperialism dreams.

The Relationship of Denmark-Norway and Sweden

The period between 1536 and 1814 can be split into four phases when it comes to the relationship between the Scandinavian kingdoms. Up until 1625, Denmark-Norway and Sweden had approximately equal military power, and they fought each other for the dominance of not only Scandinavia but also the Baltic and Cap of the North (*Nordkalotten*, the geographical area in the far north of Europe consisting of the Norwegian counties of Troms og Finnmark and Nordland, Swedish Norrbotten, Finnish Lapland, and Russian Murmansk Oblast).

Denmark used the Norwegian forces in its war efforts; thus, Norway got to experience both the Northern Seven Years' War (1563-1570) and the Kalmar War (1611-1613). Both of these wars were fought between Denmark-Norway and Sweden but for different reasons. The Seven Years' War was a product of the dissolution of the Kalmar Union, while the Kalmar War (named so after the city of Kalmar, not the union) was fought to determine who would dominate the Baltic region. During both of these wars, the Danish tactic was to attack Sweden on two fronts. One attack would come from Skåne, which then belonged to Denmark, and the second would be launched from Norway. Sweden would always concentrate on attacking Norway since it was the weaker enemy. But these conflicts didn't solve the domination problem between Denmark and Sweden. The balance of power remained unchanged until 1625.

The turning point came with the Emperor's War (1625-1629). Denmark wanted to intervene in the Thirty Years' War in the Holy Roman Empire. King Christian IV of Denmark aspired to help the Protestants fleeing the empire, but he also had his interests in the territory of northern Germany. But his meddling in the Thirty Years' War resulted in great military and political losses for Denmark. Instead, the king of Sweden, Gustav II Adolf, won both territories and influence in northern Germany. Sweden gained dominance over the Baltics and became a serious threat to the Danish heartland. They didn't hesitate to take advantage of their new political and territorial position, and in the next two wars—the Hannibal controversy (1643-1645) and the Charles Gustav Wars (1655-1660)—they took Danish territory in what is today southern Sweden and what was once Norway's Bohuslän and Jemtland-Herjedalen, both of which are today in modern Sweden.

In the next two wars, the Scanian War (1675-1679) and the Great Northern War (1700-1721), Sweden took the Danish tactics and attacked from two fronts. However, other European powers got involved in these conflicts, and Sweden had to retreat. In Norway, the defense was organized by the peasantry, just like in the previous wars. However, this time, the peasants weren't enough, and Norway had to create a professional army. Danish and German officers were hired and spread around Norway to enlist and train soldiers from the ranks of the peasantry. Each area consisting of several villages had to provide one soldier. The military effort resulted in Norway being able to provide sixteen thousand soldiers during the Great Northern War.

The Norwegian war efforts became the stuff of legends, as the simple farm boys proved they could put up a serious fight. The Norwegians used these stories to boost their national spirit and mock the Danes, who they saw as acting superior. The Norwegians started feeling proud of their army, which they regarded as a distinctive force separate from the Danish army. As for the naval force of the Denmark-Norway union, it was always based in Copenhagen, but most of its crewmen were recruited from the western coast of Norway. There was no conscription in northern Norway, neither for the land army nor for the naval force.

The Crisis Years

During the American War of Independence and the Revolutionary Wars in France, Denmark-Norway remained neutral so it could strengthen its southern fringes and prepare for a possible attack from continental Europe. The period between 1720 and 1807 was peaceful because Sweden and Russia chose to remain neutral in this conflict. The Norwegian shipping enterprise bloomed because of this neutrality because Great Britain, which was involved in both of these conflicts, lost the markets in its former colonies. However, the Revolutionary Wars turned into the Napoleonic Wars (1803–1815), and with this change, the neutral countries were forced to choose sides. Sweden stood by Great Britain, while Russia chose France. Denmark-Norway didn't have the opportunity to choose. Fearing their great fleet would end up in Napoleon's hands, Great Britain sent its army to besiege Copenhagen in 1807 and forced the kingdom to surrender its navy. Denmark was furious, and its king, Frederick VI, decided to side with Napoleon.

Because Denmark lost its neutrality, its union with Norway became an international point of interest. Denmark chose to side with France, not only because of Britain's act of burning the Danish fleet but also because the kingdom had an age-old fear of being invaded from the south. To prevent this, they chose Napoleon over Britain. However, this choice also plunged Denmark into the conflict against the British allies of Sweden and Russia.

The new wars and the Norwegian involvement in them led to the loss of exports. The presence of the British naval force in Norwegian waters also disrupted the domestic traffic, and most of the links with Denmark were cut off. The Norwegian Army was mobilized, but it waited for further orders at the eastern border. In 1807, the kingdom organized a special committee headed by Crown Prince Christian August to govern Norway during this time of military tension. The prince acted as the commander-in-chief of the Norwegian Army of the south. The first hostilities began in 1808 when the Swedish Army reached the Glomma River. The Norwegians easily defended their position and pushed the enemy back. The Swedish then moved their troops to the Finnish front, where they would fight the Russians. This allowed Norway a brief period of rest. However, the whole country started experiencing famine, especially in 1809. The situation was worst in Østlandet, where an epidemic of dysentery also started spreading throughout the army camps.

But Sweden didn't have much luck on the Finnish front, and the Russian army marched into northern Sweden. The development of these events led to several Swedish officers organizing a coup against their king, Gustav IV Adolf. They put Charles (Carl) XIII in his place. Since the new Swedish king had no children, the Norwegian commander-in-chief, Prince Christian August, was chosen as the heir-apparent to the throne of Sweden. This was done because Sweden aspired to acquire Norway, and Prince Christian was very popular there. They also regarded him as a friend because he refused to attack Sweden while its army was busy on the Finnish front.

By December 1809, Sweden and Denmark-Norway had achieved peace. In 1810, Sweden, Denmark-Norway, and Russia ended the conflict in the north, especially when Sweden decided to abandon its claim over Finland. When Great Britain decided to ease the trade blockade, it seemed that the crisis in Norway was about to end, at least for the time being. But that same year, Christian August, who had changed his name to Carl August, suddenly died of a stroke. Sweden then chose French Marshal Jean Baptiste Bernadotte as the crown prince, who then changed his name to the more appropriate Karl Johan. Although French, Karl (Charles) refused to be Napoleon's puppet and was against a retaliatory war against Russia. In 1812, when Napoleon launched his Russian campaign, Karl Johan abandoned him and sided with Great Britain and Russia, as both of these countries promised Sweden would get Norway for its military help against France.

Sweden long aspired to acquire Norway, but instead, through military conquests, they wanted the Norwegian people to voluntarily agree to the union. Thus, they promised Norway would have equal status with Sweden and would acquire the very liberal Swedish constitution. The Danish government was well aware of the Swedish aspirations toward Norway, and Danish King Frederick VI approached Britain and Russia in an attempt to dissuade them from giving Norway to Sweden. But it was already too late, and once he was declined, Frederick tied

Denmark even more closely to Napoleon's France. To keep Norway, Frederick sent his heir, Prince Christian Frederick, to be the commander-in-chief. Christian Frederick and Swedish Karl Johan would be the leading actors in the dramatic events that would soon shape Norway's destiny.

Independence in the Union with Sweden

In 1814, Karl Johan defeated the Danish army just north of the German Duchy of Holstein. He forced Danish King Frederick VI to sign a peace in Kiel on January 14th, in which Norway was ceded to Sweden. Norway thus entered a union with Sweden but as a kingdom of equal status. Christian Frederick received the news of the Peace of Kiel on January 24th, and he decided to proclaim himself as the king of Norway and disturb the Swedish plans. To do so, he needed the loyalty of the Norwegian people, and he planned to visit Trondheim in February, where he would be crowned. However, he was unsure of popular opinion, and instead of immediately taking the crown, he decided to rule as regent until the meeting of the popular assembly that would promulgate a constitution for Norway and elect a king.

Christian Frederick also feared that the Swedes would meddle in this matter. He decided to force the members of the assembly and the representatives of the twelve congregations to swear an oath by which they promised to defend the independence of Norway. To emphasize the seriousness of the oath, they all had to swear in writing. By the end of March, the assembly elections were completed, although the north of Norway did not get involved. The first popular assembly meeting took place on April 10th at Eidsvoll, and the new constitution was drafted by May 17th. Norway was officially restored as an independent kingdom, and a wide spectrum of people gained political rights due to the new liberal constitution.

The Peace of Kiel was thus set aside. But this was only possible because the Swedish Army was busy fighting Napoleon on the European continent. A political vacuum was created between the signing of the Peace of Kiel and the actualization of the Norway-Sweden union, and Christian Frederick took advantage of it. However, this newly created independent Norway had yet to survive the wrath of Sweden.

Karl Johan couldn't let go of Norway, and he wanted to reinforce the agreement made with the Peace of Kiel. He summoned a delegation of the Great European Powers (Great Britain, France, Russia, Italy, the Habsburg Empire, and Germany) to Copenhagen to investigate if Frederick VI had anything to do with the events in Norway. But the delegation cleared the Danish king of any suspicion, and they continued to Oslo. The delegation expressed they felt obliged to accommodate the Peace of Kiel, though they sympathized with Christian Frederick and the Norwegian government he had founded. The conclusion was that the union with Sweden had to be fulfilled, but Norway would receive good conditions in this union.

But Karl Johan was impatient, and he moved his Swedish Army to the border with Norway, demanding the immediate abdication of Christian Frederick. Christian offered his abdication, but he would not allow Sweden to forcefully occupy Norwegian territory as Karl Johan intended. The war between the two neighboring countries began on July 27th, 1814. This conflict was very brief, as the Norwegian Army stood no chance against the more experienced Swedish troops. The first negotiations took place a month later, and the peace was concluded with the Moss Convention on August 14th. Christian Frederick was forced to hand over Norwegian military fortifications to the Swedish Army. But politically, Christian Frederick won because he forced Karl Johan to accept the creation of a special Norwegian constitutional assembly, the Storting, that would determine the conditions of the union with Sweden. Only after the convocation of Storting would Christian formally abdicate.

The first meeting of the Storting was on October 7th, 1814, and Christian gave up his rights to the Norwegian throne as promised. The assembly then confirmed the Norwegian constitution and revised it to fit the new weaker monarchy and the union with Sweden. The constitution was ready by November 4th, and Karl Johan was elected as the king of Norway. The Norway-Sweden union would last for the next ninety years.

The Constitution

The most important legacy of the events of 1814 is the Norwegian constitution. It was the foundation of Norway's political life, and the country's basic civil rights rest on it even today. For more than two hundred years of its existence, the constitution went through changes, though the underlying principles and the institutional framework it represents were never changed. It was created by the 112 representatives sent from various communities around Norway, who met at Eidsvoll in Viken county.

In actuality, two constitutions were created in 1814. The first one was on May 17th, and it was intended for an independent Norway. It was based on the principles of popular sovereignty. According to this constitution, the king would have the executive power, while the assembly (Storting) would legislate and determine the taxes. The judicial power would be in the hands of an independent judiciary. This constitution was written for a strong monarchy. It would give the king the power to appoint all *embedsmann* and ministers. The king would also have the power to determine Norway's involvement in wars and peace and make decisions about foreign policy.

The second one was a revision and adaptation of the first constitution, and it was designed for Norway's union with Sweden. It is called the November Constitution, as it was issued on November 4th. The second constitution was based on the same principles as the first one, but it had adjusted the relations between the powers. The king no longer had the power to determine the defense and foreign policies, and the government was given a greater degree of independence. A separate document was issued in 1815 named the Document of the Realm, in which the regulations relating to the actual union and joint institutions were determined. The first lines of the constitution state that Norway is a free and independent, indivisible, and inalienable country, one united with Sweden by the same king. It is clear that although Norway was in yet another union, it had finally received its independence.

Chapter 7 – The New State

A 19ᵗʰ-century mining town of Røros, Norway.

Norway's European borders were finally set in 1826 when a frontier agreement was signed with Russia. During the period between the world wars, Norway would gain territories in the Arctic and Antarctic, its first lands outside of Europe. Christiania became the capital of the country and the center of Norway's political life, but it would not change its name to Oslo until 1925. Since the town had Norway's only university, it also became the center of scientific and cultural life. In 1840, the royal palace and new university were constructed. In 1866, the Storting was built, and in 1898, the national theater was established. Until then, the largest city in Norway was Bergen, but Christiania surpassed it in both population and wealth.

Since the unification with Sweden, Norway started experiencing economic growth as well as a great deal of social change. The population started increasing again and reached 2.2 million in 1900. Today, Norway has around 5.3 million people. Aside from the population increase, the majority of people moved from the countryside to towns. Society and the whole country transformed itself from being the backward fringe of Europe to one of the continent's most developed nations, both economically and culturally. The bulk of the population prospered.

But when Karl Johan was finally crowned in 1818, the whole of Europe assumed an anti-democratic stance, and he thought this was a good time to attack the Norwegian constitution and integrate the country into Sweden's sphere of influence. He planned to cut down the powers of the Storting, which would benefit only the Crown. But first, Karl Johan needed to persuade the parliament to change the written constitution. At first, he chose to do so by force. In the summer of 1821, he gathered the Swedish and Norwegian armies in front of Christiania. However, he changed his mind and decided to take the legislative path instead of the coup d'état.

Karl Johan sent a proposal to the parliament in which he demanded that his power to delay legislation be turned into the power of absolute veto. He also wanted the Crown to have the power to dissolve the Storting and dismiss the *embedsmann*, to have the right to nominate the president of the parliament, and to reduce the Storting's power of impeachment. The king hoped the Swedish population would support his demands regarding Norway and that the Great Powers would at least be sympathetic toward his efforts. But the Swedes thought that if Karl Johan became the absolutist monarch in Norway, he would soon demand the same constitutional changes in Sweden. The Great Powers remained neutral regarding the Norwegian question and opted not to help Karl Johan. After all, they wanted permanent peace in Europe after the Napoleonic Wars. Norway's constitution remained unchanged, and the country got to keep its independence.

Recovery and Growth of Norway

Independent Norway came to be during an economic crisis. The harvest was poor, and the country had low stocks of food. Markets were also closed to Norwegian exports, and the last war drained had all their reserves and provisions. The ensuing inflation meant new problems for the government's finances. However, it took Norway only sixty years to completely recover from this economic disaster, and at the end of the 19th century, the state had a firmly established financial foundation. Even the population doubled in size due to the better living conditions. However, Norway had to go through a process of growth and recovery to reach the status of a well-off modern country.

The population of Norway exploded during the 19th century, and there are two main reasons for it: the economy and medicine. The agrarian society of Norway improved production, and the increased food import rates brought food surpluses and eliminated famine. Better eating habits also helped the population in Norway to resist various diseases. The survival of infants significantly rose during the 19th century, and the overall life expectancy of the people increased. One of the medical explanations for the increase in the population is the introduction of the obligatory smallpox vaccination in 1810.

The population growth didn't choke the country's economy. Norway managed to avoid the so-called Malthusian trap due to emigration. During the 1850s and 1860s, many Norwegians decided to leave the country in search of religious freedom. They also left because of agricultural failure and the high cost of living. However, the largest movement of the population happened within the country. Many farms in the interior were abandoned, as people moved to the shore where they could enter the fishing or timber industry to sustain themselves or the cities where they could acquire work in the important ports.

After the unification with Sweden, Norway lost Denmark as its biggest market for iron and glass. The industry was hit hard by this loss, especially because British production was its main competitor. But through hard work to overcome these marketing problems, Norway's industry was revived in the 1840s. In just twenty-five years, the demand for new workers jumped, and in 1850, there were twelve thousand people employed in the ironworks. In the 1870s, there were more than forty-five thousand people employed in the same industry. The dominant industrial area was the shipyards. Here, employment jumped from 1,000 to 5,700 people between 1850 and 1870. The sawmills were developed during the 1860s, and by 1868, the new steam-powered sawmills were introduced to Norway. In the timber industry, employment between 1850 and 1870 rose to thirteen thousand. The new Norwegian industries were the textile factories and engineering workshops.

The modernization of the country started, especially when local entrepreneurs saw the possibility of replacing imported goods with domestically produced ones. The Norwegian tariff of 1842 also protected local enterprises, as they got lower rates on raw materials and semi-finished products. Many of the new producers, especially in the textile industry, had previous experience in the trade, so they knew the market well. They had less trouble opening the production lines and offering their products than the completely new entrepreneurs. They were clever businessmen, and instead of building their factories from scratch, they would import all the technology they needed and focus their attention on what they knew best: marketing. The Norwegians also often traveled to Great Britain, where they could learn the production process and all the technical know-how in the sphere of their industry.

Aside from the expansion of the industry from the 1840s onward, Norway also went through changes in the economic framework of the state. The new and modernized institutions helped the state take on new financial initiatives that boosted the country's economy. By doing so, the state reinforced the development of capitalism. The Bank of Norway focused its efforts on the prevention of inflation and the defense of the value of the Norwegian national currency (the Norwegian krone). The state helped the development of industry by taking up foreign loans, especially in times of crisis. In 1851, the Norges Hypotekbank was founded as a state credit institution that drew foreign capital into the country and gave the citizens long-term real estate mortgages. The private commercial banks found Norway a prospective market and started opening their offices around the Norwegian towns.

The government also realized they needed to invest in roads and communication networks. With the opening of new and modernized roads, transport prices dropped, and postal services were extended to include many new areas. Between 1855 and 1870, the state built a national telegraph network, which was immediately linked to the effective international communication system. Because of increased postal needs, the first steamships were introduced to Norway as early as 1826. However, the peak of steamboat use came in 1855, and the state alone owned eleven of them. With the steamboats came modernization and development of harbors across Norway.

But the railway became Norway's most prominent symbol of modernization. The first line was opened in 1854, and it connected Christiania and Eidsvoll. In the next 20 years, the Norwegians constructed 594 kilometers (369 miles) of railroads, with firm plans to build another 1,000 kilometers (621 miles) in the near future. This program was finished by 1883, with the state taking full responsibility for the construction and operation of the lines. No foreign companies were employed. The result of the state's devotion and investment, as well as of industry expansion, was the economic growth and improved standard of living for all the citizens of 19th-century Norway.

The Embedsmann State

The period of Norway's development that took place between 1840 and 1870 was known as the age of the *embedsmann* state. This was a period of great political stability and harmonious cooperation of the Storting and government. However, this harmony was occasionally disturbed by the stirrings of the opposition within the Storting. This opposition was the peasants, whose political body was established in the 1830s. It would become a permanent feature of the 19th-century Norwegian parliament.

The leading parliamentary figure of the 1840s and 1850s was Ole Gabriel Ueland, a son of a farmer. He was one of the greatest leaders of the peasants and one of the first peasants who took up politics. Another peasant leader was Søren Pedersen Jaabæk, who was an active member of parliament from 1845 to 1890. During this period, the peasant opposition in the Storting had a very narrow-minded agenda. They demanded the immediate realization of issues concerning the peasantry and were deeply anti-bureaucratic. One of the main goals of the peasants was to curb the power of the *embedsmann*, but they never sought to take up the leadership themselves.

The *embedsmann* had other opposition in the Storting during the mid-19th century. There were the business owners, craftsmen, and academics who didn't become *embedsmann*. This opposition was organized by a young lawyer named Johan Sverdrup, who would become the prime minister in 1884. This opposition group attempted to ally with the peasants in 1851, and together, they organized a tight opposition within the Storting called "the men of freedom," although they later changed their name to "the reform society." But the efforts of the organized opposition ultimately failed.

The main danger for the parliament came from the Thrane movement, which was active between 1848 and 1851. Named after its leader and founder, Marcus Thrane (1817–1890), the movement represented one of the most remarkable protests in Norwegian history. It was the first popular movement in Norway, numbering over 30,000 members within 414 associations. The movement itself began as a protest organization of the laborers and craft workers in the towns, but it soon spread to crofters and the petty peasantry in the countryside. The Thrane movement was ambiguous in its demands. It wanted the implementation of "one man, one vote," which is very democratic. But it also demanded that the king personally act to protect the interests of the commoners. The movement came as a response to the growing pressure on Norwegian society and the increase of the crofter system due to the population growth.

In 1850, the movement presented a petition to the king and the Storting, demanding the equal status of all people when it came to the law, a universal voting system, the abolition of taxes on essential goods (mainly food), state support for poor farmers, and better education for the commoners. The petition had thirteen thousand signatures, but it didn't achieve anything. Thus, the movement turned to revolutionary ideas, but Thrane stopped this idea from escalating. Nevertheless, he was arrested in 1851 and spent the next eight years in prison. With Thrane absent, the movement ended. He later emigrated to the United States and spent twenty-seven years there. His body was returned to Norway only in 1949, and it was put to rest in an honored grave in Oslo.

The *embedsmann* managed to hold power against all the opposition groups because they took the political initiative. Two shining examples of these initiatives are Anton Martin Schweigaard and Frederik Stang. They were both born in 1808, and they were lawyers and members of a youth intellectual movement in Norway, the *Intelligens*. In the 1830s, this movement developed a program in which the Storting and the government were bound to cooperate and take a proactive role in the modernization and development of the country. Stang was a member of the government (1845–1856) and even its leader from 1861 until 1880. Schweigaard, on the other hand, became a member of the Storting in 1842 and remained in that position until he died in 1870. Due to their positions, the two men had the opportunity to implement programs, especially in the areas of the economy.

The Beginning of Modern Norway

At the end of the 1870s, it seemed that the government and parliament had exhausted the fuel that was feeding the Norwegian economic growth. At the same time, the fishing industry started failing, as the spring herring disappeared from the Norwegian waters. The forests were mostly cut down, and the timber industry couldn't afford to export its produce. Sweden became Norway's timber competitor, as it still had dense forests. All domestic industries started suffering as the government failed to secure their protection against foreign competition. Norway had no other choice but to turn to new products, mainly to mechanization and industrialization. It was the only way Norway could keep up with the modernization that occurred throughout Europe.

Ever since its union with Sweden, Norway had its ups and downs in regards to the economy and development. The parliament's initiatives were a push forward, and they took the country out of the depression that preceded the 1840s. Although the industries, economy, and society grew, it all came to a halt between 1877 and 1887. The growth then resumed, though moderately, and it lasted until the second half of the 1890s. A new depression started in 1900, but it lasted for only five years. Norway started yet another wave of development when World War I happened, making it impossible to maintain the economy. All the various industries Norway developed were suddenly unable to work to their full capacity.

Norwegian modernization was slow, and although it progressed, it was always behind other European countries, especially Norway's immediate neighbors of Sweden and Denmark. But the modernization brought more people from the countryside to the cities, where they found employment in crafts and industry. Although Norway had once consisted mainly of peasants, its demographics had changed. Only a small portion of its population continued to practice agriculture.

The turn of the century saw a dramatic shift in demographics. The people became very mobile, and the cities started counting their population in the millions. While in 1875, only 25 percent of the population lived in towns, by 1900, that number grew to 45 percent. But Norway also lost some of its population during this period, as the emigration to the United States intensified during the 1880s and 1900s. The dominant groups that left the country were young, unmarried men and women, with the majority of them from the rural areas of Norway. In forty-five years, half a million people set sail to America. They did so because of the new labor prospects the United States offered.

Political Changes

After 1884, Norwegian politicians started organizing political parties and recruited for the offices in the Storting and the government. At first, only the Conservative (*Høyre*) and the Liberal (*Venstre*) parties existed. But the two-party system didn't last for long in Norway, and it was quickly replaced by a multi-party one. In 1888, the right-wing oriented members of the Liberal Party separated themselves, and the Moderate Liberal Party emerged. The Norwegian Labour Party was founded as early as 1887, but it didn't win its first seats in parliament until 1903. In 1909, a new splinter party from the Liberals appeared called the *Frisinnede Venstre* (Free-minded Liberals). All the new parties entering the political scene of Norway meant the end of the classic rule by a single party. However, only two of the parties dominated the Norwegian political scene until 1918: the Conservative and the Liberal.

The main point of conflict in Norwegian politics was the union with Sweden, and it remained dominant until 1905. In general, the union was seen as part of the framework of a nation's life, and it didn't pose any massive political questions. However, from time to time, dissatisfaction would rise, and the people expressed their views on the union. Some of their frustrations were over the national symbols, such as the Norwegian flag and coins. Although they took some time, these conflicts were resolved without major disturbances to the population. But some dissatisfactions had a deeper meaning for Norwegian integrity and identity.

One of the issues that Norway had with the union was the fact that the king had the right to appoint a viceroy who would lead the Norwegian government instead of the king. This meant that Norway was a dependent country. In 1859, the Storting annulled the office of the viceroy of Norway, and it was a general belief that the king would approve this decision. However, the Crown backed out of this approval due to the pressure imposed by the Swedish authorities. But in 1860, the Storting made it clear that Sweden had no right to meddle in Norwegian constitutional decisions. The conflict about the viceroy would remain one of the most serious issues that the Norway-Sweden union ever experienced.

Norway had a long history of trying to create a national identity and patriotism. The 1850s and 1860s saw the rise of Scandinavianism, an ideology that claimed that the three Scandinavian countries (Denmark, Sweden, and Norway) were culturally and linguistically very similar. The most prominent advocates of Scandinavianism considered the differences between these three nations to be on a level of regionalism in other European countries. But the political background of this ideology involved the Great Powers, which were posing a threat to the small countries in the north.

Prussia attacked Denmark in 1864, and it wanted it to join the German unification. When that happened, the reality of the Great Powers' threat increased. But the royal line of the Bernadotte family (the Swedish royal house) saw Scandinavianism as a means of uniting all the Scandinavian countries under their rule. However, this was not to be, as Norway declined all the proposals of the Swedish government to tighten the union. One of the Swedish government's proposals was to create a joint cabinet between Norway and Sweden, whose delegates would together make decisions about war and defense. But since Norway refused this, the decision remained completely with the king, his foreign minister, and his cabinet, all of which were Swedish.

Only the Norwegian prime minister, who resided in Stockholm, was allowed a seat in this cabinet, and even then, he was only allowed to attend the meetings that involved Norway. The Foreign Office had two separate bodies: the diplomatic service and the consular service. All the diplomats were Swedish, but the consuls were chosen from the joint cabinet of the Swedish and Norwegian governments, mainly because they had to deal with trade and shipping matters.

But when the Swedish government tried to change the balance in the joint cabinet of the consular service and employ more Swedish consuls, the Norwegians reacted. By doing this, the Swedes would admit they saw Norway as their subordinate. The Norwegian political opinion on the union was now radicalized. During the election campaign of 1891, the Liberal Party promised that, if elected, they would install a Norwegian foreign minister. They won the parliamentary elections, but in light of union politics, they chose to ignore their promise. As an alternative, they demanded a completely Norwegian consular cabinet. The negotiations with the Swedish government about this would last until 1905. The Swedish authorities finally accepted the creation of a separate Norwegian consular service, though it remained under the control of the Swedish Foreign Office.

The Storting decided to establish a separate Norwegian consular service, even though the king had already vetoed it. But the issue was much deeper than that. The Storting interpreted the constitution in such a way that the king could execute his rights only if he had the agreement of his cabinet. Since this was not the case, and since the king didn't form another government that would legitimize his veto, then he was no longer a legitimate ruler. The Storting didn't only establish a separate consular service; on June 7th, 1905, it broke the Norway-Sweden union. According to the Norwegian interpretation of the November Constitution, the king was the only tie between the two countries, and since Norway no longer considered him legitimate, there was no union.

The Norwegian decisions about the end of the union didn't sit well with the outside world. But in the autumn of 1905, Sweden agreed to the dissolution of the union if Norway made certain concessions. The Karlstad negotiations began in August and ended with the Swedish recognition of Norwegian independence on October 26th. King Oscar II renounced his claim on the Norwegian throne, but the Storting offered to elect one of Oscar's younger sons as the king of Norway. But the king refused this offer, and Norway elected Danish Prince Carl as their new monarch. Carl accepted the offer and took the traditional Norwegian royal name Haakon, ruling as Haakon VII (the last Norwegian king with that name was Haakon VI from the 14th century). The Great Powers had nothing to gain with the upkeep of the union, and in 1907, they decided to guarantee Norwegian territorial integrity as an independent state.

Norway Stays Neutral

Norway was independent for nine years before the outbreak of World War I (1914-1918). In those years before the war, the country had to organize its institutions, one of them being the Foreign Office. Since the Norwegian industry mainly consisted of shipping and the export of fish, and since the country still needed to import great quantities of supplies, the Foreign Office decided early on that Norway should remain a neutral country when it came to alliances. Being on the fringe of Europe, Norway was never of much interest to the Great Powers, and the country didn't want to bind itself to any foreign state that would pull Norway into military conflicts on the continent. The outbreak of the Great War was the first test of Norway's neutrality.

Norway's neutrality was also built on the wish to be left alone so that the country could build itself. The industrialization and modernization of the country were in full swing before the outbreak of the war. Norway was the second country in Europe to introduce female suffrage (after Finland), and it did so in 1913. Besides all the progress that occurred, Norway still had trouble with its food supply, as the number of citizens grew to 2.5 million by 1914. Because of this, Norway had to assume an active international trade policy, and its foreign minister, Jørgen Løvland, believed that Britain was Norway's best trading partner. The Norwegians also believed that if war occurred, Britain would defend Norway.

Norwegian foreign policy was based on their trust in international law and the rights and duties of the neutral countries, which were outlined and drawn up in the Hague Peace Convention (1907) and the London Declaration of 1909. But this trust Norway had in international law was blown to pieces with the outbreak of World War I. Although Norway had no desire to fight in the war and managed to stay out of the conflict, the country couldn't escape feeling the realities of the war. The world was paralyzed, and there was no need for Norway's shipping anymore. The food supplies on which the country was so dependent couldn't be sent to Norway since each country redirected its export surpluses to feed its army. Norway's economy was crushed by the war, even though Norway didn't fight.

As soon as Germany declared war on Russia on August 1ˢᵗ, 1914, all the Scandinavian states issued their declarations of neutrality. But for a newly independent country, this wasn't enough. Norway couldn't afford to be drawn into the conflict, so to reinforce its neutrality, the country issued another declaration of neutrality. To feel safe, the government mobilized the navy and sent Norwegian soldiers to man the coastal fortresses. Thus, the neutrality defense was set in place, even though politically and militarily, Norway was in no position to join the war. The government concentrated all of its efforts on maintaining the supply lines so that the people could be fed and the economy protected. They still remembered how Britain had blocked Norway during the Napoleonic Wars, which resulted in famine.

The people were aware of the consequences a war might have on their country, even if the fighting never reached them. The sale of food products increased, and prices rose dramatically. By August, the banking sector started panicking because the interest rates had started rising uncontrollably. Luckily, by mid-August, the people and banks had calmed down, and the panic was gone. However, the government issued a declaration by which the export of domestic goods was prohibited. Another declaration concerned the price regulations, and more would follow soon after. Norway was also prohibited from selling its ships to other countries. This was done so that the government would have full control over the Norwegian economy.

Norway heavily depended on its merchant fleet because it generated income and hauled the imported supplies. The war at sea caused great distress for Norwegian everyday life. Great Britain declared the North Sea as a militarized area on November 2nd. By doing this, the neutral Scandinavian countries were forced to oblige Britain's wishes. Norway found itself under British control and thus became a neutral ally. If they declined the British control, they would risk running their ships into minefields in the sea.

A month before the North Sea Declaration, Britain established a new policy of commerce toward Norway to block Germany. On October 15th, 1914, Britain sent a formal letter to the Norwegian prime minister, informing him that Norway had to stop re-exporting supplies that were considered contraband. Norway already had prohibitions on exports, and including the British ones meant its neutrality would be compromised. But Norway also couldn't simply ignore Britain's wishes because Britain kept the Norwegian economy stable. British interference in the shipping of the neutral countries managed to provoke the Germans.

Norway could only hope that the war would end quickly. The prolonged conflict in Europe would demand additional planning, which would only bring new problems to a young government such as Norway. Up until 1916, Norway managed to upkeep its economy, mostly through the workings of Foreign Minister Nils Claus Ihlen, who was a successful businessman. But the foreign minister believed in peace, and he was sure the war would be short. Unfortunately, his ad hoc policies failed due to the prolonged conflict. Germany wanted Norway to remain neutral, as it could keep shipping supplies to Germany if it was. Britain, on the other hand, wanted Norway to join the economic blockade of Germany and deny the enemy much-needed supplies.

By cutting off the export of Norwegian goods to Germany, Norway would lose a great client. It needed to find some kind of compensation, and Britain jumped in, promising to buy all the Norwegian products, mainly fish and copper pyrite, meant for Germany. This was not a great move economically for Britain; the country didn't need that much fish or pyrite since it had full control over American exports too. Norway offered a solution, and soon, the two trade agreements were signed between Britain and Norway. The "Fish Agreement," which was signed in August of 1916, stated that Norway could sell 15 percent of its fish and fish products to Germany, and the rest would be bought by Britain. A similar agreement was made about copper pyrite, in which Norway was allowed to sell only a small portion to Germany. Thus, Britain continued to control Norwegian neutrality, even though by international law, neutral countries were allowed to trade with both warring parties equally.

Norway's business continued to boom during World War I, but only some individuals managed to make a profit. The rest of the population saw an increase in prices and inflation. Nevertheless, there was no need for the introduction of rationing until 1918. The government took certain measures, such as the prohibition of alcohol made from potatoes and grains, the regulation of prices for vital commodities, and an overall prohibition on the selling of alcohol. But the shortages of food and fuel couldn't be avoided, and the black market started operating. This only increased the prices of basic foodstuffs.

Even then, Norway refused to introduce rationing, but it finally did so in 1918 after being pushed by the United States.

The cost of living rose by 250 percent between the years 1914 and 1918, and Norwegian society was divided into those who could afford the food no matter the cost and those who couldn't. The businessmen who were in the shipping industry got quite rich during the war, and so did the fishermen who sold fish to the Germans on the black market, despite the blockade imposed by Great Britain. Even those who refused to sell to the Germans earned good wages because Britain said it would purchase all Norwegian fish meant for export. But the city dwellers, crafters, clerks, farmers, and labor class starved.

Although the government was financially in ruins, Norway realized it was possible to keep neutrality in times of great wars. But the real reason this was possible wasn't the government's capability to deal with the political, economic, and social difficulties that war brought. It was Norway's geographical position. Since it was on the periphery of Europe, none of the Great Powers had any real interest in this remote country. With Russian and German power reduced after World War I, Norway had nothing to fear. Its independence was secured, and Norway felt confident that neutrality should remain their defense policy in the future. However, in 1940, they realized that staying neutral was no longer an option.

After World War I, when the Treaty of Versailles was signed, the archipelago of Svalbard was given to Norway. Previously, these islands belonged to no nation, and anyone interested in exploiting the waters around them was free to do so. The whaling industry was flourishing there, and the whaling companies of England, Denmark, Russia, Japan, and Norway took advantage of the rich waters. But once mineral deposits were discovered under the ground of Svalbard, and the mining industry was established there, a government needed to be established that would regulate the laws for everyone living in the archipelago. This honor was given to Norway in 1920, and the administration of Svalbard was established in 1925. The Treaty of Spitsbergen (Svalbard's previous name) made a condition for Norway to allow the citizens of all signatory countries (France, Japan, Italy, Denmark, the Netherlands, the United Kingdom, Sweden, and the United

States) to freely settle and start businesses on the island, including whaling and mining. Over time, whaling and mining were replaced by research and tourism industries. Today, the Svalbard archipelago is one of the greatest attractions that Norway has to offer. It is a very remote and desolate place, inhabited by polar bears, arctic foxes, reindeer, and around three thousand people who choose to live there, though many of them leave the archipelago to spend their winter in warmer climates.

Chapter 8 – World War II

The sinking of the German cruiser Blücher in the Oslofjord.
https://commons.wikimedia.org/wiki/File:German_cruiser_Bl%C3%BCcher_sinking.jpg

The years in between the two world wars were difficult for Norway. Small political parties became popular, but it seems that they couldn't keep the government together for long. On average, these small parties would run their term for an average of eighteen months. Norway progressed slowly after the Great War, and it did not amount to much since another war soon broke out in Europe. As planned before, Norway immediately assumed a neutral stance. But this time, the country on Europe's periphery became a significant strategic point, and four of the Great Powers that were involved in the war suddenly needed Norway. These powers were France, Great Britain, Germany, and Russia.

The actions of Russia at the start of World War II proved that Norway was an important territory for the Western powers against Russia. Only three months after the start of the war, Russia invaded Finland under the excuse that their government was fascist and could become a power base for Germany. But the League of Nations proclaimed this attack illegal, and the fighting ended only three months later, with Russia suffering heavy losses. The Winter War convinced the Western powers of the strategic value of Norway and Russia's military weakness. It also served to convince the Nazi leader, Adolf Hitler, to launch an attack on Russia and to occupy Norway since it would serve Germany's military ambitions at sea.

On April 9th, 1940, Germany started its occupation of Norway. They needed the Norwegian harbors from which they could control the militarized Atlantic Ocean and organize a defense against Great Britain. Norway would also greatly help in transporting the iron ore mined in Sweden back to Germany. The Nazis were aware that the Allies wanted Norway for the same reasons and that their invasion had to be quick. The German invasion of Norway was so well organized and coordinated that even the Western powers admitted it was a daring and unthinkable action. All the ice-free harbors between the Oslofjord and Narvik came under Nazi control early in the morning of April 9th, and Germany suffered practically no losses. The man behind this very successful occupation was General Nikolaus von Falkenhorst, and in his planning of the invasion, he only used a Norwegian travel guidebook.

To finalize the occupation of Norway, Germany needed to paralyze its political life by capturing the king and the whole government. But the Nazis failed to do this, as their warship *Blücher* sank in the Oslofjord once it engaged in close-range combat against the guns mounted on the Oscarsborg Fortress. This delay gave the king and the government enough time to discuss the situation and decide their actions. The president of the Storting, C. J. Hambro, and King Haakon VII decided Norway should keep fighting the Nazis. The Storting then proceeded to empower the government, creating a constitutional basis for exercising governmental powers under extraordinary circumstances.

Although the government decided to keep fighting against the occupation, they were aware of the hopelessness of it. All the major harbors were already in the hands of the enemy, and most of the arsenals had been lost. The country was already occupied when the mobilization of the army started, and it was painstakingly slow. Even when the soldiers were deemed ready for the front, they had no more than forty-eight days of active training. Because Norway had assumed neutrality would always be an option, the military equipment the country possessed was outdated and in poor shape.

Soon enough, the Allies came to help Norway. Britain responded first and sent troops and military equipment to Norway by the middle of April, with French and Polish troops following behind. Together, the soldiers of Norway, France, Britain, and Poland fought the Germans in the northern regions of the country. Although they were initially repulsed, they took the offensive and freed Narvik on May 28th, 1940. However, they were under constant pressure from the Nazis, and the campaign for Narvik wouldn't end until June 7th. Unfortunately, the Allies had to withdraw their forces to use them in France, and they had to let go of Narvik, which once again came to be the enemy's possession.

When the Allies left Norway, the government had to make a difficult decision. The options were either to completely surrender to the enemy or to continue fighting without the help of the Allies. The government came up with a unique solution. Both of those options were discarded, and it was finally decided to continue the war against Germany but from outside of the country. The king and all the members of his government escaped the country and formed a "government in exile" in London.

Norway Becomes an Ally

Occupied Norway had to break away from its neutrality, and by establishing a government in Britain, King Haakon VII bound his country to the Allies. In 1905, Great Britain offered to guarantee Norwegian independence, and it was implied that Britain would defend Norway in case of an attack on its territory. This is why Norway sought to bind itself more tightly to Britain, and the Storting had this in mind when they chose the Danish prince for their king, as he was married to a British royal, Maud of Wales, the daughter of Albert Edward, Prince of Wales (later Great Britain's King Edward VII). The Norwegian royal family thus had a strong connection to the British royalty, and it was unlikely Norway would ever willfully join Britain's enemies.

The best asset the Norwegian government in exile had to offer the Allies was its merchant fleet, which managed to stay out of German hands even after the occupation. This fleet made up 18 percent of the world's tanker tonnage. Norway also had the most modern fleet in the world, and since the beginning of the war, it was contracted to the Allied war effort. In April 1940, the government requisitioned its merchant fleet and put it under the management of the Norwegian Shipping and Trade Mission in London. The merchant fleet was the economic foundation on which the government in exile managed to sustain itself. But it was also one of the strongest fleets the Allies possessed in the war against Nazi Germany. As such, it was highly respected and revered. Around three thousand Norwegian sailors lost their lives proving the worth of the merchant fleet. Norwegian soldiers also fought in World War II on the side of the Allies, and they were dispatched around Europe.

Before leaving Norway, the king and the government were sent an ultimatum by the Germans. They demanded the king's abdication and the installment of the leader of the Norwegian fascist party, Vidkun Quisling, as prime minister. At the time, the legitimate government and the king escaped to northern Norway and established the capital in Tromsø. The king proclaimed he would do whatever the Storting decided and that he would offer his abdication if the ministers chose to follow Germany's demands. However, the Storting wanted to continue fighting, and they wanted to defend their king. They refused to legitimately elevate Quisling to the position of prime minister, and because of this, they were forced to flee the country.

Germany finally managed to make Quisling the prime minister. He was the perfect choice because he was willing to cooperate with the Nazis and become the leader of the puppet regime in Norway. Germany then proceeded to prohibit all political parties in Norway except the National Union Party (which was led by Quisling). Hitler appointed Josef Terboven as Reichskommissar, giving him the power to solely appoint all ministers. The "national government" was finally established on February 1ˢᵗ, 1942, by Terboven. Quisling then became the minister president, and the Nazification of the Norwegian society began.

A resistance movement developed in Norway, and it was, in a way, led by the king in exile. Although he had little official contact with the resistance itself, the members of the resistance often wore the king's anagram on their jewelry or clothing as a sign of loyalty to the old regime. Haakon VII became the symbol of the Norwegian resistance movement, and he often used the British BBC worldwide radio network to read proclamations and encouragements to his people suffering under the Nazi regime.

The Country and Society under the Occupation

In the autumn of 1940, the Germans started the Nazification of public institutions and voluntary organizations. There were no more elections for the local councils. Instead, the Nazis appointed individuals who they saw fit. They also tried to get rid of all the clerks and civil servants who were not members of the National Union Party, or at least they tried to force the people to join the party so they could keep their jobs. The bishops and the priests didn't want to suffer this pressure, so they collectively resigned their posts. The teachers who refused to join the regime were deported to the remote parts of northern Norway.

The Nazification of the volunteer organizations proved to be an impossible job. Large sections of the public were involved in these organizations, and it became impossible for the Nazis and the National Union Party members to assert full control over them. The sporting and religious organizations were the first to resist Nazification, and they were soon joined by others. By May of 1941, around forty-three national volunteer organizations protested the Nazification of Norwegian society. The result was the replacement of organizations' legal administration with Nazi ones. The ultimate plan of the National Union Party was to use these replacements to eventually form the "National Council," which would legally replace the Storting.

Living under the Nazi regime wasn't easy for regular citizens. They were forbidden from singing the national anthem or displaying national symbols of any kind. Yet many did so in pure defiance to the occupation. Unfortunately, many people paid for this defiance with their lives. Death was a common punishment, and it was implemented even for simple disobediences, such as listening to enemy radio shows or reading foreign newspapers. Food was sparse, and rationing was implemented everywhere. The urban areas had it much harder than the countryside, as many farmers were able to grow their own food, while city dwellers had to rely on rations. Even toys, books, and furniture were rationed, as well as all imported foodstuffs. Eventually, even locally made bread, butter, milk, and vegetables were rationed.

To get their rations, each family member was given a ticket, also known as a ration book, with which they were given the right to purchase a certain amount of food. To prevent starvation, many people turned to fishing and hunting. Some urban areas were abandoned, with people moving to farms where they could grow potatoes, turnips, cabbages, and carrots. In some towns, the local administration divided parks and green spaces and allotted them to people so they could grow food. Even the flowerbeds between the street lanes were turned into potato patches.

Norway's Resistance Movement

In the beginning, the resistance of Norway was marked by the defiance of the people and the open display of Norwegian royal symbols. But gradually, the resistance started organizing itself into a movement and took military dimensions. In 1942, underground operations began, and by the end of the war, they became one of the main factors of the country's defense. The movement was named *Milorg*, a simple abbreviation of *militær organisasjon* ("military organization"). At first, the resistance only engaged in intelligence activities, both domestic and foreign. *Milorg* contributed significantly to the sea battles between the Allies and the Axis powers. The resistance also helped Norwegian refugees cross the border to neutral Sweden. Sweden alone received some forty thousand Norwegians fleeing the war. The communists in Norway had their own resistance, and throughout 1942 and 1943, they formed a guerilla military organization that specialized in sabotage.

Once *Milorg* engaged actively in the battle against the Nazis, the need for internal organization and leadership rose. They were recognized as the legitimate defense body by the Norwegian government in exile, and an attempt was made to collaborate with the British Special Operations Executive (SOE), a secret organization that coordinated various resistance movements in occupied European countries. But *Milorg* had trouble coordinating things with SOE, which resulted in a series of incidents that caused the loss of civilian lives. The main problem was that *Milorg* became an integral part of the Norwegian High Command in London, which made it answer to British Field Office VI. SOE, on the other hand, worked completely independently and was never able to coordinate events with the Norwegian resistance. SOE finally changed its policy of independence and started working together with *Milorg*. By the end of the war, the resistance gathered forty thousand militarily-ready men. The communist resistance movement remained, operating independently.

However, the Norwegian resistance movement took an active role in the defense of the country only at the end of the war. By then, most of the public institutions were under the Nazis' firm grip, even the police and the press. There was no resistance to Nazification by the local authorities and manufacturing industry. People started voluntarily joining the National Union Party, which gathered around seven thousand members at the start of the war; it had forty thousand members only three years later. Around six thousand Norwegian men joined the German armed forces and contributed to the oppression of their fellow citizens or even went abroad to fight together with the Axis powers.

Norway's civilians were constantly under the pressure of bombing raids. Many cities were continuously bombed by both the Nazis and the British. Narvik, Kristiansund, Molde, Bodø, and Elverum were almost destroyed as early as 1940. Once the Nazis started retreating from northern Norway, they used scorched-earth tactics, leaving Finnmark and Troms devastated. This was considered a national catastrophe, as many people would starve to death. The retreating Germans left only smoke and ash behind them.

After the War

World War II ended Norway's neutrality. The country realized that even though it was on the fringe of the continent, it was an integral part. Its future was deeply connected with the future of Europe. During the post-war years, anti-communist sentiment rose, especially after Russia proposed to share the government of Svalbard. Communism lost all influence in Norway after 1948 when the Communist Party performed a coup d'état in Czechoslovakia. Norway was confident in its neighbors, Denmark and Sweden, even though it had been forced into a union, first with one, then the other country, not that long before. Norway began negotiations with its neighbors to form the Scandinavian defense system. However, these plans were abandoned in 1949 when NATO (North Atlantic Treaty Organization) was formed. Norway decided to become one of its founding members. This meant that Norway was now aligned with the Western powers via a treaty.

Political life went back to normal in 1945, with the Liberal Party continuing its pre-war dominance of the parliament. But the country was devastated by the war and the five-year-long occupation. It needed to focus on reconstruction. Around twenty thousand homes were destroyed by military operations and air raids. In Finnmark and North Troms, all of the buildings were destroyed by the retreating Germans after the Russian invasion of 1944. The production lines and communication networks were neglected during the occupation, and many of them were rendered useless. Many roads and bridges were blown up, and factories were destroyed. This hampered the country's ability to rebuild itself quickly. The influential contemporary economists of Norway estimated in 1945 that the war cost their country some 17.5 billion kroner in its pre-war value.

Norway suffered heavy unemployment before the war, and the situation didn't look much better after it either. With many factories and industries destroyed, the people had nothing to return to after the occupation. It certainly didn't help that inflation was looming, especially because the German occupation took eleven billion kroner from the Bank of Norway during the war. That money was put into the pockets of high officials and never went into circulation to help the economy stand on its feet.

But the politicians at the time were aware that no matter what state Norway was in, it had to rebuild itself. The reconstruction work had to begin. The society was eager to work, and it took Norway just one year to reach the output and private consumption of the pre-war period. The manufacturing and fishing industries took two years to recover and reach the pre-war level, while agriculture did so in 1948.

The fear of unemployment proved to be unnecessary. Norway's labor force would rebuild the country, and the economy had to run under its potential. Inflation continued to be a serious threat, but the government held it in check by implementing new rationing policies and employing a strict regulatory system that was kept active until the 1950s.

With the arrival of the 1960s, Norway experienced its first general prosperity after the war. The people were finally able to devote their attention to something other than the reconstruction and rationing of products. During these years, the Norwegians could relax and start focusing on strengthening their ever-growing economy. In politics, the central place was given to the idea of a state based on society and the contribution of that society to the economy. Thus, the idea of Norway as a welfare state was born. Political stability was a major influence on this idea, as all political parties supported the principles of the welfare state. Equality soon became one of the main principles of Norway, which allowed all people to have the same opportunity to secure a good and steady income through their work. Material goods and welfare were equally distributed through society, and the state set up a safety net of social benefits, which would protect the people from poverty due to the loss of income. What made the Norwegian welfare system different from other post-war welfare states was that everyone benefited from it, not only the most endangered groups.

Conclusion

Norway is famous for being one of the most expensive countries in Europe. However, the state didn't reach this status because of its ability to rebuild and develop its economy after World War II. Many European countries could claim an amazing GDP rise and increase in their economy in the years following the war. Although Norway had a unique welfare system implemented, which would help it become one of the most prosperous countries on the continent, it didn't differ much from the rest of Europe at the time. But everything would change during the 1960s with the discovery of oil in the Norwegian waters, away from the shores. When the American Phillips Petroleum Company declared it would start investigating the Norwegian continental shelf in search of oil, the government was quick to issue a decree proclaiming the ocean floor and the underground and underwater areas of the coast under Norwegian sovereignty. This meant that any natural deposits found in these areas could only be exploited by the Norwegian state or through licensing.

In 1965, the Norwegian government issued additional decrees that regulated offshore drilling. Through these decrees, it became clear that Norway wouldn't follow the example of the United States, which distributed allocations through an auctioning system. Instead, Norway followed the British system by which the oil companies had to apply for the allocations. If approved, the government would have financial gains through taxes and royalties after the oil was found. But no oil was yet found, and

Norway needed to attract international oil companies to do research. Incredibly low taxes and royalties were set up, especially for foreign companies, as the economy at the time demanded foreign currency. But this doesn't mean Norway discouraged local companies from taking part in the new industry and its development. The biggest Norwegian shipping and industrial companies took part in the early stages of the oil industry.

In 1965, Norway allocated seventy-nine blocks, and almost all of the big international oil companies took part in the research. Only twenty-nine blocks were allocated to the foreign companies that had Norwegian partners. The first drilling started in 1966, and it was the Phillips Petroleum Company that first found oil in the autumn of 1969. The next year, they confirmed that the finding was huge. It contained 534 million Sm3 (standard cubic meters) of oil and 158 billion Sm3 of gas. This discovery was made in the southwestern corner of the Norwegian shelf, and it became obvious that more oil would be found farther north. Realizing this, the Norwegian politicians decided to increase the participation of Norwegian companies in new research and discoveries. In 1971, the Labour Party politicians established a state-owned oil company named Statoil. But this company wasn't fully operational until 1972. After the referendum in which Norwegians decided not to join the European Economic Community (later transformed into the EU or European Union), Statoil started its work.

Statoil would not only bring money to the government. It also served as a regulatory body that determined the pace of oil extraction. It checked the labor and safety standards of the industry and ensured the safety and preservation of the Norwegian environment. But to be able to control and regulate oil extraction, Statoil needed to penetrate all sectors and stages of oil processing. Norway became Europe's largest oil producer in the 1990s and the second-largest exporter. The newly found wealth from oil extraction and processing gave Norway a renewed wind to broaden the social reforms and increase the welfare system. The industry also attracted migrant workers, most of all Pakistanis who came searching for jobs on the oil platforms. The state had enough money to start large investments, such as the

National Hospital, Oslo Airport, Gardermoen Line, and many subsea tunnels that connected the country.

In 1994, Norway had yet another referendum, in which it was decided to turn down membership in the EU. Those who opposed the membership won, taking 52.2 percent of the votes. Even though the Norwegians didn't choose the EU path, the country did join the European Economic Area (EEA), allowing it access to the European international market. The EEA is strictly a commercial treaty and is different from the EU. Later on, Norway joined the Schengen Area, which allowed it to remove border controls and the usage of passports with other member states.

The discovery of oil in the waters of Norway surely propelled the country into the modern era and the 21st century as not just Europe's but also one of the world's most prosperous countries. With its intriguing history and modern ideology of equality, Norway attracts many migrants from all over the world, as well as tourists. Today, Norway is often seen as one of the best countries to live in because of its prosperity, excellent education system that results in extremely high literacy rates, welfare system, low crime rates, and general happiness of its society.

Part 3: History of Denmark

A Captivating Guide to Danish History

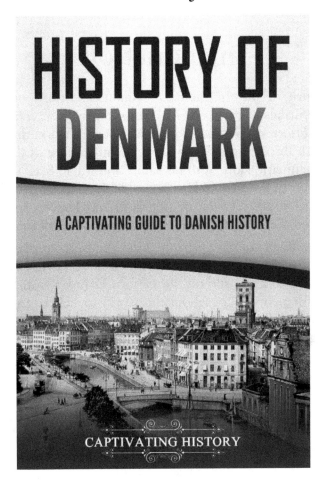

Introduction

At the turn of the 16th and 17th centuries, British playwright William Shakespeare wrote his famous play *The Tragedy of Hamlet, Prince of Denmark*. In Shakespeare's work, the heir to the Danish throne struggles to keep his inheritance as the future king of Denmark, along with his sanity and will to live. The most famous part of the play is Hamlet's soliloquy, which begins with the famous words "To be or not to be" as Hamlet speaks his thoughts on life, its turmoil, and his contemplation of suicide.

Hamlet does not have a happy life. The twists, turns, and the setting of the play (Elsinore Castle, which is the English name for the real Kronborg Castle on the eastern Danish coast) have led non-Danish people throughout the world to believe the Danes and their Scandinavian brethren from Norway and Sweden are a brooding, taciturn lot.

In actuality, over the past twenty years, the Scandinavians have been consistently considered some of the happiest and most satisfied people on the face of the earth. At the end of this book, you will find a link to the United Nations-sponsored World Happiness Report, which has named Denmark the happiest country in the world a number of times. It has been in the top five or ten since the report began in 2011.

The report reflects data on life expectancy, health, income, literacy/education, peace/war, social security, incarceration rates, and more. Over the past four years, Finland (another

Scandinavian country) has claimed the number one spot, but in 2021, Denmark was once again in the top five, coming in at number two.

We will talk more about what exactly makes the Danes so "happy" toward the end of this book. Much of this book will be spent telling you about the long and sometimes very painful and warlike history of the oldest kingdom in Europe.

Chapter 1 – Before the Vikings

Modern Denmark. "Kattegat" from the TV series Vikings is not a town but a
waterway/bay.
https://commons.wikimedia.org/wiki/File:Elling_on_denmark_map.jpg

Denmark is a small but strategically placed country. For centuries, the control of Denmark meant not only power and influence but also incredible riches due to its access to the North and Baltic Seas. The kingdoms most affected by Denmark's control of the access into and out of the Atlantic were Sweden and Russia, although every nation east of Denmark on the Baltic Sea was affected by that control.

Of the nations that lay east of Denmark on the Baltic coast, only Sweden and Russia posed a true naval threat, but that was not until the 1500s for Sweden and the late 1600s for Russia. To the west, German coastal cities and what became the Netherlands (also referred to as Holland) eventually caused naval economic competition, but this did not really affect the Danes until the 14th century when the Germans formed the famed Hanseatic League. The Netherlands would become more of a competitor beginning in the 17th century.

Of course, centuries before the Bronze Age, which began in central Europe in about 1900 BCE, the peoples of Europe were relatively isolated and lacked the ability to create true sea-going ships. Therefore, most of the raiding and trading in Denmark was done along the Danish coastline and that of modern Germany and Sweden. When we speak of "raiding" before the Late Nordic Bronze Age (the development of bronze technology came to Scandinavia about a hundred years after Central Europe), we're talking about small and sporadic tribal raids. These were not the famous raids that happened a few hundred years later during the Viking Age.

As time went by, local, regional, and national rulers built fortresses and coastal defenses to protect themselves and control seaborne traffic traveling through the straits on Denmark's eastern coasts. This did not happen in earnest until the Late Nordic Bronze Age (c. 1700–500 BCE).

The Stone Age People

Denmark has been peopled since the Late Stone Age, after the ice sheet that covered most of central and northern Europe receded some eleven to twelve thousand years ago. A series of primitive cultures lived in the area of Denmark, beginning with the hunter-gatherer cultures known as Ahrensburg (named for significant archaeological discoveries near the town of Ahrensburg, north of Hamburg, Germany) and Swiderian (for the Swider River in modern Poland). Both the Ahrensburg and Swiderian cultures were nomadic or at least semi-nomadic. They had no real permanent settlements in the area around Denmark, and it is possible they did not interact with each other.

The semi-nomadic Maglemosian culture was the first permanent culture in Denmark (including the area of today's northern Germany on/near the Danish peninsula known as Jutland). In Danish, *magle mose* means "big bog." Many finds from this culture (8000–6000 BCE) have been well-preserved by the cold, wet bogs found in the area. Scholars have found the remains of huts and the body of the "Koelbjerg Man," which was discovered in 1941 and dated to 8000 BCE

Over the millennia, a variety of different cultures rose and supplanted one another, with each making a contribution to the evolution of culture in the area. From 6000 to 5200 BCE, the culture known as Kongemose (for the village near a number of 20ᵗʰ-century discoveries) lived in much of modern Denmark. Like the Maglemosians, they were semi-nomadic hunter-gatherer people. Their stone, bone, and wood tools were more advanced than those of the previous culture, and the people had to be quite adaptive since many climatic changes took place during this time. Around 5000 BCE, the last of the Mesolithic (Middle Stone Age) cultures, the Ertebølle, spread in the area (ø sounds like the "u" in burn). The Ertebølle people developed comparatively advanced pottery making and added artistic flourishes to their work. The people of the Ertebølle culture lived not only in Denmark but also in the coastal areas of southern Scandinavia. They began to venture farther into the seas, killing whales and seals with simple harpoons. These early vessels were long canoes around thirty-five feet in length. They were sturdy enough for coastal fishing and also revealed early skills in Scandinavian navigation. Skeletal remains found in Denmark and southern Sweden have been found with arrowheads in them.

We also know that trade existed, at least on a limited and primitive level, as works from the Linear Pottery culture from the Rhine River area of Germany have been found in Denmark. Evidence of food from the northern coastal or riparian areas has been found as well. In the latter part of the Ertebølle culture, their pottery was marked by an increase in decorations, and remnants have been found throughout the area. Archaeologists have also found works from the culture that would replace the Ertebølle in Denmark: the Funnelbeaker culture. Its name comes from their pottery, which was marked by funnels and beaks for easier pouring and decoration.

The Funnelbeaker culture was important since they were the first people to inhabit Denmark, coastal Scandinavia, Germany, and Poland. They made the transition from semi-nomadic hunter-gatherers to a relatively settled farming lifestyle. They raised cattle for milk and meat, and they planted wheat and barley. They also raised pigs, goats, and sheep and used oxen to plow their fields. The Funnelbeaker culture also built early longhouses made of clay with thatched roofs. They were the first people in the area to erect megaliths to mark burial sites of men, women, and children; however, it is not known if these megaliths were marking the importance of the people or not.

The Funnelbeaker culture lasted from c. 4300 to c. 2500 BCE. They were replaced by the Corded Ware culture; they are known for the cord designs on their pottery. Rudimentary defensive works that were put up by the Funnelbeaker people have been found, which strongly suggests internal conflicts were going on while the Corded Ware culture moved in. The Funnelbeaker people soon found themselves at war with more than just themselves. Still, there may have been more than war going on between the two cultural groups, as DNA evidence has suggested that a gene that allows people to digest cow's milk has been found in the three cultures of the area: Linear Pottery, Funnelbeaker, and Corded Ware. Even to this day, southern Europeans are more likely to be lactose intolerant than their northern neighbors.

The Battle Axe Culture

The first people to be recognized as ancestors of the modern Danes (as well as the Swedes, Norwegians, and northern Germans) were from the Battle Axe culture, which appeared in the area around 2800 BCE. This culture was unique for their custom of placing small- to medium-sized stone battle-ax heads in their graves. These graves, unlike those of preceding cultures, were not communal but singular, which means they held only one body. The Battle Axe culture bodies that have been found resemble later Viking Age burials. They were highly standardized, with the men facing east and the women west. The battle-ax heads were placed north to south.

Small symbolic ax heads found in Battle Axe culture graves. Hundreds of Battle Axe graves have been found in Scandinavia, as well as about three thousand ax heads.
Terker, CC BY 3.0 <https://creativecommons.org/licenses/by/3.0>, via Wikimedia Commons https://commons.wikimedia.org/wiki/File:CordWareBoatAxe.jpg

The Battle Axe culture's DNA profile included hunter-gatherers from northern Europe, farming cultures from Anatolia (present-day Turkey), and herders from the Eurasian Steppe known as the Yamnaya people.

Another important development at the time of the Battle Axe culture was linguistics. At the time of the Battle Axe people, Indo-European languages were making their way from central Asia and southern Europe into present-day Germany and Scandinavia. At this time, European language branches began to split off. What became the Germanic family of languages developed in the area.

It is fair to say that the likelihood the Battle Axe culture was engaged in violence on a much wider scale than previous cultures was high. Aside from evidence of DNA spreading (which may have come from both consensual and forced sexual encounters), the fact that the battle-ax was so important to these people is likely proof enough. It seems highly unlikely that the ax would've been so venerated if the only thing it was used for was chopping wood.

Chapter 2 – The Nordic Bronze Age

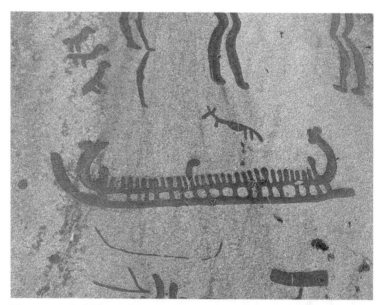

These petroglyphs in southern Sweden depict events such as raiding and animal domestication during the Nordic Bronze Age. They date from 1700 to 300 BCE and even include a depiction of what is believed to be a blue whale.

The Viking Age is the most famous period of Danish history. Literature (both academic histories and fiction), television shows, movies, and songs (there is a large sub-genre of rock dedicated to songs about or written as Vikings) are full of the same images: violent barbarian raiders who appeared out of nowhere in the late 700s CE. While it may be true that individual Viking raids did seem to appear out of nowhere on the horizon of medieval Britain and France, the Vikings and their raids did not appear "suddenly." In fact, the Viking Age was a culmination of events and developments. One of these was the Nordic Bronze Age, which took place from about 1700 until circa 500 BCE, when it was succeeded by the Iron Age or, more specifically, the Germanic Iron Age. (Iron came to northern Europe later than the rest of Europe.)

As you have read, the cultures occupying Scandinavia used walrus ivory, stone, flint, and wood for their tools and weapons. The development of bronze changed all of that. Bronze is lighter than stone and generally more durable. It's also much more durable than wood, and ivory was also used to make jewelry and other luxury items. With the advent of bronze, more ivory could be used for these highly sought-after and more valuable items. Farming became easier and more productive. For example, farmers could fasten bronze to the end of their plows, leading to deeper and more efficient planting.

Bronze was also used for everyday items, such as cups and cooking pots. Additionally, bronze was highly prized for jewelry and other decorative items. Lastly, bronze was used for weaponry, such as spearheads, swords, axes, and arrowheads. It was lighter, longer-lasting, and easier to hone to a razor-sharp edge.

The problem for the Scandinavians was that there weren't enough of the main elements that went into making bronze: copper and tin.

Roman cups found in a Bronze Age grave in Denmark.
Leif Plith, Museum Lolland-Falster, CC BY-SA 4.0

Bronze came to Germanic Europe by way of the Celtic people of central Europe, which were centered on the modern Austrian town (and tourist paradise) of Hallstatt. Known as the Hallstatt culture, the Celtic people had, among other things, a wide-ranging trade network reaching from the Atlantic coast of France to Roman territory and as far east as the Danube in Hungary. For about three hundred years, beginning in about 2000 BCE, the people of what is now northern Germany and Scandinavia traded with the Hallstatt culture for bronze. To "pay" for their bronze tools, weapons, and jewelry, the Scandinavians traded furs, ivory, and amber, which was a highly prized item that was almost impossible to find south of the North and Baltic Seas.

So, you can see that the Nordic Bronze Age marked a point in history for the Scandinavians, as they came into close contact with much of the rest of Europe. They knew of the parts that they did not trade directly with from trading with people who did. It seems as if almost every day for the last few years archaeologists have been finding new and wonderful Roman artifacts in Denmark and the rest of Scandinavia. They were brought there during the Bronze Age, as well as the time that followed (the Vendel period, named after one of the peoples in the area) and into the Viking Age.

Aside from establishing trading connections with other parts of Europe, the people of Scandinavia made the transition from semi-nomadic hunter-gatherers to settled people. Their lives were based on agriculture and the raising of animals, both for food and labor.

So, when did the people who were living in today's Denmark and southern Sweden become "Danes"? The first time that we know of the word "Dane" being used to describe the people in Denmark was in a Roman history of the Gothic peoples of the north. (The Goths were one of the people who originated and dominated the area of Sweden, along with the Svear, whose name lent itself to the name Sweden, in the year 551 CE.) Still, most historians and archaeologists used the term "Germanic" to describe the people of Scandinavia. It was not until about 700 CE that subtle but distinct differences in the people emerged, becoming Danes, Norwegians, and Swedes.

There is one mystery of the Nordic Bronze Age that has yet to be solved to everyone's satisfaction: the mystery of the Jutes. You may remember them from high school or college history courses when studying British history. You were probably told that Britain was invaded by the Angles, Saxons, and Jutes. We know that the Angles and Saxons migrated from areas of today's Germany into coastal Europe, then crossed the English Channel around 400 to 450 CE, around the time Roman rule in Britain was crumbling. At the same time, another Germanic tribe, the Jutes, also made the crossing.

For many years, historians have debated the origin of the Jute tribe. The widely accepted version is that the Jutes hailed from the Jutland Peninsula that makes up most of Denmark; it is believed that the name "Jutland" derives from the tribe's territory. The theory goes that the Jutes were forced out of their territory in approximately 200 CE by another Germanic tribe from southern Sweden: the Danes. They relocated to the Frisian coast (the coast of the present-day Netherlands and northwestern Germany), where they likely came into conflict with the Frisian people, a fierce people group that was frequently in conflict with or joined raids with the Vikings. The Jutes then voyaged to Britain. The Jutes seemed to have settled mainly in the southeastern area of East Anglia and joined with the Angles and the Saxons in their war against the native Britons.

Other historians believe that it's possible the Jutes were actually from Frisia and were pushed out by more dominant tribes. A newer theory holds that the Jutes were from the mountains on the border between Norway and Sweden, northeast of today's Oslo. They moved to greener pastures in Denmark (Jutland) and from there went to Britain. If you can recall your history classes, you might remember that after the Britons had been either killed or pushed into present-day Wales, the Jutes disappeared. They were most likely absorbed through marriage and cultural assimilation by the dominant Angles and Saxons, who merged to become what we know today as the Anglo-Saxons.

Though we don't see the use of the word "Dane" until 550 CE in a Roman work, it is likely that the Danes became a separate people group between 200 and 250 CE, when they separated from the other Germanic tribes living in Sweden and moved to what is now Denmark.

The culture that developed in Denmark, like those in Sweden and Norway, was based on the tribe and the clan. Danish society was divided into three main classes, though some suggest there were more. These were the tribal chieftain and his family, free people, and slaves. Slaves were sometimes traded for or seized from surrounding areas. The Danes "raided" before the Viking Age, though this was done mostly overland.

By the time the Danes became a separate people group, they had developed into fierce warriors whose religious beliefs had already evolved to include the notion that dying a brave death would lead to everlasting life. We have seen how the earlier Battle Axe culture had made a weapon (or a smaller replica of one) into one of the most important symbols of their people; it was so important that people were buried with one in preparation for the next combat-ridden world.

As you may know, the Germanic people that the Romans came into contact with south of Denmark along the Rhine fought differently than they did. The Romans fought in highly disciplined formations and were commanded by non-commissioned officers and commissioned officers. Germanic tribes generally fought en masse, not in disciplined individual formations. They may have been told where to go by their chieftains, but when the battle began, the Germans fought as individuals. While Roman soldiers, of course, recognized an individual's bravery, for the most part, awards or mentions went to the unit, not a man. Germans fought for honor and prestige, both in this world and after. Prowess as a warrior could make a commoner a ruler, as word of his prowess on the battlefield could spread far and wide.

The myths that would develop over time and become today's Norse mythology exalted war, combat prowess, cunning, and bloodshed. The gods watched men as they fought. It is safe to assume that even the most average Germanic warrior was a force to be reckoned with.

Of course, the Danes and other Germanic tribes of the time did not always fight "foreigners" or members of other tribes. Sometimes, disputes between individuals or groups took place. When they did, they were often settled by violence, a certain amount of which was sanctioned by the tribe. However, when this inter-tribal violence threatened to spread, chiefs called for a *thing*. The *thing* was a meeting of all the freemen of the area or tribe; there, problems from food supplies to violent feuds were settled. The *thing* developed long before Viking times, and these meetings have often been depicted in movies and TV shows.

The Germanic longhouse, a communal building, also predated the Viking Age. The longhouse could be the home for the chief and his family, but it was also a communal space where daily matters were discussed, children were communally cared for, and people and animals took shelter during rough weather. There might be a smaller longhouse in a larger village, which would be the home for a local chieftain, and the buildings would grow in size depending on the social stature of the inhabitant and the importance and size of the surrounding settlement.

Though the many Viking-related programs (both dramatic and documentary) today talk about the Viking tradition of cremating a dead warrior in a longship, these "boat-burials" often did not take place at sea. While some of them did include interment in an actual vessel, most of those excavated by archaeologists were boat-shaped stone burial plots.

In either case, the person buried was more than likely an important, powerful, and respected person. Whether a Bronze or Viking Age person, they were surrounded by weapons, treasure, bones, or actual sacrifices. These sacrifices could be animals or people. They were usually slaves, but occasionally, children with finer clothing or jewelry were discovered. This means they were likely a family member who died at the same time, probably from sickness. Most of these burial sites have been found in Norway, though a number have been excavated in Denmark.

Chapter 3 – Vikingr

Vikingr is Old Norse for "Viking" or "Vikings." It is believed by many that a Viking was simply a man who lived in or near a bay, as *vik* is the word for a body of water. It may also have meant someone from the town of Vik in today's Norway, though it's not possible that all Vikings came from that small town on the coast. No matter what its origin, "Viking" has become synonymous with the warriors who began to raid the coasts of western Europe and a large part of western Russia and Ukraine.

For those of you who are unfamiliar with the Vikings and their story, Captivating History's *History of the Vikings* will give you a better overall picture of the Scandinavian warriors. Our purpose here is to give a basic outline of the history of the Danish Vikings. To do that, we will first discuss a couple of things about the Vikings in general before telling the stories of their most well-known leaders.

As we mentioned at the end of the prior chapter, the people of Scandinavia built longhouses for their chieftains and their families. The size of the longhouses seems to have been based on the importance of both the individual ruler and the importance of the settlement they were located in. Naturally, a great king, such as the great Danish Viking Harald Bluetooth (yes, the technology is named for him), would have had a larger longhouse than one of his loyal chieftains in a remote part of Denmark. More than likely, any local leader building a larger longhouse was challenging the overlord and was likely a fool.

In Norway, in 2018, archaeologists discovered the remains of the largest longhouse found so far. It was rebuilt and added to over the years, beginning in about 700 CE, shortly before the Viking Age began. It measures 220 feet long and 33 feet wide. That's more than two-thirds the length of an American football field. We also know that at least some of the Viking elite used lime-based paint to cover the walls of their longhouses. The most widely accepted theory is that this was done to impress visitors. A clean, shining home would imitate the hall of Odin in Valhalla, the afterlife awarded to Vikings slain in battle. The whitewash might also have served to brighten the days and nights of the long Scandinavian winters.

The longhouse was also the center of local Viking life. It would have been used for safety in times of danger (yes, Vikings raided other Vikings), for meetings about communal events, and for a plethora of other things. One thing is for sure, especially in the case of the giant longhouse mentioned above: the great halls of Viking leaders, like the castles and fortresses throughout the world at the time and later, were meant to awe visitors with the owner's power and wealth.

Remember, much of what we know about the Vikings does not come from the Vikings themselves but from firsthand accounts of foreigners (the famous account of Arab traveler Ahmad ibn Fadlan describes his experiences with Swedish Vikings in Russia), secondhand accounts written by Viking enemies (most often by the literate clergy of western Europe, who were certainly biased), and the sagas. The sagas were typically written much later than the events they describe.

More than likely, Viking leaders traveled with a retinue, most of whom were bodyguards, though family members, servants, and slaves would be there as well. From the outside looking in, it makes sense that a Viking lord would travel with berserkers as his bodyguard, but that's probably not what happened. From what we know, the berserkers were likely outcasts in Viking society. While, of course, there were likely famous or esteemed warriors that did go "berserk" in battle, most of those considered to be berserkers were likely antisocial and somewhat dangerous people to be around. They were also unpredictable. In other words, they were not bodyguard material. Accounts of berserkers include them killing their comrades accidentally while in a rage in the heat of battle.

"Berserk" means "bear-shirt." Some believe that these warriors wore actual clothing made from bearskins, which did happen in the cold north. However, what makes the most sense is that the term is a metaphor. When a warrior entered a trance-like state before battle, which was usually brought on by alcohol, bloodlust, or hallucinogenic mushrooms, he put on the "bear-shirt." In other words, he "clothed" himself in the attributes of the bear: he was insanely strong, fast, and vicious. The Ulfhednar, those who became wolves, were considered berserkers; they can be seen in the Netflix series *Vikings: Valhalla.*

Though the longhouse and the berserkers are synonymous with the Vikings, nothing says "Viking" more than the famous Viking longships, sometimes called dragon-ships for the carvings on their prow. Viking longships were fast, had a shallow draft that allowed them to sail upriver, and were purposely made to be flexible, as the Vikings did not want them to easily break apart in rough seas. At the time, the Viking longship was the height of shipbuilding technology, at least in Europe.

We know the warriors from Scandinavia by other names besides Viking. In English and French accounts, they were often referred to as "Northmen" or "Norsemen." The former is an accurate term, as the Vikings came from the north, but the latter name would technically only describe warriors from Norway. Since the words are similar, both today and back then, it is easy to understand the confusion. Besides, no literate monk was going to ask one of the Vikings where they were from and what they preferred to be called. In the heat of the moment, Danes became Norsemen, and Norsemen became Danes. The Swedes were often called "Rus" from the Finnish word *Ruotsi,* meaning "rowers." (However, some believe the word "Rus" comes from the inhabitants of what is now Russia, who called the Swedes "red" for their red hair, beards, and ruddy complexions.)

The Danish Vikings raided mostly to the west—the eastern coast of England and France. However, it's more than likely that, given the close ties between Viking clans in different areas, there were Danes on Swedish voyages to the south and on Norse raids to the northeastern and western parts of England, Ireland, and Scotland.

The popular TV series *Vikings* depict Ragnar Lothbrok (Lodbrok), a legendary Viking chieftain, as a Norwegian whose home was Kattegat, the name of a body of water that lies between Denmark and Sweden. (Ragnar may or may not have existed; it is thought that Ragnar may have been a conglomeration of many Viking legends.) Dane and Swedish legends have it that Björn Ironside was one of Ragnar's sons. Therefore, it's highly doubtful that the Great Heathen Army was motivated by vengeance for the murder of Ragnar. It was more of a giant war party whose aim was not merely riches but also settlement and perhaps the conquest of England itself.

As you likely know, the Anglo-Saxons of Wessex under Alfred the Great (r. 871–899) and his descendants were, at one time, the only Anglo-Saxon kingdom left in England. For a time, the Danes and a number of Norwegians ruled East Anglia, Mercia, and Northumberland. This was the famous Danelaw, the territory in which Danish law was prominent.

This simple map gives a good idea of the extent of the Danelaw. In Scotland and the area around Liverpool and Chester, the Norsemen seem to have been more numerous than their Danish brethren.

Hel-hama, CC BY-SA 3.0 <https://creativecommons.org/licenses/by-sa/3.0>, via Wikimedia Commons https://commons.wikimedia.org/wiki/File:England_878.svg

Who were some of the more famous Danish Vikings? One of them was Guthrum (c. 835–890). Although Guthrum is depicted in the Netflix series *The Last Kingdom* as a treacherous and disloyal man, he was likely no more disloyal than any other Viking of the time. He was a leader in two armies. A large raiding force took place in the spring and early summer of 871 known as the Great Summer Army, and it joined forces with the famous Great Heathen Army, which had landed in England five years before and was waging a campaign to take over England.

Guthrum was a nephew of the Danish King Horik II, and he likely was an accomplished warrior in his own right. By the time he met up with the Great Heathen Army, Guthrum was thirty-five, which was relatively old, both in general for the time and specifically for a Viking warrior. In the winter of 878, Guthrum led a surprise attack on Alfred's court at Chippenham, which was a great defeat for the English. Alfred was forced to take to the marshes for safety.

Unfortunately for Guthrum, he was captured at the Battle of Edington later in 878. He was forced to convert to Christianity to save his life and status, and he was eventually given lands in East Anglia, which he governed for Alfred. He also had to fight future Viking raiders should they come. Guthrum's Christian name was Æthelstan (for those of you familiar with the series *Vikings*, Æthelstan, an English monk, was a main character for the first three seasons). Guthrum maintained peace in his area, though isolated raids did occur. He must have been greatly respected since he was recognized by both the English and Northmen as the "king" (under Alfred) of East Anglia.

A similar situation occurred in France some forty years later. This one involved the famed Rollo, who is also a main character in *Vikings*. Rollo's name in Old Norse is Hrolf Ganger, which means "Hrolf the Walker," as he was reputed to be so tall that he could not sit on a horse without his feet dragging on the ground (hence, he walked). Most evidence points to Rollo being a Dane, though many believe he may have been Norse. In 911, King Charles the Bald of France gave Rollo and his warriors land in what became Normandy ("land of the Northmen") to bribe them to stop raiding and defend France. Rollo's great-grandson, Richard II, would be the first official duke of Normandy about one hundred years later.

In the early 900s, the English began a campaign to take back the land under Danish law. In 954, the last Danish king in England, the treacherous Eric Bloodaxe, was killed in battle. While the Danelaw still existed under local Danish rulers, they all swore fealty and paid taxes to the English king, who at this time was Eadred (r. 946–955).

This situation lasted until 1002 when English king Æthelred the Unready (when translated from Old English, his actually means ill-advised, not unprepared) decided to launch a campaign on St. Brice's Day (November 2nd) to eliminate all of the Northmen in England. Today, this is known as genocide. His desire to do this didn't come out of thin air. The Viking raids had increased, but Æthelred was also deeply into spreading the Christian faith. He also sought to rule all of England without Danish help. Æthelred's forces killed an estimated twenty to thirty thousand Danes and Norwegians. One of the dead was the sister of a Danish king with a formidable reputation named Sweyn Forkbeard.

For the next ten years, Sweyn and his men, as well as other Vikings who were encouraged by Sweyn and the promise of great riches, land, and vengeance, raided England with increasing ferocity. With the help of English ealdormen, who changed sides due to bribes, dissatisfaction with Æthelred's rule, and/or threats, Sweyn took control of London and the area around it. Sweyn's son, Cnut, would go on to even greater heights and become known as Cnut the Great (c. 994–1035). Many times, especially in accounts written in the 19th and early 20th centuries, Cnut (or Canute) is depicted as something of a madman, standing or sitting at the edge of the ocean as the tide rolled in. Cnut became the master of not only Denmark but also England, Norway, and parts of Sweden. His power was unrivaled, and the early stories say that Cnut stood in front of the waves, commanding them to recede, only to be disappointed that his power was not *that* great. However, the more likely story, which is still probably apocryphal, has Cnut going to the water's edge to show the earls and generals around him that his power *was* limited, no matter how much they might believe otherwise.

Cnut was not a madman; he knew the limits of his power, which was indeed immense. After the death of his father, the English king Æthelred was invited to return to England by his former ealdormen and the first Norwegian king to convert to Christianity, Olaf Haraldsson. Olaf led an attack on London Bridge and then helped drive out the Danes from London and the area around it, which was their stronghold in England. Cnut, who had become the master of London after his father's death, decided to return to Denmark and solidify his rule there but not before massacring his English hostages and leaving them to rot on the beach as a warning.

In that same year, 1015, Cnut returned with a large fleet of two hundred ships and perhaps ten thousand men. Over the next year, Æthelred's heir, Edmund II (sometimes known as Edmund Ironside for his success in repelling a number of Danish attacks), and Cnut waged a vicious war for control of England. Æthelred died in April 1016, making Edmund the new king. In October, Cnut and Edmund fought the vicious Battle of Assandun in Essex. Though Cnut and the Danes were victorious, it was a costly battle, and Edmund vowed to continue the fight. With this being the case, Cnut and Edmund came up with a reasonable solution: Edmund would rule Wessex (the area south of the Thames River, at least generally speaking), and Cnut would rule the rest of England.

For Cnut, the only problem left in England was the territory of Northumbria, which had formerly been a kingdom but was now an earldom under the English king. However, the earl of Northumbria, Uhtred, refused to recognize Cnut's authority. Cnut's allies assassinated Uhtred in his own hall, and Cnut ruled all of England except Wessex. (You might recognize some of the strands of the story from Bernard Cornwell's books on Viking Age England and Netflix's interpretation of them in *The Last Kingdom*). In late November 1016, Edmund II died, and Cnut, with the support of the English lords in Wessex, became the king of England shortly after.

Cnut's early rule was marked by actions that could only be described as "Viking" in nature. He gave a sizable amount of land that had been taken from the English nobles to his Danish allies. He also had Edmund's brother, Eadwig, killed; a number of Englishmen were killed, as Cnut believed they might give him trouble in the future. One of these men was the powerful Mercian lord Eadric Streona, who had turned against his kinsmen to join Cnut and then seemed to engage in plots to make himself king.

One of the Viking chieftains allied with Cnut was known as Thorkell the Tall, and he was given authority over East Anglia. Thorkell was a member of the Jomsvikings, which can best be described as a Viking version of the later Knights Templar, an order of fanatic Christian knights that rose to prominence in the 1100s. The Jomsvikings were reputed to be fanatic believers in the Norse gods and were some of the greatest warriors at the time. Eventually, the Jomsvikings were defeated in 1043 by Magnus I of Norway, as they had become less of a religious military order and more mercenary in nature. They had contributed to a lot of instability in the region.

Thorkell was apparently an untrustworthy and/or power-hungry man. He had aided Æthelred in his conflict against Sweyn Forkbeard and then switched sides to aid Cnut. By 1021, Thorkell had apparently begun to plot to become king himself. He was removed from power by Cnut and sent back to Denmark, where he died shortly thereafter.

By 1018, Cnut had either distributed enough English lands or paid off his men to their satisfaction. In that year, a new chapter in England began. Cnut began to entrust more of his realm to English nobles, and Englishmen outnumbered Danes on his privy council. Cnut also maintained English laws and traditions in the country and his court. When he needed English help to put down problems in Denmark in 1019, he got it. In 1027, he and Scottish King Malcolm I came to terms. The Scots recognized Cnut's overlordship of their land, but he never truly ruled their country.

In Denmark, in 1026, Cnut's brother-in-law, Ulf, attempted to seize control, uniting with Swedish and Norwegian lords to do so. Through warfare, diplomacy, and bribes, Cnut managed to gain control of lands in southern Sweden and all of Norway. One of the most famous battles of the later Viking Age was between the forces of Cnut and those of Norwegian King Olaf Haraldsson. At the Battle of Stiklestad on the Norwegian coast, Olaf was defeated. After being wounded, he fell off the prow of his ship and succumbed to the waves. Cnut titled himself the "King of all England and Denmark, and the Norwegians, and some of the Swedes." What was known as the Great Northern Empire was created, though it did not survive long after Cnut's death in 1035.

Cnut is remembered, not only in Denmark but also in England, as a wise and fair king. And by all accounts, this seems to be true. Adding to his prestige was his meeting in Rome with the pope and the Holy Roman emperor, where he was seen as an equal, at least in terms of temporal (earthly) power.

Cnut died in 1035 and was succeeded by his son Harald, which is usually spelled the English way as "Harold." He ruled for a short five years and was followed by Cnut's youngest son, Harthacnut, in 1040. Harthacnut was not his father; during his reign, the Danish rule in England weakened. When Cnut the Great died, the son of Olaf Haraldsson, Magnus I, became the king of Norway, depriving Harthacnut of a large portion of his kingdom. Harthacnut died in 1042; he was the last Viking king of England. The English put forward Edward the Confessor, the son of Æthelred and Emma of Normandy. She had married Cnut after the English king's death, making Edward Harthacnut's half-brother. Edward was one of the last Anglo-Saxon kings of England, dying in 1066, shortly before the Norman Conquest.

The Great Northern Empire of Cnut the Great was short-lived, but it illustrates the power of Denmark, which would only continue to grow in the next several hundred years.

Chapter 4 – Christianity

Since the time of the great Frankish Emperor Charlemagne (r. 800–814), the Danes and other people in northern and central Europe had had to deal with the expansion of Christianity. Charlemagne sought to eradicate pagan beliefs from most of Germany. Some historians consider Charlemagne's wars against the Saxons to be genocide, as likely tens of thousands were killed during the Frankish emperor's campaign. Many others were forced to convert at the tip of a spear, and anyone caught reverting to their pagan ways would suffer a grisly death. It even got to the point where Christianized children reported on parents and other relatives.

By the 900s, most of Germany and parts of today's Austria and Poland had been Christianized by the Franks. Fortunately for the Danes, Charlemagne's sons and later descendants were too concerned with fighting each other than to carry out the Christianization of Denmark. That was not the only factor, though. By the time of Charlemagne's death, the Danes and other Scandinavians had become a mighty force that terrorized much of Europe from the 800s onward. This means the Frankish kings had little time or ability to worry about making Denmark and Norway Christian.

In England, the Vikings' numbers matched well against the divided forces of the Anglo-Saxons. But they would have little hope against a united Frankish empire determined to spread

Christianity. The Franks outnumbered the Danes, and the Vikings were not equipped to deal with a full-fledged land campaign on the border of their homeland.

To keep the enemy at bay while they raided, the Danish Vikings took the prudent step of building fortifications throughout the southern part of their homeland. In the late 7th century, the Danes began building what has become known as the Danevirke (Danework), a series of deep trenches, walls, and the occasional tower to keep the Danes safe from an attack from the south. Over the centuries, until the late 1800s, the Danevirke was added to, eventually becoming a formidable line of defense. Only the coming of modern warfare in the mid-1800s made it obsolete.

Within Denmark and southern Sweden, which may at the time have been "Danish," we know of seven Danish ring fortresses, which are also known by the Old Norse name Trelleborg ("fort built by slaves"). These forts have been dated to the Viking era, specifically during the reign of Harald Bluetooth (r. c. 958–986). These fortresses were quite large and peopled not only by warriors stationed there to guard the territory but also by their families, livestock, and slaves. These fortresses might have had intimidating armies, but they were likely a magnet for traders from other regions of Europe. They also attracted missionaries.

At first, there was just a trickle of monks traveling into Denmark. Some were never heard from again, at least at the beginning of the Viking Age. Later, as the Scandinavians became more exposed to Christian people and ideas and as their contact with more of Europe increased, a number of Vikings converted to the new faith.

Arguably one of, if not the most, successful Viking of all, Cnut the Great, was Christian, although he did not hesitate to war with other Christians when it was to his advantage. Just a short time before Cnut's rise, the idea of a Christian Viking would have been an oxymoron, but by the first decade of the 2nd millennium, more and more Vikings were converting. For some, Christianity, with its tale of a resurrected son of an all-powerful being, sounded familiar to the Norse. In Norse mythology, Baldur, the son of Odin, the All-Father and supreme deity of the Viking universe, was said to rise again after his death set in motion Ragnarök, the final battle between light and darkness. After the gods and the forces of darkness (giants, the goddess of death, and the damned who died a coward's death) had destroyed themselves, Baldur would be resurrected as the god of light, and a new age would begin. Some Scandinavians based their conversion to the new religion on this, and it was a notion that many of the monks were more than happy to let the Vikings believe. (As a side note, conversion was a much easier process in Denmark and Sweden than it was in Norway, where it took another one hundred years and much more bloodshed.)

The first Danish king to convert was the aforementioned Harald Bluetooth, who likely improved the Danevirke and built a number of the ring fortresses. He eventually converted in the 960s. By the time he did, a large segment of the population was already Christian and, for the most part, existed side by side. One archaeological discovery that helped advance this idea was a blacksmith's mold dating from the period, which could make crosses and Thor's hammer.

A number of theories exist about why Harald Bluetooth chose that moment in time to convert. Some say that he had become a true believer, that he actually continued to believe in the "old ways" while acting Christian, or that he did so for political and economic reasons. Christianity seemed to be dominant in Europe. The Christian nations were powerful and more technologically advanced, especially in regard to architecture. But perhaps most importantly, these countries seemed to be tremendously wealthy.

Raiding could bring you quick riches, but raiding was much less regular and more costly than trading. Many people are under the impression that the Scandinavians of the Viking Age were either raiders/warriors or farmers. We know that some of the largest trading centers in northern Europe were off the coast of Sweden and Denmark and that Scandinavia was economically tied to places as far away as India and possibly China. Within Europe, trading with other Christians seemed to bring better terms and an early form of "most favored nation" status for its traders and kings.

Over the course of the next century, the Danes rapidly converted to Christianity. To many in the country, the tide seemed to have turned against the old gods, as those who held on to the old ways found it in their best interest (economically, militarily, and spiritually) to move on from Thor, Odin, Freya, and the rest. In Sweden, a relatively similar process occurred. Despite some incidents, on the whole, Sweden's conversion, like Denmark's, was relatively peaceful, especially when compared to the conversion process in Norway, which included civil war, forced conversions, and violence on a large scale. The Norwegians didn't become a Christian kingdom until the 1100s.

Chapter 5 – Margaret, Queen of Denmark, Norway, and Sweden

The Viking Age came to a rather abrupt end in 1066 when the last great Viking warrior, Norwegian Harald Hardrada ("hard ruler"), attempted to assert his very tenuous claim to the English crown upon the death of Edward the Confessor. Harold Godwinson defeated Hardrada. It is believed that Harold Godwinson was named Edward's successor on his deathbed. Unfortunately for Harold, he had previously sworn to the duke of Normandy, William, that he would honor William's own claim to the English throne while he was William's "guest" in Normandy after a shipwreck on the Norman coast. But after returning to England, Harold forgot all about his promise and moved to make himself king, necessitating William's successful invasion. Harold would die in the famous Battle of Hastings, marking a new age in England.

In the years between 1066 and the formation of the Kalmar Union, which consisted of Denmark, Norway, and Sweden, in 1397, Denmark began to withdraw back into itself. When the Danes lost England after the death of Harthacnut, Norway separated, and only a part of southern Sweden belonged to Denmark. By the 1100s, Denmark had turned inward to a degree, though it did become tremendously wealthy due to its position as the "gatekeeper" of the Baltic Sea. Denmark also benefited, at least for much of the time, from being closely involved and located near the growing economic powerhouse cities of northern Germany, which began to rise to prominence in the late 1100s. These independent German city-states would unite in one of the world's first commercial trading blocs. They were known as the Hanseatic League, and it would both support and war against Denmark in the coming centuries.

By the middle to the late 1300s, Denmark was still a power to be reckoned with, but its direct influence was not felt throughout Europe as it once had. With the Danish kingdom reduced in size (though it did hold lands in southern Sweden, which were populated mostly by Danes and, to an extent, German traders), most of its international affairs had two purposes. The Danes wanted to make money, which was becoming more difficult due to competition from the Hanseatic League, and prevent other powers, such as England, Russia, and the Hanseatic League (which had armies and navies of its own, including well-paid mercenaries), from reducing Denmark's power and territory.

Margaret (or Margrethe) was destined to unite the Scandinavian people, but not in the way her father had envisioned. Her father, King Valdemar IV of Denmark, knew, like so many rulers, that a noblewoman's value came not from anything she achieved herself but from the connections, wealth, and potential children she could bring to a union. Most marriages in the Middle Ages, at least within the European nobility, were not matters of love but of politics. A local chief might marry his daughter to a neighbor and rival in order to end a feud or gain access to land. It was not that different at the top of society: kings and queens married their daughters off to gain a political advantage. If their daughter was both pretty and knowledgeable, it was easy to make a match. Most of the time, pretty was good enough. Wars could be ended or new alliances made to gain an advantage. Riches for a much-sought-after princess would change hands. The boundaries of territories might change, and new kingdoms formed that would change world history.

Initially, that was Margaret I of Denmark's role to play. She was betrothed at the age of ten to Haakon VI of Norway, who was sixteen years her senior. There was no expectation of any sort of physical intimacy until after the marriage, and Margaret stayed with her father until she became of child-bearing age.

Margaret's marriage to Haakon was intended to place the three Scandinavian countries under one crown. Haakon was the son of Magnus IV Eriksson (the Swedish royal naming protocol has the number before the last name), who was the king of Norway and Sweden. At the time, Sweden did not include all of the Scandinavian Peninsula as we know it today, as this was Danish territory. It was expected that Haakon would become king after the death of Valdemar IV.

The union of the ruling houses of Denmark with that of Sweden and Norway would also put one of Denmark's and Valdemar's rivals, the noble family of Mecklenburg, into contention for the Swedish throne. No matter how careful one is, something unexpected usually happens. In this case, the Swedish nobility, who had a say in who became the king, did not want to take the chance with Magnus and find themselves under Danish control. At the time, Denmark was a more powerful and prosperous kingdom than Sweden, and many Danish kings had had their eyes on conquering Sweden.

So, the Swedish nobles on the royal council forced Magnus out and invited Albrecht of Mecklenburg to become the Swedish king. Unfortunately for Denmark, Valdemar, who had reunited Denmark when it had defaulted on its debts and was temporarily under the sway of the Hanseatic League, was not a popular man. The Swedes allied with the Norwegians, some Danish nobles, and the Hansa (a common term referring to the Hanseatic League). They forced Valdemar to relinquish certain rights he had unilaterally imposed on the passage from the Baltic to the North Sea (this included taxes, tolls, fishing rights, and right of passage, among other things). The Hanseatic League also forced Valdemar to give it certain commercial rights in Denmark and a say in the succession to the Danish throne. The Danes were not happy about this outcome. By the time of his death in 1375, Valdemar had succeeded in putting down a number of rebellions in Jutland and was in the process of making an ally out of Pope

Gregory IX in order to strengthen his position and that of his dynasty. However, he passed away on October 24th before he could make that a reality.

When Valdemar died, his daughter Margaret maneuvered behind the scenes to get her son Olaf named the king of Denmark. The political skill Margaret showed to get her son named king should have been (and probably was) a sign that she was a force to be reckoned with. On top of that, Margaret arranged to have herself named regent, and she ruled Denmark from that point onward, even after the death of her son and the adoption of her sister's eldest son, who became Eric VII. Margaret was the true power behind the throne in Denmark.

Some historians have called her the first great queen of Europe, but for many years, she was overlooked and ranked under other great European queens, most notably Elizabeth I of England and Isabella I of Spain. While she might not have world-shaking effects like these other women, Margaret managed to stabilize an unstable region and unite the Scandinavian people together in a union that lasted into the 19th century (albeit in different forms). Margaret was intelligent and had the best education available to a woman of the time. She also must have been a keen observer and quick learner, as she spent her years before joining Haakon in true marriage watching and listening to the palace intrigues in Denmark. She observed the ebb and flow of war and became acquainted with the men in power.

In 1387, Margaret and her son Olaf were about to launch an attack on Sweden on the basis of what they believed were better claims to the Swedish throne than what Albrecht of Mecklenburg had. By this time, Olaf had come of age and ruled with his mother. However, just before the invasion was to be launched, Olaf died of a mysterious illness. (In 2021, an excellent Danish movie, *Margaret, Queen of the North*, was made. It includes the story of the "false" Olaf, a pretender who asserted that he was Olaf and that he had never died; much more is made of this story in the movie than occurred in real life, however.)

When Olaf died, Margaret adopted her sister's son and was named regent of both Denmark and Norway. During 1387 and 1388, Margaret worked with disenchanted Swedish nobles who were angry at Albrecht, as he had given their lands to his allies and Germans from the Hanseatic League. The Swedish nobles joined Margaret and named her Sweden's "sovereign lady and rightful ruler." A war with Albrecht was inevitable. Although Albrecht was strong in the southeast of the country and on Sweden's islands in the Baltic, he was ultimately defeated. He was captured by Margaret's forces and held prisoner until the forces loyal to him surrendered six years later.

By 1389, Margaret was the ruler of Denmark, Norway, and Sweden (as well as Finland, which was a Swedish possession). Being a monarch in the 14th and 15th centuries was not easy, and that goes double for a woman with actual power. Though Margaret was called insulting names, sometimes even in front of her by opposing nobles (such as King Breechless or "King without pants"), she was admired by many and inspired loyalty. There were other names that were not so denigrating, such as Lady King and Semiramis of the North, the latter of which is derived from a legendary queen of Babylon.

In 1396, Eric was declared king, but all the power rested in the hands of Margaret. At Kalmar, located on the coast of southern Sweden, the queen attempted to forge an official union of the Scandinavian countries in 1397. Each would have a king that would act as a governor of their respective countries, but Margaret would be the overlord or empress, so to speak (this word was not used, though). One of the issues that were left unsettled was whether the kings would follow the laws and customs of their own countries or be told what to do by Margaret. This was never settled to anyone's full satisfaction, but as long as the kings were responsive to the military needs of the Kalmar Union, Margaret did not mind too much if the kings oversaw local laws.

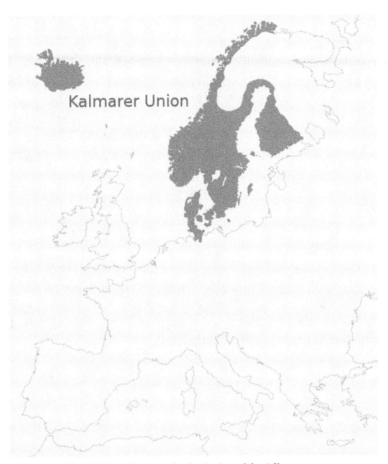

Kalmarer Union

The Kalmar Union at the beginning of the 16ᵗʰ century.

NordNordWest, CC BY-SA 3.0 <https://creativecommons.org/licenses/by-sa/3.0>, via Wikimedia Commons https://commons.wikimedia.org/wiki/File:Kalmar_Union_c._1500-de.svg

The Kalmar Union was declared when Eric was made king of Denmark, Norway, and Sweden on June 17ᵗʰ, 1397. The union was a tremendous achievement for the time. For all intents and purposes, it ended when the Swedes under Gustav I Vasa (considered the "Father of Modern Sweden") rebelled and successfully split Sweden from the union and became the Swedish king in his own right in 1523. Though Norway eventually became more of Denmark's vassal than a partner, the Kalmar Union, at least in name, continued through 1814, which was when Sweden took Norway. In 1905, Norway split from Sweden. Although the Kalmar Union had been dead in any real sense since the 1500s, all traces of the union ended at that time.

From the time of the Kalmar Union until the day Margaret died in 1412, she had gradually assumed more and more power. She limited the power of the nobility, especially in Denmark, and gained great power in the country by establishing a system of local sheriffs and constabularies to keep order and keep an eye on potential enemies. She also levied taxes on some church properties, which at the time was almost unheard of, although she maintained good relations with the pope. She also worked hard to limit the influence and power of the Hanseatic League, whose cities were on or close to the Danish border. Just before her death, she entered into a war with the Duchy of Holstein, a much-disputed territory before her time and long after she was gone. Margaret died before the war ended.

Today, Margaret is seen as a great uniter of the people, though she was authoritarian at times (it's almost impossible to see her succeeding back then without being so). Today's Danish queen took the name Margaret (or Margarethe in Danish) at her coronation in honor of the "Lady King."

Chapter 6 – Christian II

A bit more than one hundred years after Margaret's death, the Kalmar Union, at least as she had envisioned and formed it to be, ceased to exist. There were a number of problems with the union. First, Scandinavia is huge, spanning thousands of miles—and that's just the coastline. At the time, it was not possible to know with any certainty or swiftness what was happening in every corner of the union.

Second, the kings of each nation, barring Denmark, might have felt their interests did not side with Danish interests. One of the biggest reasons for Sweden's break from the Kalmar Union had to do with Denmark's interactions with the Hanseatic League. Denmark bordered or was near many Hanseatic cities and had many economic interactions with them. The relationship between Denmark and the Hansa was a balancing act and sometimes led to bloodshed. However, in Sweden, which was farther away from the Hansa, there was resentment. The Hansa merchants had become quite powerful in Sweden and had even been granted their own lands by various kings at the expense of Swedish noble families. In some places, German merchants were essentially governing Swedish towns, which was much resented. Additionally, the Swedes felt they had enough economic clout on their own due to commodities like furs, endless timber, and amber that no one else had. They did not want to go through Hansa middlemen and wanted the profits for themselves. They also did not want to be dragged into a war because the Danes and the Hansa demanded it.

Third, despite the similarities in language and culture, the Danes, the Swedes, and the Norwegians were not the same people. They had their own customs and traditions. While the Kalmar Union did not attempt to change those customs, the fact that Sweden was ruled by a Danish ruler often made the Swedes feel like second-class citizens.

When Margaret died, her nephew, Eric VII, became the true king of the Kalmar Union. However, he was unpopular, especially in Sweden, where a rebellion caused the nobles of all three countries to force him off the throne in 1439. For about ten years, the local lords ruled their countries, but disorder and disagreement about the succession forced a temporarily but weak reunion of Kalmar with Norway. This first happened under Christopher of Bavaria, who had family ties in Denmark, and continued until Christian II became the king of Denmark.

Christian II is one of the most controversial kings in Danish history for a number of reasons, which we will discuss in a moment, but his main claim to history was his determination to reform the Kalmar Union as it had existed during Margaret's time. To do that, he had to conquer Sweden. At the time of his enthronement as the king of Denmark and Norway, Sweden was in a state of near civil war, with various nobles vying for the throne or increased power. A number of them wished to rejoin the union, but to do so would cause a full-blown civil war in the country. When Christian was crowned, the Swedish delegation was asked what their position was. They replied, "We have the choice between peace at home and strife here, or strife at home and peace here—we choose the former." The question of who would be the king of Sweden would be postponed until the Swedes decided on a king for themselves, accepted Christian as their monarch, or were conquered by the Danes. They could not do the former, would not do the latter, and Christian began his campaign against Sweden in 1517.

Within Sweden, two main factions existed. One faction was the anti-Danish faction, which consisted of nobles and their followers led by the powerful regent Sten Sture the Younger, who had ambitions to become king himself. Opposing them was the faction that supported uniting with Denmark. This faction was led by Archbishop Gustav Trolle.

Romantic Era painting of Christian II and his mistress Dyveke Sigbritsdatter, a commoner whose mother became the king's advisor after her daughter's death. Christian was married to Isabella of Austria, with whom he had three children.
https://commons.wikimedia.org/wiki/File:DyvekeSigbritsdochter.jpg

To strengthen his position, both within Sweden and with the Catholic Church, Christian asked for the support and blessing of Pope Leo X, who came from the powerful and wealthy Medici family of Florence, Italy. With the pope's help, Christian put together an invasion fleet in 1517 and sailed for Sweden to relieve the siege of the archbishop's fortress. Christian was defeated, and what's more, he was humiliated; many of Sture's men were peasant levies, not the professional or semi-professional soldiers that Christian had brought with him. The next year, Christian was back again with another fleet and thousands of soldiers. Once again, he was defeated, this time at the bloody Battle of Brännkyrka near Stockholm.

By 1520, Christian had amassed an even larger fleet. In addition to Danish soldiers, he hired a number of mercenaries from France, the German states (Germany was not a country until 1871), and Scotland. Christian was victorious in two battles: the Battle of Bogesund on a frozen lake in January in which Sten Sture was killed and a follow-up battle near the important Swedish royal city of Uppsala. A long siege of Stockholm led by Sten Sture's widow and consequent negotiations caused Christian to accede to the wishes of the Swedish nobles, agreeing that Sweden should be governed according to Swedish law and customs.

This is where things get really interesting, and it is where Christian made a fatal error, at least as far as his future as the king went. Three days after Christian's coronation as king of Sweden, the king's ally, Archbishop Trolle, declared that all of the nobles who had opposed him during the war were heretics and needed to be brought to trial for their "crimes" against the church. Christian, who was naturally paranoid and a cruel man to begin with, saw this as an opportunity to cement his rule in Sweden for the foreseeable future.

Christian summoned all of the nobles who had followed Sten Sture to a meeting at Stockholm Castle for the long festivities celebrating his coronation. Sten Sture, who had died at the battle on the lake in 1520, was declared a heretic. By custom, those who had sworn an oath to Sture were, therefore, declared as guilty as their leader. They were arrested on the spot, and over the course of two days, eighty to one hundred Swedish nobles and village elders were beheaded or hanged, including two bishops who had been enemies of Archbishop Trolle. This should have gotten Christian into hot water with the pope, who was his supporter, but the king blamed the deaths on soldiers who had "gotten out of hand." This episode in Scandinavian history has been referred to as the "Stockholm Massacre" ever since.

One of the victims of the massacre was Erik Johansson Vasa, a nobleman from north-central Sweden. His son was Gustav I Vasa. Gustav was a man of immense strength, cunning, and determination. He eventually defeated Christian in the Swedish War of Liberation (1521–1523). Today, he is known in Sweden as the "Father of Modern Sweden."

Christian was an interesting man. Although he was undoubtedly murderous, he was also a man with a keen intellect. However, certain reforms got him in hot water with the Danish nobles, who eventually rebelled and forced Christian into a relatively luxurious exile in the castles of Sønderborg and Kalundborg.

In 1521, while Gustav Vasa was busy in the hinterlands of Sweden putting together an army, Christian II visited the Netherlands, which was, as it is now, one of the most modern European nations. He even met the great philosopher Erasmus and secretly converted to Protestantism, though he reverted to Catholicism upon his return to Denmark four months later.

When Christian returned to his kingdom, he issued two royal edicts: the Town Law and the Land Law. The Town Law reorganized the trading system in Denmark, which was only to be done in the towns (as opposed to on nobles' lands or homes, for example). The towns were to be governed by the king's appointees. This also made tax collection both easier and faster. Additionally, the Town Law forbade nobles from selling or trading peasants. (Since the late 1100s and early 1200s, peasants had been treated almost like slaves in Denmark, as they were tied forever to the land they were born on and had no real rights). The peasants were also given the right to negotiate their terms of tenure (how long they would work and wages, for example) with the nobility. Though it was designed to weaken the nobility, Christian's Town Law was an early step toward real reforms. It should be known that Christian's mistress and her mother were both commoners, which likely had an effect on Christian's attitude toward the peasant class.

The Land Law was likely a result of Christian's visit to the Netherlands and his exposure to the ideas of Lutheranism and Protestantism. Christian declared that priests could marry in Denmark, and some rights of the church were taken over by the state. Though the peasants and traders of Denmark approved of these reforms (Christian was known by some as "Christian the Good"), the powerful nobles and higher clergy did not.

Worse still, as far as Christian's position as king was concerned, he raised tolls on traffic through the many waterways controlled by Denmark that led to the North Sea and the Atlantic. Some of those who had to pay tolls came from the powerful Hanseatic cities of Lübeck (almost on the Danish border) and Danzig (on today's Polish coast). These cities allied themselves with Gustav I Vasa in Sweden and, in combination with the disenchanted Danish nobles, finally overthrew Christian. They voted in a new king (this time just of Denmark and Norway), Frederick (Frederik) I, who reigned for nearly ten years until 1533.

Chapter 7 – The Protestant Reformation in Denmark

During the Late Middle Ages, the European economies grew at an amazing rate. The establishment of the double-entry ledger (which counted not just the inflow but also the outflow of wealth), the expansion of trade through the building of roads and canals, and the beginning of the international credit system meant that Europe, especially western Europe, was becoming vastly wealthy.

With that wealth came a higher standard of living, more institutions of higher learning, and, of course, corruption. Corruption had been an age-old problem, but with the immense wealth being amassed, individuals and families could buy positions of power or even rise to rule a kingdom. You have already read about this happening with the Hanseatic League, which was an economic union of a number of northern European cities (mostly German, but there were also Dutch and Polish areas) that banded together for both profit and protection. From the 1300s to the early 1500s, the Hansa cities became powerful enough to tip the balance of war and even make or break kings. Though the Hansa cities were not corporations as we know them today, the Hanseatic traders and others, such as the famous Dutch East India Company, had many similarities to today's business world. Making business even more profitable was the development of the early stock market in Antwerp in

1531. This idea quickly spread throughout northern Europe and increased profits.

These ideas, along with the discovery of the Western Hemisphere, increased trade, and colonization in Asia, allowed even small countries like the Netherlands to become amazingly rich. Denmark also became wealthy; its control of the many straits leading out of the Baltic gave it power and riches beyond its size. And combined with modern developments like corporations (the Danish East India Company, which began in 1616, is one example) and credit systems, the control of the Danish Straits made Denmark one of the more wealthy and powerful countries in Europe, at least until the early 1600s.

With all of this wealth, there is no wonder that corrupt and greedy individuals took as much advantage of the economy as they could. For many honest individuals, especially in the rising middle class of Europe, the corruption was tolerable, if not excessive. At times, riots and uprisings by the middle or lower classes erupted. Although these disturbances sometimes resulted in change, they often ended with the rioters being put down harshly, at times with barbaric violence.

While corruption among the upper classes and the newly developed non-noble upper middle classes (such as the Medici in Florence and the Fuggers and Rothschilds in today's Germany) was common and more or less expected, it was difficult to tolerate corruption in the Catholic Church. Though much of eastern Europe was Orthodox Christian, its unity, influence, and power were not as great as that of the Catholic Church, which had an elaborate organization under the rule of the pope. The pope was (and still is) seen as the representative of Christ on Earth by Catholics. There were also Christian sects, such as the Copts, in places like Egypt and Ethiopia, but they were much smaller in both believers and power than the church in Europe.

That being said, for all of western and central Europe, the Catholic Church was the *only* church. Economists will tell you that when a person or group of people has absolute control of the market, corruption (both in terms of economics and power) occurs. The Catholic Church had grown in power since the legalization of Christianity by Roman Emperor Constantine in

313 CE. To the Europeans, the Catholic Church was the only way to reach heaven.

For centuries, the popes in Rome had rivaled the great kings and queens in power and wealth. Corruption had always existed, but by the early 1500s, people throughout Europe were questioning not only the church's behavior but also its monopoly on God. You see, the Bible and all other important Christian documents were written in Latin. Sermons were delivered in only Latin. After the demise of the Western Roman Empire in the 400s, more and more people began to speak their own national languages and not Latin. Latin became the language of diplomacy and the upper classes (for a time), and it was the only language in which the Word of God was printed. Parishioners had to take it on faith that their priest or bishop was teaching them the Bible's lessons correctly. The people could not generally access the Bible for themselves, even if they were a part of the increasingly small minority that spoke Latin. Imagine going to church every week—some went every day—and having the sermon be delivered in a language you could not understand. This alienated the people from having a personal relationship with God and Christ and alienated them from the clergy and church.

In the early days of the Catholic Church, priests, bishops, and even popes were allowed to marry and father children. In the early 1100s, the church banned priests from getting married, insisting they remove themselves from "worldly desires" as much as possible. Priests were the most numerous and visible agents of the church, and this edict was enforced more on priests than it was on bishops or archbishops (many of whom came from rich, influential, or noble families), the College of Cardinals in Rome (the body that administered church doctrine and law and advised the popes), and the pope himself.

All the way up the ladder of the Catholic hierarchy, officials had mistresses or women who were all but wives in name. Some also kept company with women "of ill repute." Many bishops, cardinals, and a number of popes had children.

This did not please many, but it was tolerated to a degree, depending on the country and time. What finally broke the Catholic Church's monopoly on religious beliefs was corruption.

In the last chapter, we mentioned how Pope Leo X aided Christian II's conquest of Sweden. The pope loaned money to the Danish king to secure his power, which was not uncommon. However, Leo X was from the Medici family of Florence, who had risen from obscure wool traders outside Florence to arguably the richest family in all of Europe (the wealth of the Medici circa 1464 was equal to about 110 billion US dollars today). Florentine politics had forced Giovanni di Medici, who took the name "Leo X" on becoming pope, and his cousin Giulio, who became Pope Clement VII in 1523, into exile for some time. While these men were not poor by any means, they did not live according to their former standards while away from Florence. When Giovanni became Pope Leo X in 1513 and his cousin became a cardinal and papal advisor, the church entered into a period of corruption that had never been seen before.

Aside from Leo X's unbelievably lavish dinners that were the 16th-century equivalent of Hollywood's parties and galas today, he was a great collector and sponsor of art. He was responsible for commissioning Michelangelo's Sistine Chapel, among other famous projects. He also spread the wealth to his friends and supporters in other countries to influence events. No one is quite sure how much wealth Leo X spent, borrowed, and squandered, but it was a vast amount—so vast that it threatened to bankrupt the Catholic Church. And that's where a monk from the German town of Eisleben enters our story.

The immediate impetus to Martin Luther's rebellion against the Catholic Church was the sale of indulgences. An indulgence was essentially a "get-out-of-jail card" (in this case, jail was hell) for Catholics who felt they had sinned. An indulgence was simply a slip of paper that essentially forgave a certain sin for a price. So, if you commit a sin, you could just buy your way out of it. For minor sins, such as eyeing your neighbor's wife with lust, a smaller price was paid. If you needed a blanket indulgence for the past year, you would have to pay a higher price. If you were a noble, you would likely buy your way out of a number of sins for a higher price than a peasant. And the people believed this slip of paper would save their souls.

You might be wondering why. Most people still believed in both the infallibility of the church and its representatives. Since indulgences were approved by the pope, who was Christ's representative on Earth, most people believed in them. Making the con even worse was the fact that virtually none of the average people and many nobles could read Latin, so they had to take the clergy's word for it. Those in opposition to the sale of indulgences, such as Martin Luther, saw what was happening. The priests, monks, and other clergy who were selling indulgences were taking advantage of the poor and ignorant to line the coffers of the church and their own pockets. Charlatans even posed as clergy to make a quick buck.

Indulgences had existed for some time, but Leo X used them to full effect. Within a relatively short time, his coffers were being filled again, and since the mid-1400s, with the development of the printing press, the church could turn out indulgences in what would have been unimaginable numbers.

Indulgences were the main reason for Luther's rebellion against the church, but there were others. Luther knew of the corruptions plaguing the church, which included bribery, violence, and sexual abuse.

However, there were other more theological issues that Luther had issues with. One of them was the Catholic Church's monopoly on the Bible and other holy works. In Luther's eyes, the people were subject to the interpretation of others; the clergy could twist the words of the Bible to suit their needs very easily. Luther also had issue with one of the bedrock principles of the church: that faith alone was enough to see one's soul into heaven. "Faith without works is dead" was one of the guiding principles of Luther's Reformation. It was not enough to simply say one had faith in God and Christ; one also had to show it. Most of the clergy (especially the parish priest, monks, and nuns) did do good works every day, but at the top, corruption and the disregard for the poor were ruining the church from within, at least according to Luther and others.

On All Hallows' Eve, Luther nailed what has become known as his *Ninety-five Theses* on the doors of the main church in Wittenberg, Germany. With that, the Protestant Reformation began. The *Ninety-five Theses* was a call for reform within the church, not a call for a break with it and the pope. But after

Luther refused to renounce his statement, he was excommunicated (removed from the church, with the caveat that all Catholics shun or arrest him for heresy on sight).

Within a short time, Luther's ideas spread. He was supported by many disenchanted clergy in other parts of Europe, especially in the north. However, the ultimate success of the Reformation was dependent on European rulers who were willing to support the ideas with protection, money, and arms. The pope and many Catholic rulers were determined to stamp out the Reformation everywhere it presented itself. Of course, the violence was not one-sided. Many people now believed that Catholicism was completely corrupt and that they had been learning false lessons for generations. They used violence to attack their Catholic neighbors. (One of Luther's first deeds after his proclamation was to translate the Bible from Latin into German, something that was done in other areas, including Denmark. This allowed the ideas of Protestantism to spread more rapidly.) A century after Luther posted his *Ninety-five Theses*, the Thirty Years' War broke out; it was one of the costliest wars in European history.

How does this relate to Denmark? Well, no country, especially in the central and northern parts of Europe, where the ideas of the Reformation were strongest, was left untouched by the immense changes. Denmark experienced the beginnings of its Reformation in the early 1520s. While many of Luther's ideas seeped into Denmark between the time of his posting of the *Ninety-five Theses* and the 1520s, it was not until the Bible was translated into Danish in 1524 by linguists and philosophers Hans Mikkelsen and Christiern Vinter that the ideas of the Reformation became incredibly popular in Denmark.

Imagine a world where religion was the most important aspect of individual and social life for the vast majority of people. Then, imagine that the roots of that important aspect were hidden (in this case, behind Latin), so one had to take the word of the church as to both the Bible's contents and its interpretation. Once the Bible was translated into Danish and other languages, people could access the Word of God for themselves. They often did not like what they read, at least as far as the church's behavior was concerned.

One of the more immediate results of these translations was riots against Catholic churches and cathedrals on the grounds that Catholicism practiced idolatry, the worship of false idols. Christ preached against this practice in the New Testament. Idols included the elevation and portrayal of Mary (the mother of Christ), the Crucifixion, and the worship and veneration of relics, such as pieces of the True Cross, Christ's crown of thorns, and the bones of saints. Even the concept of sainthood began to be rejected since the elevation of a person to sainthood was dependent on the pope and possibly bribes paid to high church officials. Worst of all, at least for the Catholic Church, was the rejection of the pope as the representative of Christ on Earth.

The leading Danish reformer and theologian was Hans Tausen, who met and stayed with Martin Luther in Wittenberg for a year and a half. Luther was able to stay there because he had the protection of a local lord.

Viborg Cathedral in central Denmark.
Naveen Kadri, CC BY-SA 3.0 <https://creativecommons.org/licenses/by-sa/3.0>, via Wikimedia Commons https://commons.wikimedia.org/w/index.php?curid=27494947

Tausen was a well-traveled man and had been to present-day Belgium and Holland, where he spoke to some of the early Humanist philosophers, who were developing ideas about the place of mankind in the universe separate from God (to a degree, as one had to be very careful at this time), human nature, and the future of human society. Tausen spoke not only Danish but also

German, Latin, and Hebrew, which helped him immensely in both his translations and his subsequent orations on the ideas of the Reformation.

In 1525, Tausen was summoned back to his monastic order, which turned him out due to his refusal to reject the ideas of Luther and the Reformation, whose adherents had begun to be called Protestants- (those who protested against the church). He then moved to the Order of St. John in Viborg, where he delivered electrifying sermons to rapt audiences, some of whom traveled a day or more to hear him speak.

Eventually, however, even the relative patience that the Catholic Order of St. John had ran out. Tausen gave up his robes and went to the rulers of the city to ask for their protection, which was granted to him. For a time, he preached in the city's parish church, but eventually, so many people came to hear him that people were standing in the streets.

His next sermons took place in the city's marketplace, which was within earshot of not only those who wished to hear him but also those who did not. A proposal to allow Tausen to preach in the large church of the Franciscan Order was refused. Those supporting Tausen broke down the doors and surged in. With the situation about to turn seriously violent, an agreement was reached between Tausen and his supporters and the Catholic order. Within a short time, this compromise proved to be too much for the Catholic hierarchy. The local bishop summoned an armed crowd from the surrounding area and sent them to arrest Tausen and whatever followers they could lay their hands on. Because the situation was so tense, many of his followers had weapons with them, and the men sent to apprehend Tausen were turned back.

Statue of Tausen at Ribe Cathedral today.

Vincent Simar, CC BY-SA 4.0 <https://creativecommons.org/licenses/by-sa/4.0>, via Wikimedia Commons https://commons.wikimedia.org/wiki/File:Statue_of_Hans_Tausen_in_Ribe.jpg

At this point, there were concerns that the violence would spread. The last Catholic king of Denmark, Frederick I, intervened and invited Tausen on a tour of the large port of Aalborg and made him one of his own chaplains. Though Frederick never renounced Catholicism, his openness was both criticized and lauded by the Danes, depending on their spiritual outlook. The king told Tausen to return to Viborg and give sermons. The people of the city were made responsible for his safety. One must remember that this was a time when even the most enlightened monarchs still used torture regularly, so this was a big step for Frederick to take. Denmark was still a majority Catholic nation, and any leaning toward Protestantism could affect both trade and Denmark's security. Frederick also had gone against his own oath, which stated that he would always be faithful to the church. Thus, doing this was a big risk.

Tausen began delivering his services only in Danish and began to create hymns and other worship songs in his native language. Sometime in the late 1520s, Tausen took an even further step away from Catholicism by marrying the sister of another reformer (his partner in creating Danish pamphlets about religion).

By this time, some of the Catholic orders in Viborg began to flee the city, and Tausen began to preach in the abandoned church of the Dominicans. Additionally, his standing-room-only sermons filled the Franciscan church, which the monks relinquished to him at the point of a spear carried by Frederick's soldiers and townspeople. It was only a matter of time, given the temper in Viborg and other Danish towns, before violence would flare up. This was happening not only in Denmark but also in much of northern and central Europe, including Norway and Sweden.

It was only a matter of time until Tausen began giving his sermons in Copenhagen (København in Danish), Denmark's beautiful capital. When he first arrived in Copenhagen in late 1529, Tausen was met with resistance from the city's bishop, who was accompanied by angry supporters. Fights ensued between Catholics and those who had followed Tausen to the city, as well as residents of Copenhagen who had read his pamphlets and were eager for him to speak. Though the Catholics prevented Tausen from speaking at the popular Church of St. Nicholas, Protestant crowds ran wild through the city, shouting insults at the church and the Catholic clergy. They ran into Catholic churches to destroy icons and paintings they deemed idolatrous.

The situation grew so serious, and the threat of civil war was so great (at least in the capital) that the Herrendag, the "Assembly of Nobles," met on July 2nd, 1530, to find some compromise between the two groups. Today, Tausen might be called a fanatic, as he did nothing to discourage the riots and demonstrations by his supporters while the assembly was meeting.

Over the next three years, this very tense situation remained in place until Frederick I died in April 1533. At that point, the Catholic hierarchy took matters into its own hands. They arrested Tausen, brought him before the Herrendag, and convicted him of blasphemy and expulsion from another parish where he had been speaking at the time. When the news was heard by the growing number of Protestants in the country, mob violence began in Copenhagen. The mob besieged the Herrendag and threatened to kill the clergy and nobles should Tausen not be released. This time, Tausen made the first move and calmed the crowd down. They escorted him to safety, and within a short time, the bishop in charge made an agreement with Tausen. He could preach safely as long as he toned the violent rhetoric. Tausen agreed.

In 1542, Tausen was made the bishop of Ribe (a Danish city), and he held that position for twenty years. Over those two decades, and with the help of his supporters and like-minded clergy throughout the country, Protestantism became the dominant Christian sect in Denmark, and it still is today. Most Danes do not attend church except for once a year for Christmas and maybe Easter, yet they do willingly pay a tax for the upkeep of the many medieval churches throughout the country.

Chapter 8 – Christian IV

There has been more than one queen of Denmark, but after Margaret I (r. 1387-1412) and until Margrethe II (r. 1972-present), Denmark's ruler was a man. Beginning with Christian II, the son of King Hans, in 1513, Danish kings have alternated in taking the names Christian and Frederick.

Many historians and Danes believe that the greatest Danish king was Christian IV, who ruled Denmark from 1588 to 1648. Though he was only eleven when he took the throne, his reign lasted sixty years, dying just shy of his seventy-first birthday.

Contemporary etching of Christian IV (notice the hair braid) by Willem Delff.
Courtesy Royal Collection Trust of the United Kingdom;
https://commons.wikimedia.org/wiki/File:Christian_IV._mit_Titel.jpg

Christian was the son of Frederick II. Frederick had lost the Northern Seven Years' War (1563-1570) to Sweden, which means he failed in his attempt to restore Sweden to the Kalmar Union and lost some coastal territories to the Swedes. Frederick had also reformed the Danish tax system, which brought more money to the crown. This allowed him to rebuild the Danish Navy, which went on to defeat Scandinavian pirates. Frederick also improved the fortifications on the Sound (in Danish, Øresund), which controlled access into and out of the Baltic Sea. This, in turn, brought in more coins. By the time Frederick's son became king, Denmark was once again a prosperous nation. However, Frederick also had a cruel streak, which provides an interesting and very Gothic story.

In the aftermath of the mysterious death of the husband of Mary, Queen of Scots, in 1567, Frederick was asked to deliberate on the fate of James Hepburn, 4th Earl of Bothwell. He had been accused of taking part in the death of Henry Stuart, Lord Darnley, who was the husband of the queen. (Mary was believed by many to have played a part in her husband's death. Bothwell had gotten Mary pregnant with twins who were stillborn, though Mary later accused him of rape.) Bothwell and Mary fought a war against the many rebellious Scottish nobles, which went badly for the couple, who had aspirations to rule all of Britain. Mary surrendered, and Bothwell was "allowed" to escape to Scandinavia. This was a long journey, and he was eventually captured in Norway and brought to the Danish king.

Frederick had good relations with both England and Scotland, and he was asked to deliberate on Bothwell's fate to avoid disputes in Great Britain that might lead to war. Bothwell had been found guilty in Scotland, but it was up to Frederick to decide his punishment, which was exceedingly cruel. Bothwell was chained to a post in the dungeon of Dragsholm Castle, west of Copenhagen, in 1573. He died an insane man after having spent five unbelievably miserable years at the bottom of a Danish castle.

Though this cruel streak did not appear in Christian IV's personality, he was at times ruthless when he needed to be, such as when he ordered Danish troops into war with the Protestant German states in the Thirty Years' War against the wishes of his nobles in 1624. This ended poorly for Denmark, as it had to be rescued by its Swedish rivals (against whom Christian had lost in 1613) in order to prevent the loss of too much territory.

Christian had won victories over the Germans and had also proved himself in battle on land and sea in his youth. He even lost an eye in battle later in life. But his losses during the latter part of his reign cost him both his reputation and prestige, though, luckily for Christian and Denmark, he did not lose territory.

However, unlike most rulers in history who lost important wars and battles, Christian not only maintained his throne but also enjoyed popularity at home. The Danes best remember him for his popularity, as he began a series of changes that would echo down to the 20th century. He has been given the name "Renaissance King." The Renaissance is thought to have begun in Italy in the mid-1300s, so one would think there should have been a "Renaissance King" by the time Christian took the throne. The Renaissance came to Denmark and the rest of Scandinavia in the 1400s, long before Christian IV came to the throne. But certain things happened during his reign that make him stand out.

First, there was a reflowering of ancient thought in Denmark during the Renaissance. This was helped immensely by the invention of the printing press in nearby Germany around 1450. However, the many wars with neighboring Sweden and the Hansa cost the Danish Crown much treasure. Their money was spent on defenses and keeping kings in power, which means their wealth was not spent on the patronage of the arts, letters, and sciences. Also, though there were, of course, painters and sculptors in the Renaissance period in Denmark, the greatest period of Danish visual art would come in the latter part of the 1800s and early 20th century. For instance, the famous statue, *The Little Mermaid*, by Edvard Eriksen (1876–1959), was created during this time; it stands in Copenhagen today. The same was true for the written word. The world knows the name and works of Hans Christian Andersen (1805–1875), who wrote "The Little Mermaid," and Karen Blixen (1885–1962), who is best known for the famous autobiography *Out of Africa* and many short stories. The famous philosopher Søren Kierkegaard (1813–1855) was also a Dane.

In the visual realm, the greatest impact the Renaissance had on Denmark was in the many churches and cathedrals that were built or rebuilt. Two prime examples of this are Roskilde Cathedral and Kronborg Castle.

Roskilde Cathedral
CucombreLibre from New York, NY, USA, CC BY 2.0
<https://creativecommons.org/licenses/by/2.0>, via Wikimedia Commons
https://commons.wikimedia.org/wiki/File:Roskilde_Cathedral_aerial.jpg

Another factor affecting the arrival and influence of the Renaissance in Denmark was the establishment of Protestantism. The Catholic Church encouraged the expression of the visual arts during the Renaissance period with religious works, such as Michelangelo's famous Sistine Chapel and *The Last Judgment*). This encouragement bled into other areas, such as portraiture and ancient and mythological themes. However, one aspect of the Reformation was the rejection of what many saw as idols. The rejection of any likeness of a person or the divine had an immediate dampening effect on the spread of the visual arts in not only Denmark but also Norway and Sweden. After Martin Luther, other more militant reformers arose, most notably John Calvin in Switzerland. Calvinism was a more extreme branch of Protestantism, and while it was rejected by the mainstream Protestant Church in Denmark, many Scandinavians embraced the stoic, grim, fatalistic, and determined sect. Many have called Calvinism a "joyless" sect. Although this is an overstatement, the advancement of Protestantism, with its frowning outlook on artistic expression, prevented the visual arts from fully blooming in Denmark and elsewhere in northern Europe for at least a century and a half, if not more.

So, why was Christian IV called the "Renaissance King?" "Renaissance" means "rebirth," and in much of Europe, this "rebirth" had to do with the arts and letters. So, although Christian suffered defeats in war and died a somewhat bitter man, he reformed and restructured the Danish economy, reformed aspects of its society, and built (and rebuilt) universities, churches, and public buildings throughout Denmark. He provided both scholarships and loans to students personally. He also founded new castles and palaces, some of which were at the cutting edge at the time. "Renaissance King" also alludes to the fact that, at heart, Christian was a "Renaissance man," as he valued learning and had many interests.

Christian even founded entire towns and cities, the most famous of which was Kristiania, better known as Oslo today, the capital of modern Norway. Though he commissioned the establishment of various cities, he also took part in the design and layout of some of the towns named for him. The port of Christianshavn (*havn* meaning harbor in Danish) in Denmark, which has been subsumed by the growth of Copenhagen, and Kristiansand in western Norway were established by and named for him, as were Kristianstad and Kristianopel in Sweden.

Personally, Christian was loved by most of his people, though his son-in-law did lead a rebellion of nobles that resulted in the diminishment of his power. He was seen as a Falstaff-like character to many. He was larger than life, a lover of beer, a prankster with a joke at the ready, and a man of action. Christian also studied Latin and theology, grilling prospective candidates for the upper clergy for their knowledge of Scripture, theology, and Christian history. He developed new types of guns and undertook to test them himself for both safety and effectiveness. He was also a truly able sea captain and had taken part in a few sea battles as a young man. He joined his admirals and shipbuilders in designing and testing his warships.

Christian lost money, men, and prestige due to his military defeats, though luckily for both Denmark and the king himself, by and large, Danish lands were not lost. The reestablishment of Danish rule in the now German state of Schleswig-Holstein was also a result of Christian's rule. Denmark, as a nation, took a giant step forward during Christian's reign due to his efforts or to the weakening of monarchical power, which evolved in the 19th and 20th centuries to become a fully-fledged constitutional monarchy.

Sadly for Christian, he died an unhappy man at the age of seventy in 1648. He had been born into a warrior family, so he was extremely disappointed that his efforts to grow Danish influence, power, and territory came to naught.

Chapter 9 – Danish Life and Changes in It, From Top to Bottom (1700–1814)

In 1647, Christian IV's eldest son, who was also named Christian, fell ill and died. In 1658, Christian IV's eldest surviving son, Frederick III, who had become king in 1648 after his father's death, signed the Treaty of Roskilde, ending the Second Northern War with Sweden. This defeat cost the Danes their remaining holdings in southern Sweden and two valuable provinces in Norway. They also lost the island of Bornholm in the southeast of the tip of the Swedish peninsula. This was a valuable fortress and fishing and agricultural area. While the Danes eventually regained the island (it is still Danish today), the end of the Second Northern War essentially marked out the European territories Denmark holds today. At this time, Iceland was Danish (it gained independence in 1944), as was Greenland (it is still officially part of Denmark but has a great deal of autonomy) and the Faroe Islands, which is halfway between Scotland and Iceland (it is an autonomous territory today).

Frederick III in 1656 by Karel van Mander.
https://commons.wikimedia.org/wiki/File:Frederik_III_i_rustning.jpg

Though Denmark would take part in wars after 1658, for the most part, the conflicts were few. Successive Danish governments since then have largely concentrated on peaceful pursuits. Repeated defeats by Sweden from the mid-1500s and then the rise of Prussia in northern Europe and its subsequent leadership in uniting the German states as one nation (1864–1871) meant that, in population, riches, and territory, Denmark was no longer able to initiate wars as it had previously. One glaring exception exists in 1864, which we will talk about in Chapter 11. (As a side note, by the mid to late 1600s, Sweden had risen to be a great power in European affairs. It was supported by an excellent military and had kings who were ahead of their time strategically, tactically, and politically. This ended with the Swedish loss at Poltava in Ukraine to the Russians under Peter the Great in 1709.)

Christian IV's defeats and efforts to concentrate more power in the hands of the monarch at the expense of the nobility caused a backlash. The nobles of Denmark wrested a considerable amount of power back from the monarchy by the end of Christian's life in 1648. Under Frederick III, who inherited his father's dislike of the nobility, major changes would occur in the structure of the Danish upper classes and the people.

While the Danes naturally played a political (and, to an extent, military role in northern Europe from 1658 onward and built strong defenses to prevent attacks, the focus of the monarch, the nobles, and the people gradually turned inward.

To a large degree, Frederick blamed the nobility for the defeats against Sweden during both his and his father's reign. The nobles filled the officer class and were his top commanders. To a degree, "donations" that financed the war came from the nobility, although they may have been coerced in one way or another to donate. The nobility had been exempted from taxes for some time.

In the 1400s, there were around 250 noble families in Denmark. Christian IV took measures to strip many nobles of their rank, and by 1640, the number of noble families had been reduced to 140. As you can see, there were many reasons why the nobles wished to wrest political power from Christian during his reign, which was successful to a large degree.

Frederick was determined to regain the power his father had lost. He used threats, promises, and the prestige of his position to gain support for a decree in which he pronounced the monarchy "hereditary for all time." This means that the king or queen had to be one of his descendants. This not only guaranteed the title for his lineage, but it also meant that Frederick would rule as an absolute monarch, as would his future children, grandchildren, etc. Shortly thereafter, the Danish nobles were stripped of most of their tax exemptions. One of their remaining exemptions, paying tax on their land, was removed by Frederick's son Christian V (r. 1670–1699) in 1688.

Another one of Frederick III's reforms was his opening of the bureaucracy to "commoners." These men (and they were only men) were "common" in the sense that they were not of the nobility, but they were not small landholding farmers or shoemakers. These "commoners" were of the growing middle class who lived in the cities of Denmark. Today, the majority of these men would be considered upper class or even part of the "1 percent," but at the time, in virtually all European countries, the middle class was very small. These were men of wealth who did not hold titles. Frederick's reform was a revolutionary change in Danish affairs, considering the centuries of traditions and laws broken by this action, and set the nation on the path that resulted in the amazingly egalitarian Denmark of today.

These middle-class bureaucrats would come to head the king's "colleges" (in this case, a synonym for "government department") of commerce, war, the navy, and finance. They would administer these areas for the king and would also serve as an advisory cabinet to the monarch. These men helped devise a new tax system that would take Denmark into the 1800s, and they worked with the king to promulgate a written, formal nationwide law code. Elements of this code took power or at least prerogatives out of the hands of the nobles.

One of the many results that came from adding men of ability rather than birth to the government infrastructure was Denmark's defenses were strengthened. Though Denmark's time of offensive warfare was over, it was still surrounded by nations that had proven themselves hostile many times in the past. From the early 1600s through the early to middle part of the 1700s, Sweden's search for power, riches, and influence brought it into conflict with Denmark. Now that the Danes had lost southern Sweden to the Swedes, there was very little preventing the Swedes from attacking Denmark directly. So, the Danes built a growing series of fortifications on its coastline and southern borders in the area of today's Germany. At the same time, the Danes also spent much money modernizing their navy, which, along with the forts lining the Sound, would ensure Denmark controlled access from the Baltic to the North Sea and out into the Atlantic.

Sofia Magdalena by Carl Gustaf Pilo.
https://commons.wikimedia.org/w/index.php?curid=52113251

In 1780, under Frederick III's 3x descendant Christian VII, Denmark signed a neutrality agreement with Russia, the Netherlands, and Sweden. The Swedes were the main concern, but in 1766, Swedish King Gustav III married Danish Crown Princess Sofia Magdalena. It was an unhappy marriage, but it went a long way to establishing peaceful relations with the two former enemies.

Before we move on to the changes within Denmark itself, we should at least mention Denmark's empire in the Western Hemisphere. The Danes acquired the islands of St. Thomas, St. John, and St. Croix in 1672, 1718, and 1733, respectively. (Today, these islands are known as the US Virgin Islands, which were bought from Denmark in 1917 during WWI.) These islands, especially St. Croix, were rich in sugar, a commodity that was in high demand. To grow, harvest, and package this and other crops, Denmark, like the other European nations with colonies in the New World, used slaves. By 1740, about 90 percent of St. Croix's population was enslaved people.

During Viking times, the raiders seized slaves from every area they raided and sold them in their and other territories. A large number of these people were Irish, but many were from today's England and France. The Danes also sold or bought enslaved people from the Swedes, who raided and traded in the Baltic states, Poland, Russia, and Ukraine. It was exceedingly rare for the Vikings to have slaves from the Middle East or Africa in Scandinavia, but considering the contact they had with the Byzantine Empire, which sat between Europe, Asia, and Africa, it would not have been impossible.

However, as the Europeans moved farther down the African coast, the slave trade between that continent and the Western Hemisphere increased. The Danes traded in people via the Danish East India Company, but the enslaved African population became nearly self-sustaining by the late 1700s.

In 1792, the Danes made slavery in Denmark illegal, though it continued in the Virgin Islands until slave rebellions in 1848 resulted in their emancipation. However, the Danish East India Company merely switched its route and became a minor but significant part of the slave trade from Africa to the American colonies.

One sadly ironic part of this stain on Denmark's history was that as the nation increased its participation in the slave trade, with all of its pain and misery, events and people at home were taking steps to move toward a freer society, one that would lay the groundwork of one of today's most free, happy, and economically satisfied nations.

Though slavery did not exist in Denmark after 1792, the country had long been based on blood and nobility. For most people, especially those in the countryside, which would make up the majority of the population until the late 1800s, they were often tied to a specific area or noble for their entire lives or the majority of it. Peasants were not allowed to leave the land of their birth unless they had permission from the local noble, and it was not unusual for peasants to be "lent" to friends or permanently given to them as a type of non-monetary trade. Peasants were rarely given away like this as Denmark moved into the modern era of the 1700s, but life as a peasant was still not an easy one.

Throughout most of Danish history, especially after the establishment of feudalism in the 11th and 12th centuries, peasants were subject to corvée, which required them to work the lands of the nobility. They also often had to pay a percentage of their own crops. It was not until the reforms of the late 1700s that most Danish farmers were given the legal right to own their own land.

In the 1720s, the nobility attempted to increase the amount of time required by the corvée to three days a week from two. At the time, fewer than three hundred noble families owned 90 percent of the land. They had a workforce that was just one step up from slavery that cost them nothing to utilize. The nobles had immense power over the peasantry for much of Denmark's history.'

Many modern Danish small landholding farms look much as they did from the later 1700s onward. This is a typical farm, but it was owned by the famous Danish author Isak Dinesen, which was the pen name for Karen Blixen, the subject of the film Out of Africa.

Male peasants were required to spend forty years working the land of their lord, though they were able to commute this to six years if they served in the military. The problem was the nobles decided which of the peasants on their land could serve. Not only did this give the aristocracy great power over the lives of the peasants, but it also gave them considerable negotiating power with the king. Unless the king hired mercenaries, which was expensive but often done, he was dependent on the nobility's willingness to raise an army for him. If the king was strong, they were very willing. The same could not be said about weak kings, though. For those kings who were not very powerful or merely a figurehead, negotiations would have to take place in order for the king to raise an army. This would result in an incredibly Byzantine series of favors and negotiations that weakened the king or the nobility, depending on the current state of affairs and the negotiating skill of those involved.

On a more local level, nobles were essentially *the* law in their domain. A peasant could not testify against them in court, and the nobles were allowed to inflict corporal punishment, which included beatings, whipping, the stocks, and more, on peasants they found "breaking the law." As you might imagine, sexual predation was rife, with women and girls outside of the aristocracy virtually without any legal recourse from being assaulted. It is important to note that these situations were not unique to just Denmark, although they are terrible to think about.

From the early decades of the 18th century to the rise of Napoleon Bonaparte, Europe and the brand-new United States went through an amazing period known as the Enlightenment. Those who live in Western-style democracies today can thank the men and women of the Enlightenment for the idea that people are endowed with certain rights, such as those of speech, movement, and redress from the government. These people opened the way for those today to have a say in the rules and laws under which they live instead of the often-arbitrary wishes and desires of some noble or king. The Enlightenment is one of the most fascinating periods of human history, but we don't have much time to dwell on it in this particular book. Suffice it to say that, for our purposes here, Enlightenment thoughts, coupled with the desire for greater profits, spurred great changes in Denmark, Europe, and North America in the 1700s and onward to today. Oftentimes, people think about the freedoms that are enjoyed in the West in a political way, and without a doubt, new and different political changes began to occur in Denmark in the

1700s. These changes were not the temporary changes that had been made throughout Danish history in regard to who would have power in the country. Rather, they involved the way Danes lived and worked. The 18th century marked a turning point that truly laid the foundations of Danish society today, from top to bottom. Denmark was no different in this than other western European countries (with the exceptions of Portugal, Spain, and many of the states of Italy). These countries were all making advances in agriculture and industry, beginning what would become known as the Industrial Revolution.

Though it may sound odd at first, what spurred many of Denmark's economic gains was the legalization of the free press in 1770. With the opening of a public forum where the issues of the day could be discussed and debated, new developments in farming technology and techniques began to spread. (Denmark opened its educational system to all Danes in 1814, and for the time, Denmark was a relatively literate society, especially in the cities and especially in Copenhagen.)

Changes that large could not simply arrive without affecting other parts of life. One of the hindrances to more modern farming practices was the poor land records and boundaries resulting from the inefficient central administration and unrecorded land exchanges between nobles over the years. This caused disputes between nobles, leading to the rise of "common land," which traditionally was worked for the peasants for themselves. The land owned or used by those other than the nobility in the first part of the 18th century was only about 10 percent, and a large portion of this was owned by the Protestant Church.

The other problem was more personal to most Danes than nobles' land boundaries. This was, of course, the corvée. The corvée required peasants to work their noble's land for a proscribed number of days per week. Since the peasants had little incentive to work under the corvée, output remained low, and new methods were not sought.

In 1759, the system of enclosure, which fenced in and formally drew boundaries, was enacted. There was very little resistance to this move, unlike in England. Enclosure made clear farm boundaries, eliminated many legal and personal conflicts, and resulted in the establishment of the Royal Danish Agricultural Society in 1769. This society supported and encouraged new developments in farming and farming technologies. Enclosure also opened up, both by design and accident, many of the lands outside of the reach of the nobility and clergy, and a growing number of Danish farms were created over the course of the next decades. The nobles were compensated for losses, and a number of fairly large farm holdings, which were run by the growing middle class, sprang into existence. (There are farms and ranches in the United States and Australia that are larger than the entire country of Denmark, so "large" is a relative term.) The number of small landholding family farms increased as well. But although many reforms were enacted in the 18th to the mid-19th century, small peasant farms were still subjected to a large number of restrictions.

During the 1760s, the corvée was reformed, allowing farmers to concentrate on their own subsistence farms or seek work with someone other than their lord. Though it does not seem "modern" today, this change, which allowed farmers to pay a fee rather than work the land, gave farmers more time. This, in turn, incentivized labor, which contributed to a rise in production never before seen in Denmark. Many of these changes were implemented in Norway (which, at the time, was still a Danish territory), though the land in Norway was (and still is) less productive than Denmark.

From 1784 to 1788, the Great Agricultural Commission of Denmark, which was formed by order of King Christian VII (r. 1766–1808), studied agriculture in Denmark and made recommendations for reforms. The growing power and numbers of the middle and lower classes made this reform urgent and also welcome. From the peasants' point of view, the most welcome reform was the elimination of the laws tying a peasant to the land of their birth. To help create new farms, the government would issue low-interest loans to purchase the land.

Chapter 10 – Napoleon and the Aftermath of the Napoleonic Wars

Ever since the end of the Second Northern War in 1720, Denmark had felt peace. The French Revolution and the turbulence it caused was felt in Denmark, as it was in most of Europe, but the nation managed to remain relatively untouched by the domestic tumult caused by the ideas of the French Revolution.

Some of the ideas of the French Revolution did spread into Denmark and ultimately affected change within the country, but the Danish monarchy was relatively unaffected. When the French Revolution began in 1789, the king of Denmark was Christian VII. His son, Frederick VI, was conservative and strongly protected the rights and prerogatives of the monarchy. Though he was popular at first, Frederick ended his reign as a defeated and increasingly out-of-touch king. The reason for this decline was simple: Napoleon Bonaparte.

Frederick VI in a portrait from early in his reign by Friedrich Carl Gröger
https://commons.wikimedia.org/wiki/File:Fiedrichvidenmark.jpg

Denmark's location has been both a positive and a negative throughout its history. As you know by now, it was situated between the North and Baltic Seas, which provided it with both power and coin. Throughout most of its history, Denmark managed to control the straits and sounds knifing through and around the country, allowing Denmark to become one of the region's greatest powers for centuries.

However, by 1800, Denmark's position near France brought it into possible conflict with its leader, Napoleon, due to its renown as a regional sea power. Napoleon Bonaparte had gained more and more power after his takeover of the French government in 1799. In 1794, both Denmark and Sweden declared themselves neutral in the conflicts that were taking place in Europe. In 1800, as a result of Napoleon's pressure, both Russia and the powerful German state of Prussia joined this neutrality pact.

There was one problem with this pact: Britain, France's greatest foe, was not "neutral" at all. Strictly speaking, these neutral countries said they would trade with anyone, but the reality was most of their trade (including the resources needed to make war) was with France. When Napoleon came to power in his own right, he created the Continental System, which forbade any European power from trading with Great Britain. (The success and failure of this system have filled volumes; suffice it to say that it was only partially successful for a variety of reasons, one of them being the wealth and naval power of Britain.)

Adhering to this system brought Denmark into conflict with Britain, and in 1800, the British Royal Navy sought to end the use of the Danish fleet as a go-between in France's trade in the Baltic. The British attacked and destroyed most of the Danish fleet in Copenhagen Harbor. Like many of the nations affected by the Continental System, the Danes went on to trade with Napoleon, but they increasingly entered into secret agreements with the British, something that continued until 1807.

By 1807, the remnants of the Danish fleet had been augmented by new ships. While this fleet was not as powerful as it had been, the British feared that it could be used by Napoleon. The French Navy had been almost completely destroyed by the British Royal Navy under the famous Admiral Horatio Nelson at Trafalgar in 1805, and despite having been weakened considerably at sea, it was not out of the realm of possibility that Napoleon might use Danish ships as part of a French invasion of Great Britain. This possibility, which the British thought they had prevented with their victory at Trafalgar, reared its head again when Napoleon and Russian Tsar Alexander I (r. 1801–1825) signed a treaty of friendship at Tilsit (now located in the Russian Baltic enclave of Kaliningrad). This caused the British to fear that Napoleon might once again focus on invading England, as his eastern flank was now protected.

In response to this and to take control of the entrance to the North Sea itself, the British attacked Denmark in August 1807, occupying the island of Zealand, the location of the Danish capital of Copenhagen. The city was subjected to a ruthless bombardment, which set fire to parts of the city and killed hundreds, if not thousands. Seventy-five percent of the city was destroyed, and the Danes were forced to accede to British demands, which included the seizure of the Danish fleet.

The Terrible Bombardment of Copenhagen by Christoffer Wilhelm Eckersberg "Father of Danish painting"), c. 1807

Naturally, this drove the Danes into the waiting arms of Napoleon, who, despite his loss at Trafalgar, was at the height of his power in Europe. On Halloween 1807, the Danes joined Napoleon against the British. Once again, the Royal Navy returned, this time imposing a blockade on Denmark. One of the most significant aspects of this blockade was that important shipments of grain (both Danish and European) to Norway were curtailed. Norway nearly reached famine-like proportions. Even the relaxation of the blockade in 1810 did not wipe out the hunger in Norway. It convinced many there that independence was the future. (Norway became part of Sweden in 1815 as a result of the Concert of Europe, which redrew the map of Europe after the defeat of Bonaparte, but it gained its independence in 1905.)

By 1813, the tide had turned against Napoleon. In 1812, he turned on and was then defeated by the Russians. He was forced to retreat with an ever-dwindling number of starving, disease-ridden troops back to France. Nation after nation turned against him, including Sweden. However, Denmark did not. Its weakened state and size, combined with a hatred of Britain for the destruction of Copenhagen, meant that the Danes remained Napoleon's allies.

The Swedes had become allies of the British in 1813 and declared war on the Danes shortly thereafter. (Ironically, Sweden was ruled by King Karl XIV Johan (or Charles XIV John), the founder of today's Swedish royal family. He was actually the former French Marshal Jean-Baptiste Bernadotte, a noted general in Napoleon's army and the husband of a former fiancée to the French emperor. He had been chosen by the Swedes as their new monarch in 1809 after a revolution against their former king.). The Swedes surprised the Danes by invading the country from the south. The Treaty of Kiel in January 1814 saw Denmark relinquish Norway to the Swedes. A Norwegian rebellion led by the heir to the Danish throne, the future Christian VIII, who was the governor, was met with defeat.

Denmark's relationship with Napoleon had been a disaster. Europe's greatest powers had either opposed or turned on the French at some point, but Denmark remained tied to France until the end. Both political and economic relationships were soured for years. Copenhagen had to essentially be rebuilt (though, for us in the 21st century, this was a blessing, as the rebuilding of Copenhagen, which lasted through the rest of the 19th century, resulted in one of Europe's most beautiful cities). Denmark's economy was also in shambles, and to make economic matters even worse, the British imposed extremely high duties on Danish grain, a move that other nations followed. Farmers, both rich and poor, had to sell their lands, and many nobles were forced to sell estates that had been in their families for perhaps hundreds of years. All of the reforms that had begun in the 1700s were brought to a standstill.

Most of Denmark's overseas trade was taken over by the independent German city of Hamburg. Inflation made life almost impossible. In 1813, just before the first defeat of Napoleon (he would come back in his famous "Hundred Days" to rebuild his army, only to be defeated at Waterloo), Denmark declared bankruptcy.

From 1813 to 1818, Denmark suffered from economic depression and uncertainty. In 1818, however, the establishment of an independent national bank led to the economy's recovery and kept the treasury out of the hands of the king and his advisors. Denmark slowly moved out of the worst depression in its memory. By 1830, the economy had recovered. Prices were stable, the land reforms of the 1700s were starting to take real effect, and Danish overseas trade began to make a comeback.

Frederick VI, who had once been popular, remained in power, but he held on to conservative principles and refused to consider the new economic and political ideas that had come to Europe via the Industrial and French Revolutions. His advisors were all conservative nobles, and what changes were wrought were often a result of long protracted debates with the king and his close advisors.

Things began to change in 1830 when a wave of revolutionary protests swept western Europe. These people opposed many of the conservative policies that followed after the defeat of the French. They brought up the revolutionary ideas France had initially fought for. In Denmark, this forced the king to allow the formation of national and regional assemblies, whose role was to advise and consult with the king. Unfortunately, most of these assemblies did not have the right to make or pass laws. Over the next two decades, change happened in Denmark, but it happened slowly. One of the ways the urban middle class and sometimes the farmers made themselves known was in the independent liberal newspapers, which began to rise in number. These newspapers excoriated the king and the nobility for being unwilling to enact reforms that most of the country was calling for.

Frederick VI died in 1839, and his cousin, who became King Christian VIII, took the throne. He was thought to be more liberal in his views than his uncle. However, by the time Christian took the throne, he had grown more conservative and believed that change was happening too quickly. He believed (and he may have been correct) that Denmark needed time to absorb the changes, which had been increasing in speed since the late 1700s. Christian concentrated his efforts on developing an efficient government and administration. These reforms gave more power to local governments, and, partially through them, more and more liberal policies were experimented with and refined.

A momentous change was to come in the 1840s. One reason for this was the rise of the farming class in what has become known in Denmark as the Farmers' Movement. Originally, the movement was more of a religious revival, but as time went by, farmers began to call for additional reforms, with representation in government being the most consequential.

Christian VIII died in January 1848. The brevity of his reign, which was only nine years, was unusual, for many of his predecessors since the late 1600s had ruled for decades. His death, though, could not have come at a better time for Denmark. Christian's death, combined with a new wave of revolution in 1848 (with many of the disturbances occurring to Denmark's immediate south in the many states of what was to become Germany), led to the beginning of a new age in Denmark.

The new king, Frederick VII, appointed a cabinet that included the liberals Orla Lehmann and Ditlev Monrad, who were both sons of middle-class families. Both of them would hold important positions in the government and lead the new National Liberal Party. On June 5th, 1849, Denmark had a new constitution, one that eliminated the absolute monarchy and replaced it with a constitutional monarchy, similar to Britain's. The king and his cabinet were balanced by two new representative bodies, which were similar to those in Britain. The Folketing was the Danish version of the House of Commons, and the Landsting resembled the House of Lords. An independent judiciary was created, which protected the rights now enshrined in the new constitution: free press, free speech, the right to assemble, and religious freedom. Last but not least, the vote was given to all adult men, regardless of class, which was a monumental shift in how the country ran. (Women were given the vote in 1915.) Today, the Danish government consists of a unicameral assembly (the Folketing), with a prime minister as the head of government.

The second half of the 19th century would prove to be momentous for Denmark. While the nation sustained a humiliating defeat in a war against Prussia and Austria in 1864, its economic trajectory was mostly upward, helped by the great changes taking place throughout Europe and North America. Railways were built throughout the small nation, facilitating trade with Europe by land, and the many harbors of the country were modernized. The Danish shipping industry grew by leaps and bounds, and the importation of coal and iron from Germany fueled new industries. Farming production increased, and Danish bacon and butter, which today are both highly prized commodities among restaurants and foodies, became world-renowned.

The changes in the government protected the individual to some extent, but economically, many Danish workers were at the mercy of ownership. Like many other nations in Europe, especially in the west, Danish workers in many industries began to form labor unions and trade cooperatives. While there was some resistance to these developments among the upper and upper-middle classes, it did not resemble the intense opposition to unionization found in other industrial countries, especially the United States. In the last quarter of the 19th century and into the first decade and a half of the 20th century, the Danish economy enjoyed virtually uninterrupted advancement.

Chapter 11 – The Second Schleswig-Holstein War

The two southernmost provinces of Denmark in 1864 were Schleswig and Holstein. Due to an agreement many centuries prior, Danish kings also carried the title duke of Schleswig and Holstein. At times, due to negotiation, war, or both, the king was only the duke of one or the other. For a time, both provinces were controlled by German princes/dukes, and they were part of the Holy Roman Empire. When they were Danish, the king/duke ruled them as his personal property. The reforms of the 1800s were, of course, felt, but ultimately, the king ruled one or both provinces as an absolute ruler. Today, the former duchies of Schleswig and Holstein are combined into one German state: Schleswig-Holstein. Schleswig is the northernmost of the two.

What became known as the "Schleswig-Holstein Question" was complicated, as it involved ethnic identity, royal power, the wave of nationalism (which had arisen in 1848 and had not abated), and the rising power of Prussia. Prussia, under its chancellor, Otto von Bismarck, was in the beginning stages of creating a new nation, Germany, with the Prussian monarch at its head.

Following the French Revolution and the revolutions of 1848, the people of Europe began to think of themselves as nations of people (usually people of the same ethnic and linguistic group, generally speaking) rather than subjects of a king or queen. For these nationalists, a nation was only complete when all of its ethnic relations were within the same borders. In Holstein, the majority of the population was German. In Schleswig, the majority was Danish, though there was a substantial German population.

Making things more complicated was the fact that, when the Congress of Europe met to settle the borders of Europe in 1815 after the fall of Bonaparte, Holstein was included in the German Confederation and subject to its laws, although it was still the personal property of the Danish king. As the 19th century continued, more and more people in Holstein wanted closer ties with Germany and an end to its role as the Danish king's backyard.

In Schleswig, the German population, which was a more liberally minded group of people for the time, wished to end its role as part of Denmark's personal holdings and its union or affiliation with Holstein and the German Confederation. This clashed with feelings of nationalism in Denmark, which only increased as more power was shared with the people. Germans in both duchies rebelled in 1849, and a low-level insurgency continued until 1851, when, despite receiving aid from Prussia, the rebels were defeated. This was known as the First Schleswig War.

Though the Danes were victorious, the great powers of Europe (Britain, France, and Austria-Hungary) forced the Danes to agree that Denmark would not annex Schleswig or tie it to Denmark any more than the majority-German Holstein was. However, the two duchies still belonged to the Danish king, and none of the reforms passed in 1849 had any effect on either of the two territories. The terms of the peace, known as the London Protocol of 1852, stated that the people of Holstein would be subject to the same constitutional changes as the rest of Denmark. In 1863, the new king, Christian IX, who was not Prussia's preferred choice, declared that all of Denmark's laws would be enforced in Holstein as well, something that virtually none of the people of Holstein wanted. On top of that, it was a violation of the London Protocol.

This last point gave Prussian Chancellor Bismarck the opening he was looking for. He realized that the situation in Schleswig and Holstein was the perfect opportunity to neutralize any possible moves Denmark might make to prevent the unification of Germany. More importantly, it would stymie the plans of Prussia's rival (and ally in 1864), Austria-Hungary.

In 1864, Austria-Hungary was still a power to be reckoned with, but it was not the world power it had been. Still, the Austro-Hungarian emperor and state still had immense influence in the German states, some of which were actually Austrian properties. If Prussia couldn't remove Austrian influence in the smaller states of Germany, it would never be able to unite them under its own banner.

Strangely enough, in order to weaken Austria-Hungary and create a pretext for war against it, Bismarck needed to defeat Denmark. Denmark had violated the terms of the London Protocol and attempted to basically annex Holstein, which gave Bismarck the excuse he needed. The Austrians were the power behind many of the northern German states, and it could not afford to have Denmark or Prussia gain influence in the area. In order to keep itself a player in the area, Austria allied itself with Prussia, and the Second Schleswig War began on February 1st, 1864.

The war lasted until October, but by the time a formal peace treaty had been signed, the Danes had been long defeated on the battlefield. The armed forces of Prussia and Austria separately were too much for the Danes. And when combined, Denmark did not have a chance, though it attempted to create a defensive line along the ancient Danevirke (Danework).

This defensive system had a number of flaws. First, it had not been kept in good condition, especially since the 1700s, when Denmark enjoyed a long period of peace. The Danework in 1864 was a series of trenchworks and high berms, and it was no match for the modern weapons of the Prussians and Austrians. What's more, these fortifications did not run across the whole of the southern part of Jutland; they ended on marshy land in the east, which was believed to be impassible by large forces. You can probably guess what happened: the Prussians flanked the bulk of the Danish forces by going through the marshes.

The Treaty of Vienna (1864) stipulated that Prussia would administer Schleswig and that Holstein would be administered by Austria-Hungary. Bismarck was aware that a problem would likely arise, as Prussians would need to pass through Austrian-controlled territory to administer and trade with Schleswig, and he was correct. Adding fuel to the fire was the fact that a delegation from Schleswig attended meetings of the German Confederation, which was dominated by Austria, despite being forbidden to. Prussia accused Austria of attempting to annex Schleswig, and both sides began to mobilize troops. The resultant Austro-Prussian War was the second phase of Bismarck's plan to unify Germany under the Prussian royal family. The defeat of France in 1871 in the Franco-Prussian War was the final step, and in 1871, Germany as we know it was created.

At the end of WWII, the boundaries of the country were drawn again. Rather than push for both Schleswig and Holstein to be given to Denmark, the Danes asserted that the northern part of Schleswig should be given back since it was majority Danish. The borders of Denmark have been the same since.

For the Danes, the defeat of 1864 was truly the end of Denmark's role as any kind of substantial power in Europe. Since that time, the Danes have not been involved in any major way in any world conflict, though the nation was overrun by Hitler's Germany on April 9th, 1940.

Chapter 12 – The Twentieth Century to WWII

At the beginning of the 20th century, Denmark was a much different nation than it had been at the start of the 19th century. Tremendous reforms had taken place throughout the 1800s that resulted in a nation that was more equitable and freer in 1901. Though the old aristocratic families still enjoyed some privileges and status (after all, thousands of years of law and tradition do not simply disappear overnight), the legal and cultural playing field was being leveled. Although there was some overlap, the nobility was no longer the only class with influence and power, as the new industrial class was taking over. Something similar happened in much of western Europe.

Luckily for Denmark, many in the rising class of industrialists had been raised at a time when liberalism was the order of the day. In 1901, the conservatives, who tended to back a stronger monarchy, saw the writing on the wall vis-à-vis the king. They came to an agreement with their liberal colleagues in the Folketing, which asserted that the king's role was to appoint the government from the assembly, not from his inner circle or the nobility. This custom was only enshrined into law in 1953, though it had been honored for fifty-two years.

Over the course of the first decades of the 20th century, Denmark began on the path that has resulted in its population being one of the happiest and most satisfied nations on Earth today. Education reforms opened the doors to virtually all Danes, and entry into Denmark's large number of universities became easier for the lower economic class. Tax reforms increased the state's coffers, and many loopholes were closed.

Lastly, free trade measures were put into place. This meant that many tariffs on imported goods were removed, giving Danes more choices and improving, for the most part, international relations. In return, many European nations lowered their barriers to Danish goods, which benefited both sides.

However, as you likely know, the early part of the 20th century was a time of great anxiety. Germany, a new nation of sixty-four million people, had been asserting its power since the accession of the young Kaiser, Wilhelm II. Wilhelm had dismissed the brilliant Otto von Bismarck in 1890 and took foreign policy matters into his own hands. Believing that Germany should "have a place in the sun" (meaning a share of the glory and land that was being claimed by European countries throughout the world in a new age of imperialism), the Kaiser knocked heads with the British, the French, the Italians, the Chinese, and the Moroccans—and the list goes on from there. Though Germany finally achieved the overseas empire that the Kaiser and many Germans desired, these territories in Africa and Asia cost the Germans more than they profited from them.

Bismarck believed that Germany had grown to its natural size and that any attempt to expand it beyond its boundaries of 1871 was a mistake that would likely provoke a hostile response. The creation of Germany came at the expense of France, which had been humiliated in the Franco-Prussian War of 1870–71. France had been the most populous and richest nation on the European continent, but virtually overnight, it was supplanted by Germany. France had also lost the provinces of Alsace and Lorraine to Germany but vowed to get them back. France, along with Britain and Russia, began a process of rearmament after 1871 that put it on a collision course. Naturally, Germany did the same, and after things had been ironed out with Austria, the empire joined Germany in a defense pact and armed itself heavily as well. The stage was set for World War I.

You'll notice that Denmark and the valuable territory of Norway were not mentioned in the paragraph above. Neither were the Netherlands nor Belgium. Although these nations were valuable in their own ways (the Netherlands was, as it is now, one of the wealthiest European nations), they were not perceived as military threats to any of the Great Powers mentioned above. All of them, despite having leanings toward one nation or another, wished to stay out of any conflicts. Denmark and the Netherlands both declared neutrality. Belgium was aligned with France and Britain, though it maintained fairly good relations with Germany. It had to; Belgium and Germany shared a border. In 1910, Belgium's population was just under 7.5 million. Denmark's population was just over two and a half million, and Denmark did not share a border with France to help back it up.

Denmark is surrounded on three sides by water, so the Danes also had to take into account the actions of the British Royal Navy. Relations with Great Britain in 1914 were good, but the Danes knew from bitter experience that the British would not allow control of Denmark to fall to the Germans. This would increase the area from which the growing German Navy (*Kriegsmarine*) could operate would give them control of not only Denmark's excellent harbors and shipbuilding sites but also its powerful coastal fortresses. There was also the possibility that if the Germans conquered Denmark or secured passage of its troops through the country, the resource-rich nation of Sweden would be an easy conquest, as it was just a mile or two away across the straits.

For Germany's part, it wanted to prevent British control of Danish ports. If Britain gained control, they would have a closer base of operations from which to move against German ports on the North Sea. This would make it vastly easier for the British to attack German ports on the Baltic (Kiel, Germany's naval base, is on the Baltic Sea). The Germans let the Danes know, in no uncertain terms, that should Denmark allow the British access through its waters into the Baltic, Germany would seize control of the country and its ports. The phrase "between a rock and a hard place" could not be more apt.

Between 1902 and 1910, the Danes looked for a way to protect themselves. The Danish Defense Commission was formed in 1902 to examine the situation from every angle and make recommendations regarding Denmark's future military choices. Denmark's "defense" consisted, for the most part, of its coastal defenses, which allowed it to play an outsized role in the region since it controlled sea traffic. However, since 1864, the Danes had made the conscious decision to limit their defense spending to only cover what was deemed necessary to dissuade a potential enemy. They did not seek to create a military that would pose a threat to anyone or be able to prevent a determined invasion from the south (and there was only one country on its southern border: Germany). In the end, the Danes had to choose which threat to address, and the more immediate threat to their country was Wilhelm's Germany.

In the few years before the war, the Danes entered into detailed negotiations with the Germans to try to hammer out an agreement that would guarantee the Danes a modicum of security while allaying German fears of British occupation. There was no formal result to the talks, but the British knew of them and created their own policy to deal with Denmark should war break out, which it did in August 1914.

Denmark was involved almost immediately. The Germans gave the Danes an ultimatum: they could either mine the entrances to the Baltic to block the British (and give Germany the maps detailing the mines' location), or the German Navy would do it on its own. This means the Danes would not know where the mines were, curtailing their trade with Sweden, Finland, and other countries to the east, namely Russia.

Danish King Christian X was a known friend of the British, and even he thought it was best to mine the Baltic approaches. The prime minister, along with the defense and foreign affairs ministries, were unsure of what position to take, so they let the king take the lead. What they did not know was the king had arranged for the mines to be laid but not armed. This was shortly relayed to the British, who remained skeptical, especially when a fishing boat exploded after hitting one of the "disarmed" mines. The question of mining the straits did not, in the end, have any great effect on Denmark's position during the war, but it does illustrate the desperately tight jam that the country was in.

The Danes enjoyed the diplomatic expertise of Foreign Minister Erik Scavenius from the beginning of the war until 1920. Scavenius managed to walk the tightrope between Germany and Britain and somehow managed both sides to allow Danish trade to flow to both the Allies (Britain and France) and Germany. Scavenius convinced both sides that it was in their best interest to allow Denmark to trade freely. The British, who at times during the early part of the war were desperately short on food, received Danish food exports, mostly ham, cheese, and butter. The Germans were able to access Denmark's resources, and Denmark also served as a conduit for Swedish and Norwegian goods to be sold in Germany.

A picture of Erik Scavenius.
https://commons.wikimedia.org/wiki/File:Erik_Scavenius_1_(cropped).jpg

Due to Denmark's position between the two sides, it was uniquely qualified to broker peace between them. Throughout most of the war, Scavenius, King Christian X, and Prime Minister Thorvald Stauning (the leader of the powerful and increasingly influential Social Democratic Party of Denmark) made overtures to both the British and Germans. But since each side believed at different times that "victory was just around the corner," neither of them had much incentive to make a peace that would likely be costly in some manner and anger significant portions of their respective populations. It was hard to agree on peace when millions of soldiers had sacrificed their lives for victory—whatever that might look like.

Toward the end of the war, the Danes were increasingly fearful that Britain might move to occupy Denmark as a way to end the trench warfare on the Western Front, which would likely result in the Germans moving troops into the country. That would make Denmark perhaps the last battlefield of the world's deadliest conflict, at least at that point in history.

The Danes entered into talks with their southern neighbors about the possibility of German troops entering Denmark. These talks were headed by Erik Scavenius, who tempted the Germans with the hope that they might be able to control access to the Baltic themselves, as well as access to all of Denmark's export goods. Scavenius deliberately drew these talks out and pretended to need "further consultation" with the government and the Danish king every time the Germans pushed him to sign an agreement. Scavenius had connections in the British government, as did King Christian X, who was British King George V's cousin (one the British king liked, as opposed to one of his other cousins, Kaiser Wilhelm II, whom he did not like at all). The British kept them apprised of much of British policy throughout the war.

By the time Germany began to unravel with the entry of the United States in 1917 and the failure of its 1918 Spring Offensive, the Germans had put the Danish question on the back burner. Every man was needed at the front, not in Denmark. When the war ended in November 1918, the Danes had managed to stay out of the conflict and had limited its losses to a relatively small number of ships that either struck mines or were accidentally fired upon by one side or the other.

During WWI, Denmark was able to concentrate much of its energy on continued reforms, something that many of the war's belligerents could not. The changes that took place were revolutionary and would lay more of the groundwork for the modern Danish state that emerged after WWII.

In 1915, the Danes wrote a new constitution, appropriately known as the 1915 Constitution. Though most of it was similar to the Constitution of 1864, a few advanced laws were amended, including a law that said there were to be two houses of parliament, giving women the vote, establishing health insurance and safety protocols for industrial workers, and the breaking up of some of the remaining large landholdings, which were then redistributed more equitably. One must remember that Denmark is smaller than the US state of West Virginia, and the population was (and still is) large for its size. With so many large estates, much of the population did not have a chance to own land. What's more, not all of those estates were farms, so breaking them up for farmland increased Danish productivity in a significant way.

Lastly, the parliament began to use taxation to not only raise revenue but also steer Danes toward widely shared goals or beliefs. During WWI, alcohol taxes were increased, but food subsidies were given with the money. After the war and to the present day, Danish lawmakers, with the input of constituents, have continued this policy. Today, the biggest example is the tremendous tax on cars that burn gas or diesel. This is a response to the environmental crisis, but it also discourages the almost-continuous traffic jams found in many urban areas of western Europe and the US. Part of the tax on these vehicles goes directly to fund renewable energy in the country, particularly wind power.

Though the Danes did not share in the physical devastation of WWI or have to rebuild their economies, the Danes did suffer from the economic consequences of the war and the Great Depression.

Aside from the collapse of the worldwide economy in 1929, the economy of Denmark suffered due to the conflicts between the political parties in the country, which were thankfully non-violent. For virtually all of the 20th century, Danish politics was dominated by the same four parties: the Liberals, Conservatives, Social Democrats, and Radicals.

The Liberals were liberal in the sense that they followed the principles of 19th-century political thought: free speech, free press, removing hereditary power, and limiting the power of the landed elites.

The Conservatives, generally speaking, believed in a free-market system with very little control by the government. They wanted a hard limit to the reforms that resulted in expensive insurance and welfare schemes, which were brought about by the dominant Social Democrats and Radicals. The Conservatives were also in favor of a stronger monarchy and opposed most moves to increase the power of parliament and the lower classes.

The Social Democrats believed in the equitable sharing of power and land. They were willing to put these policies into law when they were in power, which was opposed by the Conservatives and some Liberals. Some of the rhetoric of the Social Democrats, who were in power from 1930 until 1940, alarmed many in Denmark. At times, they sounded like statements coming from Joseph Stalin's Soviet Union, which was the enemy of capitalists, conservatives, and others at the time. The Social Democrats came under much criticism for some of their statements; for instance, their leader, Thorvald Stauning, once said that his party wanted to "reform society and then control it," which sounds quite ominous. Stauning was forced to make his intentions clear. Although there was still opposition from Conservatives throughout Denmark, in the end, the policy that emerged was not that of a communist takeover of the industry but shared and collective ownership, along with shared responsibilities. The creation of a large "social safety net" is still the hallmark of Danish society and politics today.

The Radical Party (today's Danish Social Liberal Party) was not as radical as its name might suggest (at least not in today's terms). They surely were not Stalinists, as many wanted to believe at the time. Though they did share some ideas with more leftist parties in other nations, such as France, they were never as radical. The Radicals believed many of the same things as the Social Democrats, but they also hoped to change the culture of the country to bring it in line with their beliefs (equality for all, women's rights, criminal reform, educational reform, and free access). They spurred on the Social Democrats, with whom they often collaborated.

Denmark suffered from incredible inflation during the early 1920s, much like its German neighbor. Part of this was to pay for subsidies and support for farms (there was a near famine in Denmark for a period in the 1920s) and industries suffering from the worldwide economic depression. Unlike many other nations at the time, the Danes managed to come out of the worst of the Great Depression by the early 1930s by reforming the monetary system. Trade began to slowly increase as the decade went on.

By 1940, Denmark was a relatively stable country. It enjoyed an economic rejuvenation and was generally free from the political strife that the rest of Europe felt. There was only one real concern: what would Adolf Hitler, who gained power in 1933, do?

The Danish Nazi Party (The National Socialist Workers' Party of Denmark or *Danmarks Nationalsocialistiske Arbejderparti*, the "DNSAP") was not popular in the years before WWII, but during the war, the DNSAP acted as an auxiliary and secret police role at the behest of the Gestapo (Hitler's secret police).

WWII began on September 1st, 1939, with Germany's invasion of Poland. On September 3rd, Britain and France declared war on Hitler, fulfilling a promise made to Poland. For nine months after the invasion of Poland, the world waited to see what would happen in the spring. On April 9th, 1940, the Danes would find out.

Chapter 13 – World War II

Denmark was fully aware of its position as Hitler's northern neighbor. With a population of about five million compared to Germany's seventy million and with an army barely the size of Berlin's police force, the Danes knew that any opposition to Hitler, should he decide to invade, was virtually useless. When the invasion did come on April 9th, 1940, some Danish units put up a resistance. They were brushed aside easily. Some fired a few bullets or shells toward the Germans for the sake of "honor," but most simply went home. Late in the afternoon of April 9th, the Danish government announced that it was surrendering to the Germans to prevent the destruction of its cities by air. The Danish Air Force was virtually nonexistent. Germany's air force (the *Luftwaffe*) very much existed and in great numbers.

Denmark is an unusual case in the history of WWII. Given its proximity to Germany, there was less open opposition to the Nazis than there was in Norway, for example, but unwritten rules of behavior toward the occupiers were followed by most Danes, except the relatively small (but growing) number of Danish Nazis. Women were not to "consort" with Germans. German commands were to be followed slowly. More than likely, many German soldiers and officers ingested a great deal of Danish saliva in their restaurant meals during the war.

Though life under Hitler's regime was not easy for anyone, comparatively speaking, it was for Denmark. The two nations had shared a border for an incredibly long time, much trade was done between the two, families were intertwined, and the ethnic similarities (both real and imagined by Hitler) were great. Hitler adopted a *relatively* benevolent attitude toward the Danes because of his racial worldview, which included the Danish people. This worldview, of course, was his nebulous fantasy idea of a group of people called the Aryans. To Hitler, the Scandinavians were the epitome of his "racially pure Germanic race." Their relative isolation had left them "unsullied" by intermarriage with "lesser" European peoples outside of Germany and Austria, the latter of which was Hitler's homeland. (As a side note, Hitler occupied Norway later that spring, while Sweden walked a fine line of neutrality.)

The Danes were allowed to run their own internal affairs as long as they fell into line with Nazi plans. Even Social Democrat Thorvald Stauning was allowed to remain prime minister, and he tried to walk a very fine line. King Christian X remained in the country, despite calls for him to go into exile. Christian played a very subtle game with the Nazi occupiers. He used coded language and symbols of resistance to show his opposition to the Nazis and the occupation. For most, he became an inspiration, though stories of him wearing a Star of David in support of Denmark's Jews are apocryphal (as is the legend of Copenhagen's Danish citizens doing the same).

Christian X on his daily, unguarded ride through Copenhagen, surrounded by adoring citizens. This continued virtually uninterrupted until the war's end. Christian (d. 1947) was one of the most popular kings in Danish history.
https://commons.wikimedia.org/wiki/File:Christian_X_of_Denmark_on_horse_at_Gyl denl%C3%B8vesgade.jpg

Despite the preferred treatment received by the Danes, they were still required to fill a certain number of Waffen SS (the military branch of Hitler's dreaded organization). A battalion-sized Danish Legion was formed, and a certain number of Danes volunteered for the all-Scandinavian Waffen-SS division (the 5th SS "Wiking"), but this number was never near the total that Hitler had hoped for.

Of course, like every other nation occupied by the Nazis, the Danes were subjected to Hitler's oppressive laws against Jews. Danish Jews were to be deported to the extermination camps being planned and erected in Poland.

Though anti-Semitism did have adherents in Denmark, the level of this was quite less than in other German-occupied territories, especially in eastern Europe. The Danish Nazis, the SS, and the Gestapo were responsible for rounding Jews up in September 1943. The following account is one of the bright stars in the incredibly dark sky covering Europe from 1939 to 1945.

The German command received orders to "evacuate" the Jews of Denmark, which included a number of German Jews who had fled before the war. The estimated Jewish population before the war was approximately 7,500, with 1,500 being German Jewish refugees. Most but not all of Denmark's Jews lived in Copenhagen or its suburbs.

In Denmark, the German commander, Georg Duckwitz, knew what "evacuation" for the Jews meant. Most Germans in high places did, and if they did not know the exact final result, they knew that, at the very least, "evacuation" meant great suffering. Duckwitz flew to Berlin and asked for clarification of his orders and for them to be rescinded; of course, he was rebuffed. He then secretly flew to Stockholm, Sweden, consulted with Swedish Prime Minister Per Hansson, and asked the Swede if his government would give the Jews a safe place if they could manage to cross the narrow straits to his country.

Hansson's answer was yes, and Duckwitz returned to Denmark. Through back channels and informants, he was able to make contact with the Danish resistance movement. Over the course of the next two weeks, Danish fishing vessels hid their Jewish brothers in their holds and smuggled them to Sweden, where they remained in safety throughout the war. Seven thousand Jews managed to make the dangerous trip. A few lost their lives when a few boats were fired upon, but less than five hundred Danish Jews were rounded up during the war. Most of these were sent to the so-called "Artist's Camp" of Theresienstadt in Czechoslovakia, where most survived due to pressure from the Danish Red Cross. Though the numbers could have been much worse, it should be remembered that some 120 to 130 Danish Jews died in the Holocaust.

As the years of occupation continued, more and more Danes rose up or took part in resistance movements throughout the country. As the war went on, the Germans requisitioned more Danish food and other goods. Shortages began to be felt, and the people began to go hungry. The Danish police, which was virtually all Nazis (though some were plants by the Danish Resistance), were brutal in their pursuit of resisters and were at times more rabid than the Nazis themselves in their methods. This caused more resistance, as did reports of both German atrocities throughout Europe and the turning of the tide against Hitler. By 1943, the Danes had managed to sabotage hundreds of German facilities or industries that contributed to the war effort, and the Nazis cracked down.

This crackdown led to widespread strikes, which led to more arrests, torture, and even more strikes. In the first part of the war, there were many Danish resistance groups, most of whom worked without coordinating plans, which sometimes led to bungled operations and arrests. In September 1943, the Danish Freedom Council was created to unify and coordinate the different groups. Eventually, some twenty thousand Danes (men, women, and children) joined the resistance movements, and many more aided them covertly.

One of the more famous resistance movements in Denmark was known as Holger Danske, named after a famous Middle Age hero who would be reborn in Denmark's hour of greatest need. One of the many functions of Holger Danske and other groups, especially in Danish cities, was the intimidation and occasional assassination of Danish collaborators. Toward the end of the war, many Danish police officers and other figures had seen the "writing on the wall" as far as Germany's defeat went and changed sides. Others were scared of possible retribution after the war was over, and they supplied the resistance movements with insider information about German plans. The amount of information increased after D-Day, which was the invasion of Normandy by the Western Allies in June 1944.

The months and weeks before D-Day saw the Danish Resistance spring into mass action in coordination with the British secret operations unit, the SOE (Special Operations Executive). So many instances of resistance and sabotage took place that the Germans were not able to send troops from Denmark to France to help repel the Allies. This caused the Germans to take direct control of policing the country, and in the last months of the war, sabotages, assassinations, arrests, and executions went up. Street battles were fought in Copenhagen toward the war's end. One of the more tragic episodes of the war was the bombing of "Shell House" (Shellhus), the police headquarters in Copenhagen where the Gestapo kept those suspected of being in the Resistance. The Resistance believed the Germans were about to get information that would result in the destruction of the movement, so the decision was made to bomb Shell House. It was hoped that a number of those in the Resistance would be able to escape, but if not, their deaths would prevent important information from being divulged. The result of the bombing was tragic. Though eighteen Danish resistance fighters were able to escape, the inexact nature of bombing at the time meant that there were many civilian casualties (of the 125 Danes killed, 86 were children). Eight prisoners had also died; they had been "housed" within the roof beams as human shields to prevent this type of attack from happening. The building was all but destroyed, and forty-five collaborators were killed, as well as fifty-five Germans.

Denmark and Norway were both liberated largely by themselves, though the Nazis had begun to flee to Germany before the end actually came. Before the war ended, the Western Allies made Denmark a priority, even over Berlin. Control of Denmark by the powerful Allied navies and a large number of British troops in the country meant that the Soviet Union, which was driving hard to obtain Denmark, could not expand its influence to the tiny but important nation.

(For more on Holger Danske and the bombing of Shell House, watch *Flame & Citron* and Flame" (currently on Amazon Prime Video) and *The Bombardment* on Netflix.)

Conclusion

After WWII, Denmark was quick to protect itself from the growing power of the Soviet Union and joined NATO (North Atlantic Treaty Organization) as one of its original members in 1949. While passing the Danish straits is "toll-free" today, Denmark and Norway, which is also a NATO member, would be called upon to close sea traffic to Russia in the event of war. Though the Royal Danish Army is small, it is highly trained and has taken part in peace-keeping missions and combat duty in Afghanistan. The Royal Danish Navy is regarded as a small but highly effective force. The Royal Danish Air Force, which is soon to be equipped with a number of the most advanced American fighters, is Denmark's largest and most effective military branch.

After the war, the Danish social welfare state as we know it today was refined and added to. The most noticeable element of this social safety net is universal free healthcare. Since the advent of universal healthcare, the rate of most major diseases caused by lifestyle is much less in Denmark than in other Western countries outside Scandinavia. Cigarettes and alcohol are highly taxed, as are some types of food, especially those with excess sugar.

Women's rights were expanded in the 1950s and 1960s, and laws protecting women's careers due to pregnancy were passed. More jobs had been opened to women to the point where there is almost gender parity in most workplaces today. Abortion was legalized in 1973. In the late 1990s and into the 21st century, Danish men began taking a significant role in parenting. Paid paternal leave and maternal leave have allowed parents to retain their role in the workplace and have improved the quality of child-rearing in the country. Guaranteed universal daycare also helps. Seventy-five to eighty percent of Danish women between sixteen and sixty-six have jobs.

Denmark was one of the first nations to recognize the rights of people of different sexual orientations; it did so in 1933, though discrimination based on sexual preference continued for some time. Same-sex marriage was allowed in the late 1980s, but same-sex marriage in the Danish church was not allowed until 2012. In 2010, same-sex couples were given the right to adopt.

Today, Denmark is one of the freest nations in terms of sexual preference, with legal protections enshrined in its constitution. It has also recognized transgender people. Danish transgender people were protected by the law when the possibility of gender reassignment surgery became a reality in the late 1970s, but they were forced to become sterilized and had to receive medical approval. The sterilization element was removed some time ago, and in 2014, transgender people were able to get gender reassignment surgery without medical approval.

Today, Denmark spends about 50 percent of its tax revenue on public expenditures, like medical insurance and education. This does mean that its tax rate is one of the highest in the world (it is behind Sweden), but in recent years, it has come down. However, most Danes support higher taxes for the efficient administration of these social programs.

So, we end where we began. For all of the reasons mentioned in this book, especially in the last chapters, Denmark has enjoyed being the "happiest nation on Earth" a number of times. And when it hasn't been declared *the* happiest, it's always in the top five, usually in the top three, along with other Scandinavian countries, such as Finland.

Part 4: History of Iceland

A Captivating Guide to the History of the Land of Fire and Ice, from the Viking Age to the Present

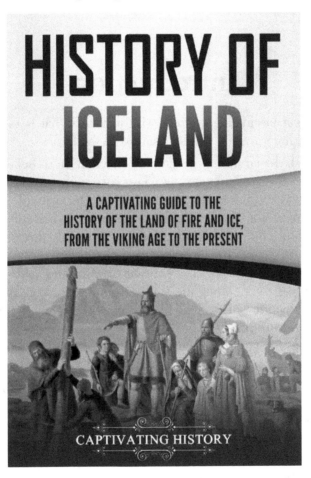

Introduction

Iceland is a fascinating country with a history that is more than just its Viking warriors. But let's start with the basics.

Beneath Iceland is a pocket of magma. It is believed that around seventy million years ago, lava rose to the ocean's surface, cooled, and began to form the island. Because of Iceland's location near the Arctic Circle, it can be an incredibly harsh environment, but it is moderated by the Gulf Stream, which brings heat from the tropics to help temper the climate. However, only 20 to 25 percent of Iceland is habitable, specifically the area along the southern and eastern coasts. Much of the remainder of Iceland is dominated by lava fields, cold deserts, and tundra. Due to its volcanic and icy terrains, Iceland is known as the land of fire and ice.

We do not have much information about the island prior to the arrival of the Norse, which is partially why they get the most attention in history books. However, we do know much about its early establishment as a country after the Norse arrived, mainly because of two important works: *Book of the Icelanders* (*Íslendingabók*) and *Book of Settlements* (*Landnámabók*). In addition, the sagas and the eddas have provided significant details about the early Icelanders; these stand as works of literature on their own, telling the stories of the Viking Age people living in Iceland.

The *Poetic Edda* is the earlier of the two works. It is a collection of poems composed by an anonymous writer about human heroes, some of whom were historical figures, and mythological tales. The *Prose Edda*, on the other hand, was a textbook on poetry, explaining the complexities of skaldic poetry and discussing meter and language. The final section of the *Prose Edda* is called the "Beguiling of Gylfi." In this section, which is written as a dialogue, Snorri Sturluson tells the tale of Gylfi, a Swedish king who learns the details of Norse mythology when he visits Asgard.

While the two eddas are important, the sagas of Icelanders provide many details of how they lived. Family sagas focus on the events of the 9th, 10th, and early 11th centuries. These stories act as source materials for those studying the struggles and conflicts of Icelandic society. They were first passed down orally but were eventually written down, mostly in the 13th and 14th centuries. While it is not known who recorded the sagas, some scholars believe that Snorri Sturluson, who worked on the *Prose Edda*, may have written down *Egil's Saga* since Snorri was one of the descendants of the saga's hero.

These texts have much to tell us about the history of early Iceland, its settlement, and the culture that shaped the country. In about 850 CE, the Vikings discovered Iceland, which was uninhabited by natives. There was a lot of open land for the taking. The Vikings were not the first to discover this land of fire and ice, but they were the first ones to settle there permanently. The first to discover the island may have been the Greeks, although they did not establish any lasting settlements.

Iceland was mainly influenced by the Scandinavians, and you can still see the evidence of this in its culture and language. Here are just a few things to note as you read this book.

The Icelandic language is the closest language to Old Norse. The original settlers were mainly Norwegian, and they brought their language with them, of course. However, their language was not strongly influenced by other languages. For instance, English was originally a Germanic language. For modern readers, reading Old English is like trying to read a foreign language. The modern English language was shaped by events like the Norman

Conquest in 1066. The Norman rule made significant changes to the language. Iceland didn't have any grand conquest by a foreign power, so Icelandic has remained relatively similar to what was spoken in the past.

With that said, Icelandic has a number of letters that are not familiar to English readers. Below is a list of a few of them with their approximate pronunciations.

Æ (lower case æ): This is pronounced similar to a long "I," as in "twice."

Ö: This is pronounced similar to a short "u," as in "fluff."

Ð (lower case ð): This letter is pronounced in different ways depending on the letters that surround it. One pronunciation is a voiceless sibilant fricative, similar to the "th" sound in "bath."

Þ (lower case þ): This letter, which is called thorn, was also used in Old English. It was replaced by "th," which is close to its pronunciation. It is similar to "thick."

Icelandic also uses a number of other variations on the Latin alphabet, particularly the accent marks over vowels, as you will see when you are reading this book.

In Iceland, the process of naming is different. Individuals did not take the surname of their fathers. Instead, their surname is patronymic, which means their surname was the first name of their father, coupled with "-son" or "-dóttir." So, if the person was the daughter of Jon, they would have the surname of Jonsdóttir. Her brother, on the other hand, would have the surname Jonsson. In more recent years, people have started to use matronyms as well (using the mother's first name). With the matronymic surname, they use the mother's first name followed by "-ar" and then "-son" or "-dóttir." However, there are those who use family names (the surname is passed down from their parents) since Iceland was once a Danish colony. Also, keep in mind that when a couple married, the woman typically did and still does not take her husband's last name. One last thing you will notice is that many of the historical figures are referred to by their first names. It makes it a bit easier to keep track of the movers and shakers of Iceland's history without getting too distracted by the similar-sounding last names.

And with that, we are ready to begin diving into the history of Iceland. Enjoy!

Chapter 1 – Early Explorers

Perhaps the earliest known encounter of Iceland occurred when the Greek explorer Pytheas of Marseille traveled in the Atlantic Ocean. Around 400 BCE, he found an uninhabited land he called Thule, which was six days north of Britain. When he returned home and began to share accounts of his adventures, people did not believe his stories of the sun shining through the night, which happens during the summer solstice in Iceland. Based on his descriptions of Thule, as well as the time it took to travel there, it seems that Thule may have been Iceland.

The Irish monks were most likely the next to arrive in Iceland when they were exploring the Atlantic Ocean to find solitary lands. They reached a land that fits the description of Thule. In 730 CE, Bede, the famous English historian and monk, mentioned their voyage, though the land he described may or may not have been Iceland; the descriptions do seem to coincide, though. About a century later, the Irish author Dicuil wrote about stories he heard from priests thirty years prior who had arrived at Thule. However, they might have landed in the Faroes since the Faroes are only 450 kilometers (280 miles) away from Iceland. The monks visited the Faroes in the 6th century, and the Vikings settled there around 650.

Although it is not known for certain if the Irish monks went to Iceland, there is evidence to support it. In Kverkahellir, a manmade cave, archaeologists found sediment deposits that indicated people were living there around 800 CE. In a nearby cave, they identified crosses that appeared to be in the Hiberno-Scottish style carved on a wall. Additionally, a cabin found in Hafnir was built prior to the accepted settlement date of 874; it had been abandoned between 770 and 880. However, it is unclear whether it was built by people from Ireland, Scotland, or Scandinavia. There is additional evidence to support the claims of Irish monks living in Iceland in the *Book of the Icelanders* or *Íslendingabók*, which was written by Ari Þorgilsson, an Icelandic priest, in the 12th century.

Once the Vikings started constructing ships that could sail the oceans, they started to head out into the world, embarking on some of the raids that helped to establish their fearsome reputation. In 793, the Vikings had their first documented raid on Lindisfarne, an island off the coast of Northumberland and England. The Vikings' sole purpose in venturing away from Scandinavia was not raiding but a desire to explore the world. They discovered not only Iceland but also Greenland and Newfoundland.

It is unclear who was the first Scandinavian to arrive in Iceland, even in the *Book of Settlements*, also known as *Landnámabók*. The *Book of Settlements* talks about the Norse settlement of Iceland in the 9th and 10th centuries. The original has been lost, but surviving copies were made in the 13th and 14th centuries. According to one of the versions, Iceland was discovered by Naddodd, who may have been thrown out of Norway because he murdered someone. He was heading to the Faroes and went off course, landing in Iceland.

Naddodd saw nothing that made him want to stay, but he did go ashore. When he did, snow started to fall, so he gave Iceland the name "Snowland." Although Naddodd did not want to stay, he told people about what he saw.

In another version of the *Book of Settlements*, a Swede who owned land in Denmark, Garðarr Svavarsson, was married to a woman from the Hebrides. He set out to claim his inheritance from his father-in-law in the Hebrides in 860 and sailed into a storm. He ended up going off course, heading north until he reached the eastern coast of Iceland. Garðarr then circumnavigated Iceland, becoming the first person to discover that it was actually an island. He built a house and stayed for the winter at Skjálfandi. When he returned home, he called Iceland *Garðarshólmi* after his own name.

While Garðarr's fate is not known, his son, Uni danski (Uni the Dane), emigrated to Iceland. Uni attempted to win Iceland for the Norwegian king, but local farmers learned of his intent. They refused to help him, although he eventually befriended a man named Leidolf. Uni became involved with Leidolf's daughter, Thorunn, and got her pregnant. Uni didn't want to settle down and tried to escape more than once. When Leidolf found Uni, he killed him.

Both versions of the *Book of Settlements* agree that the island was named Iceland by Hrafna-Flóki Vilgerðarson. Flóki was the first to deliberately sail to Iceland. He was Norwegian, but he set out from the Faroes in 868 with his wife and family, along with other travelers. He brought three ravens with him. Flóki sailed for a while before setting them free. One of the ravens returned to the Faroes, while the second one flew up and returned to the boat. The third flew to the northwest. Flóki surmised they were near land, so he followed the raven, eventually finding Iceland. Because of his three ravens, he became known as Raven-Floki or, in Old Norse and Icelandic, Hrafna-Flóki.

One of the men accompanying Flóki was named Faxe. He gave his name to the bay (Faxa Bay or Faxaflói) the travelers spotted as they approached what would later become Reykjavik.

Flóki and his fellow sailors camped in Vatnsfjörður at Barðaströnd, which is located in northwestern Iceland. In the spring, after a difficult winter, Flóki hiked up a mountain near his camp, where he noted Ísafjörður. Because the fjord was full of drift ice, he decided to name the island Iceland ("Land of Ice"). This, of course, was the name that stuck. He and his companions eventually returned to Norway. Flóki claimed the land they had found was worthless, but he returned to Iceland and settled there, living out the remainder of his life in Iceland.

Ingólfr Arnarson is considered the first permanent settler of Iceland. He and his wife, Hallveig Fróðadóttir, are considered the founders of Reykjavik, as they built a farm there. He is also the one who named Reykjavik, a name that translates to "smoky bay." The name came about because Ingólfr came ashore near a thermal vent and saw what he thought was smoke. According to the *Book of Settlements*, Ingólfr settled in Iceland in 874. Although the date is not known for sure, Icelanders celebrated the one-thousand-year anniversary of Iceland's first permanent settlement in 1874. Incidentally, 1874 was also the year the king presented the people with a written constitution.

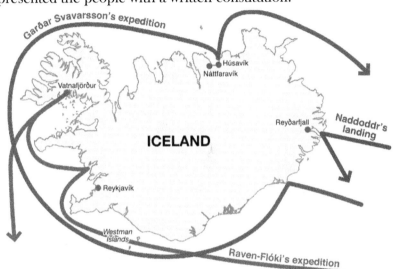

What the early Norse explorations of Iceland looked like.
https://commons.wikimedia.org/wiki/File:Settlement_of_Iceland.svg

The Settlement Period

For the next sixty years, people began to flock to Iceland. The time period became known as landnám ("land-taking"). During landnám, between ten thousand and twenty thousand people settled in Iceland since the land was basically free for the taking.

The *Book of Settlements* details the arrival of four hundred of these settlers. They established their farms in places that they named, and they retain the same names today. The settlers were predominantly Norsemen, although there were some women and people of Irish and Scottish descent. One of the women who went to Iceland was named Aud the Deep-Minded (also known as Unn or Unnur Ketilsdóttir). Her story is told in the *Laxdæla Saga*. She was the daughter of Ketill Flatnose, a wealthy Norwegian chieftain who fled Norway to escape King Harald

Fairhair's tyranny. Aud married Olaf the White, the self-proclaimed king of Dublin, and they had a son named Thorstein.

Aud traveled to the Hebrides with Thorstein after the death of her husband. There, Thorstein married and had many children. He became a warrior king in northern Scotland, but his people betrayed him. Aud was at Caithness when she heard of Thorstein's death. She saw no need for vengeance; instead, it seemed as if she was ready to move on to a new land. Aud commissioned the construction of a knarr (a type of Viking ship built for long voyages). She captained the ship first to Orkney and then to Breiðafjörður, which is a large bay in western Iceland, settling there in about 892. She had around twenty men and prisoners from Viking raids around the British Isles under her command. Once they arrived in Iceland, she freed these prisoners. These men didn't have all the rights of a freeborn man, but their status was better than a slave. Aud also gave them land to farm so they could make a living.

Aud made her mark on the place names in Iceland. The place where she ate her breakfast is called Dögurðarnes ("Breakfast Headland"). When she sailed up the Hvammsfjörð, she lost her comb at a place now called Kambsnes ("Comb Headland").

Aud also had the distinction of being a baptized Christian, and she has been credited by some with introducing Christianity in Iceland, although most people wouldn't adopt it until later. On a hill on her land, she erected crosses so that she could pray; this is now known as Krosshólaborg.

Although there were a few settlers like Aud who came from the British Isles, the settlers were mainly Norse, as evidenced by the Icelandic language. Even Aud had connections to Scandinavia. The settlers arrived in boats called knarrs, which were capable of making the journey over the harsh Atlantic. These boats were fifty to eighty feet (sixteen to twenty-five meters) long and were kind of like a Viking Noah's ark in that they transported people, goats, pigs, dogs, geese, cats, sheep, cows, and other livestock. All told, the knarrs could carry up to fifty tons. The settlers also needed to carry provisions for the long journey and essential implements, including weapons. Iceland was not heavily forested, so the explorers brought timber, though they were able to find driftwood on the beaches.

A model of a knarr.

Once the settlers arrived, they had to establish themselves. The first thing they did was build structures for themselves and their livestock before the arrival of winter. They also had to create hay for the cows if they wanted to have any milk for the winter.

It is unclear why people headed to Iceland, especially considering the fact it was seen as undesirable at first. Most likely, everyone had their own motivations. According to the *Book of Settlements*, the Norwegian king, Harald Fairhair, was a bit aggressive. The sagas reveal how Harald Fairhair originally inherited a kingdom in eastern Norway but set out to unify the Kingdom of Norway because of his desire to have a concubine. This did not sit well with Norway's minor leaders. Many of them, including Ketill Flatnose, fled once Harald Fairhair conquered all of Norway, with some of them going to Iceland. While this accounts for some of the settlers, it does not account for all of them. Some might have simply been participating in the spirit of expansion, which was part of the Scandinavian culture.

As the settlement of Iceland continued, society needed to be organized. With this came the development of the *goðar*, or the chieftain. Within each district was the *hofgoði*, who was a wealthy, respected man responsible for the maintenance of the *hof* (communal hall). In this hall, they held community feasts and religious observations. The *goðar* (plural form of *goði*) had leadership over a *goðorð* (or chieftainship), and there were many *goðorð* at first. The *goðar* may have had a religious role at first, but over time and with the establishment of Christianity as the official religion, they became simply liege-lords or chieftains. The position of *goði* could be traded or inherited, but it could also be shared or sold. Although women did have some power in early Iceland, they were not allowed to become *goðar*. If they inherited a *goðorð*, they had to pass the chieftainship to a man.

The *goðar* were involved in more than just the country's legal issues. They were also responsible for the organization of local assemblies: the *várþing* in the spring and the *leið* in the autumn. They also redistributed wealth, held feasts, made loans, and priced and distributed imported goods.

Near the end of the settlement period, which is traditionally considered to have lasted from 874 to 930, the Althing was established; this assembly was a gathering of all free males and served several purposes. The central purpose of the Althing was legislative in nature. The *goðar*, as the most powerful leaders in the country, proclaimed new laws, reviewed old laws, adjudicated disputes, punished the guilty, and acquitted the innocent. They even engaged in some trade during this two-week-long gathering.

The Althing was the main social event. Farmers, traders, craftsmen, and storytellers came, along with their families in some cases. During the Althing, the attendants lived in *búðir*, which were temporary camps. The legislative meeting was held at Þingvellir (Thingvellir), which basically means "Thing Fields" or "Assembly Fields." Lögberg (Law Rock) was at the center of the gathering, where the presiding official, the Law Speaker (*lögsögumaður*), took his seat. The Law Speaker held the office for three years after being elected by the Law Council.

A 19th-century depiction of what Law Rock might have looked like.
https://commons.wikimedia.org/wiki/File:Law_speaker.jpg

To begin each Althing, the men proceeded to Law Rock. The Law Speaker called the Althing to order and recited the laws and procedures they were to follow during the Althing. Interestingly, this recitation seems to indicate the laws were actually memorized prior to being written down. Since Ingólfr Arnarson was the first Scandinavian to settle permanently in Iceland, the holder of the *goðorð* of his descendants had a ceremonial role. They were called the *allsherjargoði* ("all-people *goði*) and were responsible for sanctifying the Althing each year.

The first Althing was held in 930 and marked the establishment of the Icelandic Commonwealth, which lasted until 1262. During the first Althing, the Icelanders adopted the

Gulathing Law. Úlfljótr, who is seen as Iceland's first Law Speaker, introduced the Gulathing Law after spending three years in Norway studying Norwegian law. While we know some details about the establishment of the political system in Iceland, many of the details are unknown, as the sagas were written for people who were already aware of it. Two sources do provide information, though: the *Book of the Icelanders* by Ari the Learned and the written law code of the Icelandic Commonwealth called Greylag (*Grágás*). The Greylag is also known as the Grey Goose Laws, although the origins of the term are unknown.

There were two important bodies: the Law Council (*Lögrétta* or "law rectifier") and the judiciary body. The Law Council was comprised of the Law Speaker, who governed the meetings, and forty-eight *goðar*. Each of the *goði* had two advisors who sat behind and in front of him. The Law Council met on both Sundays of the Althing, as well as on the last day, although the Law Speaker could call for additional meetings. The meetings convened on a platform and were public, but only members of the Law Council were allowed on the platform.

In 960, the land was divided into quarters—North, South, East, and West—which influenced the establishment of the judiciary body. Within each quarter, there were three Things (assemblies), although the North had four. Each of these quarters had a court with judges who were nominated by the *goðar*. Between 1004 and 1030, a Fifth Court was established. While each of the four courts dealt with cases from their part of the country, the Fifth Court was established to contend with cases that could not be settled in the district courts.

Due to this chieftainship system, Iceland lacked a central government. There were no "officials" to carry out sentences, and if an individual was wronged, he was expected to carry out the sentence himself with support from his *goði*. Typically, the penalty was compensation or banishment. A banishment could last for three years, although, depending on the crime, a person could be banished for life.

The victim often had to ask a more powerful individual for help. For example, if a neighbor claimed part of a farmer's land, the farmer would have to ask his *goði* for help, basically giving his land to the *goði*. If the *goði* managed to reclaim the land, the farmer would have to give some of the land to the *goði*. Based on the evidence in the sagas, most disputes did not head to court but were instead arbitrated. Unfortunately, this arbitration system favored stronger and wealthier individuals.

The lack of a central government also meant that individuals needed to rely on their *goðar*. Because of the lack of a police force or an army, the relationship had some reciprocity. They could only depend on the group of people they were supposed to protect. The law stopped the *goðar* from acting as tyrants since farmers were free to leave the chieftaincy of their *goði*. The *goði* was also able to disavow any of his followers. Essentially, the chieftaincy was not defined by geography but was instead based on a group of households. Interestingly, if a *goði* was sufficiently unpopular and enough of his men deserted him, he would have been unable to nominate any of his men to the courts and would have essentially been finished.

Although the system seemed to be democratic, that democracy was limited. Women did not participate in the ruling system, although they could own and run farms and could also run chieftaincies. However, they still had to hire a man to act as the *goði*, and women were not allowed to sit on the court or testify.

One of the best-known early Icelanders was Erik Thorvaldsson, better known as Erik the Red. Erik the Red, who was probably called this because of his red beard, was born in Norway in 950, prior to the end of the settlement of Iceland. The story of Erik the Red serves to illustrate two important aspects of Iceland: the punishment of crimes and the spirit of exploration, which drove many of the Vikings. Erik's father, Thorvald Asvaldsson, killed someone in Norway and was banished, taking his son Erik with him to Iceland. Once his father Thorvald died, Erik married Thorhild, a woman from a wealthy family. He inherited a large farm from them. Erik cleared the land, built a home, and named the farm Erikstad. Although he had several children, perhaps his most well-known child was his son, Leif Erikson (Eriksson), who was born around 970.

In 982, Erik the Red found himself in some trouble after his servants caused a landslide and destroyed his neighbor's house. The neighbor killed the servants, and Erik killed the neighbor as retribution. He was forced to move, but trouble followed him. Erik once again got in trouble with his neighbors after killing two of his neighbor's sons.

The court decided to banish him, and he decided to head west in the spring of 982, looking for a land he had heard about, Greenland. Gunnbjorn had named the land Cronland, but Erik decided to call it Greenland since he found green meadows on the island. Erik remained in Greenland for three years, exploring the new land. Once his exile was over, he sailed back to Iceland. In the summer of 985, he left Iceland again, bringing additional people and animals on thirty-five ships to Greenland. Once they landed (some did not; some ships returned to Iceland because of the weather, and some were destroyed during the voyage), they established two colonies and a few smaller settlements. By this point, Erik had four children: Leif, Thorvald, Thorstein, and Freydis, his daughter.

Erik's son Leif traveled to Norway in 1000. During that winter, he stayed with King Olaf Tryggvason, a Christian. Leif converted before returning to Greenland, and once he returned, he began converting others to Christianity. By the time Leif returned to Greenland, Erik had heard about a land to the west of Greenland. The two planned to explore this land, but Leif headed out without him, accompanied by a crew of thirty-five men. As they sailed, they encountered three lands, which Leif called Helluland, Markland, and Vinland. Leif returned to Greenland, where he lived for the rest of his life. He continued to convert people to Christianity and ran the settlements until his death, which is presumed to be around 1020.

Chapter 2 – Early Icelandic Society

Before 1000, Icelanders practiced a folk religion. The Scandinavians did not have a word for religion but used a word that roughly translated to custom (*sidr*). These customs were not homogenous, nor were they centralized in the way that we think about religion today. It might be best understood as a collection of rituals, sacred acts, and the worship of gods, whom they called the Æsir and Vanir.

Some of the gods they worshiped included Thor, Odin, and Loki, just to name a few. It is believed the Norse worshiped close to seventy gods. The gods were not perfect; they were flawed and suffered tragedies like humans. They also weren't immortal, as it was believed they would die in a cataclysmic event called Ragnarök.

Since the Norse pantheon is so well known, we will not spend much time on it in this book. However, we will discuss Iceland's conversion to Christianity in more depth.

The Conversion

Around 1000, Iceland became a Christian nation at the Althing. Although some settlers, like Aud, were already Christian, it was not widespread until this point. Olaf Tryggvason, who, according to later sagas, was the great-grandson of Harald Fairhair, ruled as the king of Norway from 995 to 1000. Olaf was a Christian and was determined to convert Norwegians and those in Norse settlements to the Christian faith. First, Olaf sent an Icelander, Stefnir Thorgilsson, who ended up resorting to violence to convert the nation. He destroyed the sanctuaries and images of the old gods. In response, he was banished from Iceland. At the Althing, they passed the "kin shame" legislation, in which Icelanders could prosecute family members if they blasphemed against the old gods or committed other irreverent acts.

After this mission failed, Olaf sent Þangbrandr, a foreign missionary, to Iceland to spread the faith. Ari states in his *Book of the Icelanders* that Þangbrandr successfully baptized several chieftains. However, Þangbrandr did not last long in Iceland, as he was forced to leave after killing a few men (it is not known why). In retaliation, Olaf took the sons of four pagan Icelandic chieftains as hostages and closed Norwegian ports to Icelanders. The two rival religions were antagonistic toward each other, and the Christians became more determined to convert the country and end the pagan traditions they deemed offensive. As the Christians moved to create a separate court system and government, the country inched closer to a civil war.

Hjalti and Gizurr, two Icelanders, had been converted thanks to Þangbrandr's efforts. However, they were exiled due to blasphemous statements and went to Norway. They later returned to Iceland, bringing a priest with them. They actually arrived in Iceland just in time to attend the Althing. Once they arrived at Law Rock, they shared their message, but it was not necessarily accepted. The Law Speaker at the time was Thorgeir Thorkelsson, a pagan. The Christians asked a man called Hall of Sida, who had accepted Christianity, to proclaim the law Christians should follow, as the two groups did not believe they could live side by side and believed they needed separate laws. Hall and Thorgeir struck a bargain and declared Christianity the official religion in Iceland. A small concession was made to the adherents of the old religion. They could sacrifice to the old gods in private, but if they were seen doing so, their actions could result in a three-year banishment.

The Icelanders accepted the conversion without much conflict. Historians have reached different conclusions as to why

Thorgeir and the other Icelanders accepted this so easily. One suggestion is that King Olaf bribed Thorgeir, while another is that Thorgeir received a prophecy that he should change sides. The reasons why the remainder of Icelanders readily accepted Christianity are unclear. Some scholars believe the Icelanders were fearful of Olaf Tryggvason; when Olaf sent Hjalti and Gizurr on their mission, he held the sons of four pagan chieftains hostage. Nevertheless, it appears that Icelanders peacefully converted, and there were few prohibitions against pagan practices in the written law.

Daily Life in Early Iceland

Iceland began as a subsistence system. As such, they did not have much to trade, exporting walrus ivory and sulfur. According to written sources, they also had cottage industries that produced dairy and woolen goods. The Icelanders had a barter system and used goods for payments to landlords and for debt settlements.

Even though Iceland is an island, the Icelanders did not have a ready supply of ships. For a simple trip down the coast, they usually traveled by horse, so a system of horse paths traversed the island. The Icelanders did have boats constructed of driftwood, which they used to fish extensively. Although they hunted for seals, their ships were not equipped to hunt for whales. When whales washed ashore, they were a huge boon since they provided huge amounts of meat and blubber. Of course, the Icelanders did not have refrigeration, so they stored the meat in whale storage pits or *hvalgrafir.* In these pits, the meat was fermented, which acted as a method of preservation. Coastal communities also ate seabird eggs and seabirds.

Icelanders were able to use seal and shark oil in indoor lamps. These lamps were created by chipping out a stone to create a bowl, and they used cotton grass (*fífa*) as wicks. Seal fat had another important use: boatbuilding. Iceland did not have pine forests to provide people with tar to caulk ships, so they used seal blubber. To do this, they placed strips of homespun wool or *vaðmál* between each plank, which they then coated with hot seal oil. According to the *Saga of Erik the Red*, the boats could resist wood-boring sea worms.

Because the Icelanders were a farming society, each farmer needed to have grazing land available. Although they could have milked the ewes, they chose not to since a sheep that is not milked produces higher quality wool, which would fetch a better price. Instead, they milked cows. The most important dairy product they produced was skyr, milk that is curdled with the introduction of rennet (enzymes). They stored skyr in large wooden vats partially buried in the ground. Skyr met the Icelanders' dairy needs during much of the year, particularly in the winter when fresh milk was not available. Their focus was mainly on growing hay to feed livestock, although they did grow grain in the southern and western areas until the 15th or early 16th century.

As subsistence farmers, the Icelanders were always at risk of having a bad year, which could result in starvation. If a farmer faced starvation, he could turn to his *hreppur* for help. *Hreppur* were communal units organized by geography, unlike loyalty to a *goði*. Each *hreppur* was comprised of at least twenty Thing-tax-paying farmers. The *hreppur* were independent groups and did not appear to be political in nature but were connected to the subsistence economy. They organized grazing lands and communal labor, offered fire and livestock insurance, and provided a local forum for resolving disputes. They also helped the poor; those unable to provide for themselves were assigned to neighboring farms, which would then provide assistance. People could not easily move around under this system, as they needed to have recommendations and formal approval. This may have been designed to keep the number of poor manageable.

The first abodes in Iceland were built using turf, which is an excellent insulator. The longhouses were between sixteen and ninety yards long and between five and a half and seven and a half yards wide. In the center of the longhouse was a fire. Over time, annexes were added to the longhouses, including kitchens and bathhouses or saunas. These bathhouses were also called *baðstofa*. With the arrival of the Little Ice Age in 1303, people spent most of their time in the *baðstofa*. They also began constructing *baðstofa* over the livestock sheds and slept together in the same space to stay warm.

Although these turf buildings were warm, they didn't let in any light, and the air inside became stale. The Icelanders developed a solution: a sort of primitive skylight. They cut one or two holes in the roof. The hole had a *skjár* to keep the warmth in and the weather out. A *skjár* was essentially a screen made of a wooden ring from a barrel and the amniotic sac from a cow. Icelanders were able to remove and reinsert the screen as needed.

During the long winter, which lasts about six months, the lack of light was not solved by using the screens since the nights were so long. Therefore, they had a practice called the *kvöldvaka*, which roughly translates as "evening wake." Essentially, it was anything the people could do to stay awake and busy during the darkness. This included their winter work, such as knitting, spinning, and making tools. Children's education was also part of the *kvöldvaka*, and the people told stories and participated in the *að kveðast á*, which was extemporaneous poetry creation. One person would create a line, another person would follow, and so on.

Each night from September until May, immediately following rökkurstund ("twilight hour"), they had ljósatími ("light time") from 6 to 10 p.m. each night. During *rökkurstund*, which lasted for about an hour as darkness was falling, Icelanders conserved light and spent the time quietly, as it was a time of rest. *Ljósatími* began with the mistress of the house formally lighting the lamp.

The Icelanders' clothing was made of homespun wool, and they used animal skins to create shoes. They also used animal skins for oilskins and parchment. They kept goats, geese, sheep, pigs, and horses. The horses were used for transportation and moving goods. One breed, the Icelandic pony, was particularly sure-footed, which made it possible to move animals to the summer breeding ground and to travel to the Althing at Þingvellir.

The Social Structure in Early Iceland

Prior to the 12th century, slavery was common in Iceland. The slaves (called thralls) were often Irish. Sometimes, thralls were bought to the island by slave traders. Occasionally, if a person was unable to pay a debt, they became a slave, but their condition was only temporary, as they were free once the debt was paid off.

If an individual could not afford to raise a child, they could sell that child into slavery. Slavery in Iceland ended sooner than it did in neighboring countries, and it has been concluded that it did so because of economic factors.

In terms of kinship, Iceland mainly had what is called a cognatic kinship system. In cognatic kinship, the lineage of both parents is equally important. The kin group was defined in relation to the individual and was comprised of a number of people who were not related to each other; thus, the individual was at the center of their own kin group. After marriage, the woman continued to belong to her parents' families, which helped to give women more independence since they could rely on their fathers or brothers for help if they needed it. However, the system also created the potential for conflicts.

Although women were not involved in politics, they were able to own land. However, they were not the first in line to inherit. If a man had a son and a daughter, the son would inherit the land. A woman could only inherit land from her father if he had no legitimate sons. When a woman married, she brought the *mundr* (bride price or dowry). This belonged to the woman. If the marriage ended in death or divorce, the property was divided.

Women had little say in who they married. They were unable to refuse a marriage unless they decided to enter a convent. If her father was no longer alive, she might have had a slight opportunity to negotiate with her relatives. However, forcing a woman into a marriage was generally not advisable.

On the surface, divorce was easy, but according to the law, divorce had to be granted by the bishop. A woman could only leave her husband if it was an exceptional situation; for example, if he proved to be impotent for three years, she had grounds to remarry. If she did leave, she took her property with her.

During the time of the Icelandic Commonwealth, reputation was valued above all else. To achieve a good reputation, a person had to preserve and increase their honor. This was done by demonstrating bravery and honesty. The people also admired physical strength and respected moderation, or hóf. Neither physical strength nor wealth alone was enough to give someone a good reputation.

Violence was a legitimate solution to restore justice in the Icelandic Commonwealth; it actually became a duty because it allowed one to display courage. As an example of how the Icelandic system worked, imagine that your relative was killed. It was seen as shameful if the killer managed to get away with it. Typically, it was acceptable to demand compensation for the murder. However, the individual whose relative was murdered may not find this satisfactory and might not believe that money could replace the loss. They could demand further justice, which could either be accomplished through blood revenge or full outlawry. Full outlawry was a person's complete and permanent exclusion from Icelandic society. Because of the nature of Icelandic society, this was often a death sentence, as the criminal could be openly hunted.

Other than the judgment of outlawry, certain circumstances made killing legal. According to the Greylag, a man had the right to kill the perpetrator of a sexual assault if the victim was his wife, daughter, mother, sister, foster daughter, or foster mother. However, there was a sort of statute of limitations; if a woman was raped, the man had the right to kill the perpetrator until the next Althing.

Chapter 3 – The End of the Commonwealth and the Old Covenant

For the most part, Iceland continued to exist as an independent nation until the 13th century, with limited contact with Norway. Norway itself had become too involved in its own issues to concern itself with what was going on in Iceland. During the 12th and 13th centuries, the most powerful *goðar* started to accumulate tremendous wealth. Power began to be consolidated, allowing a few clans to become more powerful than others. By the 13th century, the *goðorð* in the Icelandic Commonwealth was controlled by five or six families. Families at this point were sometimes united under what is currently called *storgoðar* (great *goðar*) or *storhöfðingjar* (great chieftains). There were power struggles between these *goðar*, and on top of this, the Norwegian king desired to control Iceland. Eventually, the Icelandic Commonwealth came to an end.

Before the Icelandic Commonwealth came to an end, Iceland was in the midst of the *Sturlungaöld*, or the Age of the Sturlungs, which was documented in the *Sturlunga Saga*. This era saw violent internal conflicts that lasted for approximately forty-two years. The Sturlungs, after whom the time is named, were the most powerful family clan.

Concurrently, the king of Norway, Haakon the Old, was seeking to exert his power in Iceland, and he did so by making the *goðar* his vassals. If they did what the king wanted, they would be given gifts and respect. In 1220, Snorri Sturluson, who was one of the Icelandic saga writers and the *goði* for the Sturlung clan, became a vassal of the Norwegian king. Snorri went to Norway to settle a dispute between the Oddaverjar family and some merchants. When Earl Skúli Bárðarson, the king's father-in-law, threatened to send the navy to Iceland to settle the dispute, Snorri agreed to help the king impose his will in Iceland. However, Snorri did not follow through on this agreement.

Snorri's nephew, Sturla Sighvatsson, was a little easier to convince. Sturla came to power as a chieftain of Hvammur around 1200. In 1235, during a return trip from Rome, he stopped in Norway, where he became a vassal of Haakon the Old. When he returned home, he started battling with the other *goðar*. Sturla's plan was to capture individual chieftains and send them to Norway. The king would gradually take over all of the chieftaincies in Iceland, essentially bringing the country under the crown's control. Sturla joined forces with his father, Sighvatur (who was Snorri's brother).

They first went after Snorri, who fled, allowing Sturla to take over Borgarfjörður. Over the next year, Sturla and Sighvatur solidified their positions. In 1238, Sturla summoned Gissur Þorvaldsson, *goði* of the Haukdælir clan, and captured him. Gissur swore to sail to Norway, but while he was a captive, he allied with Kolbeinn the Young, *goði* of the Ásbirnings, who was nervous that he might meet the same fate.

On August 21ˢᵗ, 1238, the combined forces of Gissur and Kolbeinn met Sturla's and Sighvatur's men at Örlygsstaðir, a farm in Skagafjörður, a district in the northern part of the country. The battle did not last long. Sturla and Sighvatur both lost their lives, along with fifty of their men.

Snorri had remained in Norway, still allied with Skúli Bárðarson. When Skúli was killed during an attempted coup, Snorri found himself in a difficult position. When he returned to Norway, Gissur Þorvaldsson (who was another one of the king's vassals) followed through with the king's orders to kill Snorri.

Gissur and seventy of his men came to Snorri's farm in September 1241 and assassinated him. This led to the rise of Gissur and Kolbeinn, both of whom became the most powerful *goðar* in Iceland.

In 1242, Snorri's brother, Þórður Kakali Sighvatsson, came back to Iceland for revenge. His father and brothers had been killed in the Battle of Örlygsstaðir, and he wanted to reclaim the land the Ásbirningar family had taken. In 1245, Kolbeinn the Young gave up the eastern portion. Despite this concession, Þórður killed Kolbeinn's son and successor, Brandr Kolbeinsson. With Brandr gone, Þórður took over the Ásbirningar clan after he secured the people's consent.

Gissur was the most powerful ruler in the south, while Þórður was the most powerful in the north. They did not know who should rule Iceland for the king, so they traveled to Norway to hear the king's decision. King Haakon, whose goal was still the subjugation of Iceland, sent Þórður back to Iceland with the mission of bringing the country under Norway's rule. Gissur remained in Norway. When Þórður returned to Iceland, he was the most powerful man in the nation. However, he seemed to neglect the king's goals, focusing more on his own power. Þórður was forced to return to Norway, where he died six years later.

Gissur was sent back to Iceland in 1252 with two courtiers. One of these courtiers was Þorgils Skarði Böðvarsson. His return led to more fighting between the Sturlungs and the Haukdælir clan. Gissur's farm was attacked, and his enemies burned the buildings and killed his wife and sons. Gissur hid in a barrel of sour whey to avoid being massacred. In 1254, Gissur was summoned to Norway, but the king began to place his trust in Þorgils Skarði instead. Þorgils Skarði was able to convince the Northern Quarter farmers to accept tax obligations to Norway.

In 1256, with the death of Þórður Kakali Sighvatsson (Snorri's brother), Steinvör Sighvatsdóttir (Þórður's sister), one of the most powerful women in Iceland, became Þórður's heir. When she was unable to successfully claim the dominion, she handed it to her son-in-law, Þorvarður Þórarinsson, who was the chieftain of the Svinfellingar family. Þorvarður had Þorgils Skarði killed due to a dispute over territory.

In 1258, King Haakon sent Gissur back to Iceland as his earl to try once again to get Iceland to submit to Norway's rule. When Gissur failed in his mission, the king sent Hallvarður Gullskór to exert pressure on Gissur. Despite all of the infighting, the important Icelandic chieftains decided to sign the Old Covenant (*Gamli sáttmáli*). The *goðorð* system came to an end, and Iceland joined Norway. The first to sign and swear allegiance to the king and his son was the Northern Quarter and the westernmost districts of the Southern Quarter in 1262. By 1264, the Icelandic Commonwealth had officially ended.

After the Commonwealth

The Old Covenant essentially guaranteed three important things. First, the Icelanders became the subjects of Norway. In return, Norway had to protect the peace in Iceland. Iceland was also considered a separate legislative district. And finally, the Icelanders were subject to heavy taxation.

After Haakon's death, his son, Magnus, became king. King Haakon had explored a policy of expansion, but Magnus's focus differed. He revised the Norwegian law, and in 1271, he sent a new legal code to Iceland based on the new Norwegian laws. This code was called *Járnsíða* (ironside). With these new laws, the institution of the *goði* was formally abolished, and the system of the Law Council changed. The Law Council became, in essence, an appeals court, and the Quarter Courts and the Fifth Court were also abolished. The king's representative was to appoint the members chosen by the farmers. Additionally, the concept of wergild was established. With wergild, the murder of an individual was not only a crime against the family of the victim but also a crime against the king. This limited the old practice of blood revenge, as the perpetrator was instead required to pay a fine for their crime.

In 1280, Magnus sent a new legal code to Iceland called Jónsbók. It was named after the man who brought it to Iceland, Icelander Jón Einarsson, who was also most likely one of the code's main authors. This new code helped to bring Icelandic law closer to Norway's laws.

The Icelanders were not overly enthusiastic about the new law, and it had some opposition at the Althing in 1281. Three groups opposed Jónsbók, and the king's representative, Loðinn Leppr, declared that it was the king's prerogative to determine the laws and demanded that they accept the new code. Despite the continued resistance, the Icelanders eventually accepted the code. Jónsbók became popular over time and was the law of the land for four centuries.

With Jónsbók, the law was a little bit amorphous, as the king could amend it at any time. The Althing still had some say in the decrees, which they could pass and send on to the king, who would then choose to accept or reject them. One of the important points to note, though, is that if a law was passed in Norway, it didn't automatically become law in Iceland, thus ensuring that Iceland retained some independence and remained an independent law district.

There was an interesting twist in regard to the Old Covenant. Essentially, Icelanders had signed the Old Covenant, swearing allegiance to Haakon. This allegiance to the king and not to the country of Norway meant that whenever a new king came to power, Iceland had to renew the Old Covenant, which could result in the addition of new stipulations. Thus, in 1302, a stipulation was added that might have been fueled by nationalism. Essentially, only Icelanders who came from the families that had surrendered the *goðorð* could become lawmen (essentially enforcers of the law) and sheriffs.

The church also experienced some changes in its power in 1269, shortly after the end of the Icelandic Commonwealth. After Árni Þorláksson was ordained, he took over the bishopric of Skálholt. At this point, the staðamál, which was the struggle over church property, began when the archbishop of Niðaróss, Árni's superior in Norway, stated that all tithes should go to the bishop.

During the autumn and the following summer of his first year as bishop, Árni traveled to the Southern and Eastern Quarters of his diocese. He informed them of the dictate. Those on the small church farms and those in the Eastern Quarters conceded. Those who were on more profitable farms did not comply easily. One notable place of resistance was Oddi, a church in Rangárvellir in southern Iceland. In 1270, at the Althing, a resolution was passed that stated Oddi was the property of the Catholic Church. However, this didn't solve the dispute over who owned Oddi, as the keepers of Oddi maintained that it had been bought by their mother, Steinvör Sighvatsdóttir.

When the conflict couldn't be resolved, they sent the issue to higher authorities. The king judged that the *staðr* ("church") of Oddi and the church farm of Vatnsfjörður belonged to the Catholic Church. Prior to this ruling, the Catholic church only owned half of the church farm. Árni continued to lay claim to church farms after this, and Steinvör's sons were among those forced to leave their patrimony.

After this victory, Bishop Árni introduced reforms and had a new Christian law passed at the Althing. Árni's victory was never completed, as the king died in 1280. His son, who was only twelve, inherited the throne, and an anticlerical government came into power. They declared all of the church legislation passed by Magnus to be invalid. In 1283, Hrafn Oddsson returned to Iceland from Norway, bringing a decree that restored the church farms back to the laymen.

The conflict did not end there, though. In 1291, after King Eric came fully to power, Árni once again tried to hand over the church farms to his clergy. In 1295, a decree came from Norway in an attempt to reach a compromise. In the end, approximately one hundred church farms were under the church's control, while approximately two hundred church farms remained in the hands of laymen.

Chapter 4 – Foreign Powers and Their Influence on Iceland

Drama in Scandinavia

Because of the connection between Norway and Iceland, the history of Iceland is tied to events in Norway and the rest of Scandinavia.

In Norway, Haakon V Magnusson moved the capital from Bergen to Oslo in 1299 after he came to power. Haakon V then betrothed his daughter, Ingeborg, to Eric, a Swedish prince. Ingeborg was only two years old when she was betrothed and only twelve years old when she married. The couple had a son named Magnus. In 1319, when Magnus was three, he inherited the thrones of both Norway and Sweden, as his father had passed away the year before. This inheritance led to a period of extreme unrest in Scandinavia. On top of this, the Black Death ravaged Europe in the 14th century and was particularly deadly in Norway. Because of Iceland's isolation, it was spared from the devastation, although it would contend with its own plague later on.

The Norwegians felt that Magnus, the son of Ingeborg, was more closely tied to Sweden, so they removed him from the Norwegian throne in 1355 and installed his son, Haakon VI, on the throne in his stead. In 1365, Magnus was held in captivity for six years by Duke Albrecht (Albert) of Mecklenburg, Magnus's nephew and a contender for the Swedish throne. Throughout this time, Magnus kept Iceland, which helped to dissolve the union between Iceland and Norway. Although Magnus co-ruled over Sweden with his son, the two were deposed in 1364, with Albrecht taking the Swedish throne. In 1374, Magnus drowned after his ship sank.

The problems did not stop there. Haakon married Margaret, the twelve-year-old daughter of King Valdemar IV of Denmark, in 1363, creating an alliance between Denmark and Norway. The couple had a son, Olaf, who took the Danish throne when he was five years old in 1376. When Olaf took the Norwegian throne four years later, Iceland became a subject of the Danish Crown. The union of Denmark and Norway lasted until 1814, but Iceland remained a Danish subject much longer.

Margaret took over the rule of both Denmark and Norway when Olaf died in 1387. Then, in 1389, an opposition party in Sweden deposed Albrecht. Margaret had the foresight to ally with the opposition, and she became regent of all three countries after an election in Sweden. She adopted her six-year-old great-nephew, who was from Pomerania (modern-day Poland). Upon his adoption, she renamed him Eric. In 1397, what came to be known as the Kalmar Union began. Eric of Pomerania was crowned king of Denmark, Norway, and Sweden at Kalmar, Sweden. Denmark became the dominant power in this union, although Sweden broke away in the 1520s, ending the union. At this time, Iceland was still considered part of Norway, so Eric ruled Iceland as Eric III of Norway.

A map of the Kalmar Union.

With the seat of power in Denmark, Iceland became more isolated from the rest of Scandinavia. Iceland was, in essence, a dependency of a dependency. Greenland, the other North Atlantic island that had been settled by the Norse, was pretty much forgotten by that point.

Sometime between 1260 and 1340, Iceland started exporting fish. The centers of power and culture in Iceland had been in two episcopal sees (where the bishop's seat is): Skálholt in the south and Hólar in the north. Both of these sites were far from the coast. However, as fishing became more important from the 14th century on, prosperous families began settling in the coastal areas. During the summer months, they farmed, and in the winter, the men fished. The women remained on the farms for the most part, raising the children and tending to the crops. Essentially, the men who worked as farmhands during the summer months caught fish during the winter months and shared a portion with the year-round farmers.

The spawning of cod helped to determine the fishing season. During the spawning season, cod came close to the southern and western coasts. This lasted from approximately January or February until May, which means there was a slight overlap with the farming season. While the men were fishing, they lived in primitive fishing camps. These camps were seasonal, but once fishing became a year-round occupation in the 19th century, fishing towns began to appear.

To fish, the men set out in open rowboats. These boats had twelve to fourteen oars and a mast; they could use a sail if the wind was right. Fishing required significant skill. The men typically used the line and hook method, and they had to use landmarks to locate and recognize fishing banks. Additionally, because of the challenges that storms might pose, they had to be able to forecast the weather. Finally, they had to be able to make difficult landings on the sandy beaches.

Interestingly, in the 7th or 8th century, people began to shift from fasting during Lent to allowing the consumption of fish, which led to a profitable fish trade for Iceland, which would become a central part of the nation's history.

The Plague

From 1402 to 1404, Iceland contended with a plague, although few details are known about it. During the 15th century, unlike the rest of Icelandic history, most written narratives were not kept, so, unfortunately, many of the details of the plague were lost. However, the *New Annal* provides some information. The first death came in August, and at that point, the plague began to spread throughout the island nation. By Christmas, it reached the bishop's see at Skálholt and the district of Skagafjörður in the central north. The year 1403 was called the "year of great mortality" in the *New Annal*. The plague remained in Iceland for nineteen months. It appears that shortly after Easter 1404, the plague receded. The annal also lists the names of those who died from the plague in the central Westfjords and in the central Eastern Quarter.

The plague arrived once again in 1494 and lasted for a year. There is even less information about this second plague. Based on the limited evidence we have, we know it arrived in the southwest area of Iceland sometime in 1494 and persisted through the winter. The death rate is also unclear, but the mortality rate was extremely high based on the extant sources, including an annal written by Jón Egilsson in 1605 and eyewitness reports.

England's Role in the 15ᵗʰ Century

Iceland had something the English wanted: stockfish. Stockfish mainly come from varieties of cod (although other types of whitefish, such as haddock, can be used). They are unsalted and dried in the sun and wind. Although the origins of the English term "stockfish" are unknown, it may come from the wooden racks the fish are hung on to dry or from the appearance of the fish once they are dry (they look like a stick). Drying fish on wooden racks is cheap, so huge amounts of fish can be dried within a few months. Typically, the drying process takes place in the winter when the fish are less likely to be destroyed by mold, insects, or bacteria, which have a harder time surviving in the cold temperature.

To make stockfish, the fish is gutted and its head removed. After this, the fish is either dried whole or split along the spine. During the drying process, fermentation takes place, and once the drying process is complete, the stockfish needs to mature for another two to three months, typically under a roof.

Although this is a recent picture, it gives you an idea of what drying cod might have looked like.

Since cod was such an important Icelandic commodity, in 1415, emissaries from the Danish-Norwegian monarchy asked the king of England to prohibit English ships from sailing to Iceland to fish. The first time English fishermen were noted in Icelandic sources was in 1412, when an English fishing boat arrived east of Dyrhólaey, the southernmost point of Iceland. The year after that, five English fishermen remained in Iceland after they had gone ashore, possibly to find food, although they may have been left behind. In 1414, a ship showed up with a license from the Danish-Norwegian Crown to fish; around thirty ships arrived in the waters around Iceland that year. Based on records, it is safe to say that at least one hundred English fishing boats traveled to Iceland each year between 1430 and 1550. The men on these large ships were sometimes heavily armed, with the ships carrying between one hundred and four hundred tons. Needless to say, the English typically got what they wanted, and this period of Icelandic history is sometimes called "the English century."

In 1425, the English captured Hannes Paulsson, the Danish governor in Iceland, for trying to enforce the ban on foreign traders. Hannes was taken to England, where he compiled a list of the crimes the English had committed in Iceland. However, he did not show much respect for the Icelanders, noting their gullibility. There is reason to doubt the veracity of the governor's statements since the New Annal does not describe any such actions by the English, and it doesn't seem the Icelanders were too upset by the kidnapping. At least one of Hannes's accusations seems to be true: the English theft of Icelandic children. Back in 1429, Jón Gerreksson (also spelled as Jöns Gerekesson), a Danish bishop of Skálholt, traveled to England and confirmed that thirteen Icelandic children had been stolen.

Jón Gerreksson himself met a mysterious fate. When he died, the New Annal ended, so there is no clear account of his death. It is known that he was killed in the spring of 1433, and it is assumed that his killers were from Iceland.

Another annal wasn't written until around one hundred years later. The new writers asserted that the responsibility for the murder rested on the shoulders of the bishop's foreign pages. According to the claims, the pages kidnapped and imprisoned two young upper-class Icelanders. However, the two youths escaped and sought revenge. They captured Jón Gerreksson, put him in a sack, and drowned him in a river. This explanation made sense when the annalists made the claim, especially since the people believed that having foreigners in positions of power was not desirable. However, today, there is little support for the theory that the pages were involved in the murder.

With a shifting understanding of history, this story has come under question lately. One possibility for the murder was that Bishop Jón had committed a crime against the Crown, which then led to his assassination. Another possibility is that Icelandic allies of the English committed the crime, possibly even doing the bidding of the bishop of Hólar, an Englishman named John Williamson Craxton.

There was another high-profile death during this time that was not shrouded in mystery. In 1467, Björn Þorleifsson, the king's governor who was a native Icelander, was murdered when a conflict arose between the kings of Denmark and England. The Danish Crown tried to impose a fee on foreign ships, which the king of England did not agree with. When English merchants went to Iceland, they were most likely expelled because they did not have a license. Angered, they killed Þorleifsson and stole gold, silver, and clothing from his family. They burned down houses and confiscated the taxes that had been collected for the king.

Interestingly, the story of Þorleifsson spawned a myth: the myth of his wife's revenge. According to one story, Ólöf Loftsdóttir, Þorleifsson's wife, gathered troops. In another, she had every Englishman she could find in Iceland executed. There is no evidence to support these stories of her heroism, though.

Some like to see Björn's death as the event that helped to spur decisive action against England. From 1468 to 1473, Denmark and the Hanseatic League (a German trading confederation) fought a war against England. By the end of the war, Germany was more involved in Icelandic trade.

At the end of "the English century," the Icelanders had not really transformed. While they did have a variety of new goods, including shoes, clothes, tools, and wine, the English did not have a lasting effect on life in Iceland. They did not affect fishing traditions, and the English fishing camps did not become permanent fishing villages. Since the English didn't have a permanent presence in Iceland, their culture did not spread very much.

The Germans

The Hanseatic League, which had its beginnings as a loose association of German traders and towns, was established as a formal political power in the 14th century. The purpose of the Hanseatic League was to protect its members and advance commercial interests. As such, the League tried to reduce trade barriers and helped to create financial prosperity among its members. However, the League was not some grand nation; it was nothing more than a confederation of city-states. In the mid-14th century, the first German Hansa (a guild of merchants) was established in Bergen, Norway.

Around 1470, German merchants who were not residents of Bergen made their first trip to Iceland. By 1481, these German merchants were perceived as a threat to those Germans who lived in Bergen, and the resident Germans complained to the Hanseatic League. The League listened and asserted that all German trade was to originate from Bergen; the German merchants could not just travel to wherever they liked in Iceland. However, members of the League did not always obey the dictate, as the German-Iceland trade was also run from Hamburg.

At first, the Germans were fishing for stockfish off the coast of Iceland, which they then sold to the English. However, this changed around the turn of the 16th century when they started to bring most of their catch back to Hamburg.

Around 1490, King Hans of Denmark began to try to accumulate allies since he wanted to regain the Swedish throne. He confirmed the privileges of the Hanseatic League and made a treaty with England, allowing the English to sail to Iceland for fishing and trade, provided they purchased an annual license from Denmark and paid the requisite duties and taxes. He also allowed the Dutch to trade freely with Iceland.

When the Icelanders learned about King Hans of Denmark's actions, they passed a new law, Pining's Verdict, at the Althing. It was named after the governor of Iceland at the time, Didrik Pining. It is unclear who initiated the law; it may have been Pining himself, but it also could have been Icelandic officials or wealthier farmers.

Pining's Verdict addressed the potential issues with England's new access to Iceland. First, the Icelanders wanted all British and German merchants to keep the peace while in Icelandic waters. Icelanders were not to trade with any merchants who did not follow this term.

Foreigners were forbidden from wintering in Iceland, although there were a few exceptions, such as if their ships were damaged or if they were wounded or sick. If they had to stay, they could not sell goods for a higher price than in the summer, and they could not employ Icelanders. Icelanders who illegally housed foreigners were to be punished.

And finally, cottars (peasant farmers who lived in a cottage and worked a small plot of land) were not allowed to remain in the country unless they met stringent wealth requirements. If they were unable to meet those requirements, they had to work for farmers.

Pining's Verdict managed to keep the extant policies in place and helped to maintain the system that benefited the wealthy. Anyone who was unable to afford to run a farm of his own was forced to work as a farmhand. It also kept people from using trade as their only job.

However, the rules regarding foreign merchants not remaining in Iceland during the winter and foreign merchants maintaining peace between themselves were not enforceable. Records of conflicts exist. When ships captured a competitor's ship, the captor often stole the cargo and killed the sailors.

One particular conflict is of note. This particular conflict began in April 1532 in the harbor of Básendar, a small town on the Reykjanes Peninsula when two English ships, carrying a total of 140 men in all, fought a crew of 30 Germans. The German crew was small, but more Germans and Icelanders joined them. Ultimately, with the help of cannons, crossbows, and spears, the

Germans defeated the English. They ended up beheading two of the English and torturing two others. The English were forced to surrender more than forty tons of stockfish. Only one of the two ships was allowed to leave the harbor, with the other one being left behind.

The surviving ship fled to Grindavík, one of the most important English harbors in Iceland. In June, a German-Icelandic force attacked the British at Grindavík. The attacking force consisted of 180 to 280 men, and they defeated the English once again. One of the English ships tried to flee, but it got stranded, and all of the crew drowned. All other Englishmen were either expelled from Grindavík or killed. This also included the English who were not involved in the conflict.

Obviously, this was not a small conflict, so the kings of both England and Denmark got involved. Together with the Council of Hamburg, the two parties created a peace treaty in 1533. According to the treaty, those from England and Hamburg were allowed to sail freely to Iceland during the summer. However, the Althing restricted fishing vessels because foreign fishing took finances from both Iceland and the Danish king, a ban that was aimed mainly at the English since they were the ones fishing off the coast of Iceland. The Norwegian Council of State agreed on the treaty.

This did not completely end the conflict, nor did it stop the English. In 1539, before the English were expelled, for the most part, from Iceland, three Englishmen were sentenced for attacking people, pillaging, and charging exorbitant prices. Although they were driven out of Grindavík, they had a permanent camp on the Westman Islands, located off Iceland's southern coast. They maintained this camp until 1558 when the Danes confiscated it. However, the English continued to sail to Iceland. Around sixty fishing ships annually sailed to Iceland, and these ships engaged in illegal trade, and their crews occasionally pillaged.

Iceland's relations with Hamburg stayed the same, at least for a period of time. The Germans established a permanent settlement in Hafnarfjörður, where they built timber frame houses. This didn't last long, though, as King Christian III of

Denmark and Norway started a new policy in which Denmark would benefit from Iceland. In 1542, he renewed the policy of prohibiting foreigners from living in Iceland during the winter, and within a year or two, he began confiscating German fishing boats in the Reykjanes area. This began a slow withdrawal of the Germans from Iceland.

Although the rest of Europe during this time period was generally engaged in greater communication and trade, Iceland did not follow this pattern, instead remaining a satellite of Denmark, which was itself only a minor trading power.

The Effects of the Reformation

The Reformation began in 1517 when Martin Luther criticized the sale of indulgences in the Catholic Church. Luther's believed the worship of saints and the reverence of holy relics, two components of the Catholic Church, be forbidden. He also advocated for individualism, essentially emphasizing the individual's contact with God. This eliminated the distinction between clergy and the common man and essentially disposed of monasteries, convents, and clerical celibacy. Although Luther didn't set out to change Christianity, his actions ultimately led to a major shift in thinking. In Germany and Scandinavia, the Reformation largely ended Catholic supremacy and put power in the hands of national and regional princes.

In Scandinavia, Lutheranism became a popular religious movement. Part of the reason it was so popular is related to property ownership. The Catholic Church owned property in Scandinavia, and Scandinavia viewed this property as a potential source of income. Hence, Lutheranism began to rapidly spread, with the Swedish Crown severing all ties with Rome by 1527. Nine years later, the Danish Crown followed suit. In Norway, there was a revolt led by the archbishop of Trondheim, but this was swiftly crushed. Once the revolt was crushed in 1537, the Norwegian Council of State was abolished.

Iceland did not have a Protestant movement, and Lutheranism first appeared around 1537 (at the latest) in Hafnarfjörður. The service was most likely performed in German, as the church there had been built by German merchants. During these early years, there were only four known

Lutherans in Iceland, all at the bishop's see in Skálholt. They were unable to advance their cause, but they didn't have to wait too long. King Christian III created the Church Ordinance of 1537, which introduced Lutheranism in Denmark. The ordinance first spread through Denmark before making its way to Iceland. In 1540, the bishop of Hólar, Jón Arason, rejected the ordinance.

An image of Jón Arason.

Navaro, CC BY-SA 3.0 <https://creativecommons.org/licenses/by-sa/3.0>, via Wikimedia Commons; https://commons.wikimedia.org/wiki/File:J%C3%B3n_Arason_-_gr%C3%B6f.jpg

It seems as if the Danish Crown was not in a particular hurry to impose Lutheranism in Iceland. However, Lutheranism became a tool to improve the king's and his bailiff at Bessastaðir's situation. In 1539, on Whit Sunday (the High Holy Day of Pentecost), the bailiff, Didrich von Minden, went to the nearby monastery of Viðey with thirteen men. They stole food and livestock and began running the monastery as a fief of Bessastaðir. Didrich von Minden did not stop there. In August of the same year, he took a group of ten men with the intention of taking the convent of Kirkjubær and the monastery of Þykkvibær. Unfortunately for all involved, they took a detour to Skálholt. They stayed the night there and decided to remain the next day, even though the bishop warned them against it. The steward of Skálholt summoned a group of farmers, and they killed every one of von Minden's men except for a twelve-year-old boy. The monastery at Viðey was retaken.

An image of Viðey today.
Navaro CC BY-SA 3.0 <https://creativecommons.org/licenses/by-sa/3.0>, via Wikimedia Commons; https://en.wikipedia.org/wiki/File:Videy_085.jpg)

Ögmundur Pálsson was the bishop of Skálholt, and he was almost completely blind. He had already begun to prepare his successor, Gissur Einarsson. Oddly, Gissur was a prominent member of the Lutheran Skálholt group, while the bishop was Catholic. Why Gissur was chosen as the successor is unclear. It is possible that Gissur was able to hide his Protestantism from the bishop, who was going blind, or it may be that the bishop had decided to surrender to the power of the Danish Crown. Although the reason is a bit uncertain, Gissur was sent to Denmark to be ordained, and he remained there until 1540. He did not return as an ordained Protestant bishop or "superintendent," as they were called. He was instead nominated to be a bishop by the king. Upon his return, Gissur took over Skálholt.

For reasons that are unclear, Ögmundur wrote to Bishop Jón Arason of Hólar complaining about the way Gissur was running things. Ögmundur suggested that Jón should convene a court of priests to judge Gissur, hinting that the most desirable result would see Gissur kicked out of office. This did not work out for Ögmundur, as Gissur ended up getting the letter. A Danish naval officer arrived in Iceland to restore royal power in May 1541, and Gissur contacted him immediately. A few days later, Ögmundur was captured and brought to Denmark. His fate is unknown, but his considerable lands became the Crown's property.

Gissur died in 1548, and after he was gone, Jón Arason began a counteroffensive against Protestantism. He attended a synod in Skálholt in June of that year, where he had a staunch Catholic abbot elected as bishop. Jón Arason himself was chosen to be the provisional administrator of the see, essentially giving him the power of a bishop. Jón Arason's opponents chose their own candidate, Marteinn Einarsson, a man appointed by the Danish Crown and ordained as "superintendent and bishop."

In response, Jón Arason built a fortress at Hólar, which he planned to arm with cannons and guns. Jón Arason and his two sons managed to capture Marteinn Einarsson. He was held captive in the fortress throughout the winter.

This did not sit well with King Christian III of Denmark and Norway, who decided that it was time to do something about Jón. The king wrote to Marteinn's brother-in-law, Daði Guðmundsson, who was a sheriff, asking him to capture Bishop Jón. However, Daði did not follow the king's requests. Jón went to Skálholt that summer, bringing the captive Marteinn with him. After making threats against Marteinn, he managed to have the see surrendered to him. Jón reconsecrated the church and had Gissur's body unearthed just so that he could throw it in a pit.

After this, Jón headed to the Althing, where he declared himself the overlord of Christianity in Skálholt. Supposedly, he proclaimed, "Now the whole of Iceland submits to me, except for one and a half cottar's sons." Historians are not quite sure who the cottar's son was, but they generally agree that the "half son" he referred to was Daði.

It is not clear what Jón's long-term plans were, but that doesn't matter because he wouldn't live for much longer. He took two of his sons and thirty men to Sauðafell in Dalasýsla, which was near Daði's home. However, Daði showed up with men who were superior to Jón's forces. Jón's men fled, and he and his sons were captured in a church and taken to Skálholt. Their captors had to decide the best way to keep them secure before they could be transported to Denmark. It turned out that the best way to keep them pacified was to dispose of them. On November 7th, 1550, they were beheaded.

Things weren't settled yet. In January, about sixty men came south seeking revenge for the executions. It is believed the group was led by Þórunn Jónsdóttir, one of Jón's daughters. They killed the bailiff and started to kill any Danes they could find. They killed fourteen men in all, wiping out the Danish administration in Iceland.

The news of Jón's death did not reach the Danish Crown, so King Christian sent warships to Iceland. Once there, they discovered what had happened and convened a court to try the traitor (who was, of course, already dead). He was declared rightfully executed, and the Crown claimed his land.

After the Reformation

During the late medieval period, bishoprics were the largest Icelandic institution and were quite wealthy. They received a quarter of the tithe annually. Each one also owned hundreds of farms, which it rented to tenants. Additionally, the bishoprics received a large portion of fines from people who went against the church and Christian law. This would change under King Christian III, who abolished the bishoprics. He also instituted the "superintendents" but decreed that the superintendents were to be limited. He did not want them to be better off than a wealthy farmer, so their household was not overly extravagant. For instance, they could only have two maids.

This policy took place in both Denmark and Norway but did not reach Iceland until later. By the late 18th century, the bishoprics in Iceland had been completely abolished. While the Danish Crown did not completely abolish the bishoprics in Iceland, they took the bishop's share of the tithe in 1556. The tithe was a necessary component in keeping the bishoprics and schools running. After this was discovered, the tithe was reintroduced, albeit with some changes. Half of the district paid the king's tithe, while the other half paid the bishop's tithe.

Landed property within the bishoprics remained intact, at least for the most part. As a result, the bishoprics ran seminaries for future clergymen and university students. These Latin schools remained the only formal educational institutions in Iceland for hundreds of years. Iceland was a rural country and a land without an educated bourgeoisie. The sees were the only permanent centers for learning.

The Crown granted permission to Bishop Gissur Einarsson to establish schools in dioceses throughout Iceland. However, he did not create schools; instead, monks and nuns continued to occupy the buildings. The opportunity to introduce more widespread education slipped from his grasp. The nuns' cloisters became royal fiefs run by commissaries, and the remaining farms were rented to tenants. The Danish Crown became the second-largest landowner in Iceland, owning 17 percent of the land; the Lutheran Church remained the largest landowner.

The church also lost a significant chunk of its judicial power after the Reformation. In 1564, a law was passed at the Althing called the Stóridómur (the Great Verdict). The rules against sexual behavior became stricter and an exclusively secular matter. Prior to the Great Verdict, the Catholic Church, for the most part, would forgive most moral crimes with a fine. This strict new law established a death sentence for offenses involving incest or for committing adultery three times.

Sexual crimes were not the only ones that were punished, although they were considered some of the more serious crimes.

For lesser crimes, punishments included whipping, outlawry, and fines. Men who faced the death sentence were beheaded, while women were drowned. Over the course of the two centuries that the Great Verdict was the law, it is estimated that one hundred people were executed.

The Lutheran Church became involved in the education of commoners. The church, of course, held that every individual should be familiar with scripture and be able to interpret it correctly. The relatively recent invention of the printing press helped to facilitate this education. It is ironic that the printing press was introduced to Iceland in the days of Jón Arason; he may have actually been the one responsible for facilitating it, although that is not certain.

Prior to the arrival of the printing press in Iceland, books and hymnals were printed in Danish and German. Because of the Bible's prominence in Iceland, it posed a threat to Icelandic poetry, as some of the poetry's characteristics were lost in the translations to other languages. The poetry lost its regular alliteration and its regular rhyme. Often, words were borrowed from Danish, and if the melody required the declensions of Icelandic to be dropped, it did so. Essentially, only the religious message remained.

Luckily for Icelandic poetry, Guðbrandur Þorláksson was appointed the bishop of Hólar in 1571. He bought a printing press and hired a typographer. Nearly 110 books were published at Hólar. In 1584, they printed five hundred copies of the Bible in Icelandic. The Icelandic Bible cost the price of two or three cows, although the price was determined by the buyer's means. Each copy was illustrated and included vignettes and ornamented initials. Other books published by Guðbrandur include a prayer book and a hymnal, which formed the basis of Icelandic church singing until the 19th century.

As much as Guðbrandur helped to preserve Icelandic poetry, it was destructive. He published his *Vísnabók* (*Verse Book*) in 1612. In this book, he attempted to get rid of two types of secular poetry: the ballad and the *rímur*. According to Guðbrandur, the ballad was amorous verses. A *ríma* (the singular form of *rímur*) was an epic poem. Essentially, it has two to four lines per stanza (although four is typical), rhyme, and alliteration. They also follow a metrical pattern and use kennings (a compound word that uses figurative language in place of a common noun) and *heiti* (a synonym in place of a more common word; for example, instead of saying "sea," one could say "salt.").

Although Guðbrandur wasn't successful in getting rid of ballads and *rímur*, his contribution was exceedingly important. When the Lutheran Church moved toward using the vernacular rather than Latin, Icelandic was preserved, and the language remained close to the medieval Norse language.

Chapter 5 – The 17th Century

The 17th century is considered one of the low points in Icelandic history, as it was marked by a trade monopoly and a period of absolutism. This century also saw two dreadful occurrences: the Turkish Raid of 1627 and the witch hunt.

The Danish Crown was unable to expel the German traders from Iceland, so they sought other pathways to deal with them. Frederick II of Denmark and Norway (r. 1559–1588) had begun a policy of leasing Iceland's harbors to merchants, which led to a lively trade but also led to an increase in the cost of goods. Christian IV (r. 1588–1648) adopted the policy of mercantilism, which was popular at the time. Under this system, the state aimed to increase its wealth by promoting trade, using the tools of monopolies and privileges in particular. On April 20th, 1602, Christian IV issued a decree creating a trade monopoly. Under this decree, the citizens of Copenhagen, Elsinore, and Malmö (which was, at that point, part of Denmark but is now in Sweden) were given exclusive trading rights with Iceland for twelve years. This restriction on trade was to last for 186 years! Around 1620, thirty-six of the merchants founded the Icelandic, Faroese, and Nordic Trade Company, which was successful for about forty years. It faced problems during the Danish-Swedish War, which lasted from 1657 to 1660. It was dissolved in 1662, as the war caused the end of the company's regular trade with Iceland.

After the war, the merchants began leasing harbors again, although they were leasing them in pairs in auctions. One harbor was used for the export of stockfish, while the other was for the export of mutton and woolen products. Iceland itself was divided into trading districts, which were organized around the harbors. This meant that Icelanders could not pick and choose to get a better deal. If they did, they were punished. On the other hand, merchants were given free rein to trade outside of their district.

The merchants then took it a step further. They believed the trade regulations prevented people from carrying exportable goods between districts. Essentially, if a peasant journeyed elsewhere in the country to fish, that peasant was required to sell the catch in the trade district where it was caught; they could not bring it home to sell. The merchants also pressed charges against the bishop of Hólar, who tried to bring rents from other districts back to the see. Overall, though, the trade monopoly had some positive effects. It helped with price fluctuations, allowed the smaller, less wealthy communities to get some trade, and favored farming, although fishing was more profitable.

One of the other problems Iceland faced during this century was the Turkish Raid of 1627. Historically, Iceland was defenseless. While the trade monopoly existed, the Danish Crown sent warships to protect trading ships as they traveled to Iceland. Occasionally, during the summer months, the warships remained in the waters. Their goal was to keep foreign fishing boats away from the coast while the trading vessels were in the harbors.

Iceland's lack of a defensive force was not usually problematic. But once pirates from North Africa began roaming the North Atlantic, its lack of a military force became a problem.

In 1627, four pirate ships from Algeria and Morocco arrived in Iceland. Although they were not from Turkey, they were called "Turks" in Iceland because Algeria and Morocco were both part of the Ottoman Empire; in Iceland, they referred to the empire as the Turkish Empire.

One of the four ships arrived in the harbor of Grindavík and captured fifteen Icelanders and a few Danes. After this, they captured a Danish cargo ship. The two ships started to sail to

Bessastaðir, the residence of the Danish governor, Holger Rosenkrantz. Once Rosenkrantz heard the news, he set up cannons in the small fortress near his residence. Because of the weight of the ships' cargo and captives, one of the ships was stuck near Bessastaðir for two days. The pirates tried to lighten the load by shifting the cargo and their captives.

One of the members of the defense force was Jón Ólafsson. He was an experienced cannoneer and had served in the Royal Danish Navy. He saw the opportunity to open fire on the pirates, but the Danish governor stayed his hand. It is not known why, but the pirates were able to sail home with their ill-gotten gains.

Two of the other ships went to the East Fjords. They sailed around the coastline for a week, taking at least 110 prisoners and killing at least 9. After meeting up with the last ship, the three ships set sail for the Westman Islands. Over the course of 2 days, they captured 242 people, killed between 30 and 40, and destroyed property, burning churches and warehouses.

The descendants of the Vikings were not able to put up much of a fight against the invaders. However, they did stay true to their natures as composers of stories, as they wrote down the details of the invasion. One of the writers, Klaus Eyjólfsson, came to the island about a month after the attack and interviewed those who had survived. He provided the excruciating and sometimes graphic details of the invasion. Björn Jónsson, a self-educated farmer and annalist who wrote the *Story of the Turkish Raid*, also made a number of observations about the raid itself and the individuals who appeared to enjoy killing and mutilating people.

The pirates transported their captives to Algeria, where they were to be sold in the slave market. Over time, some of the captives died from diseases. Some got free of their own accord, and a few converted to Islam. Those who converted to Islam had the opportunity to return to Iceland, but they declined.

One of the captives, a Lutheran minister named Ólafur Egilsson, was sent to Denmark to negotiate a ransom for the captives. It took him six months to reach Copenhagen. When he arrived, Denmark did not have the money to meet the ransom because its funds had been depleted from the Thirty Years' War. Ólafur returned to Iceland penniless and without his family.

Eventually, ten years after they were taken captive, the remaining thirty-four Icelanders were ransomed and returned to Iceland. Ólafur's wife, Ásta, was among those who returned. In 1639, three years after Ásta returned, Ólafur died. He was seventy-five when he died, but he had managed to write of his unfortunate travels upon his return to Iceland.

One of the other individuals who eventually returned to Iceland was Guðríður Símonardóttir. Guðríður was captured while she was living at Stakkagerði with her husband, a fisherman named Eyjólfur Sölmundarson. Eyjólfur evaded capture, but Guðríður faced a much different fate. Once she arrived in Algeria, she was sold as a slave and became a concubine. Although she saved money to pay her ransom, she did not earn enough. However, once the ransom for the remaining Icelanders was paid, she was also released. She returned, but her son, who had also been captured during the raid, decided to remain in Algeria.

Before the captives were returned to Iceland, they were transported to Denmark so they could be reeducated. Guðríður was taught by a theology student named Hallgrímur Pétursson. Guðríður and Hallgrímur fell in love, and she got pregnant. When they returned to Iceland, Guðríður discovered her husband had died. This was fortunate for her; with her husband out of the picture, she had committed the offense of concubinage rather than adultery. In 1637, she gave birth to a son, whom they named Eyjólfur after her first husband. The next year, the couple married. Hallgrímur, who was ordained as a minister, became known for his poetry and hymns, particularly his works about the life and death of Christ called the *Passíusálmar* (*Passion Hymns*). This collection of fifty hymns continues to be published, and there is a custom in Iceland in which the dead are sometimes buried with copies. Each day during Lent, one hymn is read on the radio.

Unfortunately for Guðríður, she became the focus of gossip and was given the derogatory nickname Tyrkja-Gudda ("Gudda the Turk"). Some later folktales said she seduced Hallgrímur and kept Muslim idols in secret. As Sigurður Nordal, an Icelandic writer and scholar who defended her, noted that this did not make sense. If she was Muslim, she would not keep or worship idols.

The 17th century was also the time of the witch hunts in Iceland, which got their start in 1625. That year, the first victim was burned to death in Eyjafjörður. He had been accused of conjuring a ghost and sending the ghost to one of his neighbors. The ghost supposedly committed several appalling actions, including the murder of some horses. The man did not confess to the crime but was found guilty after the court found he had sheets bearing runic inscriptions.

After this first execution, witchcraft accusations were infrequent until the middle of the 17th century when a new sheriff came to power: Þórleifur Kortsson. This new sheriff most likely learned the European manner of dealing with cases of witchcraft during his time in Hamburg. In his first year as sheriff, Þórleifur burned three men at the stake in Strandasýsla.

Three years later, a clergyman named Jón Magnusson in a nearby town became ill with a strange illness. Jón Magnusson levied accusations against a father and son, both named Jón Jónsson. Incidentally, Jón Magnusson had suffered from a similar illness earlier in 1627. The clergyman wrote of his illness in his account *Píslarsaga*, describing his physical suffering and demonic visions. The father and son were arrested in 1656 and confessed to using magic spells and trying to kill Magnusson, but they denied being in league with the devil. On April 10th of that year, they were burned at the stake.

After their death, Jón Magnusson's illness continued, so he assumed witchcraft was still at work. He figured that it must be the oldest daughter of Jón Jónsson, Þuríður Jónsdóttir. She was able to flee. But even with her gone, Jón Magnusson's madness continued, and in the second part of the *Píslarsaga*, he documents his continued problems and claims that the authorities were allowing witchcraft to run rampant throughout the country. In 1658, Þuríður Jónsdóttir was acquitted of the charges against her after several witnesses spoke for her. Jón Magnusson only had one witness, Erlendur Ormsson, who was a "wandering prophet." Even though Þuríður Jónsdóttir had been absolved of any possible guilt, he still wrote the *Píslarsaga* to help justify his actions. He remained pastor of Eyri until he retired in

1689.

A few years later, another woman fell ill: the wife of Páll Björnsson, another clergyman in the Westfjords. Þorleifur Kortsson had risen to be the lawman, and as such, he dealt with the case. By the time this particular case ended, seven people had been executed.

Denmark had an absolute monarchy by 1661, and the Danish tried to stop the witch hunts. However, the Icelanders were hesitant to bring them to an end. All told, twenty-three men and two women were executed for witchcraft during this time.

The final element contributing to the problems of the 17th century was the rise of the absolute monarchy in Denmark. Before 1661, the country limited the monarchy's power with the Council of State, which had significant power, and a diet, which chose the new king. While the diet typically chose the king who would have inherited the throne anyway, it restricted the new king's power by forcing him to accept a charter. This charter's conditions meant that nearly all power went to the council.

From 1657 to 1660, Denmark fought a war with Sweden and had to give up all lands east of the Sound, which meant the loss of population and any control of the traffic in the Sound. Because the aforementioned charter gave so much power to the council, which was comprised of the nobility, the council was blamed for this massive defeat. In 1660, the unprivileged classes, the clergy, and the burghers (wealthy citizens) forced the Council of State to free the king from his charter. This meant Denmark's government became an absolute monarchy. This was followed by a reorganization of the top administration, which was divided into colleges. Although none of these colleges were located in Iceland, three were important: the Chancery, the Treasury, and the Supreme Court (this became the highest court of appeals for Iceland until 1920). From then until the 1830s, no representative political organization convened in Denmark.

In 1662, the king wrote a letter to the people of Iceland announcing that the governor, Henrik Bjelke, was to oversee Iceland's oath of allegiance to the king at the Althing. The letter did not mention absolutism. The Icelanders may not have known what was going on in Denmark and what this would all mean for them. One hundred nine representatives signed a document that acknowledged the absolute sovereignty and hereditary rights of the king two days after their arrival at Kópavogur. That same day, the representatives wrote letters to the king in which they explained their acceptance of his rule was contingent on the idea that the "old law of the land, peace, and freedom, with the rights that the previous praiseworthy kings of Denmark and Norway" would be maintained.

Despite the acceptance of absolutism, the situation in Iceland did not change until Henrik Bjelke resigned. After his resignation, the administration was reorganized. The new governor was called the *stiftamtmaður*. The first *stiftamtmaður* was the king's five-year-old illegitimate son. The position involved no responsibilities and very little work, but it did confer financial benefits. In other words, the office could be held by a child. The *stiftamtmaður* did not even live in Iceland until 1770, and once they did, they more directly influenced the Icelandic government. This would be the case until 1872 when the position changed to the *landshöfðingi*. The governor's assistant was called the *amtmaður*. Another new position was the treasurer or *landfógeti*, who looked after the royal properties in the country. These positions would continue to exist until 1904, which was when home rule was introduced.

During the period of absolutism, the Althing continued to pass judgments and create legislation, although the Althing shrank in size and dignity. In 1720, farmers were no longer nominated to pass sentences at court, with the duty being transferred to the sheriffs, who passed sentences in their home districts. At that point, Law Council members simply acted as witnesses. The number of farmers required to ride to the Althing declined from eighty-four to ten, all of whom came from the three districts closest to Þingvellir (before this, they came from all over Iceland).

Iceland maintained its separate existence from Denmark since royal decisions that applied to Iceland were made with the country in mind. Icelandic officials were also contacted prior to a decision being made. If the Icelanders were in consensus that a measure would not work, the Danes typically conceded. The sheriffs and lawmen were almost always Icelanders as well.

It can also be said that although Iceland did not formally have any nobility, the country was a feudal society (if a feudal society is defined by being ruled by men who made their living through the exploitation of the peasantry).

Chapter 6 – Reforms and Literature in the Early Modern Period

Language and Literature

By the end of the Late Middle Ages, the height of Icelandic literature had mostly passed. However, there was a revitalization in the second half of the 16th century with the *Annal of Gottskálk*. In 1593, *On Bishops of Skálholt before and around the Reformation* was written. The text, which Bishop Oddur Einarsson most likely wrote, was taken from the tale of a farmer, Egill Einarsson. One of Egill's sons, Jón, a clergyman, lost some of his fingers. Oddur brought Jón to Skálholt, where the latter wrote *Bishops' Annals* in 1605.

Pastor Jón Halldórsson wrote sagas about the first bishops in Iceland up to his time period, the early 18th century. Bishop Finnur Jonsson, Jón Halldórsson's son, expanded on the work, creating a four-volume history of the church in Iceland. The grandson of Bishop Guðbrandur (the man who brought the printing press to Iceland), Bishop Þorlákur Skúlason, hired Björn Jónsson to compose an annal about the period starting around 1400. Björn did so in the late 1630s, and his work helped to develop annal writing in the 17th and 18th centuries. Although his work revived the old scholarship, it was not comparable to the medieval sagas.

The annals were not the only significant work at this time, as geographical literature also became popular. Bishop Guðbrandur, who was a geographer and Iceland's first cartographer, had issues with the descriptions of Iceland and hired Arngrímur Jónsson to correct some of these. Arngrímur published *Brevis Commentarius de Islandia* to correct the falsehoods about Iceland. However, the booklet was not successful because it was the truth; people preferred adventurous stories. After this, Arngrímur wrote his most influential book, *Crymogæa*, which was published in Hamburg in 1609. Arngrímur got around the challenge of writing the history of a nation that had never fought a war against another country by writing stories about the heroes of old and their bravery in contending with troublesome foreign princes. Here, the idea of maintaining the purity of the Icelandic language by keeping it free from foreign words was introduced. Arngrímur was a patriot and sang the praises of the early ages of the Icelandic Commonwealth as a sort of golden age. Because of this, the work has been called "the manifesto of Icelandic patriotism." However, Arngrímur's arguments were tailored since he was a Lutheran clergyman.

Arngrímur's work had an influence beyond Iceland. It helped to make scholars in Denmark aware of the fact that Icelandic manuscripts included information about Scandinavia's history. Arngrímur was hired to research the history of the ancient Danish kingdom. It is thanks to him that a saga of the Danish dynasty exists. His work on the *Crymogæa* made him the best-known Icelander among educated Europeans and brought awareness to the sagas and Icelandic mythology. As a testament to Arngrímur's importance, he was pictured on the 10 krónur banknote, although it is no longer issued today.

During this time, the Icelandic language took on new significance. Because the Icelandic language is so close to Old Norse, Icelanders were able to easily understand old manuscripts. There is a story about a twenty-two-year-old student who had been expelled from the Latin school at Hólar in 1658. This student, Jón Jónsson, who later adopted the name Jón Rúgmann, traveled to Copenhagen to appeal the expulsion. His ship was captured by Swedes, who noticed the manuscripts he was carrying. After discovering that he could read the manuscripts, the Swedes sent him to the university at Uppsala, where he learned to translate manuscripts so Swedes could understand them. He ended up working as a translator and interpreter of Old Norse texts.

Another Icelander, Árni Magnusson, a professor of Danish antiquities in Copenhagen in 1701, traveled around Iceland, surveying the country to gather information for a land register. He collected as many manuscripts as he could, which included not just whole books but also fragments. To bring his collection back to Denmark, he needed thirty packhorses to carry it all. Árni produced no manuscripts about his main study, but he did do important work nonetheless. His work existed in the comments he wrote on scraps of paper inserted in the manuscripts. Thus, he was the first to complete the work that is typical of philology.

Árni's work was almost lost in a fire that destroyed half the city in 1728. He managed to save most of the parchment manuscripts except for twelve (which contained sagas that were available elsewhere). Despite his efforts, he lost the majority of his books, a number of documents, and hundreds of paper manuscripts. Upon his death, he left what remained of his collection to the state, which used it to form the Arnamagnæan Institute in Copenhagen. It eventually became the center for Icelandic studies. In 1971, the works were returned to Iceland unless it was not considered part of Iceland's cultural heritage. Once the works were returned to Iceland, the Arnamagnæan Institute, the center for philological studies, was founded in Reykjavik.

The Census

The 17th century may have seen a renaissance in Iceland, but the end of the century brought minor famines during the winters of 1696 to 1699, as the Icelanders faced bad years for fishing and farming. The famines were not significant enough to warrant a request for help, but they did discuss them at the Althing in 1700. However, the regional governor believed otherwise and took a request to the king to meet and discuss the problems Iceland was facing.

As a result, a new price list that was more favorable to Icelandic producers was created. A two-man committee was also established to investigate Iceland's economic and social conditions. One of these men was Páll Vídalín, a theologian, sheriff, and vice lawman. The other was Árni Magnusson, a theologian and professor of Danish antiquities in Copenhagen. They were to investigate the conditions in Iceland and write proposals to improve Iceland's economy and administration.

Part of their work included taking a census to register each person's name, age, and social status. They also had to take a count of all of the livestock in the country and create a land register. The land register included ownership and rent, as well as a detailed description of each farm, actual livestock, and livestock the farm could support.

The census provides information to scholars about the Icelandic population at the time. For example, the infant mortality rate was higher there than it was in England during the same time period. The marriage rate for both men and women over the age of twenty was less than 50 percent. The low marriage rate was a consequence of the economy. In essence, the number of habitable farms restricted the number of marriages, as it was not really acceptable for a man to ask a woman to marry him if he was not able to offer her the status of a housewife.

In 1703, there were 8,191 homes, of which approximately 1,100 had a woman as the head of the household. These homes were divided into four different types: farms with definite boundaries; outlying farms, which were farms with their own houses and hayfields but had a shared grazing field; cottages, which meant the inhabitants had little to no farmland and worked other jobs; and lodgers, those who were living in someone else's home but still managed to maintain an independent status.

Approximately half of the Icelandic farms belonged to the people. The Lutheran Church owned two-thirds, and the Danish Crown owned the other third. Although a large portion of Iceland's property was privately owned, 95 percent of the farmers were tenants. About 45 percent of the land was owned by people who rented it to others. The farmers were relatively transient during the 18th and 19th centuries, as they rarely stayed on the same farm. This geographical mobility, coupled with relative social mobility, had a few effects. It created a homogenous society, there was an absence of dialects, and there was a lack of a real division between the high and low cultures in the country.

Educational Reform

In 1741, a Danish clergyman named Ludvig Harboe was sent to Iceland with his Icelander assistant, Jón Þorkelsson. Their job was to investigate Christianity and the state of education in the country, which they did for four years.

In Hólar, the children were tested by a pastor or deacon. Harboe discovered that a little more than half of them could read Icelandic. Harboe recorded the rate of literacy in the diocese of Skálholt based on the responses of the clergy. According to his findings, less than half the people were literate. Approximately 41 percent were literate in the east, while in Vestur-Skaftafellssýsla and Borgarfjarðarsýsla in the south, the percentage was between 23 and 32 percent. From Mýrasýsla to the Westfjords, literacy ranged from 32 to 50 percent.

Based on Harboe's studies, there are several possible conclusions that can be reached. For instance, one can surmise that literacy among the youth was on the rise at this time. However, the reasons for the literacy rate are not as important as the outcome since Harboe's studies are not reliable enough to allow historians to reach definite conclusions.

After Harboe's studies were finished, a number of reforms were passed on education, Christian observance, domestic discipline, and the registration of parishioners and clerical services. Most of these (if not all) were drafted by Harboe himself.

Although adult Icelanders lacked formal education, they were required to teach their children to read and teach them about Christianity. The church had some responsibility for this as well since pastors were required to visit every home in their parish twice a year. During these visits, they supervised what the children were learning. They were also responsible for visiting beggars and vagrant children. Provisions were put in place if a household did not include anyone who was literate. They were to teach the children as much as they could, no matter how little. If the pastor discovered a family could not teach the children, the children were moved to be with a family that could. The family was not allowed to object to this removal, but they could hire a literate servant to teach the children instead.

Harboe also prescribed the practice of daily religious services. It became a custom for people in Iceland to have a nightly service throughout the winter but only one per week on Sundays during the summer. Pastors were allowed to command the heads of household to purchase suitable books for services. The sermon book that came to dominate Iceland was *Sermons for the Home* (*Húss-Postilla*) by Bishop Jón Vídalín.

While Harboe's educational policy was a bit different from what was being practiced in Denmark and Norway, where children were mainly being educated in schools, it seems that it was effective. About eighteen years after Harboe's visit, a report indicated that literacy rates in Skálholt had risen from 36 to 63 percent. Reports from the church registers indicate that 90 percent of people above the age of twelve were literate around 1780. The 10 percent of the population who were not literate were elderly or disabled.

However, Harboe's revolution only considered religious observance and reading, which is a receptive act; it did not extend to writing. For example, a clergyman in 1787 complained that those who were supposed to complete reports on farming could not do more than fill in the names. This changed eventually; between the late 18th and mid-19th centuries, there seemed to be a breakthrough in writing.

Chapter 7 – The 18th Century

How Reykjavik Came into Being

Although much happened in Iceland during the 18th century, we are going to fast-forward to the mid-18th century. Reforms had happened throughout the century, although most were focused on the old ways of doing things, typically within the realms of farming and Christianity. The rest of Europe had progressed, leaving Iceland behind. For example, in continental Europe, urban centers were developing, and the people were using watermills and decked fishing boats, which were unknown in Iceland.

In 1749, Niels Horrebow, a Danish lawyer and polymath, became embroiled in an embezzlement scandal. He was sent to Iceland to complete field research into the nature of the country. He remained there for two years, recording his observations and publishing them in Danish. Similar to Arngrímur Jónsson's earlier work, Horrebow corrected false beliefs about Iceland that was present in foreign literature.

Horrebow spent the winter of 1750/51 at Bessastaðir with Skúli Magnusson, who was the newly appointed treasurer and the first Icelander to be appointed to the position. This afforded the opportunity for discussions about some of Iceland's needs, such as forestry, decked vessels for fishing, wool processing in factories, the regeneration of agriculture, and the processing of fish with salt rather than drying. While these suggestions had been made before, Skúli wanted action, not just words. That summer, during the Althing, Skúli established a joint stock company called the *Innréttingar*. Around thirteen men promised to contribute what amounted to the price of 350 cows to the company.

Skúli sailed to Copenhagen after the Althing and remained there for the winter. Because the things he wanted were in tune with Copenhagen's plans for Iceland, he was promised money and three lots of land close to his residence so the project could get off the ground. Two lots, Effersey and Reykjavik, were near Hólmurinn, a trading harbor. Hvaleyri, the third lot, included Hafnarfjörður, another trading harbor. Hafnarfjörður is now the third-most populous city in Iceland.

Skúli also bought two decked fishing boats, timber for houses, and tools for wool processing. He hired fourteen Danish and Norwegian farming families to teach Icelanders how to grow grain. That summer, he returned to Iceland, and once he landed at Hólmurinn, he started to plan construction on one-story houses with high attics. At the time, Reykjavik was a major farm with six outlying farms and a church. According to the 1703 census, there were only twenty-one people living at the main farm and a total of forty-eight on the outlying farms, but it was close to the harbor and to Bessastaðir and Viðey, the two administrative centers.

The houses in Reykjavik were to be built on the path between the extant farmhouses and the shore. This path would eventually be called Aðalstræti (Main Street). During the height of activity, around seventy people, male and female, worked in workshops, spinning wool, weaving cloths, twisting ropes, and tanning hides. A watermill was built on a nearby river to help with fulling (the washing of wool to remove oils), as it demanded more energy.

Skúli's enterprises were not successful. The Danish and Norwegian farmers he hired only remained for a few years, and the Icelandic farmers did not want to try this new farming venture. Because Iceland was competing with European industry, the attempts to produce wool and skin for export incurred heavy financial losses. In the 1750s, the wool industry was dealt another blow. People were trying to establish an experimental sheep farm near Reykjavik and imported rams from England. These rams brought an unwelcome visitor, scabies (also known as scab), which was lethal to the Icelandic stock. To eradicate the disease, they had to slaughter all of the sheep in the diseased areas. This was devastating for the wool workshops since they could not get the wool they needed. They had to turn to the Crown for financial support.

These financial losses did not sit well with royal officials, so, in 1764, they forced the *Innréttingar* to merge with a trading company that was about to assume Icelandic trade from the Crown. For a short period of time, the original owners of the *Innréttingar* became partners in the trading company. However, the merged company shrank when the owners of the *Innréttingar* sold their shares. Ten years after the merger, the Crown took over Icelandic trade once again. The Crown continued to run the workshops until they were sold to two Danish merchants in 1799.

Although Skúli's attempts to transform Icelandic society were not overly fruitful, they did have one extremely important effect: the establishment of Reykjavik, where nearly 40 percent of Icelanders currently live. At most, the *Innréttingar* employed one hundred people, and it only lasted for fifty years, but it also had a lasting effect: it attracted other institutions to Reykjavik since Reykjavik was the closest place to an urban center in Iceland. In 1770, the first prison was built in Iceland. It was a small stone house in Reykjavik. This was actually the first stone house in Reykjavik and one of the first in Iceland. Iceland no longer had to send its criminals to Copenhagen. Essentially, the construction of the prison meant the *Innréttingar* had established an official government institution.

An example of a stone church. This one is located in Hólar.
Michael Scaduto, CC BY-SA 2.0 <https://creativecommons.org/licenses/by-sa/2.0>, via Wikimedia Commons; https://commons.wikimedia.org/wiki/File:Holakirkja.jpg

While the lasting effect of Skúli's enterprises was the establishment of Reykjavik, other people also transformed the country in small ways. In the 1700s, two Icelandic students—Eggert Ólafsson and Bjarni Pálssons—studied natural history in Iceland and collected manuscripts for the Arnamagnæan Institute. Eggert Ólafsson was a well-known poet, and Bjarni Pálssons was a student of medicine who would go on to become the first director of public health in Iceland. The two climbed Hekla, a volcano, a feat they claimed to be the first to accomplish.

Eggert, who studied natural sciences, the classics, grammar, law, and agriculture at the University of Copenhagen, wrote on a number of diverse topics and had a pro-conservation stance regarding the Icelandic language. Eggert also had a fierce sense of patriotism, coupled with the desire to revive Iceland's culture. He traveled with Bjarni throughout Iceland from 1752 to 1757, visiting a number of natural sites and proposing geographical and infrastructural improvements. After their travels, Eggert published an account of the cultural and scientific studies he had completed, *Reise igiennem Island* (*Travels in Iceland*), in 1772.

Problems in the 18ᵗʰ Century

While the 18ᵗʰ century was a time of progressive thinking, it also brought the worst disasters Iceland had seen since the plague.

In 1707, Iceland was struck by a smallpox outbreak, which ravaged the country for two years. Although exact details about the number of dead were not kept, through examining the annals of individual parishes and comparing them to the 1703 annals of the same areas, it seems that smallpox killed about a quarter of the population. However, it was actually worse than those numbers show. People younger than forty were the most targeted, although children seemed to be less vulnerable. It is believed the disease may have killed most (perhaps all) of the pregnant women.

Another catastrophe struck Iceland in the 1750s: famine. In 1750, Iceland contended with unusually cold weather, which was accompanied by widespread pack ice that closed the fishing grounds. In 1751, most, if not all, of the livestock must have died in Vopnafjörður (northeast Iceland) because most of the residents became vagrants. It seems they saved their lives by leaving. Things did not improve much over the next few years. In 1755, the pack ice did not recede. It remained off Iceland's northern coast from the end of winter until September 1756. In the fall of 1755, Katla, a volcano in southern Iceland, erupted. Because of the volcano's location in the Mýrdalsjökull glacier (the icecap that covers Katla), the eruption caused damage not only from the eruption itself but also from the floodwaters it unleashed.

By 1756, the pack ice had expanded to reach the southern coast, the Westman Islands, and Reykjanes. It began to warm after this, but the damage had already been done, as much of the livestock had died. The famine reduced the population by 5,800, which is, of course, significant for a small country. The population rebounded over the next twelve years until the next disaster hit.

May 1783 was marked by regular earthquakes. By June, the earthquakes were nearly continuous and accompanied by thunderous noise. On June 8th, 1783, a dark cloud rose behind the mountains in an area called Síða in the district of Vestur-Skaftafellssýsla (southern Iceland). This cloud quickly reached the inhabited area, and once it did, the ground was covered by black ash. Two days later, the Skaftá River dried up. Two days after this, lava was flowing through the riverbed. This eruption was called "Skaftáreldar," or the "Skaftá Fires."

The situation did not end with a river of fire, though. On June 14th, a repulsive-smelling rain fell. The odor was so dreadful that some people found it hard to breathe. Birds died, and the grass withered. As the destructive rain fell, a dark cloud spread across much of Iceland. Fires could be seen burning in a fissure near a hillock called Laki. Lava would soon erupt and flow toward the farmlands.

The Laki fissure.

Chmee2/Valtameri, CC BY-SA 3.0 <https://creativecommons.org/licenses/by-sa/3.0>, via Wikimedia Commons; https://commons.wikimedia.org/wiki/File:Laki_fissure_(2).jpg

One can only imagine the fear the people must have felt. They took what they could, but the lava began to close in. One farmer managed to save his flock of ewes only to have the entire flock engulfed by lava.

The flow finally decreased in October, and in February 1784, the fires in the Laki fissures ceased. An estimated 1,903 square feet were covered in lava by the time the lava stopped flowing. This was not the end of the environmental calamities for the Icelanders, though.

The preceding winters had been so cold and snowy that the farmers had used up their stores of hay. Not much hay was harvested during the summer, and some of it was poisoned by the ash (volcanic ash usually contains fluorine). While food shortages were not uncommon in Iceland, they usually came in late winter, spring, or even as late as early summer. This time, the people were affected in early winter. In December 1783, people started to die from starvation in the northeastern part of the country. People had been fleeing the eruption in the southeast, and now they fled the frozen northeast, heading to the southwest. Unfortunately, many died on the way, and some who did reach the fishing stations in the southwest were exhausted and overate the fresh fish. Many did not survive.

The winter of 1783 weakened the Icelanders, and this continued until the summer. Other factors were at work that made recovery difficult. In August 1784, earthquakes destroyed approximately four hundred homes in Rangárvallasýsla and Árnessýsla in the south. These homes needed to be rebuilt before the arrival of winter, so the people inevitably lost some time when it came to making hay. This extended the famine, which was called the Mist famine because of the mist the eruption caused. The mist had mixed with the toxic ash that emerged from the volcano, so it poisoned the grass and reduced the air quality. This mist also caused problems beyond Iceland. According to some, it may have been one cause of a bad harvest in France, which led to a bread shortage and increased inflation. This inflation helped to fan the fire of discontent in France, resulting in the French Revolution.

The news of the famine finally reached Denmark in the autumn of 1783, too late for its assistance for the upcoming winter. Nevertheless, the Danes organized a collection to assist the Icelanders. Some of that money helped Icelanders buy livestock. It was not until July 1784 that the king stepped in to send free grain to the country. He also issued a decree that allowed the trade monopoly to distribute fish freely. This seemed to provide some relief, and Iceland began to recover.

It is hard to determine how many people died because of the famine, but it does seem the country lost a lot of its livestock. The end of the trade monopoly also brought changes to the Icelandic economy and allowed Icelanders to engage in foreign trade themselves.

After these problematic years, the population started to rebound, with growth at about 1.32 percent. They eventually rebuilt many of the farms that had been destroyed by the lava flow. The population was recorded as being 47,240 during the 1801 census. This showed a decline of three thousand people since the last census was taken in 1703.

Government Changes in the 1700s

On August 18th, 1786, the town of Reykjavik was founded by a royal decree. The trading houses had already moved from the harbor at Effersey into Reykjavik, and as free trade was introduced, more than one trader could operate in Reykjavik. Reykjavik also expanded after the 1784 earthquakes in Skálholt destroyed all of the buildings, with the exception of the church. The earthquakes led to the loss of most of the see's livestock, which resulted in tenant farmers being unable to pay their rent. The decision was made to sell the farm of Skálholt and all of the see's land. Both the bishop and the school would be moved to Reykjavik, with the move being paid for by the Danish treasury. The see of Skálholt ended after operating for seven centuries.

The Althing

Back in the 1690s, some manner of shelter was built in Þingvellir for the Law Council. In the later part of the 18th century, a timber house was built to replace it, and the Althing was held there until the end of the century. People continued to complain about the drafts and leaks in the timber structure, as recorded in the minutes for the Althing. Suggestions were made to move the Althing to another location or to split it into two courts, but no action was taken—that is, until 1798. That year, during the Althing, Magnus Stephensen, a lawman, complained of illness resulting from being exposed to the conditions in the building. He left after stating that he was too ill to continue working on his current case.

The next year, Magnus Stephensen's father, Ólafur, declared that the Althing would be held in Reykjavik. During the summer, the Latin school building was available, and the Althing used it again in 1800.

Meanwhile, a committee of four, which included Magnus Stephensen, had been appointed to study the arrangements of schools and jurisdiction. The report they issued led to a decree ending the Althing, which was replaced by the *Landsyfirréttur* (the High Court). It met in Reykjavik and was comprised of three professional judges. The end of the Althing meant the end of the Lawman; the *Landsyfirréttur* instead had a president of the court. The role of the court and its position in Icelandic society was similar to the Althing, but the court now met at least six times a year rather than annually.

Gradually, all of Iceland's administration began to consolidate in Reykjavik, including the governor, a Dane named Frederich Christopher Trampe, who rose to power in 1806 and preferred living in Reykjavik. Shortly after that, the former prison found a new purpose: the official residence of the governor.

Chapter 8 – An Odd Revolution

The Idea of Degeneration

The notion that Iceland had been degenerating since the early centuries of settlement became widespread in the 16th century and was central in Arngrímur Jónsson's historiography. Magnus Stephensen, who became the first president of the High Court and a proponent of the Enlightenment, challenged this belief. He did not doubt that life had been more prosperous during the Icelandic Commonwealth, but he did not think the era was a golden age because Danish absolutism brought peace and security.

In the late 19th and early 20th centuries, the belief in Iceland's prosperity during the Icelandic Commonwealth was connected to the belief that Iceland had gone into decline in the 13th century when it lost its autonomy. Icelanders also seemed to believe they would attain future prosperity if they could restore their independence. Increased self-rule was accompanied by economic progress in the early 20th century. However, it would be years before Iceland was granted its autonomy.

Let's start in the early 19th century to see how the Icelanders' views on self-rule progressed. During the Napoleonic Wars, Denmark was compelled to side with France against Britain. In the autumn of 1807, forty-one ships that had sailed to Iceland during the summer were making the return trip. Eighteen of those were captured and ordered to sail to England. Bjarni Sivertsen, one of the first Icelandic merchants and shipowners since free trade was introduced, was taken to London. There, he met a Danish prisoner of war, Jørgen Jørgensen, who had sailed on British ships and seemed to have sympathies with the British. Jørgensen began to develop an interest in Iceland after conversing with Bjarni.

Jørgensen met Joseph Banks, an Englishman who had led a scientific expedition to Iceland in 1772. Banks advocated for Britain's annexation of Iceland, and Jørgensen joined him. In 1808, Jørgensen met Samuel Phelps, who ran a soap factory in Lambeth and needed fats to produce his product. Jørgensen told Phelps that Iceland had tallow for export, but the war was hindering trade. Recognizing the possibility of filling his need for tallow, Phelps sent a ship to Iceland in early 1809, with Jørgensen acting as the interpreter. This attempt was unsuccessful, partly because the trading season in Iceland was during the summer months.

Phelps decided to return in the summer, securing the protection of the British Royal Navy this time around. In June, a British sloop-of-war arrived in Iceland. The captain forced the Danish governor of Iceland, Frederich Christopher, Count of Trampe, to sign a treaty granting British citizens unlimited trading rights in the country.

Despite the treaty, Trampe maintained the prohibition against trade with Britain, which Phelps and Jørgensen discovered when they arrived in Reykjavik. Having tried to take a more lawful path and failed, they decided to use force. On June 25th, thirteen armed men stormed Trampe's home, captured him, and took him to their ship, where they held him captive. Supposedly, Trampe asked people not to save him from his captivity, and no one did.

Phelps continued his trade with the Icelanders, while Jørgensen took over the rule in Iceland, a role he was quite enthusiastic about. Within one day of Trampe's arrest, Jørgensen posted two proclamations, which were written in both Danish and Icelandic. They announced the abolition of Danish authority in Iceland. The proclamation also subjected all Danes to a curfew and required the surrender of firearms, ammunition, and daggers. All native Icelanders, including royal officials, would be treated well, provided they obeyed orders. Jørgensen's second proclamation declared that Iceland would become an independent country under British protection. It would have a new Icelandic flag and an independent legislative body. After his proclamations, Jørgensen declared himself "Iceland's protector and supreme commander on sea and land." However, once the Icelanders elected parliamentary representatives, his rule would end.

As the new temporary "supreme commander on sea and land," Jørgensen needed to garner support from Icelanders to help him with the country's administration. A High Court judge in Reykjavik assumed the post of regional governor of the Southern Region (this had been part of Trampe's office). Jørgensen had eight Icelanders act as his bodyguards, and they rode with him as he tried to secure his power in the country. Jørgensen did not meet much resistance from officials in the country, as most officials decided to remain in office under him. There were those who remained true to their official oaths to the Danish king, such as the regional governor of the Northeastern Region.

The question is, why were people obedient to Jørgensen? Of course, we can never know for sure, but it seems they probably believed he was backed by the British government. However, this wasn't true. In August, a British warship came to Iceland. The ship's captain, Alexander Jones, who attended a ball given by the "supreme ruler," was initially a bit puzzled by this new government in Iceland. It is possible he might have believed that Jørgensen and Phelps were acting secretly on behalf of the British government. Jones was not duped for long, though, as he managed to get Phelps to admit that he and Jørgensen were doing this on their own.

Jones was in contact with Magnus Stephensen, who was still the president of the High Court. Stephensen asked Jones to intervene and remove the two from the country, which was accomplished on August 22nd via a two-party treaty. One of those parties was comprised of Captain Jones and Phelps, while the other was Magnus Stephensen and his brother Stefán, the regional governor who had abdicated. Jørgensen was removed from office, but Trampe chose not to return, instead heading to Britain to demand restitution.

In the meantime, Iceland was ruled temporarily by the Stephensen brothers. From England, Trampe appointed a new governing board, which the Danish Crown confirmed. Jørgensen, who had broken parole, was detained in England. He continued to lead a storied life, acting on behalf of the British secret service at times and later being sent to Australia as a convict. In Australia, he went on expeditions and studied the life and customs of the Aboriginals in Van Diemen's Land (the colonial name for the island of Tasmania).

The coup in Iceland was so inconsequential that it didn't really seem to affect the Icelanders' desire for autonomy. However, the coup had some importance. It showed how defenseless the Danish administration was in Iceland. It also demonstrated the lack of Icelandic nationalism or enthusiasm for democracy at the time; although the Icelanders simply accepted Jørgensen's rule, they did not show any real enthusiasm for his message. They didn't seem to care who was in power as long as they could continue to pursue business as usual. They did maintain a sense of ethnic identity, which could be traced back to the Viking Age; however, they didn't have a sense of political nationalism. This was reflected when Norway was severed from Danish rule five years after the Icelandic coup. No one in Iceland really said anything about it.

Reestablishing the Althing

A Danish linguist named Rasmus Christian Rask became interested in the Icelandic language during the 19th century. He believed the language was the common language of the Scandinavian peoples. He also believed the Icelandic language and literature of that time period were the same as the language and literature of the Middle Ages. He concluded that Icelandic had been spoken across Scandinavia even before Iceland was a country.

Upon visiting Iceland in the 1810s, he discovered that Icelandic was being threatened by Danish, especially in

Reykjavik. He concluded that in one hundred years, Icelandic would no longer be spoken in Reykjavik, and in three hundred years, it would be extinct. In 1816, he established the Icelandic Literary Society (*Hið íslenska bókmenntafélag*), which was devoted to promoting and strengthening the Icelandic language, literature, and learning. Divided into two departments, one in Copenhagen and one in Reykjavik, it published both medieval and modern books in Icelandic. In the 1830s, a political counterpart for the cultural movement started to emerge.

The inception of the Icelandic political movement was, in some ways, connected to events in continental Europe. The Danish king had been the duke of two duchies—Schleswig and Holstein—since the Middle Ages. Schleswig was comprised of both Danish and German speakers. Holstein, on the other hand, was entirely comprised of Germans and was part of the German Confederation, which had been established in 1815 after Napoleon's defeat. In 1830, after the July Revolution in France, people started to push for Holstein's rights. In 1831, King Frederick VI of Denmark established four diets: one for Holstein, one for Schleswig, one for Jutland, and one for the archipelago of Zealand, Funen, and the smaller islands (which was intended to include Iceland and the Faroe Islands).

Nationalist sentiment had not really come to the surface yet, but it seemed to be slowly bubbling. In the 1810s, Ebenezer Henderson, a Scottish clergyman, traveled to Iceland to distribute Bibles, but before he arrived in Iceland, he spent some time in Denmark, where he studied Icelandic and read the sagas. He got the idea that the Icelanders really missed the Althing. Around this time, a law student in Copenhagen, Baldvin Einarsson, started an annal. He also composed a long essay that argued the explicit aim of the diet, which was to awaken the spirit of the nation, could not be accomplished without some changes. He argued that one of the problems hindering this was the fact that Iceland still only had two or three men in a Danish assembly. He believed the solution lay in reinstating the Althing.

Officials in Iceland were consulted about the possibility of joining the diet of the Danish islands, but they did not have much interest. Magnus Stephensen and others wanted things to continue, as they did not take issue with the unrestricted monarchy. The other group, whose best-known member was Bjarni Thorarensen, the regional governor in the Northeastern Region, wanted an assembly of officials in Iceland. Incidentally, Bjarni is now known for other things, as he was one of the first poets to embrace Romanticism in Icelandic poetry.

The interest in reestablishing the Althing did not go anywhere at the time. However, since Iceland didn't seem to be interested in electing representatives, the Crown appointed two for the nation.

Baldvin Einarsson died in an accident before any steps could be taken to restore the Althing, but four Icelandic students in Copenhagen took up his cause two years later, establishing the annal *Fjölnir*. The *Fjölnir* occupies an important place in the history of Iceland's nationalist movement, but its specific contributions are hard to define, especially since only nine volumes were published over thirteen years. It also did not make any new political suggestions. There is no evidence that the first volumes were distributed. Volumes six through eight were sold from 1843 to 1845. During that time, they sold three hundred to four hundred copies. Yes, this is a small number; however, keep in mind that the country had limited access to printed texts, and books were read aloud in large homes and passed from farm to farm. Therefore, it probably had a wider circulation than the numbers reveal.

Although it didn't seem to stir much outrage, the *Fjölnir* made some significant contributions, such as the publication of Jónas Hallgrímsson's poetry. Jónas's poetry has become some of the most beloved poetry in Iceland, and his poems are some of the best-known poems about Iceland and its people. He is still honored today. On November 16th (Jónas's birthday), the Jónas Hallgrímsson Award is given to an individual for their outstanding contribution to the Icelandic language. In 1996, Iceland started to recognize his birthday as the Day of the Icelandic Language.

Iceland saw an increase in support for more extensive internal rule by the late 1830s. From 1837 to 1838, some leading farmers and officials set out to put a consultative assembly into place. The governors began understanding the advantages of a stronger, more centralized government. After one governor, L. A. Krieger, left his post, he suggested the creation of a cabinet of a governor and two ministers in Reykjavik, which would allow for the transfer of some of Iceland's administration to the country itself. Governor C. E. Bardenfleth, who succeeded Krieger, suggested something between a cabinet and an elected assembly, a suggestion that led to the establishment of a Committee of Officials by royal decree in 1838.

The first issue for this committee was, naturally, how to elect representatives to the diet of the Danish islands. Although the committee drafted a law regarding elections, they advanced another proposal stating that until everything was established, the king was to appoint representatives. The king, Frederick VI, did not have the opportunity to appoint any officials, as he died in December 1839 while the committee's proposal was winding its way through the Danish colleges. His successor, his cousin Christian VIII, a ruler who was suspected of having liberal tendencies, was unable to exercise those tendencies in Denmark proper, so he decided to extend a small gesture to Iceland.

This small gesture was one that his Chancery advised against. However, he asked the Committee of Officials about establishing a consultative assembly called the Althing.

At the same time, the son of a clergyman from Hrafnseyri became the new leader of the Icelandic group of nationalists in Copenhagen. This new leader, Jón Sigurðsson, had gone to Copenhagen in 1833 to study philology, which was the main training that Latin school teachers received. In 1840, his studies ended when he entered the political arena. After he failed to take over the *Fjölnir*, he and his followers started a new annal, *Ný félagsrit* (*New Society Papers*). When the first publication of the annal appeared in 1841, politically active Icelanders (mainly in Copenhagen) became engaged in lively discussions. The *Fjölnir* group argued about establishing the Althing at Þingvellir, while Jón Sigurðsson's group thought the Althing should be held in Reykjavik. The argument against holding it in Reykjavik was that the city was dominated by Danish traders and servants, making it mainly a Danish town. Jón Sigurðsson's reply to this argument was that having the Althing in Reykjavik would help to make the town more Icelandic.

Reykjavik won out, which led Jónas Hallgrímsson to compose a poem describing the Althing as a meeting of ravens on a hill instead of a meeting of hawks on a rock, which is a reference to Law Rock at Þingvellir. Most Icelanders seemed to support the return to Þingvellir, but the officials preferred Reykjavik. If they were to have it in Reykjavik, there would be no need to construct a building to accommodate the assembly.

The Danish Crown issued a decree regarding the organization of the Althing in March 1843. According to this decree, the Althing was to be comprised of twenty-six male members. Of those, all but six were to be elected, and the non-elected members would be appointees of the Crown. Each member had to be at least twenty-five years old and hold a certain social status. The elected members would each serve a six-year term and participate in the Althing three times. The eligible voting population was made up of only 3 to 5 percent of the people; only men who were thirty or older and who had a certain property status were eligible.

The new Althing was to meet every other year. The biennial meeting in Reykjavik would convene on the first weekday of July and last for four weeks.

The first election was held in 1844, and ten farmers, three clergymen, two secular officials, three other academics, and the steward of the Latin school were elected to serve. Because of the restrictions, there were only nineteen members because no one was eligible to vote in the Westman Islands. In terms of the king's appointees, one regional governor, two High Court judges, two clergymen, and one local sheriff were chosen. These men attended the first Althing, which began on July 1ˢᵗ, 1845.

One of the elected attendees was Jón Sigurðsson. He remained at the forefront of Icelandic politics for three decades after this, and after his death, he was one of the most iconic symbols of Icelandic national identity. He was not a typical nationalist, though. He lacked the romanticism of some of the other nationalists and was instead driven by modernization, economic progress, democracy, and human rights.

Gradual Separation of Iceland from Denmark

In March 1848, a delegation from Schleswig-Holstein was sent to Copenhagen with one goal: to unify Schleswig-Holstein with the German Confederation while maintaining a special relationship with Denmark. This did not go over so well with everyone, though. A meeting of more than two thousand people followed their arrival, in which many demanded a common constitution for Denmark and Schleswig. The day after a political divorce was reached, March 21ˢᵗ, Copenhageners demanded the appointment of new ministers. The king of Denmark, Frederick VII, announced they had all resigned, and the day after this, he announced he was now a constitutional monarch, bringing the absolute monarchy to an end.

The reaction was noticeably less peaceful in the duchies, where a revolt broke out when they heard that Schleswig would be united with Denmark under a single constitution.

The Icelanders heard this news with hope, but there was a danger to the island nation, both culturally and politically, because there was a question of what Iceland's status would be within Denmark's constitutional monarchy. Jón Sigurðsson was the first to try to find an answer to this question, drawing on the past to propose a legislative parliament in Iceland and a four-person government. The four men would stay in Copenhagen one at a time. This essentially translated to Iceland having a personal union with Denmark and would be the theoretical basis of Iceland's push for autonomy.

In the summer of 1848, some reacted by convening political meetings, which would be the first stirrings of democratic political activity, although they were not heavily attended. Customary summer meetings began at Þingvellir, which led to the rise of political organizations since each district developed local committees. However, these were not political parties.

One consequence, which may have been the most important one, was a royal declaration from the king of Denmark on September 23ʳᵈ,1848. In essence, the king said that he had no intention of finalizing a decision regarding Iceland's constitutional status until Icelanders had the opportunity to discuss it themselves. At the same time, the government offices in

Copenhagen were reorganized, and a separate Department of Icelandic Affairs was established. The first director of this new department, which was under the Ministry of the Interior, was an Icelander named Brynjólfur Pétursson. He had been on the board of the *Fjölnir*. Brynjólfur was among four Icelanders appointed to the Constitutional Assembly in Denmark, where they worked on writing the Danish Constitution. The four Icelanders did not have the time to set up the process of elections in Iceland, but they did ensure that there was no mention of Iceland in Denmark's constitution. This seemed to bode well for those who were pushing for independence, but this opinion shifted in Denmark and the rest of Europe by 1851 before the National Assembly had convened in Iceland.

By the time the assembly was seated, they had a visitor from Denmark. Twenty-five soldiers arrived on a Danish warship, which was stationed outside Reykjavik. They did not come empty-handed, though, as they presented a bill proposing a law on Iceland's status and on elections to the Danish Parliament. The bill was accompanied by a copy of Denmark's constitution. Iceland was expected to accept the validity of the constitution, although legislative power would be a bit different. Icelandic legislative power would stay with the king and his ministers, although the Althing would be able to act as a consulting body. Additionally, Iceland would hold six seats in the Danish Parliament.

On August 6th, the Icelanders drew up a separate proposal that called for an almost entirely independent Iceland, a proposal that was based on Jón Sigurðsson's earlier proposal. However, the proposal was rejected, and the assembly was dissolved.

Although the National Assembly ended on August 9th, the Danish soldiers remained in Reykjavik for months. The officials opposed to Denmark's proposal were banned from attending future Althings.

About ten years after the failed National Assembly met in Reykjavik, power in Denmark shifted back to the nationalist liberals, who began to resolve the deadlock with Iceland. Their goal was to start the process of separating Iceland's finances from those of Denmark. This was partly due to Denmark's inability to have any say in the finances of Iceland, but it was also due to Iceland's rising deficit. Copenhagen wanted to make sure that Iceland's problem remained Iceland's problem.

The committee, which consisted of three Danish representatives and two Icelanders, came to two conclusions. They all supported the financial separation of Iceland and Denmark, and they all agreed that the Danish exchequer should support the Icelandic exchequer with an annual allocation.

This allocation was seen as justice rather than as relief. In the past, the sees were financed by the landed property they owned. With the union of the schools and the sale of properties, the excess funds went to the Danish treasury. The treasury then assumed financial responsibility for the running of Latin schools and the Icelandic bishop's salary. Since this burden was about to be removed from the Danish treasury, it seemed only fair to provide compensation to Iceland since it would bear the cost in the future.

They did not, however, completely agree on the amount of compensation. All of the Danes and one of the Icelanders proposed an annual compensation that would be close to Iceland's deficit, with part of it being permanent and the rest being temporary until Iceland's economy recovered. The second Icelander, Jón Sigurðsson, came up with a different calculation for the amount that Iceland could rightfully claim.

A portrait of Jón Sigurðsson.
https://commons.wikimedia.org/wiki/File:Sigur%C3%B0sson_by_%C3%9Eorl%C3%A1ksson.jpg

Jón Sigurðsson considered the amount of money Denmark took from the sale of Icelandic farms, as well as a portion of the monopoly trade profit. He calculated this portion based on Iceland's population in relation to the population of the Danish realm. He also subtracted Iceland's contributions to the royal court and the central government. Jón reached the conclusion that Denmark should pay Iceland 100,000 rigsdalers (the currency used in Denmark until 1875) annually, an amount significantly higher than the 42,000 rigsdalers proposed by the rest of the committee.

When Schleswig and Holstein became part of the German Confederation in 1864, some Danish officials in Holstein lost their jobs, including Hilmar Finsen. Because he had Icelandic ancestry, he was given the post of governor of Iceland, which, for a few years, had been vacant. This move seemed to be a step in the right direction for Iceland.

During the 1867 Althing, a bill was submitted proposing an Icelandic constitution. This came after the failure to conclude Iceland's financial separation. With this new proposal, internal Icelandic affairs were to be the responsibility of the Althing and the Danish king. Iceland was to have no role in common Danish-Icelandic affairs, and the ministerial power was to rest with a minister from the Danish government. Additionally, the king would request that the Danish government allocate 50,000 rigsdalers annually (37,500 of the allocation would be permanent).

Although the Icelanders at the Althing made some minor changes to this proposal, they agreed with its major points. Governor Hilmar Finsen acted as the royal representative at the Althing and indicated that he would attempt to get the Crown's approval for the proposal. It seemed as if Iceland would finally establish a legislative parliament.

However, this did not happen because the Danish Parliament needed to agree to the allocation of this large sum of money. They kept applying conditions to the allocation, and ultimately, it failed. In 1869, the Danish Parliament submitted it once again to the Althing. Although it seemed very similar to the proposal two years prior, the Icelanders weren't happy with it.

In 1870, A. F. Krieger assumed the post of minister of justice in Denmark. This may have seemed inconsequential, but the Department of Icelandic Affairs had recently been transferred to the Ministry of Justice. Therefore, the Icelandic question became his responsibility. He was the one to decide whether the Danish Parliament should pass a law on the status of Iceland. He did, and once it was in Parliament, it passed easily. On January 2nd, 1871, the king signed it into law.

This act, called the Status Act (*Stöðulög*), basically confirmed the points made in the constitutional bill from 1867. It defined Iceland as an unalienable part of the Danish state, but it was to be considered a separate country with special rights. The act also created boundaries for internal affairs and resolved financial compensation for Iceland. Iceland was to receive 50,000 rigsdalers annually, and 30,000 of that was to be made permanent.

The Icelanders were not happy about this new law, although the 1871 Althing accepted the financial component with a caveat: the right to request additional future compensation. As for the other components, the Althing viewed them as concessions that the Danish Parliament was willing to make to Iceland.

The next year, Denmark redefined the post of governor and renamed it *landshöfðingi*. The position did not change much from the *stiftamtmaður* (the former position of governor), but it did increase the position's administrative power of Iceland since the *landshöfðingi* was not part of the local government of Denmark. However, because Denmark made the change without consulting the Althing, this led to bitterness in Iceland. One farmer, Einar Ásmundsson, put forth a theory that Christian IX was not the king of Iceland. Einar based his argument on the fact that Christian IX had come to power under the succession law of 1853, which Iceland had never validated. At Þingvellir in 1873, a meeting was convened prior to the summoning of the Althing. They declared that Iceland was a separate society in a special relationship with Denmark. However, once the Althing began, they decided they would ask the king to give Iceland a constitution the next year since it would be Iceland's millennial celebration.

Christian IX issued a constitution for Iceland's Internal Affairs, allowing the Althing to have control of Iceland's legislative affairs, on January 5th, 1874. This constitution, which was based on the Status Act, was to come into effect on August 1st that same year. Keep in mind the Althing had previously rejected the Status Act. Essentially, the Althing was to have legislative power along with the Crown, and everything else would pretty much be the same as it had been before. This constitution also included additional provisions focused on general human rights. These provisions were similar to corresponding clauses in the Danish Constitution.

The summer of 1874 saw the celebrations of Iceland's millennial anniversary, as the Icelandic Commonwealth is considered to have begun in 874. Thus, when Christian IX arrived with the constitution, the festivities led even the most ardent nationalists to remain silent about their compromises with the Crown. Although Iceland did not have full independence at this stage, it had taken the first step in that direction.

Chapter 9 – Icelandic Society in the 19th Century

Daily Life in the 19th Century

Between 1815 and 1855, the population of Iceland grew from forty-eight thousand to around sixty-five thousand, which is significant growth for a country like Iceland, which had a high infant mortality rate. The population growth pushed people farther inland or out to the fishing grounds. Before the growth, there was moorland, which was only used for summer grazing in the northeastern part of the country. With this migration, people started to build farms on the moorland. The number of livestock also increased, particularly sheep. The farmers mainly increased the number of castrated male sheep (called wethers), not ewes. The wethers produced wool, meat, and tallow, which were export goods, and this pattern indicates there was a growth in farming aimed at trade.

Some of this prosperity was linked to the shift to a relatively warm climate, which started in the 1840s, as it allowed for an expansion of farming. In addition to the rise in farming, fishing also increased, as did the importation of rye, rye meal, and other luxury items like coffee, tobacco, and sugar.

By 1870, the population hit seventy thousand, but the Icelanders ran into new problems on the farms. They had imported four lambs from England to improve the Icelandic breed. Unfortunately, these lambs brought scabies with them, which proceeded to explode throughout the southern and western regions. It killed a large number of sheep, and some of the survivors were rendered useless. The debates over how to contend with the disease raged; some thought they should try to find a cure, while others thought they should exterminate the sheep in the affected areas.

The debates over handling the spread of the disease started to coincide with the constitutional issue in Iceland. Essentially, Jón Sigurðsson, who was involved in politics, became one of the leading proponents of finding a cure. His position was the same as the Icelandic authorities. However, the majority of people did not agree, especially in areas unaffected by the disease. Jón brought three vets, including a leading Danish veterinarian, to Iceland in 1859, and they were granted unlimited authority to take any action they deemed necessary. Jón lost his seat as the speaker at the Althing. It may or may not have been caused by this incident, but he lost by only one vote.

The year 1859 was one of the coldest years on record, which, when combined with the increased population and the epizootic of scab, led to a decline in opportunities for people to marry and start their own households. The people just could not support a family at this time. The Icelanders were concerned the government would not be able to support the population. Thus, in 1859, they passed a vote to petition the king to issue a law forbidding the marriage of "notorious squanderers, drunkards, and good-for-nothings." The king refused the request, but the Althing, undeterred, asked again. They did not succeed. After this, they tried to push for even stricter limitations on marriage. Iceland's push for more conservative laws helped to fuel the movement for Icelandic nationalism.

The expansion of populations in rural areas was alleviated by two forces: emigration and movement to fishing villages. Icelanders emigrated to America, Greenland, and Brazil, although the largest number headed to Canada, drawn by the favorable offerings from Canadian authorities.

One of the indicators of the migration of people from farms to fishing villages was the growth in Reykjavik. In the mid-1800s, the population stood at one thousand, and by the 1890s, it had grown to four thousand. While the movement to towns was driven by population growth in rural areas, other factors drove people to move to fishing villages. One of these factors was the improvement in trade, while another was the use of the decked vessels introduced by Skúli Magnusson in the 18th century. The use of these vessels improved fishing tremendously. Before this, Icelanders had been fishing in open rowboats. Not only were they unable to catch large numbers of fish, particularly during a bad season, but they also faced hazards, including lost boats and drowned men. For example, 1865 saw 174 men drown and 20 lost boats. In 1700, 175 men drowned in one day alone. These numbers do not seem high until you put them in the context of Iceland's population size.

The use of decked boats helped to bring capitalism to Iceland, as individuals owned multiple boats, which allowed them to employ large numbers of fishermen. They also engaged in fish processing. The decked vessels allowed for a longer fishing season as well, allowing people to follow the shoals for half the year. The other half was spent on boat maintenance, which meant fishermen had to work year-round. However, other challenges came with the appearance of capitalism. It started to create an environment for class conflict, and the decked vessels brought the first trade unions. Oddly enough, the owners of the decked vessels created the first union in 1894 to keep wages low.

With these changes in the 19th century, Iceland still remained relatively underdeveloped. Little changed on the farms, but people were gradually beginning to change, which was reflected in the changes in their homes. Some farmers moved the *baðstofa* (living rooms that were traditionally saunas) to the front (it had traditionally been in the back). Others began to build individual chambers with gables facing the pavement in front of the house. There were also some farmhouses with front-yard vegetable gardens, although there weren't many of them at this time. The farmhouse was typically surrounded by a field of green grass fertilized by manure. In some, these fields, called *tún*, were enclosed by a low wall to keep livestock out. During this time, there were few manmade roads in the countryside. The livestock began to create narrow paths by trampling the vegetation with their hooves. It wasn't until the last decades of the 19th century that roads were created. Icelanders finally built bridges over two of the largest rivers in the 1890s.

In the mid-19th century, most Icelanders still lived in turf houses, even in Reykjavik. In 1865, 140 houses were made of turf, while 76 were constructed from timber. Only six stone houses existed in the town at that point. This began to change at the turn of the century. In 1910, the number of turf houses began to decline across Iceland. Forty percent were constructed of timber, while the number of stone or concrete houses remained at only 4 percent. However, living conditions within the turf houses differed greatly. For example, in the houses belonging to the wealthier farmers, the farmer and his wife had their own room. The rest of the household spent most of their time indoors in the *baðstofa*. A servant's space was extremely limited; they most likely only had half a bed and a small shelf.

While we would consider the use of timber houses to be an improvement over turf, this was not necessarily the case. Timber houses lacked sufficient insulation. They were colder, and people hesitated to heat them properly since it was made of wood. The cold was compounded by the windy rain in southern and western Iceland, which made keeping water out a challenge. The problem was slightly abated in the 1880s since the use of corrugated iron provided a barrier.

In terms of stone houses, stone cutting was pretty much unknown until after the Althing house was built around 1880. The Danes taught stone masonry to some Icelanders, but it didn't catch on. In the 20th century, when concrete was introduced, it overtook the use of stone as a building material. Icelanders started to use glass for windows in the 19th century, and they also shifted to using paraffin lamps for lighting, replacing the fish-liver oil lamps. In terms of clothing, they mainly wore clothes made from Icelandic wool.

John Coles, an English traveler, went to Reykjavik in 1881 and observed that it was one of the ugliest towns he had seen. There was no evidence of city planning, the houses were a variety of sizes, shapes, and colors, and there were no trees. He also observed a lack of sanitation and the stench of rotting fish.

A recent image of Reykjavik.

In regard to education during the 19th century, compulsory reading instruction had been established for years, but this was still mainly accomplished in the home, even after the introduction of compulsory education in Denmark in 1814. In 1880, Iceland finally passed a reform mandating education in writing and arithmetic. One of the first schools was established in 1852. In the 1870s, other fishing villages established schools of their own. In rural areas, the establishment of a permanent school was not practical, giving rise to itinerant schools, which were held in relatively large homes. For some students, the homes were within walking distance, but for others, they stayed at the farm during the school session, which lasted three or four weeks. Sometimes, the teacher lived at the farm, moving on to the next farm at the end of each session.

Once Iceland had its own treasury, it started to support schools financially, including the itinerant schools. One study completed for the winter of 1903/04 found that only 60 percent of students aged ten to thirteen attended school of any sort, including itinerant schools. With the education law of 1907, compulsory education was introduced for students in urban areas. In 1874, before compulsory schooling, schools targeted to meet specific needs started to appear. One school focused on providing girls with a general education and preparing them to become housewives. In 1880, the first farming school was opened, and in 1892, a school offered training for teachers. In 1891, a navigation school was opened in Reykjavik.

Further Movement toward Independence and Women's Rights

In 1879, Jón Sigurðsson, the early proponent of Icelandic nationalism, died. Benedikt Sveinsson, a sheriff in Þingeyjarsýsla, took up the cause when the Althing built itself a new stone building in Reykjavik in 1881. By 1884, interest had been renewed in Benedikt's proposal for an amendment to the constitution to "Icelandize" the ministerial power in Iceland. That year, there were at least three attempts in three different parts of the country to establish political parties, all of which advocated nationalist policies. Although they did not come to fruition, they helped support Benedikt's informal nationalist movement. Because of the concentration on the constitution's revision, it was called the Revision Movement.

At the 1885 Althing, a proposal was passed for a constitutional revision, allowing for a regent (a substitute for the king) and up to three ministers. The king did not sanction the proposals, and in 1897, Valtýr Guðmundsson, a lecturer in Icelandic history and literature at the University of Copenhagen, advanced a new proposal for constitutional change. With his proposal, only one aspect of the ministry had to be Icelandized: the nationality of the prime minister. His opponents argued that his proposal meant they were essentially accepting that Iceland was part of the Danish state. Valtýr's proposal began to gain some traction after the death of Benedikt Sveinsson in 1899; at this point, Valtýr's argument gained some ground, as some started to understand how important it was for the prime minister to reside in Iceland. Once the revision to the constitution was sanctioned, Hannes Hafstein, a poet, lawyer, and the leader of the Home Rule Party, became the first Icelandic prime minister in 1904. The government moved into the building that had once been a prison, and the position of governor was abolished.

Historically, women did not have many rights in Iceland, which mirrored the rest of Europe, but this began to change around this time. Before, women could run the farm if they were widowed but could not pursue an education or vote. In Denmark and Iceland, the old law stated that men inherited twice as much as women. However, the Althing changed this to allow men and women to inherit equally. This was passed in 1850, but men's legal guardianship over their wives did not change. In 1861, a law was passed stating that women had personal autonomy at the age of twenty-five. This law likely abolished the earlier law that said women had to obtain the consent of their parents prior to marriage.

In the mid-1880s, there was agitation to grant women more rights, although it was overshadowed by the push for nationalism. In 1894, the Icelandic Women's Society was established with the goal of obtaining women's rights to study at university. It also began advocating for women's suffrage. Once Hannes Hafstein became prime minister, he opened a modern secondary school for women. Later, when he was no longer prime minister, he submitted a bill proposing that all people, men and women, had the right to attend all educational institutions. By 1920, a new constitutional amendment was passed to allow women and other previously disenfranchised individuals the right to vote.

A new party formed in opposition to Hannes Hafstein: the Independence Party. After the Althing passed a vote of no confidence in Hannes in February 1909, the Independence Party nominated a new prime minister. In 1915, a constitutional amendment ended the requirement that six members of the Althing had to be appointed by the king and allowed an increase in the number of ministers, which led to the formation of a coalition government. Simultaneously, the king decreed the Icelandic flag could be flown in Iceland and its territorial waters. Essentially, Iceland became a separate state in a special union with Denmark.

The High Court in Reykjavik became the Supreme Court of Iceland two years after this. This change allowed the Icelandic court to supplant the Supreme Court in Copenhagen, which, up to that point, had been the final court of appeals. In addition, Denmark's annual contribution to Iceland's coffers ended, but a fund was instituted to foster cultural connections between the countries. In 1940, they decided on whether they should renew the treaty saying that Iceland and Denmark were in a special union. They did not, and Iceland became independent at long last.

Chapter 10 – The 20ᵗʰ Century

In the 20ᵗʰ century, Iceland experienced rapid modernization. Fishing became the most important driver of the economy, although there were a number of people working in agriculture and textiles.

The first attempt to run a trawler for fishing came in 1899, while 1912 saw a breakthrough in trawler fishing. From 1902 to 1930, Iceland's fishing industry became mechanized, and the take increased from 80,000 tons to 400,000 tons. The number of people who worked in the fishing industry increased by 50 percent. They primarily dry-salted the fish to process it. Herring, the second-most common fish Icelanders caught, was processed another way. Herring was rendered into oil, which was then incorporated into animal feed.

With economic growth came a change in everyday life. People began living in timber or concrete houses, although, in 1940, 23 percent of people living in rural areas were still living in turf houses. Around 1915, a fire broke out in Reykjavik, destroying twelve timber houses. Restrictions limiting timber buildings to a certain size were put in place, and soon after, timber houses went out of fashion in the country. Additionally, the Althing passed a law eliminating the creation of basement apartments.

On January 1ˢᵗ, 1915, prohibition went into effect in Iceland, although this was not done with an amendment but rather through a referendum. At the time, Iceland did not have a bad drinking problem, but they still put the law into effect. Prohibition did not last long, especially once Spain made some threats. Spain said that if Iceland did not end the prohibition on Spanish wine, it would impose high tariffs on Icelandic cod. Wine became the only allowable alcohol (except alcohol for medical use), and the government ended up having a monopoly on the alcohol trade. In 1933, the abolition of prohibition was passed, although beer with a higher alcohol content was not allowed until 1989.

Once Iceland achieved its independence, political parties arose. They were closely modeled on those of the three Scandinavian countries. There was the Labour Party, which was the most Denmark-friendly and left of center; the agrarian-liberal Progressive Party, which was right of center; the Independence Party, which was the right-wing party, partly because the other groups saw themselves as being to the left of it; and finally, the Communist Party. Because no party has ever had an absolute majority in both chambers of the Althing, the country has either been run by coalitions or short-lived minority governments.

Prior to 1930, Iceland enjoyed prosperity, but it, like the rest of the world, was touched by the Great Depression. Prices for Icelandic exports fell because of falling demand. Unemployment hit relatively high numbers, which was exacerbated by the fact that unemployed workers did not receive benefits. There were two solutions to the problem of unemployment. The first of these was charity, primarily through soup kitchens run by Christian congregations. The second was public work, which was restricted to men. Public work projects, such as laying streets in Reykjavik, were financed by state and local authorities and allocated based on need.

Despite the high unemployment rate, the population in urban areas experienced continued growth. This growth resulted in a shortage of housing. Unfortunately, the Great Depression lasted longer in Iceland than in other parts of the world, as the Spanish Civil War decreased the demand for salt fish. However, the Great Depression was eased by World War II, as the demand for fish on ice in Britain soared.

Iceland adopted a neutral stance during World War II; however, its sympathies lay with the Allies (Britain, France, and the US, to name a few). Iceland continued to remain neutral even after the beginning of the Nazi occupation of Denmark on April 9th, 1940. At this time, Britain offered its protection to Iceland, although Iceland still held to its stance of neutrality. One month later, British naval vessels arrived in Reykjavik, proclaiming they had come to ward off the Germans. Upon their arrival, British soldiers went to the German consul's home to arrest him. They found him there and used his bathtub to burn documents.

The British soldiers informed the Icelandic government they would not be interfering in Iceland's politics, and Iceland, in turn, told the people that they were to see the soldiers as guests. The British erected barracks and constructed three airfields and a naval base. However, when the German invasion of Britain became a more pressing concern, it became obvious that Britain could not offer much protection to Iceland.

An agreement was soon reached between the US and Iceland with the help of Britain's mediation. The US, which was still neutral at that point, agreed to protect Iceland with the understanding that American soldiers would leave once the war was over. When US forces arrived on July 7th, 1941, they built a new airfield and a military base near Keflavik in southwest Iceland (they are both still operational today). The arrival of these forces solved not only the problem of defense but also the problem of unemployment because Iceland had to provide significant labor for the armies.

Iceland did not participate in World War II (or in World War I), but it did suffer casualties, which were high in proportion to the population. Many of these casualties were from cargo and fishing ships that were sunk by the Germans.

At the end of the war, the US asked for permanent military bases in Iceland, but this request was denied. In May 1947, most of the remaining Americans left Iceland. An aircraft company, Iceland Airport Corporation, took over the Keflavik airport, which resulted in six thousand to ten thousand Americans remaining in Iceland beyond May.

Another consequence of the war was the dissolution of the Union Treaty. A day after Germany began occupying Denmark, the Althing temporarily dissolved Iceland's union with Denmark. A year later, the post of regent (*ríkisstjóri*) was created; this office was to replace the role of the king in the Icelandic constitution. Around this time, the notion of turning the constitution into a republican constitution was gaining some traction. In 1942, two parties emerged: one that wanted a quick separation from Denmark (they were concerned that Germany might continue to dominate Denmark) and another that wanted to wait until Denmark was liberated.

In March 1944, the Althing decided to establish a republic, and on June 17th, 1944, Jón Sigurðsson's birthday, the Icelandic Republic was established at Þingvellir. Despite the heavy rain, an estimated twenty-five thousand people (roughly one-fifth of the population) came to hear the declaration by the president of the Althing. Speeches followed, and the prime minister read a telegram from Christian X, the king of Denmark, who congratulated the new republic.

In 1952, in the midst of the Cold War, Iceland entered the Cod Wars with Great Britain, which was essentially a dispute over fishing rights. Iceland started to extend its fishing territory in 1958, increasing it from four miles to twelve miles. The Cod Wars came to an end after Iceland and Britain broke off diplomatic relations (this was after the fishing territory was extended to two hundred miles in 1975). On June 1st, 1976, the Norwegian government mediated. As a solution, Iceland permitted Britain to use twenty-four trawlers to fish for six months within the two-hundred-mile limit. On December 1st, the British trawlers left Icelandic fishing grounds for the last time.

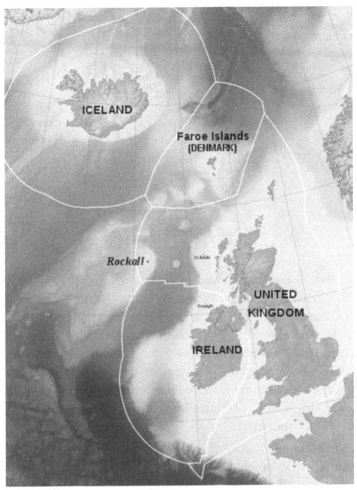

A look at the economic zones of Iceland and the United Kingdom. This map was created in 2018.

Just as fish remain central to Iceland, so, too, does its literature. Icelanders maintain a connection to their language, as it is a part of their tradition. Despite Iceland's understanding of itself as a literary nation, it wasn't until 1955 that an Icelander, Halldór Kiljan Laxness, won the Nobel Prize for Literature. Since 1980, approximately 1,000 to 1,500 books have been published annually by Icelandic writers. It is a high number considering the size of the country, and it definitely shows a connection to their past and their identity as a nation.

Conclusion

When the Norse first arrived in Iceland during the Viking Age, they found an unoccupied land and set out to create a new home. Every country needs rules, and the Vikings turned to the Althing, which has acted as the government of Iceland for much of the country's history. The settlement period also was marked by the creation of the *goðar*, the chieftain or ruling class. In 1262, the Icelandic Commonwealth came to an end, as Iceland pledged an oath of fealty to the Norwegian king. This oath led to the creation of the Old Covenant.

The Icelandic government remained connected to the governments of Sweden, Norway, and Denmark for centuries. These connections shaped Iceland's history, from religious conversions to the regulation of trade. This period was occasionally marked by strife, as Iceland occasionally found itself in conflict with Norway and Denmark. Occasionally, England entered the fray as well. Iceland also faced environmental challenges like volcanic eruptions. Their struggles marked an eventual movement toward independence from Denmark. They were finally able to attain it during World War II with Hitler's invasion of Denmark.

Iceland was slow to modernize, and while Iceland continues to be connected to its past, much of the island nation continues to evolve. The country has continued to be aware of its literary heritage and retains its traditional language. In fact, foreign words are not used in Iceland, so if a new word is required for something, the Icelanders' favored method of coming up with the term is to use old Norse roots. Fishing remains a significant industry in Iceland, but the country's abundant geothermal and hydroelectric power sources have allowed it to develop a manufacturing sector. And, of course, now that people have begun to discover the beauty of the island, tourism has boomed, becoming one of Iceland's most dominant industries.

We hope you enjoyed this look into Iceland's past and strongly encourage you to learn more about its rich history and culture.

Part 5: History of Finland

A Captivating Guide to Finnish History

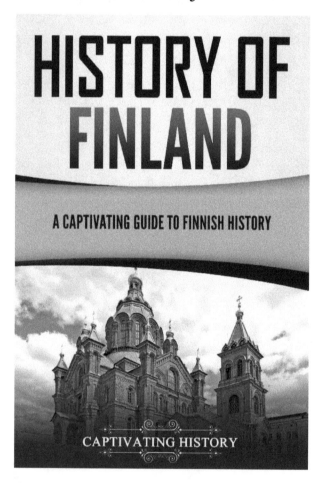

Introduction

Finland (called *Suomi* in Finnish) was in the news a lot in 2022. It has long been a non-aligned country that walked a tightrope between Russia to its east and the NATO countries to the west. Two words that describe the Finns of the 20th and 21st centuries are "fiercely independent." Still, they can only maintain that independence by standing alone in a Europe that has long been divided between East and West.

Why are the Finns so fiercely independent? Well, until 1917, Finland was ruled by outsiders—the Swedes to the west and Russians to the east—for centuries. From the times of the Vikings, areas of Finland (and sometimes even the whole country) were not "Finnish." Imagine if the British had ruled the United States from the 1600s to today. The Finns' lives would have been similar. They were subjects of outside kings, queens, and tsars until just over one hundred years ago.

Finland became formally independent in 1918 after Vladimir Lenin, the leader of the Soviet Union, officially recognized the "new" country on January 4th, 1918.

Until 2022, that independence was contingent, to one degree or another, on Finland maintaining a balance in its relationship with the Soviet Union/Russia and the West. Officially "non-aligned" with either side, Finland found itself in a position of influence with the two sides. The Finns had good relationships with both sides and often hosted or sponsored talks between them.

Still, while Finland is a relatively large country in Europe, it was dwarfed by the USSR and unfortunately found itself at odds with it in 1939 when Soviet ruler Joseph Stalin decided to reclaim Finland and annex it into the USSR as a socialist republic. Suffice it to say that while Stalin did not achieve all of his goals, the war did not go well for Finland, though it retained its independence through the brave resistance of its outnumbered soldiers.

After WWII, with Stalin at Finland's doorstep, the Finns renewed their neutrality pledge. Though constantly under the watchful eye of the Soviets, the situation benefited the Finns to a significant degree. They were one of the few Western countries with open doors to Soviet business, and a huge amount of trade in machinery, telecommunications, and much else flowed into the USSR from Finland. The Finns also did business with the countries of western and central Europe, most of whom were NATO (North Atlantic Treaty Organization) members.

The fall of the Soviet Union in 1991 and the formation of the Russian Federation did not change Russia's relationship with Finland. But when Vladimir Putin took power in Russia and gradually began asserting Russian nationalism and boasting of a massive military buildup, Finland's relationship with Russia began to change.

Though still officially non-aligned (a policy approved by most Finns until quite recently), the country began to shift slowly toward NATO. Russian submarine patrols in Finnish waters and occasional overflights of its border regions pushed the Finns, like it did the similarly non-aligned Swedes, toward the United States and western Europe. In the ten or so years before the invasion of Ukraine in 2022, Finnish forces took part in military exercises with NATO, and its intelligence services began to work more closely with the West.

Finland shares an eight-hundred-mile border with Russia. When Putin invaded Ukraine, which had once been a part of the Soviet Union, Finland wisely decided that it might be next in Putin's plans to restore Russian "glory." In spring 2022, the Finns and the Swedes applied for NATO membership, which is being fast-tracked as of this writing.

A new era has begun for Finland.

A Few Facts and Figures About Finland

Finland is one of the Nordic countries. Looking carefully, you'll see that the word's meaning is easily deduced. In most Germanic languages (Finnish is not one of them), *Nord* means "north." Many people mistakenly lump Finland in with its western neighbors of Norway, Sweden, and Denmark, the Scandinavian countries.

Scandinavia has its roots in both Latin and Old German. The Romans called the region *Scandinovia* for a new and prosperous island, which, of course, was wrong. They likely got the name from the Old German word *Scadinavia*. In Old Norse, Skaney means "south end of Sweden." In the older Proto-German language, the words are *Skaðin and Awjō, meaning "dangerous island" or "dangerous land next to water," likely referring to the rugged coastline of Norway and the frequent bad weather in the region.*

Scandinavians speak languages from the German language tree. The Finns, along with the Hungarians and Estonians, speak a language from the Finno-Uralic tree, which originated in northern Russia and the Ural Mountains.

Of the 193 countries in the United Nations, Finland is sixty-sixth in size. Over 10 percent of its 338,145 square kilometers consists of lakes. Much of the rest of the nation, especially away from its capital of Helsinki, is forested, and the Finns have been quite careful to keep it that way. Generally speaking, Finns pride themselves on being "outdoor people," even if they don't camp and "rough it" all the time.

The population of Finland is quite small for its size. In 2022, it had 5.6 million people. Though the country is 66th in size, it is 116th in population. There are 16.36 people per square mile. Finland is about 83 percent the size of California. California had a population of 37 million and a population density of 251.3 people per square mile in 2019.

Finland is not crowded, and its people like it that way. A popular joke in Finland during the recent pandemic had to do with social distancing. Since Finland is sparsely populated and the Finns are perceived as being people who like their space and privacy, T-shirts and signs mocking the need for social distancing popped up all over. It wasn't that the Finns believed the disease was a hoax (on the contrary, they were quite prepared for it). No, it was just that social distancing was already a thing in Finland. One T-shirt had a Finnish flag with the words "Social Distancing" below it. Under that was this phrase, "I'm Finnish. I've been preparing for this my whole life."

As you discovered earlier, Finland is bordered by Russia. It also shares a long border with Sweden and a smaller border with Norway above the Arctic Circle. Speaking of the Arctic Circle, Finland is cold in fall and winter, though most of the country lies beneath the Arctic Circle. Still, on average, Finland is relatively temperate, at least for its location. The Baltic and North Atlantic currents bring warmer water and air to the coasts, and the lakes have a great effect on the weather as well.

In June 2022, the average temperatures in Helsinki in the south and the city of Sodankylä in the north were 15.9°C/60.6°F and 13.8°C/56.8°F, respectively. In January 2020, a generally warmer year worldwide, Helsinki's average temperature was -3.4°C/25.8°F and -9.5°C/14.9°F in Sodankylä. Despite the warming trends of the waters, Finland is cold, and for much of the year, there is not much sun. Its lack of sunlight has to do with its location in the far north, which sees longer nights in the winter, but the weather also plays a role. Surrounded by water on three sides, there are far more cloudy days than sunny days in Finland. Sunny days in Finland generally see crowds of people outside soaking up all the sunshine they can get.

Finland is not mountainous. Most of its territory is flat, especially in the south, but there are large numbers of rolling hills and plains. A little over 70 percent of Finland is forest, and only 7.5 percent is arable (suitable for farming). Finland was once a nation with large numbers of farmers, including dairy farmers, but even when much of the population worked in agriculture, the Finns had to import most of its food. Finland faced hunger and, at times, starvation throughout its history.

Natural Resources

Finland contains and produces a variety of natural resources. As you might assume from a country covered by trees, its primary resource is timber. Like Norway and Sweden, its neighbors to the west, Finland also contains significant deposits of lead, nickel, gold, silver, limestone, copper, and iron ore. It also has a large fishing industry.

Population and Ethnic Groups

Finland's population in 2022 was 5,601,547. New York City alone has more people than Finland. The country is sparsely populated and likely has been throughout its history.

Finns, Swedes, Estonians, Romani, Russians, and the native Sami are the largest ethnic groups. The intertwined history of Finland and Sweden means that it is likely that many Finns have Swedish ancestors. The Romani people have enjoyed, for the most part, living in Finland compared to other countries, as Finland has been traditionally less discriminatory toward them than European countries in the south.

Language

Finland has two official languages: Finnish and Swedish. For centuries, Finland was a Swedish territory, and much of the western part of Finland was populated by Swedes. The Swedes and much of the urban and upper-class population of Finland spoke only Swedish. This very slowly began to change after Finland was given to Russia in an 1809 treaty, but even into the 20th century, many of the ruling and educated classes spoke Swedish.

In a 2008 poll, Finns voted Carl Gustav Emil Mannerheim (most often known as just Mannerheim), the leader of Finland for much of the first half of the 20th century, as the "greatest Finn of all time." Mannerheim had Swedish and German roots and struggled to speak Finnish. It is estimated that only about 6 percent of Finns spoke Swedish at home in 2022.

Other languages include Estonian, Russian, Romani, and three Sami languages: Inari Sami, Skolt Sami, and Northern Sami. The majority of Finns speak English to some degree or another. Most speak English fairly well and even fluently.

Finnish, like Estonian and its distant cousin Hungarian, is quite difficult to learn. Strangely enough, these three languages are more related to the Turkic languages of Central Asia and Turkey than they are to any of the Scandinavian and European languages.

Even if you cannot speak Finnish, you can easily recognize it in print. Finnish uses a lot of vowels and has many different vowel sounds. The letter "e" is the most commonly used letter in English, but "e" is not used as frequently in Finnish as "o," "u," and "a." Finnish also contains many examples of double consonants, particularly "l" and "k."

English: "Finland is a beautiful country with a lot of trees and lakes."

Swedish: "Finland är ett vackert land med många träd och sjöar."

Finnish: "Suomi on kaunis maa, jossa on paljon puita ja järviä."

Estonian: "Soome on ilus maa, kus on palju puid ja järvi."

Hungarian: "Finnország egy gyönyörű ország, sok fával és tavakkal."

Religion

Most Finns describe themselves as Lutheran. However, as in most Western countries, church attendance in Finland has declined over the last few decades. Fully a third of Finns say they are not religious at all. There is a small percentage of Finns who are Eastern Orthodox who live mostly near the Russian border. Russia is a predominantly Orthodox country, so this makes sense. Another small percent of the population is Muslim; they are mostly immigrants or descendants of immigrants from the Middle East. Most Muslims live in larger cities, such as Helsinki and Turku.

The national flag of Finland.
https://commons.wikimedia.org/wiki/File:Flag_of_Finland.svg

Government

We will be discussing the evolution of Finland from a Swedish and Russian territory ruled by various forms of a monarchy to the representative democratic government it is today. But for the moment, it is enough to know that the Finns have a unicameral legislature (one chamber as opposed to two like in the United States).

The president is the chief of state and largely conducts foreign affairs internationally but with the input and influence of the government through the prime minister and the legislature. The prime minister is elected by the people and runs the government. They are responsible for creating laws and policies that are then voted on by the legislature (the Eduskunta). The president is elected once every six years, providing stability. The prime minister is more dependent on political support within the Eduskunta, and the position is sometimes more tenuous than that of the president, depending on party politics and popularity.

As of this writing (fall 2022), Finland's president is Sauli Niinistö. He has served since 2012. The president has a two-term limit and serves for six years per term. The prime minister is Sanna Marin, who became the youngest world leader in 2019 at the age of thirty-four and the youngest prime minister in the country's history. Marin has been somewhat controversial in Finland, not so much because of her policies but because of her age, gender, and appearance, all of which have provoked deep discussions and arguments within Finland over the role and behavior of women in society.

Chapter 1 – Prehistory

It was not until the advent of Christianity in Scandinavia that we really learned much about the people of Finland. Archaeologists are learning more all the time, but compared to other nations, especially other European nations, our knowledge of Finland and the people who lived there is relatively scant.

In 1996, a number of interesting stone objects were found in Wolf Cave on the coast of central western Finland. From 1997 to 2000, paleontologists, archaeologists, and other scientists worked in the cave to determine the origin of these objects, which included two hundred artifacts and about six hundred pieces of what is believed to be "strike waste," the chips from when stone is pounded or pressed against another stone to make sharp stone tools. Some of the artifacts were made of minerals that do not naturally occur in the area, causing speculation that they were brought from outside, possibly by Neanderthals, some 120,000 to 130,000 years ago.

There were also large amounts of animal bones and skeletons of various sizes. In two deeper layers of soil, there seemed to be evidence of signs that the ground had been packed down by humans, animals, or both, though the animal bones themselves were found in the top layer of the soil, with the bones dating to only about eight thousand years ago.

Wolf Cave shortly after its discovery.
https://commons.wikimedia.org/wiki/File:Varggrottan_1998..jpg

Work is still ongoing in Wolf Cave, though it is slow since the site is dangerous with the constant threat of cave-ins. Prehistorians in Finland and elsewhere are still debating on the origin of the bones and stone, with some insisting that they are evidence of Neanderthal settlement, at least for a time, in Wolf Cave. If this is true, it would be the only evidence of Neanderthals in any of the Nordic countries. While that does not mean that the people who lived in Wolf Cave were not Neanderthals, it makes the chances of it a bit less likely.

Other scientists believe that the cave was underwater for the time period in question, while others do not. It's also possible that the implements found in the cave come from a much later time period. Studies continue, but as of this writing, the people who live near Wolf Cave in the town of Karijoki derive some income from a small tourist trade.

What We Do Know About Ancient Finland

We know that parts of Finland were occupied by at least 8,500 BCE during the Stone Age. Actually, the period is best known as the last glacial period or the last ice age. These people were hunter-gatherers who likely traveled throughout the area, perhaps including southern Sweden and northern Russia.

About three thousand years later, knowledge and culture from other parts of Europe began to arrive in Finland. In mainland

Europe, the Corded Ware culture was present. It was one of a series of cultures that replaced or built on those that had come before. In Finland, the Corded Ware culture is the first known culture to have created more advanced tools from the molding and firing of clay. The name "Corded Ware" comes from the culture's pottery (in the form of urns, pots, and smaller containers), which has a purposefully artistic corded design.

The Corded Ware culture existed not only in Finland but also in a large arc from central Europe to Scandinavia to the plains of central Russia from circa 3000 to 2350 BCE. Toward the end of the period, it is possible that semi-permanent, semi-agricultural settlements were built, at least in the southern part of Finland or near the coasts where the weather was a bit warmer. However, the development of Finnish agriculture was slow compared to other parts of Europe due to the lingering effects of the cold climate brought about by the last glacial period.

Typical Nordic decorative stone axes.
Wolfgang Sauber, CC BY-SA 4.0 <https://creativecommons.org/licenses/by-sa/4.0>, via Wikimedia Commons https://commons.wikimedia.org/w/index.php?curid=34399027

The later Finnish Corded Ware culture differed from those in other parts of Europe to a degree and has its own name: Finnish Battle Ax culture. It was named after the soapstone and decorative stone axes found throughout much of Finland. Since the discovery of these battle axes, debate has raged between Swedish and Finnish archaeologists about whether these cultures were the same people and whether a particular territory was the "home" of the culture or not.

The next significant change in Finland was the arrival of the Bronze Age, which is generally considered to have lasted from about 3300 to 1200 BCE, though the Bronze Age in Finland began and ended later than it did in more temperate and centrally located parts of Europe and Eurasia.

It's believed that bronze technology came to Finland from the area of the Altai Mountains, where China, Russia, Mongolia, and Kazakhstan meet. The earliest bronze implements found in Finland greatly resemble other artifacts from what is called the Seima-Turbino phenomenon, named for the places where these types of artifacts were first found. The term "phenomenon" is used because this tool-making culture spread in almost all directions for a relatively short period of time, just two hundred years, between 2100 and 1900 BCE.

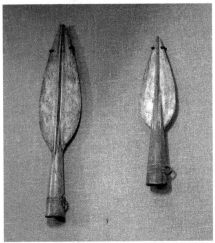

Seima-Turbino spearheads found at Borodino, Russia
Лапоть, CC0, via Wikimedia Commons https://en.wikipedia.org/wiki/Seima-Turbino_phenomenon#/media/File:Spearheads_1_Seima-Turbino_GIM.jpg

Artifacts from the Seima-Turbino phenomenon have been found in Korea, Japan, northeast China, the Russian Far East, Finland, and parts of Sweden. It's also possible that the Uralic roots of the Finnish language come from the time of this phenomenon.

The Bronze Age ushered in greater Finnish contact with the outside world. Previously, what trade existed between the people in Finland and other places occurred with those who inhabited modern-day Estonia, just across the Gulf of Finland. There may also have been trade routes overland from the southern Finnish area through the area around modern St. Petersburg to Estonia.

People in Finland began to make their own style of bronze tools and weapons around 1300 BCE and also began to import quantities of bronze from the Volga region of Russia, southern Sweden, and Norway. Though Finland remained a mystery to many people outside the region for quite some time, there was contact between people in the region, even if it was only on the coasts.

The Iron Age and the Roman Age

The Bronze Age in Finland lasted longer than it did in other parts of Europe, ending only in about 500 BCE with the coming of the Iron Age. Artifacts dated from 500 to 1 BCE indicate no real signs of contact with the great civilizations of the Mediterranean, the Middle East, or Asia. This time is called the Pre-Roman Period.

The Roman Period of the Finnish Iron Age began in 1 CE and ended around 400 CE (roughly about the time of the fall of the Western Roman Empire). As you may know, if you have read about other Nordic cultures of the time, the people of modern Norway, Sweden, and Denmark were what some historians call pre-literate, meaning they had a runic (and rudimentary) alphabet and did not keep written records of any great length or meaning beyond runestones and inscriptions on bones. Their written records indicated possession or perhaps a short snippet about boundary lines or the death of a kinsman or friend. The people of Finland may have had a runic alphabet, like the Estonians of the time. However, no written documents or artifacts from Finland from the period are known to exist.

The first written reference to the people of Finland comes from the Roman historian Tacitus in his book, *On the Origin and Situation of the Germans*, which is usually referred to as the *Germania*. Tacitus's work encompasses the lands of modern Germany and parts of Austria, Poland, Denmark, Sweden, Norway, and Finland.

Tacitus's book describes in great (but not always accurate or subjective) detail the Germanic people of present-day mainland Europe and ends with brief references to the people of Estonia, whom he called the Æsti and the Fenni. In his book, Tacitus admits that he does not know how to classify the Fenni, as he is unsure if they were German people or Sarmatians, people who lived in parts of Ukraine and Central Asia near the Caspian Sea and Persia. Even in Roman times, people were confused about which group the Finns belonged to, much in the same way that people today sometimes call the Finns "Scandinavians."

Tacitus never traveled to Finland or most of the other places he wrote about. He relied on word of mouth and ancient writings, although he probably sprinkled in some imagination as well. But even though the following quote does not paint the Fenni in a great light, Tacitus does indicate a bit of respect for them at the end of his book:

"The Fenni are astonishingly savage and disgustingly poor. They have no proper weapons, no horses, no homes. They eat wild herbs, dress in skins, and sleep on the ground ... Yet they count their lot happier than that of others who groan over field labor, sweat over house-building, or hazard their own and other men's fortunes in the hope of profit and the fear of loss. Unafraid of anything that man or god can do to them, they have reached a state that few human beings can attain: for these men are so well content that they do not even need to pray for anything."

Some other Roman writings describe the area that was occupied by the Finns. There are also place names that indicate permanent settlements on the coast. Additionally, there are also the names of a number of ancient Finnish kings and a few descriptions of their culture. However, Finland remains a mystery for the most part until well into the Early Middle Ages.

The Finns are mentioned a couple of times in the annals of the Frankish Empire during the time of Charlemagne, but the annals only mention the Finnish name for the country, *Suomi*, and a man who signed some type of peace agreement.

Two runestones in Sweden mention Finland as *finlont* and *finlandi*, but that is all the mentions of Finland until the writer of many famous Scandinavian sagas, Snorri Sturluson, talks about the land and people of Finland in *Egil's Saga*. Snorri tells of a war in the far northeast of Finland between a mixed Norwegian/Finnish war band and the Karelian people, who live in the territory between Archangel and St. Petersburg, Russia, today.

In the 12th and 13th centuries, the mentions of Finland and the Finns begin to increase. This happened due to increased Swedish activity in the country, mostly in the form of missionaries and Swedish rulers' interest in forced Christianization.

Contact with the Outside World Grows: 400–800 CE

Though there is not one moment that marks the "end" of the Roman Empire, at least in western Europe, it was in decline for over one hundred years when the Migration Period began around 400 CE.

The empire had been the glue that held the many people of western and southern Europe together. With the end of the empire and of the Roman army as a dominating force, many people in Europe began to move. At the same time, people from the steppes of modern Ukraine and Russia began to arrive in Europe, some of them just for a time, like Attila's Huns, and others more permanently, like the Magyars, the people who are today's Hungarians.

Much of the contact and trade people from outside Finland had with the Finns occurred in what is called Finland Proper (*Varsinais-Suomi* in Finnish). Finland Proper is the territory on the other side of the Åland Islands from Sweden and includes today's city of Turku. It had been home to most of the Finnish population for centuries. During the Migration Period, groups of Finns began to move eastward along the coast of the Gulf of Finland to the location of modern Helsinki.

Finland is much colder than most other European countries, but it is warmed to a degree by the currents of the Baltic Sea. The southern coasts are a bit more protected from harsh weather, so temperatures there are a bit higher on average. This means that while the southern coast of Finland is not as fertile as California's Central Valley, more varieties and more plentiful crops will grow there than in other parts of the country.

One of the more noteworthy things about the Migration Period and the end of the Roman Period in Finland was the growth in the use and production of iron. The Iron Age came later to Finland, but evidence of domestic iron production has been found that dates to the Migration Period. Additionally, the swords, axes, and knives found by archaeologists in Finland clearly show the influence of the Germanic cultures bordering Finland to the west and south.

The Early Middle Ages or the Merovingian Period

The Merovingians were the ruling dynasty in today's France from the mid-400s to the rise of the Carolingians (the dynasty that included Charlemagne) in 751. The term has nothing to do with Finland in any way; it's simply a term used by historians to indicate different periods of time.

During the Merovingian Period, Finland imported more and more goods from other nations. With a couple of exceptions over the course of 250-plus years, that meant traders came to Finland, not the other way around. Some of the more valuable items were weapons that were far beyond Finnish skills at the time. Many of these weapons were not only stronger than what the Finns made at home but were also more decorative as well, which indicates what historians have believed for some time: that Finland, much like its Nordic neighbors of Sweden and Norway, was divided into a group of small kingdoms. The remains of wooden hillforts, partially preserved by the cold weather or protected by the bogs and lakes of the country, also indicate a tribal culture consisting of various petty kingdoms.

Like the Swedes and the Norwegians, the Finnish kingdoms likely traded, formed alliances, and battled each other at different times.

One of the other important changes taking place in Finland, at least to a small degree, was the arrival of Christianity. Archaeologists have found a number of graves with Christian grave goods near the village of Orismala on the central western coast of the Gulf of Bothnia that date from the late Merovingian Period. This does not mean that most or even many Finns were Christian at the time, but it is another indicator of Finnish contact with the outside world. You'll learn more about native Finnish spiritual beliefs shortly.

Chapter 2 – Vikings?

Finnish tourists traveling in the United States or elsewhere likely have had the following conversation before:

"Hi, where are you from?"

"Finland."

"Oh, you're a Viking!"

Finns hear this more often than they would care to. People with Scandinavian heritage might think having ancestors who were Vikings is kind of cool. But remember, Finns are not Scandinavians, and they're definitely not Swedes, which was the nearest Viking civilization to Finland in the Viking Age.

However, while Finns, as a whole, were not Vikings, there were individuals and small groups of Finns that were. Although all of the people of Scandinavia during the Viking Age (793-1066) are sometimes described as Vikings, this is usually done for the convenience of the writer and is usually preceded by a disclaimer that says something like "Though not all Scandinavians were Vikings, we occasionally use the term to describe the people of Scandinavia as a whole." This is acceptable, but it is not really correct. Vikings were not an ethnic group. Vikings were mostly men who banded together to raid, war, and trade with the people of Europe during the Viking Age. Many Scandinavians (Norwegians, Swedes, Danes, and Icelanders) were not Vikings; they were farmers, fishermen, and blacksmiths.

Additionally, while most people who "went Viking" were Scandinavian, not all of them were. In Ireland, a new Hiberno-Norse culture began sometime after the Viking raids commenced in Britain and Ireland (Hibernia was the Roman name for Ireland). The same thing occurred to a degree in Scotland, especially on the coast of the Irish Sea. Additionally, men who sought adventure and were trusted by the Scandinavians as traders or allies could become Vikings. We know there were Frisian/Dutch Vikings and German Vikings. Later in the period, a new Viking culture was born out of the Swedes' adventures in Russia and Ukraine.

So, were there Finnish Vikings? Yes. We know this because a peace treaty between the Vikings of Kievan Rus' and the Byzantine Empire (Eastern Roman Empire) in 945 includes three Finnish names side by side with the Swedish ones. So, while there were Finnish Vikings (at least three of them), the vast majority of Finns were not.

Vikings and Finns

We know that the Vikings and Finns had contact. The location of Finland alone tells us they must have had contact, but other records (including Scandinavian Viking Age goods in Finland) tell us they did.

Because both Viking and Finnish cultures were pre-literate people with no contemporary written histories at the time, we know very little about the contact between the two groups of people. We know a bit about the contact between the Finns and the Vikings, mostly Swedish Vikings. Although assumption is not good historical practice, it's likely that the contact between the Finns and Vikings was similar to the Vikings' contact with other people in Europe and beyond.

In central Sweden, there is an island called Birka. During the Viking Age, the land and waterways were much different than they are now because of erosion and climate changes. Birka was one of the biggest international trading posts in Europe at the time. Goods from China, the Middle East, the Mediterranean, and elsewhere were bought, sold, and bartered for at Birka.

Runestone Gs-13 found in Sweden north of Stockholm. It mentions the death of a man named Brusi, who was killed in battle in central Finland. The carvings also indicate that Brusi was a Christian. It is dated to c. 1000.

Finns may have gone to Birka to trade and later may have traveled to the island of Gotland, which succeeded Birka as the main Swedish trading station after the waterways to Birka silted up. We don't have much evidence of Finns outside of Finland, Estonia, and a small part of northern Russia, so it may be that the Finns counted on people coming to them with goods. We know that the Finns likely traded for weapons and other goods, probably rare luxury items like glass or fine jewelry. The Finns traded or sold furs, amber, and ivory, some of which they may have traded for with the Sami people, who still inhabit parts of northern Scandinavia and Finland.

Iron Age swords found in Finland. The same style of sword has been found in all areas inhabited or visited by the Vikings.

Swords in similar styles from earlier times and in greater numbers have been found in the Viking homelands and in places they visited, so it's highly likely that these weapons originated with the Northmen. Additionally, the sites in Finland where these swords were found are near coastlines, not inland, which would indicate contact between Vikings and Finns in Finland itself. Scandinavians also sailed to Finland to trade. Given human nature and what we know about the Vikings, it's likely that the Vikings brought slaves to Finland to sell or trade and probably took Finnish slaves as well.

Finland was a collection of tribal kingdoms and clan alliances. Given what we know about Viking Age societies throughout Europe, it seems likely that some Vikings took Finnish slaves from areas where they had not established trade connections. They probably sold enslaved Finns from one area to another region or a rival kingdom.

There are a number of stories handed down through the centuries about conflicts between the Finns and the Vikings.

Many of these come from Finland and are a bit light on the details. Others are written in the sagas. The vast majority of the sagas do not mention Finland at all.

What could be the reasons for the dearth of information regarding Viking Age ties between the Scandinavians and Finns? We can make a couple of educated guesses.

First, there is no record of Finnish warships or any kind of large ship during the Viking era, although they did have boats. None of the neighboring people who were victimized by the Vikings mention raids by the Finns. So, aside from the relatively few Finns who joined Viking bands, like those in the attack on the Byzantine Empire circa 945, most of the contact between Finns and Vikings probably happened in Finland.

This contact also likely happened on the coast. This would have given the Vikings an escape route if they needed to flee. Additionally, many of the larger and richer Finnish settlements were by the ocean. Finland's coast also had much more visibility, generally speaking, than the heavily forested interior. Aside from making movement difficult, the Vikings would have been at a decided disadvantage in any battle that took place in the forest, not because they couldn't fight there but because the Finns knew the forests like the back of their hand. They knew the best place for an ambush, concealment, and camps.

One of the stories that come to us via the sagas is the story of Agne and Skjalf. The story is told in the *Yngling saga*, which was written by Snorri Sturluson, the Icelandic warrior and poet of the late 12th and early 13th centuries. The *Yngling saga* tells of the creation of the universe, Earth, and the Norse gods. It also includes stories from the first kings of Scandinavia. Many of these tales have to be taken with a grain of salt, though.

According to Snorri, there was an ancient Swedish king named Agne. Like most kings in ancient times, Agne was a warrior. While on a raid to Finland, he killed a Finnish chieftain named Froste. (One of the interesting things about the Finns mentioned in the saga is that they have Scandinavian names. Those either came down to Snorri like that, or he changed them from Finnish to Swedish-sounding names for his audience.)

Froste's son Loge and daughter Skjalf were taken prisoner by Agne, and the Swedish king fell in love with Skjalf. She agreed to marry him but told the king that he would first have to hold a funeral feast for her father that involved great quantities of beer. At the feast, Agne began to drink heavily, and Skjalf asked to see the gold he had taken from her father. This gold must have been in the form of necklaces and torques (more like a heavy decorative collar than a necklace), for Agne put the gold around his neck. He paraded around to show his new wealth before passing out.

While he was unconscious, Skjalf tied a rope to the back of the jewelry and had her Finnish compatriots hoist the king in a tree, where he hanged and suffocated. Then Skjalf and her men stole a boat and sailed away. Snorri says that Agne was killed somewhere south of Stockholm. Legend has it that he was buried in an area near Stockholm called Sollentuna, near where the modern train station stands.

Skjalf having King Agne hanged. Engraving by Hugo Hamilton, 1830.

There are a number of other myths, legends, and rumors about the Finns and Vikings or, rather, how the Vikings saw the Finns. Many of them have to do with the Vikings' fear of the deep Finnish forests and lakes. Add to the trepidation anyone feels in an unfamiliar land, especially one where people want to do you harm, was the idea that the Finns were adept spell-casters. They could supposedly make men see things that weren't there, conjure spirits that would get them lost in the forest, and change the weather. There is a story that the Vikings did not want to take Finns on raids because the Finns could control the weather, which would put the Vikings at their mercy.

All of this is understandable. Since time began, men have been attributing supernatural powers to their enemies. Why? Well, if the enemy is vanquished, then you've defeated a powerful enemy with magical powers, causing your status as a warrior or leader to go up. If you lose, then it wasn't because you're a bad warrior; it's just that you are up against an enemy who has magic.

Since Swedish settlements on the Åland Islands and the coast of Finland began during the Viking era, we can assume that many of the conflicts, whether they were military, political, or both, went to the Vikings.

However, we do know of one battle that was won by the Finns, who forced the famous King Olaf of Norway (r. c. 995–1028) to flee. Olaf, who was one of the first Viking chieftains in a Scandinavian country to convert to Christianity and was made a saint by the Catholic Church after his death at the Battle of Stiklestad, is one of the most famous Vikings described in Snorri Sturluson's saga *Heimskringla*. In the following excerpt, you can learn about many aspects of the Vikings and what little we know of the Finns:

"After this they sailed to Finland and plundered there, and went up the country. All the people fled to the forest, and they had emptied their houses of all household goods. The king went far up the country, and through some woods, and came to some dwellings in a valley called Herdaler, where, however, they made but small booty, and saw no people; and as it was getting late in the day, the king turned back to his ships. Now when they came into the woods again people rushed upon them from all

quarters, and made a severe attack. The king told his men to cover themselves with their shields, but before they got out of the woods he lost many people, and many were wounded; but at last, late in the evening, he got to the ships. The Finlanders conjured up in the night, by their witchcraft, a dreadful storm and bad weather on the sea; but the king ordered the anchors to be weighed and sail hoisted, and beat off all night to the outside of the land. The king's luck prevailed more than the Finlanders' witchcraft; for he had the luck to beat round the Balagard's side in the night. and so got out to sea. But the Finnish army proceeded on land, making the same progress as the

king made with his ships. So says Sigvat:

'The third fight was at Herdaler, where

The men of Finland met in war

The hero of the royal race,

With ringing sword-blades face to face.

Off Balagard's shore the waves

Ran hollow; but the sea-king saves

His hard-pressed ship, and gains the lee

Of the east coast through the wild sea.'"

In 2008 and 2010, archaeologists recovered two vessels that were built in the years just before the Viking Age began. These two boats were not the traditional Viking dragon ships but rather precursors to them. They were powered by oars and showed some of the characteristics of later Viking sailing ships.

The boats were found near the village of Salma on the Estonian island of Saaremaa, which lies only a short distance from the mainland. The boats held forty-one bodies, which were placed in orderly rows after their deaths, which were violent. Both boats were burial vessels, and they carried all the earmarks of a Scandinavian burial. We don't know who their enemies were. They might have been other Vikings or people from mainland Europe not indigenous to the island, but it's just as likely, perhaps even more so, that the Vikings' enemy on Saaremaa were Finns or their related Estonian cousins, who speak a closely related language and still trade with Finland.

In the later part of the Viking Age, existent records from 1042 tell of attacks on Finland by the Viking Rus' king of Novgorod, Vladimir Yaroslavich, whose father was Russian and mother Swedish.

A birchbark manuscript dating from the late 11th or early 12th century tells of attacks in Karelia (parts of which lay in modern-day Finland and Russia) by the Lithuanians between the years 1060 and 1080. At the time, the Lithuanians were a growing regional power.

Drawing of a birchbark manuscript in Finnish runes, the earliest known use of a written Finnish language.
https://commons.wikimedia.org/wiki/File:Birch-bark_letter_292.gif

Chapter 3 – The *Kalevala*

Now we're going to skip from what we know about early Finnish history to the 19th century but only to tell you about some important work done by one of the most influential men in Finnish history, though he is not a household name by any means, at least outside Finland.

His name was Elias Lönnrot. He was born in the village of Sammatti near the coast of south-central Finland in 1802 and died there in 1884. During his long life, Lönnrot and many other Finns read about the explosion of national feelings in Europe following the French Revolutions of 1789 and 1848.

Lönnrot in 1872 by Bernhard Reinhold.

Europeans had previously thought of themselves as subjects of one monarch or another, even rulers who were foreigners. The people slowly began to identify more with their ethnic and cultural roots than with a monarchy under which they had little, if any, say.

As you will learn in the following chapter, Finland was part of the Swedish Empire for centuries. Though there had been local rebellions against Swedish rule at times, these were sporadic and generally not supported by the entire Finnish population. However, by the time Elias Lönnrot began studying the evolution of the Finnish language and the oral traditions of Finland, there was an increasing sense that the Finns were losing their history and that the country, especially in the south and southwest, was becoming more "Swedish" in its culture, language, and politics. Finnish was looked down upon by ethnic Swedish, Finnish, and Finno-Swedish elites as the language of the peasants and uneducated.

During Lönnrot's lifetime, he made many trips to the more remote regions of Finland, especially in the lands of the Sami people in the central and far northern parts of the country and the Karelia region on the border with Russia. He talked to as many people as he could about the stories that had been told from one generation to the next. Many of the different groups of people Lönnrot spoke with were illiterate. However, like in other pre-literate and tribal societies, Sami and Finnish storytellers had memorized the stories of their ancestors.

Lönnrot traveled through Finland beginning in 1827 and continued making long journeys into the hinterlands for over thirty years. While writing down the many stories he was told, Lönnrot also had time to put together a guide to Finnish plant life in the Finnish language. Later in life, he compiled and published the first Finnish-Swedish dictionary.

But it is the collection of stories and epic poems that he gathered from the Sami and others that Elias Lönnrot is most famous for. This is the *Kalevala*, the epic poem of Finland. Because of the *Kalevala*, we have a basic knowledge of what the ancient Finns believed about the world, the universe, the gods, and the afterlife.

When Lönnrot sat down through the years to study, organize, and transpose his notes into a sensible and somewhat chronological account, he realized there were significant gaps and even contradictions in many of the stories he had been told. This is not surprising, considering that before Lönnrot, the stories that eventually made up the *Kalevala* were part of an oral tradition going back nearly one thousand years, perhaps more.

For many reasons, including readability, Lönnrot filled in the gaps with his best guesses and what he believed the people of earlier times might have believed. This means that the *Kalevala* is partially the product of Lönnrot's imagination, although it is still an important piece of Finnish history. Still, it makes for an entertaining read and forms the basis for modern ideas about the Finnish spirit world, creation myth, and gods. The gods and heroes of the Finns have similarities and differences with the famous Norse gods of Finland's Scandinavian neighbors.

Like many creation myths, the Finnish version begins with something already in existence, in this case, a giant bird whose egg forms the roof of the sky. Inside this half of an eggshell is the flat earth, and the sky revolves around the top of the shell, which is anchored on the North Star. Coming straight down from the North Star was an invisible energy field, imagined as a sort of "stellar whirlpool," which also served as a conduit for the souls of the dead. The souls would travel through this magical whirlpool of stars into the land of the dead, Tuonela.

At the edges of the flat earth was not a void, like many ancients believed, but another land that people could not journey to. This land was the land of the birds or Lintukoto, a warm paradise where many birds went during the winter. Today, the skies of rural Finland are almost as free from ambient light as they were centuries ago. On a clear night, it is very easy to see the Milky Way, the bright band of stars that marks the center of our galaxy as seen from Earth. The Milky Way was called Linnunrata ("the path of the birds") by the Finns, as it was believed to be the path migrating birds used to travel from Earth to Lintukoto. Incidentally, the word *lintukoto* is used by Finns today to mean a place like paradise, a place where you might want to vacation during the long northern winter, like Tahiti, for example.

The Milky Way as seen from northern Chile.

Animal spirits play a large part in traditional Finnish stories, particularly birds, who were believed to bring the soul to a human being at birth and to Tuonela at death. An invisible bird, the Sielulintu, stood vigil by a person when they slept, making sure the soul did not wander off during dreams.

The bear was considered the most powerful and revered animal and spirit, so much so that it was barely called by its proper name, *karhu*. Bears were seen as the living embodiment of ancestors and were called by other names, such as *otso* ("browed one") or *kontio* ("land dweller").

Gods and Heroes

Bears and birds were not gods, though they were sometimes depicted as supernatural. No, the gods were superhuman, and for the most part, they were depicted much like any other pagan god: muscular heroes, powerful old men, and very beautiful or very ugly women.

The most powerful of the gods was Ukko, the god of the sky and thunder. In this way, he was similar to Thor, the Norse god of thunder. However, unlike Thor, Ukko was an old man, though he did possess a stone hammer. Ukko is sometimes equated with another name, Ilmarinen, the god of thunder and blacksmiths, who is one of the main characters of the *Kalevala*. Ilmarinen and Ukko are often considered one and the same, though the name Ukko is more recent. *Ukkonen* is the Finnish word for "thunder."

In the *Kalevala*, Ilmarinen/Ukko is credited with creating the stars and making the most treasured object in the Finnish supernatural universe: the Sampo. The Sampo is a magical object that granted its holder riches and good fortune. The Sampo is created by Ilmarinen for the witch Louhi, who promises the blacksmith her beautiful daughter's hand in marriage if he can make something that will ensure her bright future. When Louhi sees the power of the Sampo for the first time, she devises a plan to steal it. After it is stolen, Ilmarinen's land and people begin to suffer. A large portion of the *Kalevala* tells of Ilmarinen's journey to recover his magical object, but it gets smashed during a battle at sea and is lost forever in the depths of the ocean.

Ilmarinen is joined on his voyage by the most famous ancient Finnish hero, Väinämöinen, who is depicted as an older, wise man who is still physically strong. What's more, he possesses a magical voice and instrument, his kantele (a combination between a harp and a lyre), which he uses to bewitch people, especially beautiful women. His voice is so powerful that he can create things with it, such as the boat he uses to sail off into the sunset at the end of the *Kalevala* after he is defeated by an especially intelligent newborn baby who chides the hero for all of his sins. Before Väinämöinen leaves the shores of the mortal world, he vows to return someday to help humanity by singing a new golden age into existence.

Obviously, the story of Väinämöinen's end presages the arrival of Christianity in Finland, and it may be that Lönnrot created the ending himself. For a time, it was thought that Lönnrot may have made up about half of the *Kalevala*, but recent studies indicate that only about 3 percent of the story can be attributed to Lönnrot's imagination. About 14 percent of the stories are compilations that he made from a variety of similar stories. The rest are mostly unchanged, except for readability and organization.

The *Kalevala* contains many more stories than just Ilmarinen's creation of the Sampo and Väinämöinen's singing. Many more heroes and villains, both otherworldly and mortal, are described within it, as are many goddesses and beautiful maidens, witches, and magical creatures.

The *Kalevala* has influenced Finns since its publication, most notably in the works of Finland's most famous composer, Jean Sibelius (1865-1957). February 28th is a national holiday and is known both as Finnish Culture Day and Kalevala Day.

Väinämöinen playing his kantele.
https://commons.wikimedia.org/w/index.php?curid=92532856

Chapter 4 – The Swedish Crusades

Most Swedes had converted to Christianity by the early 1100s. For the most part, the conversion of Sweden from a pagan to a Christian society was smoother and more gradual than it was in neighboring Norway, where pagan earls and peasant rebellions violently resisted Christianization for some time.

The Danish king (more of a powerful clan chieftain) Harald Klak had converted to Christianity in 826, but this was likely done under duress, as he was in exile in France at the time. When he returned to Denmark to seize the throne, he was supported by the king of the Franks, Louis the Pious, and returned to Denmark with an important but little-known figure of Scandinavian history, the Frankish monk Ansgar. However, Ansgar's missionary work would have to wait, for Harald Klak was defeated in his attempt to seize the Danish throne. Harald became a feared and infamous pirate, raiding the northern coasts of Europe, including France. He also appears to have given Christianity lip service and likely went back to his old beliefs.

The first Danish king to become a Christian was Harald Bluetooth, who agreed to be baptized in 965. However, this was likely only done so he could establish better trade relations with the kingdoms to his south and prevent an invasion by the more powerful Franks.

It would be another half-century before the kings of Norway converted to the new religion, and the Catholic Church would not found bishoprics there until about 1100, establishing both religious and secular ties with the ruling classes in Norway. With the coming of Christianity and the defeat of the Vikings in England at Stamford Bridge in 1066, the Viking Age came to an end, but that did not mean the Swedes were done invading other countries. Now, they invaded other countries to convert pagans to Christianity.

The three Swedish Crusades occurred circa 1155, 1239, and 1293. But before we tell you more about these events, you should know a bit more about Ansgar, the monk. Ansgar was from Bremen, the famous northwestern German port. He was given the task of spreading the gospel in Scandinavia and arrived at the famous Swedish trading station of Birka in 829, three years after his adventures with Harald Klak.

Ansgar did not convert many people at the famous trading post, but he did make important inroads for his faith by attracting rich and influential converts, like the local king's steward and a wealthy widow and noblewoman Mor Frideborg, who, in addition to being one of the first Swedish converts, is also the first woman in Swedish history whose identity can be confirmed from historical documents.

In 831, Ansgar became the bishop of Bremen, and between dealing with secular political matters and converting northern Germans and the Danes (who raided the Christian city of Hamburg and destroyed church records and relics), he did not return to Sweden until sometime between 848 and 850. Once there, he managed to avert a violent pagan reaction to Christianity. In 854, Ansgar returned to Sweden and joined the court of the powerful chieftain at Birka, Olof, who is said to have been favorably disposed toward the new faith.

Ansgar taught the rudiments of the Christian faith and educated and converted many Swedes. By the time of his death in Germany in 865, Christianity had a foothold in Sweden, though it would take another 150 years or so for most Swedes to embrace the new religion. The last pagan Swedish king was Blot-Sweyn, who reigned for three years, from 1084 to 1087.

Sixty-three years after the death of Blot-Sweyn, Swedish King Erik IX (also known as Erik the Saint or Erik the Holy) began the First Swedish Crusade into Finland. By the time of Erik's reign, Christianity had not only become the spiritual belief system of most Swedes but also a political ideology. The basis of this ideology was that, at least in theory, the unification of all people under Christ would lead to peace and, more importantly, would hasten the Second Coming, in which Jesus would return to Earth and usher in everlasting peace, prosperity, and happiness. But many believed that in order for that to happen, the gospel had to be spread to all corners of the world. The Swedes decided to begin with Finland, but religion was not the only reason they moved into the southern and western coasts of Finland beginning in 1155.

The First Swedish Crusade might not have even happened. Missionary activity had been growing in Finland, with missionaries coming from Sweden and Novgorod, which eventually grew into Russia. The Swedes, like the Norwegians and Danes, were Catholic. The Russians were Eastern Orthodox. To a degree, over the next two centuries, these two sects of Christianity would struggle to claim Finland for their respective churches. When we refer to a "crusade" in Finland, we are talking about a much more gradual one. This crusade was performed mostly by monks and Swedish nobility rather than armies of men forcibly converting the Finns. That would come later.

From the time of Charlemagne onward, power and influence in much of Europe east of the Rhine River were fought over by various popes and the Holy Roman emperors. Though, in theory, the emperor was subservient to the pope and the church, stronger and richer emperors had more power than the pope in Rome. This struggle was mostly peaceful, though it wasn't always. The pope was a secular leader as well, and he was able to field sizable armies at times because of the church's massive treasury.

What's more, though the emperors and popes had been playing political games for hundreds of years, most of these intrigues played out in mainland Europe. In other words, their conflicts did not take place in the Nordic countries. Norway, Sweden, and Finland were wide open as far as the church and emperors were concerned, and they attempted to fill the void.

The Swedes were moving toward a unified kingdom under one monarch rather than having tribal chieftains or petty kings of smaller areas. To counter the complete consolidation of power in the hands of the Swedish kings and to counter the influence of the archbishopric of Bremen in Germany, which controlled the churches of southern Sweden and was more loyal to the emperor than the pope, the church established archbishoprics in Lund and Uppsala, Sweden.

That left Finland. Across the Baltic from Finland are the modern-day countries of Lithuania, Latvia, and Estonia. There were two Holy Roman emperors for most of the 12th century: Conrad III (r. 1138-1152) and Frederick I "Barbarossa" (r. 1155-1190). These two rulers forcibly carried Christianity into the Baltic region, sometimes with great violence. The pope rightly expected that the emperors would make an effort to convert the Finns and secure their loyalty. If this happened, almost the entire northern coast of Europe would be more loyal to (or afraid of) the emperor than the papacy.

In the 1100s, the struggles for power among those who wanted to be king of Sweden allowed the popes to play one man against another while still being at the forefront of establishing a greater presence in Finland.

The leader of the missionary effort in Finland was a British monk named Henry. Henry was backed by one of the most powerful Swedish kings in history, King Erik of the Svear. The missionary work and conversion of the Finns, particularly on the western and southern coasts, went relatively smoothly, but that "easy" effort didn't quite fit in with the narrative the church wanted people to believe. A better story is that Henry, despite many troubles and much violence, managed not only to firmly establish the church but also carried out miracles while he did so.

After his death, Henry became Saint Henrik, the patron saint of the new Catholic diocese of Åbo (present-day Turku). Henry's death was one of the violent instances that marred the mostly peaceful growth of the church in Finland in the 1100s. He was murdered in his new diocese, or at least that's the legend. Finnish history records many different versions of Henry's death, with most of them involving a peasant named Lalli.

Bishop Henry killed by Lalli, Romantic-era painting by Albert Edelfelt
https://commons.wikimedia.org/w/index.php?curid=16348922

Power Struggles over Finland between the 12th and 14th Centuries

The First Swedish Crusade was launched in the name of religion, but much of what occurred in 1155 was part of a power struggle between the pope and the Holy Roman emperors.

Over the next two centuries, religion was used as a convenient cover for additional plots and power moves involving Sweden, Finland, Denmark (which was an economic and military power to reckon with at the time), and the growing strength of Novgorod. The Germanic Hanseatic League, a collection of wealthy and powerful cities, was also a major player in the struggle to control parts of Finland and the Baltic. Obtaining Finland would give a nation (or league) a strategic advantage because of its coastline, especially in the far south and southwest. A great deal of trade sailed in and out of the eastern Baltic and the Gulf of Finland, and whichever kingdom controlled the coastlines could control trade by denying ports to competitors and charging exorbitant port fees and transit taxes.

The coastlines of the Baltic countries were also contested, and in 1219, the Danes founded the port of Reval, which is now Tallinn, the capital of Estonia. In Estonian (again, a language related to Finnish), *Taani linn* means "town of the Danes." Strangely, though the Estonians later called it the "town of the Danes," most of the foreigners there were German Hanseatic traders, who would soon, with the tacit approval of the Swedes, begin to move into the villages, towns, and growing cities in Turku and the southern coasts. In both Sweden and Finland, German traders wielded considerable influence, and their power would last until it was finally controlled to a great degree by the great unifying Swedish king, Gustav I Vasa, in the 1500s.

In 1240 and 1242, two of the most famous battles in history, or at least in Russian history, took place. Prince Alexander of Novgorod defeated an army of Swedes at the Neva River, which would run through the city of St. Petersburg when it was founded in 1703 under Tsar Peter the Great. Prince Alexander is known to history as Alexander Nevsky for his victory on the Neva. This victory helped contain Swedish expansion in Finland, and much of the eastern part of the country remained Eastern Orthodox (the faith of the Russians) until relatively recently. Somewhere in the neighborhood of just 1 to 2 percent of Finns today are Eastern Orthodox, and most of them live in the eastern borderlands of the country, closest to Russia.

Despite the defeat inflicted by Alexander Nevsky (who also defeated the famous Teutonic Knights in Estonia in 1242, giving Novgorod greater influence in the Baltic), the Swedes were the major political and military power in Finland. In both Sweden and Finland, the church and the increasingly powerful kings of the Svear began to centralize power in Sweden and Finland under their control.

Sweden, at least the Sweden we know today, was not completely Swedish in the 13th century. In actuality, much of the lower part of the country, especially toward the west across the straits from Denmark, was under the control of the Danes. In many places in the area, the Danes outnumbered the Swedes. The Danes controlled the area directly through Danish princes and nobles allied with the Danish Crown and indirectly through Hanseatic German traders allied with Denmark and Swedes from the south, who often identified more with the Danes than their fellow Swedes. On top of all that, many of the southern Swedes wanted to rule all of Sweden and were not keen on seeing northern and tribal rivals consolidate power at their expense.

Though the Danes in Denmark and what is now southern Sweden wanted greater influence and trade in Finland, the Swedes would dominate Finland because of Sweden's location to Finland and the northern Swedish kings and the church (with its riches) holding centralized power in their hands.

One reason the Swedes were able to control parts of Finland was that it was sparsely populated. Aside from the Swedish far north, Finland is generally much colder and more forested. Additionally, away from the coasts, the land is much less arable than in Sweden. This meant the Finnish population was smaller than Sweden and Denmark, as it is today. The land and climate would not allow a large population at the time due to their crude understanding of agriculture and medicine.

The Swedes were able to move into western Finland with relative ease, and the colonization was not, for the most part, hostile. Finns and Swedes lived in relative harmony. Still, at the first signs of Swedish penetration into new parts of Finland (in the south and west), many Finnish tribal leaders and their people cleared and marked new areas of somewhat arable land for themselves.

It made sense for the Swedes to get along with their Finnish neighbors, even though the Finns were sparsely populated and in the minority. Though the Swedes could count on their king to strike back against any hostile act, Sweden and the forts containing Swedish troops were few and far between. Due to the difficult landscape and climate, traveling by horse was not much faster than walking. Any Swedish settlers who angered enough Finns in the countryside would be on their own.

World history is full of stories about colonizers conquering people in violent conflicts. In Finland, with few exceptions, the gradual colonization of the country, which started in the southwest and moved slowly toward the area of the modern capital, Helsinki, was peaceful. By the mid-14th century, the closeness of the Finns and Swedes resulted in the merging of cultures. By the 15th century, what historians call "Fenno-Swedish culture" emerged, which included elements of both. Many Finns and Swedes in the south and western coastal areas could speak one another's language, though more Finns learned to speak Swedish than the other way around.

The Second Swedish Crusade

In 1239, a Swedish nobleman and contender for a unified Sweden, Birger Jarl, led an expedition into the hinterlands of south-central Finland, a land called "Tavastland." The people there, known (unsurprisingly) as the Tavasts, rose up in rebellion against the Catholic Church, declared themselves Orthodox, and had been establishing close ties with Novgorod. With the blessing of the Church, Birger Jarl led a punitive expedition against the Tavasts. He put down the rebellion and built a castle in Tavastland to help keep order and administer the area in the name of Sweden. With the support of the church, the Swedes made Finland (or what they controlled of it at the time) a part of their kingdom in 1250 under King Valdemar. Swedish rule of Finland would continue for over five hundred years.

The Third Swedish Crusade

In 1293, the Swedes sought to expand their political and military power to other parts of Finland, namely Karelia, the area that borders modern Russia today. As you learned just a moment ago, most Karelians were Orthodox. Additionally, a small number were still pagan, at least partially. For religious and financial reasons, the Catholic Church wished to expand into Orthodox Karelia, and the Swedish nobility wished to enlarge the area under their control, especially at the expense of Russia, which had been growing its influence in the area. Another reason, at least according to the Swedish King Birger Magnusson, was that the Karelians preyed on trade missions and held Swedish hostages, most of whom were tortured and killed. A band of Karelians had also trekked to Sweden and carried out a raid in 1257, which cost many lives.

The conversion of the Karelians was not as peaceful as what had occurred earlier in other parts of the country. Leaders of Karelian tribes were burned at the stake and subjected to many unpleasant punishments; the Middle Ages is famous for torture.

The leader of the Swedish expedition, a Swedish noble and constable of the realm named Torgils (Torkel) Knutsson, built a fortress in the town of Viborg on the Karelian Isthmus, just north of present-day St. Petersburg. (Viborg was the Swedish name for the town. Viipuri was the Finnish name. Vyborg is its Russian name, and Russia has owned the territory since the end of the Winter War in 1940).

The establishment of a permanent Swedish settlement in Viborg helped to pacify the Karelian region and place Sweden firmly in charge of Finland. The Treaty of Nöteborg (1323) settled the border between Novgorod and Sweden and also marked the recognized demarcation point between Catholicism and Orthodoxy. The Third Swedish Crusade and the Treaty of Nöteborg are immensely important to Finnish history. The treaty brought Finland into Catholic western Europe. For the most part, Finnish culture, economy, and language (remember, Swedish is one of the official languages of Finland, and until the end of WWI, the sizable and wealthy Swedish minority wielded great power in Finland). When Russia took control of Finland in 1809, it took control of an almost completely Westernized country. For much of the time that Russia "owned" Finland, it gave the Finns freedom in their own affairs that no other territory in the Russian Empire enjoyed. That did not mean that Russian rule was benign; at times, especially after the installation of a particularly brutal governor, it could be oppressive.

By the early 16th century, the Swedes had built a number of large fortresses and castles of various sizes to control and administer the country. Near each of these castles and fortresses were the expanding diocese and archdiocese of the church. Together, the church and the Swedish Crown (which would become even more powerful with the rise of King Gustav I Vasa in the 1520s) would establish firm control over all of Finland.

Pagans

In Iceland, remnants of the old Norse beliefs still remain. Elves, gnomes, and other spirits are believed by many Icelanders to actually exist, at least sometimes. Similarly, aspects of old pagan beliefs still exist in Finland, as you saw with the word for thunder.

You may know that the Christmas tree has absolutely nothing to do with Christianity. Historians differ in their belief about the origin of the tradition of a lighted tree but suffice it to say that the holiday tree was a pagan tradition that was subsumed by Christians in later centuries. Same with the Yule log, with "Yule" being an Old Norse word. In Finland and other parts of Europe, the most obvious example of the church adjusting to "heathen" practices was the fertility rites that took place in the spring. Though the sexual aspect of the pagan rites was eliminated, the symbolic sacrifices made during the rites were changed slightly into the Catholic holiday of Whitsun, the marking of the ascension of Christ and the birth of the Catholic Church. In Finland, Whitsun became an excuse to party, just like in pagan times.

Chapter 5 – Gustav I Vasa and the Reformation

"The Father of Modern Sweden," King Gustav I Vasa, 1542
https://commons.wikimedia.org/w/index.php?curid=73305

In 1397, the Danes, Norwegians, and Swedes formed one of the earliest formal multi-national states, the Kalmar Union, named after the town in which it was officially proclaimed. In 2022, Finland, Sweden, and Estonia were all led by women, and from 1397 until 1412, the Kalmar Union was ruled by a woman, the powerful and often-overlooked Margaret I of Denmark.

Though the Kalmar Union was relatively strong under Margaret, after her death, the relatively poor economies, small populations, and internal political and ethnic strife meant that, though the union still existed in name, it grew slowly weaker after Margaret's death. However, many Danish kings still asserted their over-lordship over both Sweden and Norway. Though there were many reasons for the growing weakness of the Kalmar Union after Margaret, two of them involved Sweden directly.

First, the Danes continued to hold the southern part of Sweden. They had for centuries, but as the 16th century approached, common geography, strategies, and ethnicity compelled generations of Swedish kings and nobles, especially those from the north-central part of the country, to try and either maneuver or force the Danes out. Economically, Swedish rule of the southern part of the country would allow them to have some control over the commercial traffic passing through the straits that separated Sweden from Europe.

Second, the Danes used their position in southern Sweden to interfere in the country's politics. The Danes supported a variety of candidates for the Swedish throne, contributing to political, economic, and ethnic instability. The Danes also encouraged the settlement of rich German Hanseatic traders in many of the cities, ports, and castles of southern Sweden, which, over the centuries, became a very important issue in the struggle to unify all of Sweden under one powerful king. At that time, Sweden would have included all of what we know as Sweden today and much else, including Finland.

The man who eventually united the Swedes and established a dynasty that would drive the Danes completely out of Sweden in 1658 was Gustav I Vasa. (The Swedes have a unique method for their royal titles. In this case, Gustav was the man's first name; he was the first "Gustav" to rule Sweden. His last name was "Vasa."

Today's Swedish king is Karl XVI Gustaf. He is the sixteenth Karl, and Gustaf is his middle name, not the name of the ruling family. His family can trace its lineage back to Jean Bernadotte, one of Napoleon's marshals who was asked by the Swedes to take the throne in 1818.)

In 1520, growing Swedish power was a threat to the Danish king (who ruled Denmark and the Kalmar Union), Kristian II. That year, Kristian invaded Stockholm to put down a growing rebellion against his rule among the Swedish nobility. When he arrived in Stockholm, he invited the leading Swedish nobles to dinner and then had them arrested on trumped-up and complicated charges of heresy. Eighty-two men were executed shortly thereafter. One of them was the father of Gustav Vasa, who was traveling in disguise through the Hanseatic cities of northern Germany at the time.

When Gustav returned to Sweden, much of the southern countryside and coast that weren't already under Danish control had fallen to King Kristian, but many of the cities, like Stockholm and Uppsala, remained in Swedish hands, as did the central part of the country, where Vasa's family was from and where they were strongest. When Vasa returned, he raised an army and began a war against the Danes, which resulted in him becoming king of all of Sweden, except for the small Danish holdings on the southern coast, which were eventually made Swedish in 1658.

Gustav Vasa is considered the Father of Modern Sweden today. He was the first monarch to rule a unified Sweden. He ruled at the same time as Henry VIII of England, with whom he corresponded, and his rule was often as harsh as Henry's. Like Henry, Vasa joined the Protestant Reformation, not necessarily out of religious belief but because this would allow him, not the pope in Rome, to control religion in Sweden. More importantly, the money that the church, now the Church of Sweden, brought in would belong to him.

For the Finns, this meant yet another change in their religion because of Sweden.

Gustav I Vasa also founded the city of Helsingfors in 1550. Today, the world knows the city as Helsinki, which is the capital of Finland. Until Helsingfors/Helsinki became the capital of

Finland in 1812, the most important city in Finland was Åbo, known as Turku today.

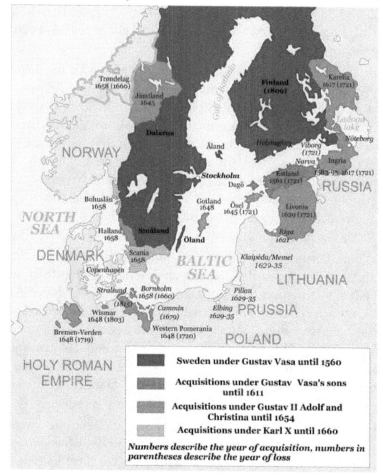

Sweden during and after Gustav I Vasa.

Under the Vasa kings and queens, Sweden grew into a great European power, and for a time in the late 17th century and early 18th century, it was a power broker in Europe. In 1630, Swedish King Gustavus II Adolphus, with a highly trained and professional Swedish/Finnish army, helped end the Thirty Years' War, which had decimated northern and central Europe. One of the more famous units in the Swedish army was Finnish, the

Hakkapeliitta, a light cavalry unit that specialized in swift, surprising raids into and behind enemy lines. In 1940, while Finland was under assault from the Soviet Union, the Finnish government resurrected the spirit of the Hakkapeliitta to encourage its countrymen, many of whom specialized in cavalry and ski raids behind enemy lines, appearing from and disappearing into nowhere.

Hakkapeliitta stamp, 1940.
https://commons.wikimedia.org/wiki/File:Hakkapeliitta-1940.jpg

Finland was formally a part of Sweden at the time of Gustav Vasa. It would remain part of Sweden until 1809, when the two most powerful nations in Europe at the time, France and Russia, forced Sweden to relinquish control of Finland.

In the 17th and 18th centuries, most Finns thought of themselves not as Swedes but as part of the Swedish Empire, and to a very large degree, this benefited them. The population of Finland has always been small, especially considering the size of the territory, and in the late 17th and early 18th centuries, Russia was becoming more powerful and established varying levels of control in the Baltic region. The Russians also claimed parts of Karelia and areas around the new city of St. Petersburg. Sweden's army was a valuable hedge against future Russian moves against Finland, though, by 1809, Sweden's army was not capable of resisting both the French and Russians, who forced the cession of Finland without firing a shot.

Chapter 6 – Swedish Rule in Finland until 1809

The end of the Thirty Years' War, codified in the famous treaty known as the Peace of Westphalia (1639), ushered in a period of peace and relative stability in Sweden and Finland. From this time until the Great Northern War, which was fought between Russia and its allies (the Kingdom of Denmark and Norway and Saxony-Poland-Lithuania) and Sweden, great changes took place within Sweden (which included Finland). Many of these much-needed reforms set the groundwork for the modern Swedish and Finnish states.

One of Sweden's benefits was the formation of an informal trade association that involved the increasingly wealthy Protestant states of northern Europe (England, Denmark, many of the German states, and Holland). This alliance allowed for greater trade between Protestant states with a bit less competition from their Catholic neighbors to the south.

In 1634, a number of administrative reforms were enacted in Sweden that streamlined decision-making within the government and military, making them more responsive to the needs of the people and defense. A formal civil service was also created. The departments of the civil service were called colleges (called "ministries" in Finland, which had its own administrative structure under a Swedish governor-general, a nobleman appointed by the Swedish monarch). The colleges were responsible for things like agriculture, trade, defense, and education, to name a few. From 1623 to 1637, Finland had two governors-general.

By the time the third governor-general of Finland was appointed in 1637, most of the reforms that had been carried out in Sweden had been established in Finland. However, Governor-General Count Per Brahe the Younger is the best-known Finnish governor-general.

Brahe was governor-general of Finland twice, from 1637 to 1641 and 1648 to 1654. Administratively, Brahe presided during a period of peace and stability within Finland and took credit for many of the reforms that had been enacted before his arrival. However, he and his administration did enact some important and beneficial reforms that caused him to be remembered long after his death. People referred to the years of his administration as the "time of the Count," and many looked back on those years with some fondness.

In 1636, the Royal Mail of Sweden was founded. Within two years, Brahe had built a post office in virtually all of the towns and cities (not villages) of Finland. This made communication administration faster and easier not only within Finland but also between Sweden and Finland.

The Royal Academy of Åbo (now the Royal Academy of Turku) is the oldest university in Finland. It was founded by the incredibly interesting Queen Kristina (r. 1644–1654), who you can read about in Captivating History's *History of Sweden*. Per Brahe supported this idea wholeheartedly and is remembered as the man who oversaw its construction and initial administration.

One of Brahe's greatest accomplishments was the building of new towns in Finland. Brahe was very much like a king in Finland, and in Sweden, the new monarch would traditionally take a tour on what was called the "Royal Route," traveling to the interior of the country and back. Brahe wasn't a king, but he did have almost absolute power in Finland.

Per Brahe, c. 1650

When Per Brahe arrived as governor-general for the first time, he knew very little about the interior of the territory. His tour through Finland opened his eyes to the hard lives of the few Finns who lived there and to the economic possibilities of the country.

In the 17th century, the new economic idea was "mercantilism," the notion that an economy ran best when it was highly centralized and governed by strict rules that were designed to give it a favorable balance of trade. Mercantilism is often associated with the establishment of colonies that would benefit the mother country. In this case, the mother country was Sweden or, rather, the Swedish government, which had been on the road to becoming an absolute monarchy for some time.

Control was very important in the economic sphere. The Swedes set up an unusual system that, on the whole, benefited Swedes and Finns, at least in the cities, larger towns, and ports. A few population centers were declared "staple towns." Only staple towns had the right to trade internationally. The small number of these towns and the concentration of trade there meant it was easier for the government to tax and control trade coming into and leaving these centers. In Finland, at least in Brahe's time, there were only three staple towns: Åbo, Helsinki, and Viborg (on the Karelian Isthmus near St. Petersburg). Greater wealth was concentrated in these three cities, which, in turn, drew more people to them, both from the Finnish interior and Sweden.

Towns that were not staple towns were only allowed to trade within Finland, and the government also oversaw this. So, those in the country towns and villages that wished to trade overseas had to go through merchants in the staple towns. They also had to pay a special tax. In turn, the staple town merchants would sell those goods overseas, and they were again taxed.

Though this system greatly benefited the Swedish Crown and Finland's governor-general, they were not the only ones. Brahe sponsored the founding of ten towns in Finland, which, generally speaking, improved the lives of many Finns. These towns, which were located in the interior of the country and on the relatively undeveloped southeastern coast, brought in Finns, Swedes, and foreigners, mostly wealthy Germans and Danes. Though Sweden and the towns of western Finland traded with Russia, most of their overseas business was done with western and central Europe. The new towns in the southeast mainly did business with the Baltic states and Russia.

Slowly, the country grew more prosperous, though Finland and most Finns were not nearly as wealthy as Sweden and most Swedes. By 1700, Finland, while still a relative "backwater" compared to Sweden, Denmark, and even poorer Norway, was much more prosperous than anyone could have expected in 1639 when Brahe began his first term as governor-general.

Trade Goods

Until the early 17th century, only about 5 percent of the Finnish population engaged in something other than fishing, farming, and hunting. Most surplus grain was paid as tax. In the early 17th century, Europe experienced the greatest economic boom it had ever known. The colonial empires of England, Holland, Spain, and Portugal supplied much of Europe with goods from Asia, Africa, and the Middle East. Spain and Portugal had begun their slow decline in the early 17th century and were distant Catholic powers that Sweden had little to do with. However, England and Holland were growing richer by the day, and Swedish economic ties with both countries went back centuries. In the later 17th and early 18th centuries, economic ties between Sweden and France, continental Europe's richest and most powerful nation at the time, also increased.

Holland and England built more ships as overseas trade increased in the 17th and 18th centuries. They built thousands of ships. One result of such a massive shipbuilding program was the almost complete deforestation of both countries. Before the use of steel to build ships, the nations of Europe that had the most forested lands had an economic boom. And no territory in Europe was more forested than Sweden, Finland, and Norway.

In Norway and Sweden, which were more technologically advanced compared to Finland and whose trees were generally more suited to shipbuilding and other finished products, lumber mills cut down trees and created lumber to specification.

Much of Finland was pine forests. Pine trees are the source of pitch and tar, both necessary in building ships. In the mid-17th century, tar (the more useful and effective of the two products) made up about 2 percent of Finland's exports. Before the end of the century, tar made up nearly 10 percent. Of that 10 percent, about 75 percent of Finland's tar production came from the eastern part of the country, which had traditionally been the poorer region. The Swedes did not have a monopoly on tar production and trade, but they dominated it and were able to control prices through the sheer volume of tar they produced and shipped. Think of the Swedes as the 17th-century version of OPEC (Organization of the Petroleum Exporting Countries), except they dealt in tar rather than petroleum.

Another benefit of the vast Swedish and Finnish forests was that the trees could be turned into charcoal, which was needed for iron- and steel-smelting. In an age before the widespread use of coal, timber was needed to make iron. The Dutch and especially the English had iron deposits, but they lacked the wood to make charcoal. This was where the Swedes came in. Though there were only about thirty ironworks in Finland, there were over three hundred in Sweden. Finished copper production also relied on wood/charcoal, and both Sweden and Finland had plenty of both. Copper and iron production in the Swedish Empire rose until the early 18th century, and even then, copper production comprised about 25 percent of Sweden's exports.

Religion

Absolute monarchies reached their greatest heights in Europe during the 17th and 18th centuries. Even in England, where the monarch's power was restrained by Parliament, the ruler held tremendous power. This was the same (albeit to an even greater extent) in mainland Europe, with the exception of Holland, which had become, at least to a degree, a republic after it won its independence from Spain in 1581.

In the Catholic kingdoms, monarchs often vied with the church for a greater share of power. In France under Louis XIV (considered the "ultimate" absolute monarch), the state, for the most part, managed to control the church's power to a large degree. In Spain, from the early 17th century onward, both the church and nobility worked incessantly to weaken or control the monarch's power, meeting much success.

In central Europe, meaning the German states and what would later become Czechoslovakia, the population was split between Protestants and Catholics, making absolute power hard to come by. The only significant German absolute monarchy was in the northeastern kingdom of Prussia, where almost the entire population was Protestant Lutheran.

In Denmark and Sweden (until relatively recently, Norway was always the "poor cousin" of the Scandinavian countries and was alternately part of Denmark and Sweden at times), the Protestant Lutheran Church was the only religion. Though there were Catholics in both countries, they were persecuted and punished economically to a large degree. This was much more prevalent in Sweden than in Denmark.

Protestantism had begun to split into a number of different sects by the late 17th century, but the teachings of Martin Luther were still the foundation for them. And though the Protestant kings and nobles fought exceedingly bloody wars for their right to choose their religion, this freedom of worship did not trickle down to the populace. In Sweden and Finland, a harsh Lutheran fundamentalism took hold. Religious toleration did not become law in Sweden until 1781, and even then, Catholics experienced widespread discrimination.

This book is meant to be an introduction to Finnish history, and unfortunately, an in-depth study of religious fundamentalism in Scandinavia is outside its scope. But suffice it to say, like most fundamentalist sects, those in Sweden and Finland established requirements for church attendance, manner of living, types of speech, and books the population were allowed to read and those they were not. The vast majority of printed works in Scandinavia and Finland at this time were religious. Reading for enjoyment or enlightenment outside of religious readings was either proscribed or severely frowned upon.

This does not mean that the Swedes established something like a modern police surveillance state. They didn't have to; peer pressure and beliefs did much of the policing for them. In virtually all Protestant churches at the time, the "fire and brimstone" sermon took root. Fear of hell kept many people in line at a time when being different or an outsider was dangerous. Much of the population was ignorant, meaning they weren't properly educated.

What education the people had came from the Lutheran Church. Since the Protestants believed the Bible was the literal word of God, they believed each person should have access to it (even if they were told how to interpret it by the clergy). Thus, literacy in the Nordic countries was (and still is) among the highest in the world.

What's more, religion was a unifying element in Swedish and Finnish societies. Most of the religious education was done in Swedish, and during the 17th and 18th centuries, this was done without much resentment on the part of the Finns. The period saw a growth in the wealth of most people, and Finnish was not prohibited. Most Finns were loyal to the Swedish Crown to some degree or other, and since much of the southwest was populated by Swedes, there was some degree of intermarriage. Ethnic conflicts between Swedes and Finns were kept at a minimum.

Chapter 7 – Swedish Decline

For much of the 17th century, Sweden was one of the great European powers. It could even be said that it was a world power. From 1638 to 1655, the Swedes even had an overseas colony called New Sweden. You might know it as Delaware. The Swedes also had a relatively unbroken series of kings who were skilled soldiers, and they had one of the first professional standing (full-time) armies in the world.

In 1658, the Swedes pushed the Danish king and most of the Danish people out of mainland Sweden once and for all. By this point, they had fought many of the armies of Europe and, in most cases, won, oftentimes with fewer men.

By 1721, Sweden's place as a European power was done. In 1809, its place as a regional power was unsteady. The defeats that Sweden sustained on the battlefield and at the negotiating table meant that the Finns were susceptible to growing foreign influence and control, with most of that influence, especially from the late 18th century onward, coming from Russia.

From 1611 to 1718, the Swedes had five monarchs: Gustavus II Adolphus (the only Swedish king called "the Great"), the controversial but brilliant Kristina I, Charles (Karl) X Gustav, Charles XI, and Charles XII. Though Kristina was not a field general, she understood strategy well and wisely appointed her generals and advisers. There is a general consensus that all of the Swedish kings of this period were gifted military leaders, though the last, Charles XII, overestimated his ability and underestimated his enemy. By the end of his reign, Sweden had become a second-rate power.

The Northern Wars

Sweden took part in many conflicts during its history, but the three we are going to examine were called the Northern Wars. There is some confusion about the name of these wars, but for our purposes, the First Northern War took place from 1558 to 1583. It was between Sweden and its allies (Denmark, Poland, and Lithuania) on one side and Russia. The war ended in a Swedish victory, with Sweden making some territorial gains. The Second Northern War (also known as the Livonian War, lasting from 1655 to 1660) was fought against Poland. The Second Northern War was fought over the succession to the Swedish throne. There had been kings of Sweden who were also Polish, and this conflict put an end to Polish claims on the Swedish crown.

The Third Northern War is also known as the Great Northern War. It lasted from 1700 to 1721 and was fought between Sweden and Russia (the latter of which was joined by Saxony, the union of Poland and Lithuania, and Denmark-Norway). The Swedes were joined by a number of allies, but most of them were smaller states, with the exception of the Ottoman Empire, which was in decline at the time. The British and Dutch also allied with Sweden, but they were too far away to make any real significant impact on the conflict.

At first, the Great Northern War seemed as if it was going to end like the other Northern Wars had, with a Swedish victory. Over and over, the professional armies of Sweden, which consisted of large numbers of Finns, were greatly outnumbered but won victory after victory in both the west and east.

In 1709, Charles XII drove deep into Russia and Ukraine. At Poltava in present-day Ukraine, Charles made some uncharacteristic mistakes. He ignored intelligence about Russian numbers and fortifications and did not give clear commands to his generals. Poltava was a disaster for the Swedes and allowed the Russian tsar, Peter I (known as Peter the Great), to proclaim a Russian Empire, which included the Baltic states, Ukraine, and parts of Poland.

Charles's return to Sweden took years, and his journeys took him as far away as modern Turkey. When he returned to Sweden in 1713, he found Sweden under siege by its enemies, some of whom had once been his allies, like Great Britain. During the last phase of the war, Sweden lost all of its overseas territories, including parts of northern Norway that had been nominally Swedish for centuries.

Though Charles and his generals won a number of victories against great odds in Europe and Norway, Charles was killed in Norway while besieging the town of Fredrikshald. He was shot clean through the head while inspecting Swedish trenches. With Charles's death, the Great Northern War ended, and his daughter, Ulrika, became queen of Sweden. One of the few territories the Swedes kept was Finland, but Swedish control of Finland would end in just a few decades.

Chapter 8 – Russian Crown Colony

At the end of the Great Northern War, Russia had gained Swedish/Finnish territory, the land bridge north of St. Petersburg and a bit beyond, through the Treaty of Nystad. In the 1740s, internal strife in Sweden led to increased Russian influence in Finland and Sweden. A period of struggle ensued among the Swedes, and another war (1741-1742) was waged with Russia over control of Finland, especially its southern ports. In the Treaty of Åbo (1743), the Russians were given more territories.

The green indicates areas given to Russia in 1721 and the yellow in 1743. Remember this map, for this would essentially be the final settlement of the Finnish border after the Winter War with the USSR in 1940.

By Janneman, CC BY 3.0 <https://creativecommons.org/licenses/by/3.0>, via Wikimedia Commons; https://commons.wikimedia.org/w/index.php?curid=757077

In 1789, the French Revolution began. The effects of the French Revolution on Finland were indirect but profound. The revolution began as a rebellion against the rule of the absolute monarchy of Louis XVI and the Ancien Régime, the "ancient" ruling class of kings and aristocrats.

Outside France, the French Revolution greatly affected the many states of what would become Germany in 1871. There were dozens of German states, which included principalities, duchies, kingdoms, and independent cities. Some were extremely small, while others, especially Bavaria and Prussia, were large. Most were controlled or heavily influenced by other nations or more powerful German states, but Austria, France, and Denmark either directly or indirectly controlled or influenced many.

In France, the rebellion against Louis XVI quickly spiraled into a violent and radical revolution that removed the king and queen (and their heads), the privileges of the nobility, and much of the Catholic Church's power. Soon, France was at war with much of Europe, whose monarchs and ruling classes feared the spread of revolutionary ideas in their territories.

The victories of the French forces, both the revolutionaries and the man who succeeded them, Napoleon Bonaparte, spread the ideas of the French Revolution, especially the ideas that emphasized democratic ideals and self-determination. In France, self-determination (a later historical term from WWI but which is appropriate here) meant the people's freedom to determine their own form of government. This applied to almost all of Europe but was more a reference to the German states being free from foreign occupation and control.

Of course, Napoleon's rule outside of France was just as oppressive as within France, but the spread of the biggest revolutionary idea, nationalism, could not be contained. In Sweden, where the monarchy's power slowly declined in the later 18th and early 19th centuries, many called for a more representative government.

In the 1780s, Swedish society was increasingly divided, at least at the top. Two factions, one supported by France and the other influenced by Russia, fought for control of the country. In 1786, the king, Gustav III, came out on top and reestablished an absolute monarchy similar to what had existed before. Like the French, the Swedish people and nobility were growing tired of the king's oppressive rule. And to add to an already volatile situation, Gustav, without seeking the approval of Parliament, which violated his own constitution, declared war on Russia in 1788. This caused a mutiny among the liberal officers in the army, and Gustav was put down ruthlessly. The war with Russia provided Sweden with its greatest naval victory in history, but it did not settle anything. The Treaty of Värälä, which ended the war, only reinforced the borders that the countries had before the war began.

However, in March 1792, things changed within Sweden. A plot by nobles, who wished to diminish the power of the king, succeeded. Gustav III was assassinated, though it took him thirteen days to die of his wounds. Some of the plotters had been supported by France.

The new king, Gustavus IV Adolf, would eventually join one of the many coalitions against Napoleon, but neither he nor the Swedish army bore much resemblance to the powerful Swedish forces of the 17th and early 18th centuries.

One of Napoleon's admirers, the young tsar of Russia, Alexander I, did not join sides in the Napoleonic Wars. A complicated series of events began when Alexander I and Napoleon met at Tilsit (today known as Sovetsk in the Russian territory of Kaliningrad on the Baltic Sea). As a result of being defeated by Napoleon, Sweden was forced to cede Finland to Russia per the agreement made between the Russian tsar and the French emperor.

In Sweden, the military defeat and humiliating loss of Finland after centuries of Swedish rule resulted in the overthrow of Gustavus IV Adolf by disenchanted nobles and the businessmen of the country (who were often one and the same). In his place, the Swedes, through a truly strange series of events too long to describe here, offered the crown to one of Napoleon's field marshals, Jean Bernadotte, who accepted and became Charles (Karl) XIV Johann of Sweden, the founder of the present-day Swedish royal family.

On the face of it, one would think that the new Swedish king would be nothing but a tool of Napoleon's, but when he accepted the Swedes' invitation and sought Napoleon's blessing, he told the French emperor that his new responsibility was to his new kingdom, not his old emperor. And he meant it. Charles XIV established a policy of neutrality, which guided Swedish foreign policy from 1810 until 2022 when, in the face of Russian aggression in Ukraine, Sweden (and Finland) applied to join NATO.

Finnish Nationalism

French revolutionary ideas included nationalism and self-determination. Though the latter term originated at the end of WWI, it works as an explanation of what began to happen in Finland, especially among the Finnish elite, including university professors, writers, poets, and higher-level bureaucrats.

It would take a few decades for the feeling that Finns should govern themselves to become a popular cause among the general population. However, the feeling grew until the last quarter or so of the 19th century when the Fennoman movement began to have a real impact, not just politically but also among the people themselves.

For centuries, Finland had been part of Sweden. Perhaps if Swedish rule had continued, the Finnish nationalist feeling would have gained traction in the late 19th century, but we do know that this feeling increased in popularity under Russian rule, especially as the 19th century headed toward the 20th century.

Russian Rule, Pt. I

In 1721, Russia took control of the Karelian Isthmus and the area around Lake Ladoga. In 1743, the Russians gained more territories and forced the Swedes to agree that Sweden would not enter into any foreign alliances without Russian approval. The latter stipulation would not last long, but in 1810, the Swedes decided on the policy of neutrality, which lasted until 2022.

In the 18th century, Russian rule in the parts of Finland it controlled was, relative to what came later, somewhat benign. Part of this was due to the nature of Russian expansionism and government. Even before the time of Peter the Great, Russia had been expanding its territory, but under Peter and his successors, this expansion increased.

Given the size of the territory, the state of communications between the 17th and late 19th centuries, and the nature of Russian absolutism, the governance of new territories happened rather haphazardly. One of the benefits of this was that, especially in Finland, the bureaucracy was left relatively unchanged. Compared to the wild and sparsely populated areas of the east and south that Russia colonized during this period, the central Finnish administrative state was advanced.

The Finns in this territory had been "Swedish" for so long and knew that the geopolitical situation meant they were left on their own. Those living near the borders of Russia, for the most part, accommodated themselves to Russian rule. For Russia, a peaceful, relatively prosperous population on their border meant more income from taxes and that thousands of Russian troops, who were needed elsewhere, did not have to be posted in Finland.

To the surprise of many, the Russians did not force Eastern Orthodoxy on the Finns and kept Swedish laws in effect. Poor landless Finns were not forced into serfdom, as had been the case in Russia for centuries. During Swedish rule, peasants had often risen up to protect their rights to certain lands and when the rule of the nobility became too oppressive. These rebellions, especially the Cudgel War of 1596–1597, were put down violently, but peasant uprisings were always at the forefront of the minds of rulers who were debating new policies. The international culture and thriving economy of the largest Finnish city on the isthmus, Vyborg (in Finnish, Viipuri), also benefited the Russians and promoted the continuance of a benign rule.

Russian Rule, Pt. II

In 1809, the Swedish defeat and the negotiations between France and Russia resulted in all of Finland being given to Russia in the Treaty of Fredrikshamn. Finland was designated a grand duchy under the control of the Russian tsar, who functioned as the grand duke of Finland. The tsar, in turn, appointed a governor who was responsible only to the monarch. At times, the Finns enjoyed a measure of self-rule that other parts of the Russian Empire could only dream of. For instance, Finns were not required to serve in the Imperial Russian Army, though quite a few did, especially among the upper classes.

Mannerheim, the man who would be declared the "greatest Finn of all time" in 2008, was a Swedish Finn whose family had roots in Germany and who spoke Swedish, German, and Russian better than he spoke Finnish. He was one of these upper-class officers and was present at the crowning of the last Russian tsar, Nicholas II, in 1896. (Nicholas took the throne in 1894.) Similar to the Swedish monarchy, the Finns were represented by a one-house parliament called the Diet from 1809 to 1906 and Parliament from 1906 to 1917. There, matters pertaining to Finland were debated, and laws were passed as long as they did not run counter to Russian policy. Mannerheim's great-grandfather was a senator and one of the very first to hold the important office of vice chairman of the Economic Division, which, despite its name, was very much akin to that of the modern Finnish prime minister. Mannerheim's grandfather was governor of the Vyborg principality for a time as well.

All Russian governors-general of Finland were members of the nobility. Most of them held political office in Russia as well. Occasionally, some of them decided to suppress "Finnish-ness" and promote more direct Russian rule. They promoted Russian culture over Finnish, including the Orthodox religion. This likely happened out of personal political reasons, a sense of Russian superiority, or because they were unfamiliar with the spirit of Finnish independence and wished the Finns to be "Russified" like many other minorities in Russia had been.

This first happened in 1824 when Russian Count Arseny Zakrevsky was appointed governor-general of Finland. Zakrevsky also held the powerful position of minister of the interior of Russia; in other words, he was the head of Russia's police and secret police, the Okhrana, among other things.

When Zakrevsky took office, he immediately began to bypass both the Finnish Diet and the Finnish secretary of state, who presented Finnish laws to the tsar for approval. Zakrevsky took that right and the influence that went with it. And like many other high-ranking Russian nobles, Zakrevsky angled for an influential position when Alexander I died in December 1825. Zakrevsky and others believed that the next tsar would be Constantine, Alexander's younger brother. In order to win favor with the new "tsar to be," Zakrevsky promoted a law that required the Finns to swear an oath of absolute loyalty to the tsar, something they were not inclined to do.

Unfortunately for Zakrevsky, Constantine lost a power struggle with his younger brother, Nicholas, who became Nicholas I, "Tsar of all the Russias," just before the New Year, 1826. Upon taking the throne, Nicholas promised the Finns that their traditional rights would be respected. Zakrevsky lost the battle but remained governor-general until 1831.

In many ways, Russian policy in Finland was unique among the other territories Russia controlled, at least in the first part of the 19th century. In many areas, particularly in the Russian-controlled parts of Poland (Austria and Prussia controlled the other two-thirds) and Ukraine, violent uprisings for independence took place, which were put down with great violence. In Ukraine especially, Russian policy included the forced use of the Russian language and direct and harsh rule by Russian governors and generals.

This did not take place in Finland, at least not directly. Zakrevsky and others within the Russian government and nobility favored a policy that became known as gradual Russification. The Russian language would be encouraged in business, and since Finland's trade involved Russia to one degree or another, many Finnish nobles, merchants, and businessmen began to learn Russian to make their way up the Finnish and Russian economic and social ladders. For instance, Mannerheim's Russian was much better than his Finnish for most of his life.

The Fennoman Movement

Despite the fact that speaking Russian was encouraged, especially among upper-class Finns, Swedish was still the language of most business transactions within Finland (especially in the south), of government, and of literature. Some Russians, both within Russia and in Finland itself, actually encouraged the use of Finnish but not necessarily out of liberal ideals. The thinking behind this was that if Russians encouraged the use of Finnish, at least among Finns, it would separate Finnish culture and the Finns themselves from Sweden, which was still a regional power.

In 1863, Finnish was recognized as the official language of the country, with Swedish being the other official language. However, about 15 percent of the country and almost all of the ruling upper class only spoke Swedish or used it as their preferred language. This is significant. If you recall, one of the main reasons that Protestantism spread throughout Europe was because of the translations of the Bible from Latin into national languages. Until that time, Christians were dependent on the Catholic clergy to educate them on religious matters.

In the same way, people who only spoke Finnish were at a disadvantage in their own country. Since most of the larger businesses used Swedish, only those who could speak that language could participate. The same held true for governmental matters and the press. Though most Finns were far from illiterate, until the second half of the 19th century, they had to rely on the goodwill of others for knowledge of what was happening in their country and the world.

For much of its history, Finland had been part of a larger whole. Luckily, its size, geography, climate, circumstances, and the occasional violent uprising kept it from suffering from the fate of so many other colonies around the world. The Finns didn't deal with the complete loss of independence, the destruction of their culture, or the assimilation of their people.

The fear of assimilation and the rise in nationalism in the 19th century caused a number of Finns, mostly from the educated and upper class (who were, most of the time, one and the same) and whose primary language was Swedish, to promote Finnish as a way of protecting Finnish culture and creating a nationalist feeling based on shared history, values, and culture.

The Fennoman movement (sometimes known as Fennomania in Sweden and Finland—and no, in this instance, "mania" does not mean a focused type of insanity; it loosely translates as "Finnishness") was a literary movement that championed Finnish in the publication of classic literature, newspapers, and newly written works, including academic works.

In the early 19th century, changes in government censorship in much of western and central Europe, education policy, and printing technology meant that more people were reading than ever before. In Germany, one of the most literate countries in the world, reading actually became a "fad" of sorts. New scientific discoveries, new and brilliant literature written in German (rather than Latin, for instance), and much else made the discussion of books and ideas extremely popular in Germany. The "reading rage," or *Lesewut*, spread to Sweden and then to Finland by the early 1830s.

This gave rise to the Fennoman movement, which became the primary movement of Finnish nationalism until Finland won its independence shortly after WWI. The most popular example of Finnish-language literature was the publication of the *Kalevala* in 1835.

You have already learned about Elias Lönnrot and the *Kalevala*, but the importance of the *Kalevala*'s publication went beyond just the use of the Finnish language in a major literary work. The *Kalevala* promoted a sense of exclusively Finnish history and culture that had not existed before.

A first edition of the *Kalevala*, 1835.
https://commons.wikimedia.org/wiki/File:Kalevala1.jpg

Two other leading figures from the early Fennoman period were J. V. Snellman and J. L. Runeberg. Snellman was a politician, journalist, and writer, and Runeberg was a priest who also published popular books and tracts on Finnish culture and history. Ironically, both men wrote exclusively in Swedish.

The Fennoman movement was opposed by a loose-knit group of writers, politicians, and professors known as the Svecomans, who promoted the continued use and spread of Swedish rather than Finnish. Others opposed to the Fennoman movement and its beliefs, which became more political and less cultural as the 19th century went on, were the leaders of the church in Finland, most of whom were either Swedes or Swedish-speaking Finns, and the Russian authorities, who were always alert to the possibility of rebellion within their empire.

The struggle to get Finnish recognized as one of the territory's official languages ended in 1863. However, to get to that point, the Finnish and the Fennomans had to endure some hard times. By the late 1840s, Tsar Nicholas I had become more and more conservative and autocratic, allowing himself to be convinced, mostly by conservative clerics in Finland, to outlaw the use of Finnish in all written works that were not religious in nature. Of course, that only encouraged the Fennomans (who, as you learned above, included a number of Swedish-speaking Finns, many of whom changed their names to more "Finnish-sounding" ones). It also caused more Finns to become resentful of foreign rule and cultural dominance.

Russian Rule, Pt. III

Just because Russian rule in Finland was somewhat more benign compared to some of the other territories of the Russian Empire does not mean that the Finns liked it. Some at the very top made the best of a bad situation and attempted to climb the Russian social ladder in St. Peterburg, which, after all, was only a few miles from Finland. Rich merchants and traders had a distinct advantage over their Swedish counterparts since most Swedes dealing with Russians used Finnish middlemen or landed in Finnish ports. The Finns also sold some Western goods in Russia, but Finnish furs, timber, and tar (at least until the end of the age of wooden sailing ships) were in high demand for most of the Russian rule.

As you just discovered, many upper-class and aristocratic Finns were part of the Fennoman movement, which gave birth to the idea of an independent Finnish nation and the importance of the Finnish language.

Finns in the lower-middle and lower agricultural class also grew bitter about the increasingly autocratic Russian regime in the last part of the 19th century. Not all were happy with Russian rule, and the people grew increasingly unhappy by the turn of the century. Unfortunately, though Finns in the lower classes had representation in the Finnish Parliament, you can likely guess they had no real power and lacked leaders who had the charisma, influence, and desire to move Finland toward independence.

In 2022, the Russo-Ukrainian War began. One of Vladimir Putin's stated goals was that Russia was concerned that NATO would spread into Ukraine. He also made remarks that Russia was against NATO expansion retroactively and made demands that NATO roll itself back to its pre-1991 borders in western Europe. "NATO expansion" was one of the ways Putin attempted to "sell" the invasion of Ukraine to the Russian people. As you may know, his invasion of Ukraine alarmed Europe, specifically Finland and Sweden, two nations that had an official policy of neutrality for decades and centuries, respectively. As a result of Putin's Ukrainian invasion, both Finland and Sweden applied for NATO membership. His plan had the exact opposite effect from what he intended.

In the same way, the Russians of the late 19th century wished to make Finland a more integrated part of the Russian Empire. The man who would carry out this more radical and sudden plan of the "Russification" of Finland was Nikolai Bobrikov, who was appointed governor-general of Finland and commander of the Finnish Military District in 1898.

Bobrikov.

Bobrikov was appointed by Tsar Nicholas II, who had taken the Russian throne in 1894. Despite the hopes of some more liberal-minded Russians, Nicholas proved himself to be the autocrat his father was and became influenced by hardline conservatives in the royal family, including his wife and the Russian Orthodox Church. The idea that Finland had a great degree of autonomy and its own parliament rankled Nicholas and many of the most powerful men in the Russian aristocracy. They felt that territories controlled by Russia should speak Russian, act Russian (by adopting Russian customs, traditions, modes of dress, and, most importantly, governance), and worship like Russians.

Though many of the Finnish elite, especially in the east of the country and in the military, did speak Russian, at least to a degree, most Finns did not want to speak Russian and made little attempt to learn how. They certainly didn't want to "act Russian" or change their religion. In 1899, the most famous Finnish composer Jean Sibelius wrote his haunting and majestic piece, *Finlandia*, in reaction to increasing Russian intrusion on Finnish life. Through music, the piece tells the story of Finnish history and is still the most famous piece of music ever written by a Finn.

Bobrikov helped ensure the Finns would resent Russian rule and be less likely to accept anything Russian, from the language to its church.

Once Bobrikov took office, he almost immediately put his plan into action for the Russification of Finland. His program included the adoption of Russian as the official language of Finland, limiting the power of the Finnish secretary of state (who represented Finland at the tsar's court), and fully integrating the Finnish armed forces into the Imperial Russian Army. This meant Finns would not be in all-Finnish units but spread among Russian forces throughout the empire. They would be far from home and far from creating any disturbances in their homeland.

In this painting, *Hyökkäys* (known as *The Attack* in English), the double-headed Russian eagle is attacking Finland, who is trying to save her laws and independence. It was painted in 1899 by Edvard Isto.

https://commons.wikimedia.org/wiki/File:Suomineito.jpg

A year after taking office, it was clear that Bobrikov had the full support of Nicholas II. In 1899, the tsar signed a decree that gave him the right to overturn any legislation passed in Finland. For the most part, the Finns had the right to make decisions within their own borders for centuries, including their time under Russian rule. In response, 500,000 Finns (about 25 percent of the population) signed a petition asking Nicholas to rescind his decree. By all accounts, Nicholas never even looked at the petition when it arrived at his palace. He should have, though, as the sheer number of signatures might have changed his mind about his rule in Finland.

In 1900, Russian was made the official language of all government business, and Russian language instruction was increased in Finnish schools. Finnish officials in certain government offices, particularly offices governing the country's many lighthouses and railroads, were replaced by Russians. Russian stamps replaced Finnish ones, which simply reminded the Finns every day of the increasing Russian control over their country. Throughout Finland, especially in the cities, Russian security officials watched to see who opposed Bobrikov's policies. As you can likely imagine, many vocal opponents of these policies were arrested. Many were tortured, which was a common punishment for those accused of sedition within Russia itself.

In 1902, the first draft of Finns for the integrated Imperial Russian Army took place. Less than half of those who were called showed up. Three years later, the Russians called off the Finnish draft, saying the Finns were "unreliable," which actually meant that the tsar was afraid of a Finnish war of independence.

The Finns call the period of time under Bobrikov until the end of World War I *Sortovuodet* (the "Years of Oppression"). Unfortunately for Bobrikov, his plan backfired. A group of Finnish nobles began a debate on whether Bobrikov should be assassinated or not. One of these men, an ethnic Swedish Finn named Eugen Schauman (who, incidentally, was born in Kharkiv, Ukraine), shot Bobrikov three times on June 16th, 1904. Bobrikov died the next day. Schauman knew that an extended period of torture would follow, so he killed himself after shooting the governor-general. Though he is remembered less today than in the period immediately after the assassination and Finland's independence in 1917, Schauman is still considered a national hero in Finland.

After the death of Bobrikov, Russia suspended some of its measures against Finland. This was not a result of the assassination but rather the Russian fear of even wider unrest in Finland. Russia itself was facing discontent, with the people growing tired of the autocratic system of the tsars and upset over the humiliating defeat of Russia at the hands of the Japanese in the Russo-Japanese War of 1905. Unrest (including the infamous Bloody Sunday in January 1905, in which hundreds, if not thousands, of peaceful demonstrators were gunned down in St. Petersburg) spread throughout Russia and threatened Tsar Nicholas II's rule. One of the byproducts of the Russo-Japanese War was the sale of weapons by the Japanese to the Finns, which were later used against the Russians and in the Finnish Civil War of 1918, which followed World War One.

However, in 1908, the second period of the *Sortovuodet* began. The measures enacted in this period went further than what even Bobrikov had pushed for. In 1910, a law was decreed in Russia that replaced all Finnish parliamentarians with Finnish officers of the Imperial Russian Army. Russia imposed a heavy tax on Finns for not renewing conscription. Also, in 1910, all power of the Finnish Parliament was given to the Russian Duma (a newly formed representative body that, until the latter stages of WWI, did the tsar's bidding). In 1912, the Law of Equality was passed, which forced all Finnish civil and governmental positions to open to Russians. During WWI, these measures were suspended for fear of an untimely Finnish revolt but were fully intended to be restored when the Russians won the Great War.

Finns of the Royal Prussian 27ᵗʰ Jäger Battalion in Latvia, also a Russian possession before the war, summer of 1917.

By the time WWI began in August 1914, many Finns had become determined to fight for their independence after the war was over. Thousands of Finns traveled to Germany and fought as Finnish Jägers ("hunters" or light infantry) on the Eastern Front against the Russians during the war. In 1918, the survivors of these formations returned to Finland to begin what they believed would be a fight against Russia. Additionally, many German soldiers traveled to Finland to join their Finnish comrades. The German military sold much equipment to the Finns to fight Russian influence, prevent weapons from falling into Allied hands, and make money. Russia's policy had clearly backfired.

Chapter 9 – WWI, Civil War, and Independence

Finland's role in World War One was relatively small. Because the conscription laws had been suspended before the start of WWI and because Russia did not want to provoke a Finnish uprising on its northern flank, only a small number of Finns (under one thousand) served alongside the Russian forces in the war. Many of these men were from the Swedish-speaking elite, including Mannerheim, who you will learn more about shortly. More Finns went to fight for Germany than for Russia. The Finns who fought were not only aristocratic officers but also a larger percentage of soldiers and non-commissioned officers and sergeants. These men provided critical leadership and training to the Finnish "Whites," the anti-communist, conservative forces of the Finnish Civil War, which would follow World War One.

By 1917, Russia's grand ideas of victory against Germany and Austria-Hungary were in shambles. Its troops were hungry and did not have enough supplies of weapons and clothing. Many of the officers (many of whom were of the hated aristocracy) seemed to care more about personal glory than the lives of their men. Sounds rather familiar.

Additionally, a variety of socialist movements, including the Bolsheviks, who were led by Vladimir Lenin, were on the verge of a revolution in the major cities of Russia, particularly St.

Petersburg, the capital. In 1917, Lenin was living in exile in Switzerland when food riots and protests broke out in Russia. Additionally, Russian troops at the front either simply left the fighting and started to head home or mutinied against their officers and formed leftist revolutionary units instead. These units were more concerned with fighting the tsarist system than the Germans and formed the core of what would become the Red Army. Of course, Lenin played a significant role in all of this.

In April 1917, Lenin found himself an unexpected ally: the German Empire. The Germans agreed to escort Lenin safely and secretly to the Russian border via Sweden and Finland and provide money for his planned revolution. In return, Lenin promised that should he become the new leader of Russia, he would immediately make peace with Germany along the front lines that currently existed, which meant that Germany would rule Ukraine and a large portion of Russia south of St. Petersburg and west of Moscow.

Surprisingly, both parties kept their word, and after the success of the Bolshevik Revolution, the new Union of Soviet Socialist Republics (USSR) made peace with Germany and confirmed its territorial gains, which Lenin likely knew Germany would lose, either through defeat by the Allies or its eventual defeat by a resurgent Russia.

Independence

One of the first things that Lenin did when he came to power surprised almost everyone, including some in Lenin's inner circle, particularly Joseph Stalin. On January 4th, 1918, Lenin recognized Finland as an independent country. Even in the time before the arrival of the Swedes in the Early Middle Ages, the Finns did not have a country but rather a number of tribal kingdoms that often fought one another.

Lenin recognized Finland's independence. He did not "grant" it. Granting something was only kings and tsars did. Moreover, with Russia's mounting losses in the war, Tsar Nicholas's preoccupation with it, and internal Russian dissent, the Finns had begun to take gradual control of their own affairs. By January 1918, they had control of their country in all but name.

The Soviet document that recognized Finnish independence signed by Lenin, Stalin, Trotsky, and others
https://commons.wikimedia.org/w/index.php?curid=28197479

Some American historians called the US Civil War the "Second American Revolution" or the "American Revolution 2.0" since many issues, from slavery to federal powers and state rights, had not been adequately settled with the defeat of Britain in 1781. Similarly, Finns (and this word now includes all the people living in Finland: Finns, Swedes, and the Sami, the native people of the north) had never had the opportunity to truly debate the form of government they would create if they gained independence.

In the last two decades of the 19th century and the early decades of the 20th, a number of different groups emerged in Finland, all with varying and sometimes widely diverging opinions of what Finland should look like as an independent nation. Even the Fennoman movement, which had become less of a cultural movement and more of a political one by the 20th century, had split into factions, with some advocating a limited Finnish monarchy along the lines of Sweden or Britain and others calling for an American- or French-style representative government. Still, others called for some form of socialism, including Soviet-style communism.

The Finnish Civil War

The early 20th century was a time of great political change and upheaval. Even the most stable countries were rocked by large and sometimes violent labor strikes and the occasional act of political terrorism. For most of Finland's history, the Finns had been able to avoid civil violence. You have just finished learning about the reasons for this: foreign control by Sweden and Russia. Independence was not necessarily a surprise, given the world situation and US President Woodrow Wilson's call for self-determination of the people. If there were ever a group of people that wanted that self-determination, it was the Finns.

Finland was very lucky in a way, for most believe that if Lenin had refused the Finnish move toward independence, war would have ensued between Finland and the Soviet Union. This might have been a war the Soviets could not win, especially since hundreds of thousands of Red Army soldiers were busy fighting hundreds of thousands of White Army troops (those who wished to reinstate the Russian royal family or establish a non-communist military dictatorship). War against Finland might have resulted in a White victory and the end of the Soviet Union.

In Helsinki today, there is a park named after Vladimir Lenin. Many foreigners wonder why the Finns would name this park after Lenin. For a time, there was even a statue of Lenin. As any Finn will tell you, this park is less a memorial to Lenin than it is a reminder of Finnish stubbornness because, after Lenin, many Russians wanted Finland back. Truth be told, so did Lenin, and the Bolsheviks had supported Finnish communists to a degree even before independence. When the Finnish Civil War began, that assistance (mostly in the form of troops and advisers, along with some weapons) continued.

This book is a general history of Finland and, by necessity, covers most, but not all, of the main events that shaped the country politically, militarily, and globally, with a bit of economics thrown in. Unfortunately, that means much of the fascinating cultural history of Finland and some of the country's internal political and economic events have to be overlooked.

As the 20th century approached and ideas about representative democracy and various kinds of socialism spread, the middle and lower classes of Finland began to play a more significant role in society and politics.

Having been the subjects of two monarchies, most Finns had never truly had a voice in the country, at least not one that could be heard beyond their village. By the time WWI broke out, Finland had experienced an interesting type of autonomy within the Russian Empire. Various governors and the last tsar, Nicholas II, attempted to slowly change Finnish society from the top down through Russification. But between an incompetent, indecisive tsar and an emergency within and outside Russia, Finland was left relatively unmolested in the years leading up to and during WWI.

Throughout that time, the Finns, the Finnish Parliament, and the Senate (which played the role of Cabinet and a sort of Supreme Court) had been gaining more and more power. By the time Lenin signed the independence document, Finland had, to a large extent, been governing itself for a number of years.

Unfortunately for Finland, the economic gap between those at the top and those at the bottom only increased in 1918. That year, a large segment of the Finnish population still worked in agriculture. The life of a Finnish farmer was incredibly hard, and famine was a recurring feature of Finnish life, especially for those who worked the land. Finland, as you can likely imagine, has a very short growing season, and the soil is quite poor, especially in relation to its neighbors to the south and Sweden, which enjoys the benefit of a slightly warmer climate brought in by warmer currents from the Atlantic. Finland does not have this benefit. Honestly, anyone who worked outdoors in Finland had a tough life in the 19th century. Many Finns migrated to other countries, especially the United States, where the winters were milder. In 1918, Finland was not much different from other countries in Europe and North America. More people were leaving farming, fishing, and forestry for the cities and the promise of a better-paying, steady job at the factories that were being built seemingly every month in southern Finland and its coastlines. However, the country was and still is primarily rural.

The Finns had experienced civil upheaval before, especially during and after WWI, as other nations in Europe did. These were mostly worker strikes and occasional protests by farmers. Both of these groups, but primarily the workers in the cities, had been heavily influenced by the rising tide of European social democracy and communism.

Adding to the usual workers' woes (inadequate housing, medical care, job security, worker safety, and pay) was the fact that many of the working class were seeing that life in Finland had been governed by the upper classes, whether they came from Sweden, Russia, or even Finland itself. While the elite of the country discussed the type of government Finland should enjoy after Russian rule, many of those at the bottom saw nothing but a continuation of rule by the elite. The fact the rulers were Finns made no difference.

For hundreds of years, the farmers and rural workers (miners, tar-pit workers, fishermen, etc.) went through their lives following the dictates of others; at least, that was how it seemed to the most radical and militant of them. The upheaval of the war, the vacuum left by Russian rule, and the fact that the elite seemed determined to "make the rules" without input from the workers almost begged for a revolution. And the fact that there was no official Finnish army or national police meant that it was the right time for a revolution.

Finnish Civil War

The Finnish Civil War began on January 27th, 1918, when armed communist groups (which had been getting arms and support from the Soviets) took control of Helsinki in much the same way the Bolsheviks had seized St. Petersburg in 1917.

When that happened, conservative militia groups, some of which had formed before Finland's independence, and many Finnish officers of the tsar's army fled the city and moved to the western parts of the country. There, they disarmed the remains of the Russian army, which had not been able or unwilling to return home after the Bolsheviks took power. The anti-communist Finns were soon joined by many of their battle-hardened countrymen who had fought with Germany. The anti-communist forces, known as the "Whites," were also reinforced by sizable contingents of German troops and officers, who were sent to Finland by their government to prevent the communist takeover of yet another northern country. The Kaiser and conservative forces in Germany, who were still fully engaged against the Allies in WWI, sent large amounts of weapons and ammunition to Finland to support the Whites against the "Reds" (the communists).

Members of the Female Red Guard of Turku, 1918.
https://commons.wikimedia.org/w/index.php?curid=52071524

When the Finnish Civil War began, the Reds controlled most of the southern part of the country, including the major cities. The Finnish Red Army has been estimated to have had around 100,000 men and women in its ranks when the conflict began, with somewhere near 80,000 in arms, 2,000 of them being women. Unfortunately for the Reds, most of these men and women had no combat experience, and only a few officers did. A number of Russian officers were embedded with the Finnish Reds, but they were too few and not well liked.

The White Army had about the same number of soldiers (who were all male), and like the Reds, most did not have army experience of any kind. However, the returning veterans from the

Jägers and many of the Finnish officers from the tsar's army gave the Whites a distinct advantage.

During January and February, the Whites solidified their hold on the northern and central parts of the country and trained their troops as much as possible before they went on the offensive. In April, they were joined by thirteen thousand German troops, which quickly established bases around the Gulf of Finland, forcing the Reds to pay attention not only to the Whites in the north but also to their German allies in the south.

The Finnish Civil War was short. By the middle of May, it was over. A slew of smaller battles had taken place during the winter, but the White Army's seizure of Helsinki (carried out in large part by German troops) and the battles for the cities of Vyborg (Viipuri) and Tampere were the major battles of this short conflict.

However, like most civil wars of any size, the Finnish Civil War was exceedingly violent, and the casualty rate was much higher than one would think for a war that lasted just a couple of months. About twenty thousand Red soldiers died in the war. A much smaller number of Whites, Germans, and some Swedish volunteers perished, numbering about five thousand.

The war was bloody for such a small country, and for the losing Reds, capture often meant death. It's estimated that close to ten thousand Red soldiers and sympathizers were gunned down in what would today be considered a war crime. There was also quite a large number (approximately twelve thousand) of Red prisoners who died in captivity or from hunger, cold, and disease. Nearly one thousand Russians who were sent to help the Finnish Revolution were killed in action. Over 1,500 were executed upon capture. These non-combat killings were not one-sided, as it's believed some two thousand White soldiers were executed by the Reds during the short conflict.

Chapter 10 – Mannerheim and between the Wars

After the civil war, the Whites were in a weaker position than they had been before the war. This was because of Germany. It wasn't as if the Kaiser sent his troops to Finland for nothing. Yes, the Germans were worried about the spread of communism, but altruism was not Germany's sole motivation. With a considerable number of German troops still in the country, the German government leaned on the Finnish Senate (which had been building a new Finnish system even before WWI) and forced a German prince on them to serve as the new king of Finland.

The Senate had no choice but to agree, and German Prince Friedrich Karl (Frederick Charles), who just happened to be the brother-in-law of Kaiser Wilhelm II, was "elected" king of Finland. As a result of this, Marshal Carl Gustaf Emil Mannerheim, who had led the White forces during the Finnish Civil War, resigned from his post.

Mannerheim was a hero to many Whites and much of the Finnish population, despite the calls of many on the left in other countries (both Red Finns in exile in the USSR and left-leaning European parties) that he be tried for war crimes.

When Mannerheim resigned from his position, many Finns wondered if another period of instability was about to begin. The short but violent and wide-ranging civil war meant the Finnish economy had declined rapidly. Hunger affected most of the country, and starvation was the norm in the southern part of the nation. International aid from the United States and western Europe helped to prevent the rise of a worse situation.

The division between Finns over the new German king ended in November 1918 when the Germans laid down their arms. The king, his German advisers, and their troops returned home to their defeated country that December.

Given the nature of the Finnish Civil War and communist propaganda, the Finnish government that came out of the conflict and the very short "German period" was amazingly democratic. On July 17th, 1919, the Constitution Act was passed, creating the first independent Finnish government. The act was amended four times throughout the 1920s, each time clarifying certain laws and the responsibility of governmental bodies.

The new government reflected a compromise of sorts. The more influential Whites wanted an appointed president who had a good deal of authority. The more moderate and popular Social Democrats wanted a more powerful Parliament. In the end, the president retained a great deal of power, but this was balanced by the universally elected Parliament. What's more, the Whites' candidate for president, Mannerheim, lost the election, which was won by the Social Democrats, who aligned with the agrarian Centre Party, which mostly represented the farmers and the rural areas of the country, to form a majority.

Though the presidency was won by a member of the Centre Party, who served from 1925 to 1931, the Social Democrats kept a majority within the country. When the party did not lean to the left as far as some radical members wanted, they split from the party and formed a new one, which advocated communism. In 1922, they won nearly thirty seats in Parliament, but by the end of the decade, most of them had been arrested or deported for revolutionary intent. Finland's new rulers were not going to tolerate Russian-supported communism.

In response to Social Democratic control and what they saw as the rise of communism in Parliament and the rest of Europe, right-wing militants formed a new party in 1929. It was called the Lapua Movement, named after the town in which it was founded.

The Lapua Movement was influenced by the rise of fascist power in Europe. In 1929, there was only one fascist government in Europe, that of Mussolini in Italy, but by 1929 (the year the Great Depression began), Adolf Hitler was one of the leading politicians in Germany. In other countries, such as Poland, for example, fascist and ultra-nationalist ideas began to take hold.

The Lapua Movement had sizable support among the conservative upper classes, but as the 1930s progressed and they and other Finns saw the result of fascist violence in other countries, support for the Lapua Movement, which advocated the use of mass violence against anyone they believed to be on the left, began to wane.

In 1932, a Social Democratic meeting in the southern town of Mäntsälä was violently interrupted by a sizable contingent of Lapua supporters led by General Kurt Wallenius, a former chief of staff of the Finnish army. Within a short time, this disruption escalated into a planned coup d'état, with Wallenius calling on the army and the former Whites to join him in marching on the capital. Luckily for Finland, no one responded to his call to arms, and a speech by President Pehr Evind Svinhufvud convinced the Lapua in Mäntsälä and elsewhere to give up any ideas of trying to seize power. Some eight months later, the Lapua Movement was banned by the government, ironically under the same law they had pushed to outlaw the Communist Party.

Mannerheim (1867–1952)

Writing a short book that spans the whole of Finnish history is hard, to say the least. Making the project even more difficult is the figure of Mannerheim, who was named the greatest Finn of all time in a national poll in 2004. So, please keep in mind that what you are about to learn is really more of a sketch of an amazingly interesting and influential life.

Mannerheim, who is often known more by his preferred title Marshal Mannerheim than his full name (Carl Gustaf Emil Mannerheim), was born into an aristocratic family that originated in Germany. His ancestors moved to Sweden in 1693 and were part of a large German minority that played an important role in trade in many Swedish cities. In the 1700s, the Mannerheims moved to Finland, looking for land and opportunity in the sparsely populated Swedish territory.

When Finland was ceded to Russia in 1809, Mannerheim's paternal great-grandfather, Count Carl Erik Mannerheim, held the most powerful position in the semi-autonomous Russian Grand Duchy of Finland. Mannerheim's grandfather and father were interested in a number of different fields, including industry, and the family made a better than modest income.

Mannerheim during the Winter War, 1939–1940.
https://commons.wikimedia.org/w/index.php?curid=14157305

Mannerheim's mother was Swedish-Finnish and the daughter of one of the richest men in Finland. Combined with Mannerheim's aristocratic title, wealth, and physical presence (he was six feet, four inches tall, and handsome), his own intelligence and amazing story put him in a position to be an influential man in Finland when his country needed him the most.

In 1882, Mannerheim attended a Finnish military academy for the upper class but went missing in his senior year, which resulted in his dismissal. Actually, everyone knew where he was: pursuing his love interest. Despite this, he attended the elite Nicholas Cavalry College in St. Petersburg until 1889, and in 1891, he was in the elite Chevalier Guard Regiment in the Russian capital.

After having two daughters, his first marriage to a Russian-Serbian noblewoman ended in a separation in 1902 (they were divorced in 1919).

Mannerheim at the coronation of Nicholas II in St. Petersburg, 1896.
https://commons.wikimedia.org/w/index.php?curid=8686448

Mannerheim's first combat experience came during the Russo-Japanese War. Though the war was a humiliating defeat for the Russians, Mannerheim was awarded for bravery and quickly rose in the ranks. By the time the war ended, he was a lieutenant general.

When the war ended, Mannerheim was sent on a journey through Central Asia to Beijing, with the ultimate goal of finding out if a Russian invasion of sparsely populated western China was feasible to offset British interests in the area. Mannerheim's journey took him all the way to China with a small four-man caravan. They judged the support of Central Asian tribes for China and got an up-close look at the terrain. He arrived in Beijing two years after his journey had begun. One of his stops included a meeting with the thirteenth Dalai Lama of Tibet; Mannerheim was the third known European to meet the Dalai Lama.

When Mannerheim returned to St. Petersburg three years later, he was one of the foremost European experts on China and provided an amazing amount of information on China's economy, modernization, politics, military, influence of Japan, and much else. His trip also began a life-long love of Chinese art, and he managed to learn enough of the language to hold conversations.

WWI

As a Russian army officer during WWI, Mannerheim was the commander of the elite Guards Cavalry Brigade and fought in southwest Russia and Ukraine against the Austro-Hungarians and Romanians. He was again awarded for bravery and was made commander of the 12th Cavalry Division in 1915.

Mannerheim was on leave in St. Petersburg when the Russian Revolution against the tsar succeeded. (This was the February Revolution that put Alexander Kerensky in power. Kerensky and his government were overthrown in the Bolsheviks' October Revolution a few months later.) Mannerheim returned to the front but was relieved of his command shortly thereafter, for he was believed to be against the revolution. He resigned from his commission and returned to Finland to what he believed would be his retirement.

We discussed the Finnish Civil War previously. Mannerheim was the commander of the White forces during the conflict. His role in the atrocities that took place is debated in Finland to this day, but most believe that, at the very least, he had some knowledge of them. Within Finland after the war and to some on the left in the country to this day, Mannerheim was the "White General" and bore the responsibility for many massacres during the conflict.

When the Finnish Civil War ended, there were some in Finland who wished to make Mannerheim the king, but that held no interest for him (nor most Finns). So, he retired once again and visited relatives in Sweden. While there, the influential Mannerheim held talks with the British and Americans. He explained to them his and many of his fellow Finns' opposition to the new German king and Finland's desire to become an independent nation. In October 1918, with Germany's defeat inevitable, Mannerheim was sent to Britain and France to confer with the Allies and seek their recognition of an independent Finland. In January 1918, the Germans, Swedes, French, Norwegians, and Danes recognized Finland's independence. Britain and the United States followed shortly thereafter.

When Friedrich Karl returned to Germany, Mannerheim was elected regent by the Finnish Senate and acted as a uniting executive of the country, though his powers were limited. Most of the time, he just added his signature to new legislation as a formality. The position of regent was discarded after the first presidential election in October 1919, which Mannerheim lost by more than two to one. He then retired to private life once again. His past support of imperial Russia and his membership in the Finno-Swedish aristocracy worked against him.

(As part of his effort to seem more Finnish, Mannerheim took to signing documents with the Finnish version of his first name, Gustaf, "Kustaa." He also simply signed as Mannerheim. He never used Carl. His friends and family called him Gustaf. He hated the name Emil and never used it.)

In 1931, with fascism on the rise in Europe and Stalin firmly and menacingly in charge in the Soviet Union, Mannerheim came out of retirement once again to head the National Defense Council. Though Finland had declared a policy of neutrality after its independence, everyone in the country knew its biggest threat came from the east.

From 1931 until just before the outbreak of the Winter War in 1939, the Finns established, built, and reinforced what became known as the Mannerheim Line. Most of the fortifications on this defensive line were built between the wars. It was located on the Karelian Isthmus south of the city of Viipuri but stretched all the way from the Soviet border to the northern end of the isthmus, which led to the Finnish interior.

Finnish-Soviet relations

The next chapter talks about the famous Winter War, which was fought between Finland and the Soviet Union, but before we can discuss that important event, it's important to understand aspects of the relations between the two countries in the years before the war began.

The Karelian people live in the border area of Finland and Russia. With some exceptions, the Karelians of Finland share much of the same culture as other Finns, though they often speak a particular dialect that sets them apart. The same holds true in Russia. Most Karelians on both sides of the border, if they are members of any church at all, are Eastern Orthodox, while most Finns are Lutheran or non-practicing. Changing times and borders have led families in both countries and segments of the population to occasionally call for the unification of all Karelians in one country. Immediately after WWI and into the early 1920s, before the rule of Stalin made the nature of Soviet communism quite clear, many Finnish Karelians and others pushed for a "Greater Finland," which included much of Russian Karelia. Not knowing what was to come, a considerable number of Russian Karelians were indifferent to these calls to join their Finnish brethren. The brutal nature of the climate and the vast forests meant that, for centuries, most Karelians crossed back and forth across the border at will.

However, the rise of communism and the virulent anti-communism of the Finnish Whites during and immediately after the Finnish Civil War meant that from 1918 to 1922, there was a conflict between White militias and the small but still sizable Red Army in Karelia. Though the Finnish government disavowed the incursions by these militias, Mannerheim, at least for a time, supported them.

In 1920, the Treaty of Tartu between the USSR and Finland recognized the rights of the Karelian people in the USSR to autonomy, and the Finns gained the White Sea port of Petsamo. The treaty also formally annulled the 1809 Treaty of Fredrikshamn, which gave Finland to Russia.

However, by 1922, many Karelians in the USSR, like so many others, were beginning to recognize the nature of the Soviet regime. Soviet Karelian militias formed and voted for secession from the Soviet Union. They were joined by a number of Finnish volunteers, but the Finnish government and army remained out of the conflict, although they secretly sent arms to the rebels.

By the end of 1921 and the beginning of 1922, the Soviets had won their civil war and had begun to establish an iron grip on the country. Exaggerated reports of Finnish support for the Soviet Karelian militias provoked the Soviet leadership, especially the chief of the Red Army, the famous Leon Trotsky, who would later lose a power struggle with Stalin and be assassinated in 1940. Trotsky vowed to "march into Helsinki." The Karelians had no chance, and the "invasion" was crushed by the end of January. Tens of thousands of Karelians fled to Finland. Many communist Finns who had fled after the civil war settled in Soviet Karelia, which they used as a base to recruit disaffected Finns (there weren't many) and to spy on their homeland for the Soviets.

The increasingly inhumane nature of the Soviet regime, the quashing of the Karelian rebellion, Trotsky's call for a "march to Helsinki," Stalin's increasing calls for a restoration of the Russian Empire under communism, Soviet meddling in Finnish affairs, and a huge Soviet military build-up were all factors in the Finns building the Mannerheim Line between 1931 and 1939, despite public Soviet declarations of peace between the two countries.

The Mannerheim Line, 1939.
User Jniemenmaa on en.wikipedia, CC BY-SA 3.0
<http://creativecommons.org/licenses/by-sa/3.0/>, via Wikimedia Commons,
https://commons.wikimedia.org/w/index.php?curid=1301558

Chapter 11 –
Talvisota/Jatkosota (Winter War/Continuation War)

Finnish troops during the Winter War.
https://commons.wikimedia.org/w/index.php?curid=549346

Before we begin, we want to let you know about another great book from Captivating History called *The Winter War*, whose sole focus is on the Winter War. You can also find that book in a larger collection called *The Eastern Front*, which covers the entire war between Germany and the Soviet Union from 1941 to

1945. This chapter will be a relatively short overview of the war between Finland and the USSR in the winter of 1939/40.

In 1932, the USSR signed a non-aggression pact with Finland, Poland, and the Baltic nations of Latvia, Lithuania, and Estonia (all formerly part of the Russian Empire). This surprising move was born from a desire to create a buffer zone between the USSR and resurgent Germany. It was also meant to reassure the smaller countries that they wouldn't fall into Germany's orbit in the near future.

To a smaller degree, the Soviets wanted to ensure, as much as possible, a neutral western flank in the face of a powerful Japan, which had recently invaded the Chinese territory of Manchuria, which lay on the Soviet border.

Though Stalin was firmly entrenched in power in Moscow, the true face of Soviet communism was slowly being revealed to those in the West. None of the nations that signed the non-aggression pact trusted the Soviets, although that was almost always the case when countries sign such pacts. Nations act in their self-interest; trust is another matter.

However, by the late 1930s, Stalin's purges of his real and imagined political rivals and the show trials and executions that followed showed the nations on the borders of the USSR Stalin's true face. Between 1937 and 1938, Stalin purged the leadership of the Red Army, assuring his place at the top but weakening the army to a dangerous degree. But for the Finns, Stalin's military purge was a gift, for the men who led the coming invasion of Finland were not the Red Army's best. Many of them were either killed on the battlefield or in Stalin's prisons afterward.

Throughout the 1930s, the Soviet Union and Hitler's Germany played a game of cat and mouse for influence and control over the Baltic nations, Poland, and Finland. The Finns were, as you know, between a rock and a hard place geographically. To the west lay Sweden, which was an officially neutral and second-class power. In the very north of the country, Finland and Norway shared a small border, which was both out of the way and militarily useless. The only other nation Finland shared a border with was the Soviet Union, and having already fought Soviet-supported communists and the Bolsheviks in

Karelia, the Finns were extremely wary of their giant neighbor.

The Finns exported natural resources to the Soviets and received both cash and grain in return. Aside from Sweden (from which the Finns bought high-quality weapons), Finland's other major trading partner was Germany. The Germans needed Finnish minerals and wood, and the Finns needed German machines, machine parts, and arms. The Finns enjoyed a relatively cordial relationship with the Germans before WWI, as well as during and after the conflict.

For the Finns, friendly relations with Germany were the best way to hedge Russian aggression, especially after the rabidly anti-communist Hitler took power. For Hitler, good relations with Finland made Stalin think that he might have a possible northern front to deal with should there ever be a war with Germany, which he expected to happen.

In the last half of the 1930s, the Finns reached out to Estonia, Latvia, Lithuania, and Sweden in an attempt to forge a kind of military alliance on the Baltic Sea, but the nature of the geography (most of the countries were separated by water, with small or non-existent navies) and the relative sizes of these nations, compared to the military giants of the USSR and Germany, caused this effort to fail.

Though Finland's relationship with Hitler was good in the late summer of 1939, Hitler was Hitler. The infamous Nazi-Soviet non-aggression pact, officially known as the Molotov-Ribbentrop Pact (the foreign ministers of the USSR and Germany, respectively) saw Hitler and Stalin agree not to go to war with one another. They also secretly parceled out northeastern Europe between them. In return for Hitler's valuable half of Poland, he agreed that Stalin could take the eastern part of Poland, the Baltic states, and Finland. This would allow Stalin to reconstitute the former Russian Empire, albeit under the red flag of communism. Neither power expected the non-aggression pact to last very long, but Stalin surprisingly expected it to last much longer than it did (it lasted just under two years).

On September 1st, 1939, Hitler invaded Poland from the west. On September 17th, Stalin's forces invaded from the east. They also quickly took over the small and militarily weak Baltic states.

In all four countries, the Red Army and Stalin's secret police began a purge of known anti-communists, the intelligentsia (professors, teachers, writers, artists, etc.), and the military, although other groups were persecuted as well. Suspicion of being anti-Soviet was enough to get one thrown in prison. Many didn't even make it to prison.

As the Germans began mass killings of the Jews in Poland (among many other minority groups), tens of thousands of Poles, Latvians, Lithuanians, and Estonians suffered the same fate. When the Germans marched eastward in 1941, many of the Baltic people joined them in an extremely violent anti-communist purge, which had vicious elements of anti-Semitism.

Many Finns saw the writing on the wall; they would be next. First, though, Stalin made demands. On and off during the 1930s, the Soviets had offered to buy or lease a number of Finnish islands off the southern coast of the country. The Soviets wanted these as naval and air bases to protect approaches to St. Petersburg. After Finland won its independence, it was not in the mood to part with any of its territory. When the USSR's offers were rebuffed, veiled and not-so-veiled threats of Soviet military action were made. The Finns rebuffed these as well and continued fortifying the Mannerheim Line and other points along their border and coast.

Shortly after completing his takeover of the Baltic states in October, Stalin made another offer to the Finns: give up the islands in the Gulf of Finland, allow a Soviet base near Helsinki, and give up the Karelian Isthmus. The Finns were determined to protect their hard-won independence and knew that any toehold the Soviets received in Finland would likely end it. So, the Finns sent Stalin "a hard no." By this time, Mannerheim was again in command of all Finnish forces.

During the last part of October and through November, the Red Army built up its strength on the Finnish border. This was done relatively openly, as Stalin hoped the show of massive strength would cause the Finns to cave to his demands. It had the opposite effect.

(It should not surprise anyone that the Finns and Ukrainians have very close relations now and that the Finns have sent a large amount of military and economic aid to Ukraine in its fight with Russia.)

"Forts, cannons and foreign aid will not help unless every man himself knows that he is the guard of his country." Mannerheim

On November 26th, 1939, Soviet secret police agents shelled their own post on the Finnish border in a false flag operation that was blamed on the Finns. No one in their right mind believed the Finns would launch a preemptive attack against their gigantic and powerful neighbor.

On November 30th, 1939, the USSR invaded Finland. It also sent its bombers to Helsinki, causing minimal damage but outraging much of the world. In response, Soviet Foreign Minister Vyacheslav Molotov announced the Soviets had not bombed Helsinki but actually dropped food packages. The Finns called these "Molotov's bread baskets." When Finnish troops engaged the Soviets shortly thereafter, one of their primary weapons against the lightly armored Soviet tanks in the dense and dark forests of Finland were bottles of flaming liquid (with gelatin and naphtha included to stick it to the desired target). The Finns quickly dubbed them "Molotov cocktails."

Soviet attacks from late November to late December 1939.
https://commons.wikimedia.org/w/index.php?curid=7224222

Most people believed the Finns would either be defeated easily or come to terms quickly with Stalin. Neither happened. All along the Mannerheim Line, the Finns held strong in the face of incredibly careless Soviet assaults, mowing down thousands of Soviet soldiers in days.

Though most of the fighting of the Winter War took place on the Mannerheim Line and was relatively static, the most famous image of the war was the Finnish ski troops in the forests to the north of the Karelian Isthmus. Most Finns then and to this day know how to cross-country ski. Many were experts at it. Covered in white camouflage, virtually silent on their skis, and knowing the country like the back of their hands, the Finns north of the isthmus fell back from the front lines in good order under massive Soviet attacks and lured the Red Army into the depths of the Finnish forests. There, mostly at night but many times throughout the day too, the Finns appeared behind Soviet lines to the left and to the right—they seemed to come out of nowhere. Many Soviet soldiers were killed or wounded by friendly fire because they simply did not know where the Finns were and panicked.

Finnish troops along the front in the trenches of the Mannerheim Line and in the forests to the north showed incredible bravery. This was doubly so when it came to the hundreds of Soviet tanks that took part in the invasion. For the first part of the attack, the Soviets launched tank attacks without supporting infantry. The Finnish soldiers, whose outfits allowed them to blend in the snow and forest, would get close enough to the Soviet tanks that they could place specially made anti-tank grenades in the exhausts or vulnerable spots in their armor. Molotov cocktails in air vents roasted Soviet crews alive.

Three of the Finns' biggest victories were along the Mannerheim Line and at Tolvajärvi and Suomussalmi to the north. In the north, the Finns lured the Russians deep into a forested area that was laced with large lakes. There were only limited areas where troops could travel between the lakes, and the Finns skillfully herded tens of thousands of Russian troops deeper and deeper into the forest. Within days, thousands of Soviet soldiers were killed. Others froze to death. Thousands simply gave up. Only one hundred Finnish died.

In January, Stalin called a halt to most offensive operations in Finland. To say he was displeased would be an understatement. He appointed a new general, Semyon Timoshenko (a future Soviet hero of WWII), to command the effort against Finland and gave him much freer rein than he had with the previous commander. It did not pay to be too much of a free-thinker in the Red Army, but Timoshenko ordered new training, tactics, and clothing and gathered new supplies for an offensive that began on February 11th, 1940.

Simo Häyhä, the greatest sniper of all time and a Finnish national hero.
https://commons.wikimedia.org/w/index.php?curid=18849139

The Finns fought valiantly. You may know of one of the most famous soldiers of the war, Simo Häyhä, the greatest sniper in history. However, the Finns were outnumbered by almost ten to one by the time the Soviets launched nearly half a million men up the Karelian Isthmus. Using new tactics and combined air, tank, artillery, and infantry attacks, the Soviets forced the Finns farther and farther back into mainland Finland.

By mid-February, Mannerheim and the Finnish government knew that it was only a matter of time before the Soviets achieved a major breakthrough and sent word to the Soviets of their willingness to negotiate. The Finns knew they were in a weak position and hoped that the Soviet demands would not be excessive.

At the end of February, Stalin was fearful that a longer war in Finland might cost him more casualties than he was willing to accept in the face of a growing threat from Hitler. So, Stalin dictated terms that were more than the Finns wanted to give up but less than they had feared Stalin would offer. At the beginning of March, the Soviets launched a massive offensive that pushed the Finns almost completely off the Karelian Isthmus and inflicted massive casualties on the tired and now ill-equipped Finnish forces. Attacks farther to the north allowed the Soviets to advance there as well.

On March 12th, the Finns signed an agreement with the Soviets. The agreement did the following:

- Finland gave the entire Karelian Peninsula and a considerable area beyond it to the USSR. Much of southern Finnish Karelia was made Soviet territory.

- In the far north, a large area around the town of Salla was given to the Soviets.

- A number of Finnish islands in the Gulf of Finland were given to the Soviet Union.

- And the island fortress of Hanko on the southwestern coast of Finland was also ceded to Stalin.

Though these concessions were distasteful in the extreme to the Finns, they knew they had no choice. Mannerheim and his officers had fought a brilliant campaign, but the numbers were not on their side, and no ally was going to come to their aid. Understandably, no Finn, then or now, likes to hear this, but considering the possible alternative, the concessions made in 1940 to the Soviet Union were amazingly light.

Part of the reason for that "lightness" was Stalin's fear of Hitler, but most of it was due to the massive casualties the Finns had inflicted on the invaders. Stalin realized what the price would be if he fought a long war in Finland.

Jatkosota

Stalin's attack on Finland drove the Finns further into Germany's orbit. There were thirteen months between the end of the Winter War (March 1940) and Hitler's invasion of the USSR (June 1941). During every month, from March to June, Finland and Germany became closer. The number of German weapons (mostly in the form of small arms and anti-tank weapons) that flowed into Finland skyrocketed, and Finland's trade with Germany also increased.

Politically, there was no question of Finland adopting Nazi policies, unlike other countries closer to Germany. Throughout WWII, the Nazis pressured the Finns to pass anti-Semitic legislation in their country. At times, the Nazis offered to take the Jews of Finland "off its hands," so to speak, but Germany's suggestions were either ignored or openly rebuffed. The Finns had just fought against one totalitarian dictator; they had no desire to slowly give up their independence to another.

When Hitler notified Mannerheim that Germany would be going to war with the Soviet Union and that he considered any of the recently lost Finnish territories to belong to Finland, the two countries came to an understanding. Hitler would gain Finland's support in the north, hopefully causing the Red Army to move troops from their border with Germany in Poland. German troops could be stationed on Finnish soil.

In return, the Finns would reclaim their recently lost territories, which would be recognized by Germany as Finnish. However, Mannerheim and the Finnish government made it very clear that Finland's goals would include nothing but the recovery of lost territory and that Finnish troops would not advance past the borders. Hitler agreed, and oddly enough, even when it became apparent to anyone (other than Hitler) that the war was going badly for Germany, the German leader never caused trouble within Finland, such as, for instance, attempting to place a pro-Nazi Finn at the head of the Finnish government.

Shortly after Hitler's invasion of the USSR on June 22nd, 1941, it became apparent that he would not need the Finns to go beyond their borders at all. The German forces were sometimes gaining close to a hundred miles a day or more. Hitler and many German generals prematurely began to believe that the Soviet Union was finished.

In the north, a German division joined the Finns when Finland declared war on Stalin on June 25th, 1941. Within weeks, Finnish soldiers had almost pushed the Soviets back to the pre-Winter War border on the Karelian Peninsula. Farther north, Finnish and German troops pushed the Soviets rearward but not with the speed that occurred farther south. The forests were thick and slowed the Soviet withdrawal and the Finnish/German advance, though by winter, much of the land that had been lost to the Red Army in 1939 and 1940 was regained.

Throughout the war, the Finns did not advance beyond their stated goals. It must be said that about 1,400 Finns volunteered to join the Nazi Waffen-SS, the armed combat branch of the SS. Throughout the first two years of the war, Finnish SS volunteers fought on the Eastern Front, far south of their home country. By 1943, they had lost about 25 percent of their strength, and during their home leave in the summer of 1943, they were dissolved by the Finnish government.

Throughout Hitler's empire, small segments of many nationalities joined volunteer units of the Waffen-SS. In keeping with Nazi ethnic theories, only people deemed "Germanic" were accepted initially, but as more countries fell under Hitler's control and more foreign volunteers were enrolled, things began to change. By the end of the war, distinctly non-Germans, such as Albanians, Frenchmen, Ukrainians, and others, made up about a third or more of the strength of the Waffen-SS, a force that numbered close to a million men in total. The vast majority of Finns were, if anything, anti-Nazi. They were just anti-Soviet and anti-Russian. *Jatkosota* (the "Continuation War") went just as well as you might imagine. Throughout the war, Soviet divisions were sent to the north to keep the Finns from advancing should they change their minds about their war aims. Though rather small in size in comparison to the battles that took place farther to the south, which included hundreds of thousands of men at a time, serious fighting still took place between the Finns and Germans on one side and the Soviets on the other.

But though the Finns held their own along the border, the same could not be said for the Germans in mainland Europe. That story has been told millions of times: the German defeats at Stalingrad and Kursk, the absolutely huge Soviet military, millions of tons of aid from the US and UK to Stalin, and the need for Hitler to defend Africa and western Europe all contributed to the eventual defeat of Hitler.

The Finns were among the first to see the writing on the wall, which became even more clear when Hitler visited Finland for Marshal Mannerheim's seventy-fifth birthday, which was declared a national holiday. One of the more amazing and rather unknown things about WWII happened during Hitler's meeting with Mannerheim in a train car in Finland.

A Finnish radio technician, who was there to record and broadcast any public statements the leaders wished to make, saw that the window of the train cabin where the leaders were to meet was open. Without anyone noticing, he was able to slide a small microphone over the edge of the window and record about eight minutes of Hitler and Mannerheim's private conversation. The recording is the *only* recording of Hitler speaking in his conversational voice, meaning he was not giving a ranting speech or press interview, which were increasingly rare after WWII began. It is also the only recording of Hitler speaking to a foreign head of state.

Hitler was a bit in awe of Mannerheim, which was clear when he spoke about him among his cronies and when they met. (Mannerheim had visited Nazi Germany in 1934.) Mannerheim was considerably taller and better looking than Hitler, and he had been a general since Hitler was in his teens. Mannerheim was also a foreign aristocrat. Hitler had often shown an old-fashioned and middle-class deference to members of the aristocracy.

Mannerheim was formal, but he was almost always formal. He did call Hitler "polite" and "informed" in their meeting, but many in Finland knew that Mannerheim didn't love Hitler. Throughout the conversation, at least the bit that was recorded, Hitler referred to the huge size of the Red Army and said that if he had known how extensively armed Stalin was, he never would have ordered an attack on the USSR. At that moment, Mannerheim realized that Hitler was not as sure of victory as he claimed. (If you are interested in hearing the full conversation, a link to it is in the bibliography.)

In the summer of 1944, in conjunction with the Anglo-American offensive in France, the Soviets launched a massive offensive along their front line with the Germans and the Finns. Operation Bagration included three million Russians. Only a fraction of those three million was involved in Finland, but that was more than enough. There were few German troops left in Finland, and those that were there were relatively demoralized, as were many Finns. For the Finns, the war had become a war of attrition, and though they were not at the end of their strength, they were fast approaching it.

From June 9th to September 18th, 1944, the Soviets attacked in great strength northward up the Karelian Isthmus. Smaller offensives occurred farther north. Though the Finns inflicted heavy losses on the Soviets, it was clear to everyone that it was only a matter of time before the Soviets took the entire country— a fate virtually no one in Finland wanted. A political squabble resulted in Mannerheim becoming president of Finland and commander in chief, and his government agreed to the Soviet Union's terms.

Those terms included, as you can imagine, the return of the Finnish territories that had been taken by the Soviets in the Winter War, reparations, the ceding of the port of Petsamo on the Arctic Sea, an openly stated policy of neutrality, and closer economic ties to the Soviet Union. Finland was in no real position to disagree.

Those Finns living in the areas that were to be given to the Soviets fled as quickly as they could, as did many Germans. Part of the agreement with the Soviets stipulated that the Finns disarm, by force if necessary, all German troops in Finnish territory. Some German troops were disarmed, but they remained in Finnish, not Soviet, custody. Most returned home. Some German units refused to lay down their arms, and battles did occur between the former allies. The Germans fought a fighting retreat and acted as the Germans had throughout the war, burning thousands of homes and other buildings on their way.

During the Winter War and the Continuation War, Finland lost over ninety thousand soldiers killed in action. Over 150,000 were wounded.

Conclusion

At the end of WWII, Finland entered into a completely new phase of history. The terms of the Soviet agreement were harsh, but they could have been much worse. The reparations payments demanded by Stalin caused a great deal of disruption to the war-weakened Finnish economy. The terms of the agreement did not forbid Finnish contact or trade with the West, but trade was limited due to the state of the Finnish economy and worries over angering Stalin.

Marshal Mannerheim passed away in 1952, ending a long era. That same year, Finland began to come out of the shadow of WWII and hosted the Winter Olympics in Helsinki. Finland did not suffer diplomatically to any great extent with the Western powers after the war. While most nations were not pleased that the Finns had aligned with Hitler, they knew the Finns were truly "between a rock and a hard place" when it came to Hitler and Stalin. Most foreigners were well aware that the Finns had refused to advance past the pre-war borders of 1939, and there was no evidence that the Finnish government or any of its branches had taken part in Hitler's crimes against humanity.

During the Winter War, France, Britain, and the US were all on the side of Finland. While Finland's reputation had been damaged to a degree by its dealings with Hitler, by the early 1950s, it was once again welcomed into the community of free nations to a degree.

That "degree" was determined by Finland's giant communist neighbor. The terms of the post-war agreements with the Soviets included:

- The territorial concessions already mentioned;

- A non-aggression pact between the two nations (neither side—although it really only meant Finland—could enter into an alliance directed against the other. This was firmly aimed at Finland joining the Western powers, specifically NATO after it was formed in 1949);

- For fifty years, the Finns would lease the naval base at Porkkala to the Soviets. This was later moved to another location close by, which today is a beautiful national part;

- The Finns would legalize the Finnish Communist Party and outlaw far-right/fascist parties, though its democratic government was unchanged;

- Reparations in the amount of $300 million (approximately $4.5 billion in 2021);

- Finland's armed forces would not be any larger than deemed necessary for the defense of its borders;

- The Soviet Union would be "consulted" of any Finnish application to economic pacts involving other states, especially with the US and western Europe.

Though Soviet restrictions on what Finland was realistically able to do internationally relaxed after Stalin's death in 1953 and again in 1956 after Khrushchev came to power in the USSR, the Finns were cautious in their dealings with the West. Even their desire to join the Nordic Council, which consisted of Sweden, Norway, Iceland, and Denmark, was viewed with suspicion, as the latter three countries were members of NATO. Finland did become a member of that council, and as the decades passed, Finnish trade with the West grew. However, it was rather small in comparison with the trade the Finns engaged in with the Soviets, its satellite nations in eastern Europe, and the non-aligned nations of the world.

Finland was not isolated from the West like other nations, such as East Germany, Poland, Hungary, and other Soviet client states, but it was not integrated with the West either. The country was situated in a strange sort of diplomatic twilight zone between West and East. The interesting thing about that is the Finns were free to find their own unique way into the future. They had a policy of neutrality and were independent of the many rules that came with membership in NATO, the European Economic Community, and the European Union. This place between the West and East and Finland's adjustment to it is known as "Finlandization." The term is often used in situations where smaller countries find themselves caught in the struggle between the larger powers of the world.

After all, the Finns had only been independent since 1917; in other words, in 1945, Finland had been independent for only twenty-eight years. Though the Finnish democratic institutions were strong enough to survive the Cold War, Finland's economy suffered a number of times in the years from 1950 to 1995 (when it joined the EU) and beyond.

Finland played a vital role in Cold War international relations. Helsinki became a hub of spy networks, where the West could spy on the Soviet Union more directly, but the Soviets were able to monitor Western activity in Finland and other parts of Europe from there as well. The Finnish government often brokered back-channel agreements between the superpowers, and in 1975, Finland was the host of talks called the Helsinki Conference. The conference not only led to limits on nuclear armaments in the USSR and the US but also laid down in writing the expected behavior of nations in regard to human rights.

Like its Nordic neighbors, Finland established a very wide social safety net in the years after the war. Though that net has been trimmed back in recent years, the Finns, like the Swedes, Norwegians, Danes, and Icelanders, enjoy a kind of social and educational security unheard of in many other Western countries, including the United States.

The story of Finland is much more than the political and territorial history that we have written here. For instance, Finland's prime minister (as of 2022) is a woman, and Sanna Marin was not the first. Achieving gender equality in Finland and other Nordic nations has been a priority. Finland has been recognized as one of the leading nations in the world when it comes to equality between genders. Finland is also at the forefront of the movement toward equality for LGBTQ people.

As of this writing, for the last five years, Finland has been ranked as the "happiest nation on Earth" in that famous yearly poll of international experts. The Finnish enjoy a high standard of living.

Some of the most pressing problems today include immigration and the limits of the Finnish economy and society imposed on it by immigration. Like many other European nations, especially the richer nations of northern Europe, the influx of refugees from the Middle East has caused Finns to debate the limits of its welfare state and the future of its unique culture.

Other issues that regularly appear in the Finnish news are the autonomy and economic and demographic situation of the Sami people, who were known for centuries, quite to their chagrin, as "Lapps" or "Lapplanders." Various groups of Sami inhabit the central and northern areas of Norway, Sweden, Finland, and, to a small degree, the Karelian Peninsula of Russia. The Sami of the Nordic countries enjoy an autonomy that allows them, within certain limits, to govern and police themselves.

You may know of the Sami people through their famous public image of being reindeer herders, but today, most Sami people in Finland and elsewhere do not make their living in herding, much of which is done for tourist purposes today. Questions about the economic future of the Sami, as well as who the Sami are, are big questions in Finland today. In 2022, some leading Sami questioned Prime Minister Marin's commitment to the well-being of the Sami and posed economic and environmental questions that involved them and their ancestral lands. (We have included links for more information on this issue and on the Sami in general in the bibliography.)

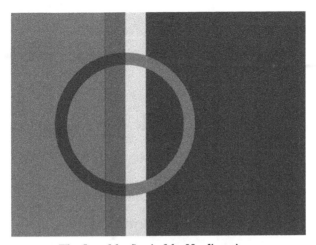

The flag of the Sami of the Nordic nations.
https://commons.wikimedia.org/w/index.php?curid=491498

This book ends where it began, with the end of the century-old policy of Finnish neutrality. Before the Russian invasion of Ukraine, most Finns continued to believe that the official policy of neutrality should continue, though most Finns clearly leaned to the West in terms of identification and culture. Vladimir Putin's behavior in the 2010s and onward caused the number of Finns supporting closer ties to the West to grow, although most Finns did not express a desire to join NATO. The Russian invasion of Ukraine in 2022 changed that opinion literally overnight.

For its size, Finland is exceedingly well armed. It is also well prepared and sends a large amount of economic and military aid to Ukraine. As you can imagine, this has not sat well with Putin and many of the Russian people. In late December 2022, a group of masked men threw bricks and sledgehammers at the Finnish Embassy in Russia. Russian police stood idly by, which tells you quite a bit about Russo-Finnish relations. (A link to the video of this event is in the bibliography.)

It is a time of great change for Finland. During the Winter War, the Finns' stoic courage in the face of the Soviet invasion was known as *sisu,* and today, that word is popular once again in Finland. The country has taken a firm stand against Russian aggression, just as it did back in 1939.

Here's another book by Captivating History that you might like

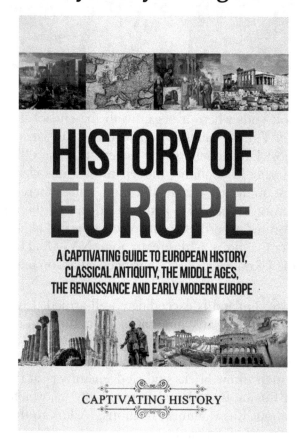

Free Bonus from Captivating History (Available for a Limited time)

Hi History Lovers!

Now you have a chance to join our exclusive history list so you can get your first history ebook for free as well as discounts and a potential to get more history books for free! Simply visit the link below to join.

Captivatinghistory.com/ebook

Also, make sure to follow us on Facebook, Twitter and Youtube by searching for Captivating History.

Youtube: Captivating History

Bibliography

"Activities & Attractions at Birka | Birka the Viking City." Birka Vikingastaden. Last modified March 23, 2021. https://www.birkavikingastaden.se/en/attraction/.

"GDP of European Countries 2019." StatisticsTimes.com | Collection of Statistics and Charts. Accessed December 2, 2021. https://statisticstimes.com/economy/european-countries-by-gdp.php.

"Giant Swedish Yule Goat Torched Again After 5-year Respite." Reuters. Last modified December 17, 2021. https://www.reuters.com/lifestyle/giant-swedish-yule-goat-torched-again-after-5-year-respite-2021-12-17/.

The Girl King. Directed by Mika Kaurismaki. 2015. Sweden, Film.

Glete, Jan. "The Swedish fiscal-military state and its navy, 1521-1721." University of Stockholm. https://www2.historia.su.se/personal/jan_glete/Glete-Swedish_Fiscal-military_State.pdf.

Heilung. "Krigsgaldr." YouTube. n.d. https://www.youtube.com/watch?v=K7ZqZVunCb4&ab_channel=Heilung. This is a music video that uses imagery taken directly from Scandinavian rock carvings. The song is based on an Icelandic poem. The title of the song translates to "War Magic."

"Historic Arabian Accounts Describing Vikings." Sons of Vikings. Last modified October 11, 2021. https://sonsofvikings.com/blogs/history/historic-arabian-accounts-describing-vikings. (Scroll to the bottom of the page for Ibn-Fadlan's firsthand account.)

Jarman, Cat. *River Kings: A New History of the Vikings from Scandinavia to the Silk Roads*. New York: Simon & Schuster, 2022.

"Monarchy & The Royal Court." Sveriges Kungahus - Sveriges Kungahus. Accessed February 1, 2022. https://www.kungahuset.se/royalcourt/monarchytheroyalcourt.4.396160 511584257f21800096.html.

Radio, Sveriges. "Are Swedes Really Tall, Blonde and Blue-eyed?" Sveriges Radio - Lokala Och Rikstäckande Radiokanaler. Last modified July 12, 2014. https://sverigesradio.se/artikel/5912864.

"The Roman Iron Age in Scandinavia." Early Medieval Archaeology | Early Medieval Archaeology Educational Resources. Accessed December 10, 2021. https://early-med.archeurope.com/iron-age-scandinavia/the-roman-iron-age-in-scandinavia/.

"Sweden." Central Intelligence Agency - CIA. Accessed November 15, 2021. https://www.cia.gov/the-world-factbook/countries/sweden/#people-and-society.

"Viking Age 'gold men' found in Sweden." The Local.se https://www.thelocal.se/20131115/viking-age-gold-men-found-in-southern-sweden/.

"Vikings in the East: Scandinavian Influence in Kievan Rus." Medievalists.net. Last modified December 25, 2013. https://www.medievalists.net/2011/10/vikings-in-the-east-scandinavian-influence-in-kievan-rus/.

Boyesen, H. H. (1995). *The History of Norway*. Cambridge: Chadwyck-Healey.

Brøndsted, J., & Skov, K. (1987). *The Vikings*. Harmondsworth, Middlesex, England: Penguin.

Derry, T. K. (2004). *The Campaign in Norway*. London: Naval & Military Press.

Derry, T. K. (2012). *A History of Scandinavia: Norway, Sweden, Denmark, Finland and Iceland*. Minneapolis: University of Minnesota Press.

Helle, K., Kouri, E. I., & Olesen, J. E. (2016). *The Cambridge History of Scandinavia. 1520-1870*.

Kendrick, T. D. (2014). *A History of the Vikings*. London: Routledge, Taylor & Francis Group.

Larsen, K. (2015). *A History of Norway*. Princeton, NJ: Princeton Legacy Library.

Lauring, P. (2015). *A History of Denmark*. Copenhagen: Høst & Søn.

Lindqvist, H., & Bradbury, R. (2006). *A History of Sweden*. Stockholm: Norstedt.

Sawyer, B. (2000). *The Viking-Age Rune-Stones: Custom and Commemoration in Early Medieval Scandinavia*. Oxford: Oxford University Press.

Sawyer, P. (2001). *The Oxford Illustrated History of the Vikings*. Oxford: Oxford University Press.

Sulzberger, C. L. (1997). *World War II*. New York: Houghton Mifflin.

Yilek, J. A. (2018). *History of Norway*. Shelbyville, KY: Wasteland Press.

"Ancient Roman Artifact Found on Danish Island." ScienceNordic. Last modified April 22, 2015. https://sciencenordic.com/archaeology-cultural-history-denmark/ancient-roman-artifact-found-on-danish-island/1416970

"A Brief History of LGBTQI+ Rights in Denmark." Scandinavia Standard. Last modified August 8, 2017. https://www.scandinaviastandard.com/a-brief-history-of-lgbtqi-rights-in-denmark

Captivating History. *French History: A Captivating Guide to the History of France, Charlemagne, and Notre-Dame de Paris*. Captivating History, 2021.

"Christianity Comes to Denmark." National Museum of Denmark. Accessed March 14, 2022. https://en.natmus.dk/historical-knowledge/denmark/prehistoric-period-until-1050-ad/the-viking-age/religion-magic-death-and-rituals/christianity-comes-to-denmark/

"The Danish Jewish Museum - 400 Years of Danish Jewish History." Accessed April 12, 2022. https://jewmus.dk/en/the-danish-jewish-museum/

"DNA Reveals Details of Scandinavian Battle Axe Culture." Life in Norway. Last modified April 20, 2021. https://www.lifeinnorway.net/dna-reveals-details-of-scandinavian-battle-axe-culture/

Ed. "'To Be or Not to Be': Hamlet's Soliloquy with Analysis." No Sweat Shakespeare. Last modified January 26, 2021. https://nosweatshakespeare.com/quotes/soliloquies/to-be-or-not-to-be/

"How a Heinous Act of Genocide Doomed Aethelred the Unready's Kingdom." History Hit. Accessed March 11, 2022.

https://www.historyhit.com/1002-attempted-genocide-englands-danes/

"How Accurate Are the Viking Sagas?" TheCollector. Last modified February 1, 2022. https://www.thecollector.com/viking-sagas-historical-mythology

Kessler, P. L. "Kingdoms of Northern Europe - Jutes (Eudoses)." The History Files. Accessed March 9, 2022. https://www.historyfiles.co.uk/KingsListsEurope/ScandinaviaJutes.htm

"King Frederik II of Denmark and Norway and Duke of Schleswig – European Royal History." European Royal History. Accessed April 3, 2022. https://europeanroyalhistory.wordpress.com/tag/king-frederik-ii-of-denmark-and-norway-and-duke-of-schleswig

"Prosperous Vikings Whitewashed Their Walls." ScienceNordic. Last modified October 13, 2013. https://sciencenordic.com/archaeoloy-chemistry-denmark/prosperous-vikings-whitewashed-their-walls/1391621

UN/Sustainable Development Solutions Network. Accessed February 15, 2022. https://worldhappiness.report/

"Árni Magnusson." Wikipedia. Wikimedia Foundation, February 9, 2022. https://en.wikipedia.org/wiki/%C3%81rni_Magn%C3%BAsson

"Aud the Deep-Minded (Ketilsdóttir)." Wikipedia. Wikimedia Foundation, July 11, 2022. https://en.wikipedia.org/wiki/Aud_the_Deep-Minded_(Ketilsd%C3%B3ttir)

Byock, Jesse. *Viking Age Iceland.* New York: Penguin, 2001.

"Crymogæa." Wikipedia. Wikimedia Foundation, May 27, 2022. https://en.wikipedia.org/wiki/Crymog%C3%A6a

Davies, J.D. "The Barbary Corsair Raid on Iceland, 1627." J D Davies – Historian and Author – The Website and Blog of Naval Historian and Bestselling Author J D Davies, February 20, 2017. https://jddavies.com/2017/02/20/the-barbary-corsair-raid-on-iceland-1627/ .

"Eggert Ólafsson." Wikipedia. Wikimedia Foundation, July 25, 2022. https://en.wikipedia.org/wiki/Eggert_%C3%93lafsson

"Erik the Red." Ages of Exploration, Mariner's Museum, 2022, https://exploration.marinersmuseum.org/subject/erik-the-red/ .

"Guðríður Símonardóttir." Wikipedia. Wikimedia Foundation, March 29, 2022. https://en.wikipedia.org/wiki/Gu%C3%B0r%C3%AD%C3%B0ur_S%C3%ADmonard%C3%B3ttir

Hansley, C. Keith. "The Complicated Life of Uni the Dane." *The Historian's Hut*. https://thehistorianshut.com/2021/06/10/the-complicated-life-of-uni-the-dane/ Accessed 9/7/2022.

Herman, Arthur. *The Viking Heart: How Scandinavians Conquered the World*. New York: Mariner Books, 2021.

"Jón Magnusson (author)." Wikipedia. Wikimedia Foundation, April 6, 2021. https://en.wikipedia.org/wiki/J%C3%B3n_Magn%C3%BAsson_(author)

Karlsson, Gunnar. *The History of Iceland*. Minneapolis: The University of Minnesota Press, 2000.

"Settlement of Iceland." Wikipedia. Wikimedia Foundation, July 30, 2022. https://en.wikipedia.org/wiki/Settlement_of_Iceland .

Sigmundsdóttir, Alda. *The Little Book of the Icelanders*. Middletown, DE: Little Books Publishing, 2021.

Anti-Finnish Russian demonstration. Video, December, 20, 2022 https://twitter.com/AlexandruC4/status/1605201446072639488

Accessed October 29, 2022. https://www.news.com.au/finance/work/leaders/sanna-marin-finnish-pms-photo-shoot-for-trendi-magazine-sparks-social-media-outcry/news-story/f01426d473d991b924775f9f3d3e9d2e

"Dancing Up a Political Storm." The New York Times - Breaking News, US News, World News and Videos. Last modified August 30, 2022. https://www.nytimes.com/2022/08/30/style/sanna-marin-partying-finland.html

Derry, T. K. History of Scandinavia: Norway, Sweden, Denmark, Finland, and Iceland. Minneapolis: University of Minnesota Press, 2000.

"Finland PM Sanna Marin 'Doesn't Care About Rights for Sámi People.'" Euronews. Last modified October 28, 2022. https://www.euronews.com/my-europe/2022/10/27/finland-pm-sanna-marin-doesnt-care-about-human-rights-for-sami-people-as-reforms-likely-to.

"Finland: Monthly Average Temperatures 2021." Statista. Last modified January 6, 2022. https://www.statista.com/statistics/743043/monthly-average-temperatures-in-finland/.

"Finland." Central Intelligence Agency - CIA. Last modified September 7, 2022. https://www.cia.gov/the-world-factbook/countries/finland/.

"The History of Finland." Edrawsoft. Accessed October 29, 2022. https://www.edrawmind.com/article/history-of-finland.html

"The History of the Sami." LAITS – Liberal Arts Instructional Technology Services. Accessed December 19, 2022. https://www.laits.utexas.edu/sami/dieda/history.htm

"Museovirasto (en-US)." Museovirasto. https://www.museovirasto.fi/en/.

"Mysterious Prehistoric Sites of Finland." SpottingHistory.com - Explore Historic Sites & Historical Attractions on Map. https://www.spottinghistory.com/featured/mysterious-prehistoric-sites-of-finland/

"Salme Ship Burials." Viking Archaeology - Viking Archaeology. https://viking.archeurope.info/index.php?page=salme-ship-burials.

Tacitus. "Germania by Tacitus." Roman History Site and Discussion Forum | UNRV.com. https://www.unrv.com/tacitus/tacitusgermania.php

The Hitler Mannerheim Recordings. (n.d.). YouTube. https://www.youtube.com/watch?v=oET1WaG5sFk&ab_channel=HistoryChannel "The Transition to Christianity." National Museum of Denmark. https://en.natmus.dk/historical-knowledge/denmark/prehistoric-period-until-1050-ad/the-viking-age/religion-magic-death-and-rituals/the-transition-to-christianity/.

"Vaka Vanha Kalevala Viehättää Yhä Taiteentekijöitä – Taistelu Sammosta on Suosikkiaihe." Yle Uutiset. Accessed December 6, 2022. https://yle.fi/a/3-12683309?s=03.

Varjus, Seppo. "Uutuuskirja: Mannerheim Innostui Aluksi Hitleristä." Ilta-Sanomat. Accessed December 20, 2022. https://www.is.fi/kotimaa/art-2000005187079.html Mannerheim's impressions of Germany, 1934.

Printed in the USA
CPSIA information can be obtained
at www.ICGtesting.com
LVHW010010080224
771084LV00003B/139